用心雕刻每一本......
http://site.douban.com/110283/
http://weibo.com/nccpub

用心字里行间　雕刻名著经典

Cross-Cultural Communication and Management

Ninth Edition

Fred Luthans
University of Nebraska–Lincoln

Jonathan P. Doh
Villanova University

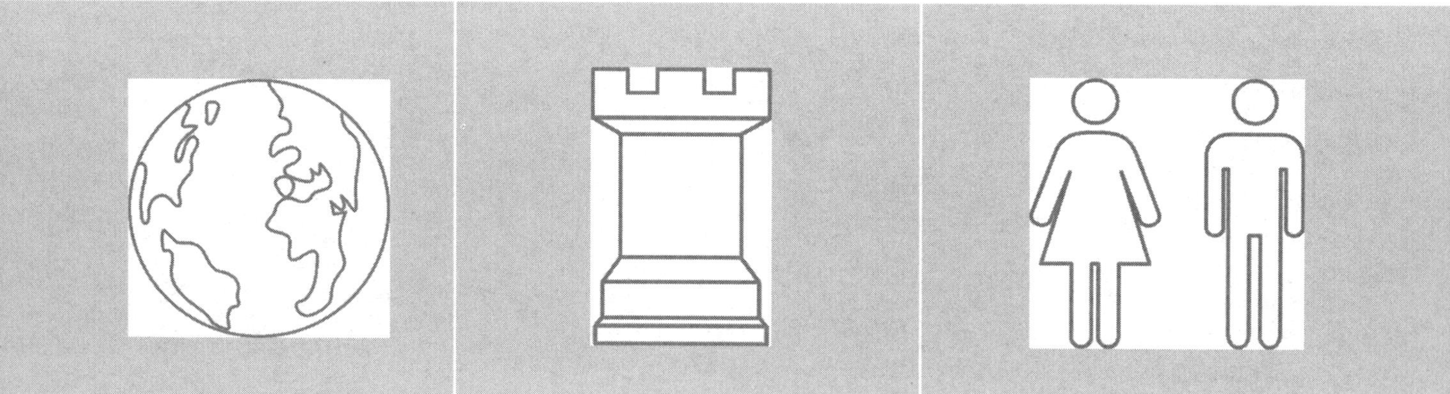

跨文化沟通与管理

第9版

双语教学版

［美］弗雷德·卢森斯
乔纳森·多 著

人民邮电出版社
北 京

图书在版编目（CIP）数据

跨文化沟通与管理：第 9 版：双语教学版 /（美）卢森斯,（美）多 著 .
—北京：人民邮电出版社，2015.12（2020.8 重印）
ISBN 978-7-115-40873-0
I. ①跨… II. ①卢… ②多… III. ①企业管理—双语教学—高等学校—教材—汉、英 IV. ① F270
中国版本图书馆 CIP 数据核字（2015）第 263241 号

Fred Luthans, Jonathan P. Doh
International Management: Culture, Strategy, and Behavior, 9th Edition
ISBN 0-07-786244-9

跨文化沟通与管理（第 9 版，双语教学版）

◆ 著　　　［美］弗雷德·卢森斯　乔纳森·多
策　　划 刘　力　陆　瑜
责任编辑　徐向娟
装帧设计　陶建胜

◆ 人民邮电出版社出版发行　北京市丰台区成寿寺路 11 号
邮编　100164　电子邮件　315@ptpress.com.cn
网址　http://www.ptpress.com.cn
电话（编辑部）010-84931398　（市场部）010-84937152
三河市少明印务有限公司印刷
新华书店经销

◆ 开本：850 × 1092　1 /16
印张：12
字数：250 千字　2016 年 1 月第 1 版　2020 年 8 月第 4 次印刷
著作权合同登记号　图字：01-2007-4966
ISBN 978-7-115-40873-0

定价：38.00 元

本书如有印装质量问题，请与本社联系　电话：（010）84937152

内容提要

本书选自弗雷德·卢森斯的*International Management: Culture, Strategy, and Behavior* 2015年的第9版。在全球化背景下，跨文化管理是所有跨国组织以及跨国管理者的重要议题。本书作者关注并尊重文化差异，同时又融入当代最新的跨文化管理的研究成果和实践经验。

全书共分为四章：文化的意义和维度；跨文化管理；组织文化与组织多样性；跨文化沟通与谈判。全文论述深入浅出，可读性、实践性强。对所有标题加了中文注释后，让读者可以迅速阅读并抓住主旨。

本书可作为工商管理、商务英语等专业的“跨文化沟通与管理”双语课程适用教材，也适合跨国企业管理者、跨国企业研究者以及从事国际贸易的广大读者参考阅读。

About the Authors
作者简介

FRED LUTHANS is University and the George Holmes Distinguished Professor of Management at the University of Nebraska–Lincoln. He is also Chair of the Master Research Council for HUMANeX, Inc. He received his BA, MBA, and PhD from the University of Iowa, where he received the Distinguished Alumni Award in 2002. While serving as an officer in the U.S. Army from 1965–1967, he taught leadership at the U.S. Military Academy at West Point. He has been a visiting scholar at a number of colleges and universities and has lectured in most European and Pacific Rim countries. He has taught international management as a visiting faculty member at the universities of Bangkok, Hawaii, Henley in England, Norwegian Management School, Monash in Australia, Macao SAR, Chemnitz in the former East Germany, and Tirana in Albania. A past president of the Academy of Management, in 1997 he received the Academy's Distinguished Educator Award. In 2000 he became an inaugural member of the Academy's Hall of Fame for being one of the "Top Five" all-time published authors in the prestigious Academy journals. Currently, he is co-coeditor-in-chief of the *Journal of World Business,* editor of *Organizational Dynamics,* coeditor of *Journal of Leadership and Organization Studies,* and the author of numerous books. His book *Organizational Behavior* (Irwin/McGraw-Hill) is now in its 12th edition and the groundbreaking book *Psychological Capital* (Oxford University Press) with Carolyn Youssef and Bruce Avolio will be out in its second edition in 2014. He is one of very few management scholars who is a Fellow of the Academy of Management, the Decision Sciences Institute, and the Pan Pacific Business Association, and he has been a member of the Executive Committee for the Pan Pacific Conference since its beginning 30 years ago. This committee helps to organize the annual meeting held in Pacific Rim countries. He has been involved with some of the first empirical studies on motivation and behavioral management techniques and the analysis of managerial activities in Russia; these articles have been published in the *Academy of Management Journal*, *Journal of International Business Studies, Journal of World Business,* and *European Management Journal.* Since the very beginning of the transition to market economies after the evolution of communism in Eastern Europe, he has been actively involved in management education programs sponsored by the U.S. Agency for International Development in Albania and Macedonia, and in U.S. Information Agency programs involving the Central Asian countries of Kazakhstan, Kyrgyzstan, and Tajikistan. For example, Professor Luthans' recent international research involves his construct of positive psychological capital (PsyCap). He and colleagues have published their research demonstrating the impact of Chinese workers' PsyCap on their performance in the *International Journal of Human Resource Management* and *Management and Organization Review.* He is applying his positive approach to positive organizational behavior (POB), PsyCap, and authentic leadership to effective global management and has recently been the keynote at programs in China (several times), Malaysia, Korea, Indonesia, England, Norway, Finland, South Africa, and soon Italy.

JONATHAN P. DOH is the Herbert G. Rammrath Chair in International Business, founding Director of the Center for Global Leadership, and Professor of Management at the Villanova School of Business. Jonathan teaches, does research, and serves as an executive instructor and consultant in the areas of international strategy and corporate responsibility and serves as an occasional executive educator for the Aresty Institute of Executive Education at the Wharton Business School. Previously, he was on the faculty of American and Georgetown Universities and a senior trade official with the U.S. government. Jonathan is author or co-author of more than 75 refereed articles published in the top international business and management journals, 30 chapters in scholarly edited volumes, and more than 75 conference papers. Recent articles have appeared in journals such as *Academy of Management Review, California Management Review, Journal of International Business Studies, Journal of World Business, Organization Science, Sloan Management Review,* and *Strategic Management Journal.* He is co-editor and contributing author of *Globalization and NGOs* (Praeger, 2003) and Handbook on Responsible Leadership and *Governance in Global Business* (Elgar, 2005) and co-author of the previous edition of *International Management: Culture, Strategy, and Behavior* (8th ed., McGraw-Hill/Irwin, 2012), the best-selling international management text. His current research focus is on strategy for emerging markets, global corporate responsibility, and offshore outsourcing of services. His most recent scholarly books are *Multinationals and Development* (with Alan Rugman, Yale University Press, 2008), *NGOs and Corporations: Conflict and Collaboration* (with Michael Yaziji, Cambridge University Press, 2009) and *Aligning for Advantage: Competitive Strategy for the Social and Political Arenas* (with Tom Lawton and Tazeeb Rajwani, Oxford University Press, 2014). He is co-Editor-in-Chief of *MRN International Environment of Global Business* (SSRN Journal), Senior Editor of *Journal of World Business,* Associate Editor of *Business & Society,* and *Consulting Editor of Long Range Planning*. Beginning in January of 2015 he will assume the position of Editor-in-Chief of *Journal of World Business.* Jonathan has also developed more than a dozen original cases and simulations published in books, journals, and case databases and used at many leading global universities. He has been a consultant or executive instructor for ABB, Anglo American, Bodycote, Bosch, China Minsheng Bank, Hana Financial, HSBC, Ingersoll Rand, Medtronic, Shanghai Municipal Government, Siam Cement, the World Economic Forum, and Deloitte Touche, where he served as senior external adviser to the Global Energy Resource Group. Jonathan is part of the Executive Committee of the Academy of Management Organizations and Natural Environment Division with increasing responsibilities culminating in the chair of the division in 2016. He was ranked among the top 15 most prolific international business scholars in the world for the period 2001–2009 (Lahiri and Kumar, 2012). He holds a PhD in strategic and international management from George Washington University.

Contents
目　录

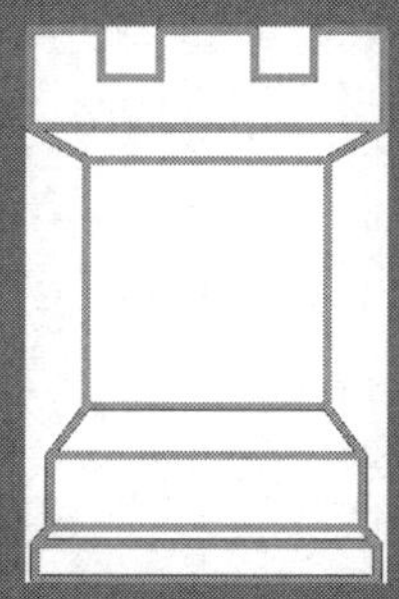

Cross-Cultural Communication and Management

Chapter 1

文化的意义和维度
THE MEANINGS AND DIMENSIONS OF CULTURE

OBJECTIVES OF THE CHAPTER

A major challenge of doing business internationally is to respond and adapt effectively to different cultures. Such adaptation requires an understanding of cultural diversity, perceptions, stereotypes, and values. In recent years, a great deal of research has been conducted on cultural dimensions and attitudes, and the findings have proved useful in providing integrative profiles of international cultures. However, a word of caution must be given when discussing these country profiles. It must be remembered that stereotypes and overgeneralizations should be avoided; there are always individual differences and even subcultures within every country.

This chapter examines the meaning of culture as it applies to international management, reviews some of the value differences and similarities of various national groups, studies important dimensions of culture and their impact on behavior, and examines country clusters. The specific objectives of this chapter are:

1. **DEFINE** the term *culture,* and discuss some of the comparative ways of differentiating cultures.
2. **DESCRIBE** the concept of cultural values, and relate some of the international differences, similarities, and changes occurring in terms of both work and managerial values.
3. **IDENTIFY** the major dimensions of culture relevant to work settings, and discuss their effects on behavior in an international environment.
4. **DISCUSS** the value of country cluster analysis and relational orientations in developing effective international management practices.

国际化管理的世界

The World of *International Management*

丰田质量危机的文化根源

The Cultural Roots of Toyota's Quality Crisis

Worldwide, the Toyota brand name has been a symbol of quality. Toyota's focus on Kaizen (the Japanese term meaning "continuous improvement") helped Toyota become the number one seller of automobiles in the world.

In light of Toyota's commitment to quality, it was shocking when Toyota announced multiple massive recalls of many of its vehicles between 2010 and 2013. In early 2010, Toyota stated that it would recall approximately 2.3 million vehicles to correct sticking accelerator pedals, and, on top of that, approximately 5.2 million vehicles would have an ongoing recall for a floor mat pedal entrapment issue. Later that year, another 1.5 million vehicles were recalled over concerns of leaking brake fluid and electrical problems. In October 2012, 7.4 million vehicles were recalled to repair faulty power window switches, and in early 2013, another 1 million automobiles were recalled due to airbag issues.[1]

In addition to a $1.1 billion class-action settlement, Jeff Kingston of Temple University Japan estimated that the 2010 recall cost Toyota $2 billion.[2] Moreover, the way Toyota managed the crises has been even worse than the financial consequences. The president of the company, Akio Toyoda, the grandson of Toyota's founder, did not appear publicly for two weeks after the 2010 recall announcement. When he did appear, Toyoda took the path of minimizing the problem, citing a software issue, rather than a defect, as the source of the pedal problems. Toyota also failed to disclose the malfunctions to the Department of Transportation within the legal 5-day window, resulting in fines of $48.8 million in 2010 and $17.35 million in 2012.[3] Some uncertainty remains as to whether the problems originated in Toyota plants in America or whether the problems can be traced to designers in Japan. Kingston asserted that Toyota's failure to be forthcoming on critical safety issues has put "the trust of its customers worldwide" in jeopardy.

Where did Toyota go wrong? How did the symbol of quality become tarnished? Some contend that cultural factors contributed to Toyota's current crisis.

日本文化如何影响丰田

How Japanese Culture Influenced Toyota

In his *Wall Street Journal* article, Kingston explained the cultural roots of Toyota's woes. He indicated that "a culture of deference" in Japanese firms "makes it hard for those lower in the hierarchy to question their superiors or inform them about problems." In addition, the Japanese tend to focus on the consensus, which can make it difficult "to challenge what has been decided or designed." In Japan, Kingston noted, "employees' identities are closely tied to their company's image and loyalty to the firm overrides concerns about consumers."[4]

One can deduce how Toyota's problems arose in this cultural environment. If subordinates noticed a problem in vehicular accelerators, they would likely be hesitant to

- Report the problem to their superiors (culture of deference)
- Criticize their team members who designed the accelerators (focus on consensus)
- Request the firm spend extra money to redesign the accelerators for greater consumer safety (loyalty to the firm over concern for consumers)

Moreover, Kingston noted that Japanese corporations have a poor record when responding to consumer safety issues. He described the typical Japanese corporation's response in the following way:

- Minimization of the problem
- Reluctance to recall the product
- Poor communication with the public about the problem
- Too little compassion and concern for customers adversely affected by the product[5]

Toyota has not been the only high-profile Japanese company to face scrutiny based on its corporate culture. When the earthquake and resulting tsunami caused a meltdown at the Fukushima nuclear power plant in 2011, outsiders questioned the delayed response by both the Tokyo Electric Power Company and the government. In 2012, an independent report, drafted by a Japanese commission, found that the meltdown was likely preventable. Communication broke down on multiple levels, and employees failed to question authority. The cultural tendency to favor the collective group delayed the implementation of emergency measures, according to the report. In the case of Fukushima, this led to disastrous consequences.[6,7]

Why do Japanese firms usually respond this way to consumer safety issues? Kingston gave three reasons. First, "compensation for product liability claims is mostly derisory or nonexistent" in Japan. In other words, Japanese corporations have little to lose by their minimal response. Second, Kingston describes Japan as "a nation obsessed with craftsmanship and quality." In such an environment, there is significant "shame and embarrassment of owning up to product defects." Corporations may seek to deny their products have safety concerns in order to "save face," i.e., to protect their companies' reputations. Third, Kingston told CNN that "Japanese companies are oddly disconnected with their consumers."[8] In an article printed in *The Wall Street Journal,* Toyota President Akio Toyada wrote: "[I]t is clear to me that in recent years we didn't listen as carefully as we should—or respond as quickly as we must—to our customers' concerns."[9]

Cultural factors can explain another aspect of Toyota's problems—public relations. Toyota has received much less negative attention in the Japanese media as compared with the American media. Professors Johnson, Lim, and Padmanabhan of St. Mary's University offer insight on why this may be: "The American culture demands transparency and action, whereas the Japanese culture assumes that taking ownership of problems and apologies will suffice."[10] Akio Toyoda publicly apologized at press conferences for the inconvenience caused by the Toyota recall and took personal responsibility for the consumer safety issues. For the Japanese media, that was enough. But not for the American media.

Johnson, Lim, and Padmanabhan explained that, while American corporations are expected to be transparent about their problems, Japanese firms have adopted the business practice of keeping problems "in-house." Americans have interpreted Toyota's reticent attitude to mean that Toyota is trying to cover up its problems. Johnson, Lim, and Padmanabhan pointed out, "Since Toyota is firmly established in the U.S., it needs to be meticulously transparent."[11]

丰田的全球战略挑战

Toyota's Global Strategy Challenge

In contrast to the cultural explanation of Toyota's issues, Bill Fischer on Management Issues.com offered a different perspective, suggesting that Toyota's obsession with growth was the cause of the problems. In his view, companies "can expand by either opening new markets or offering new competencies, but not by doing both at the same time!" Fischer emphasized that companies lack a "head-start" based on using their existing "know-how" by "moving into new product areas, in new geographic markets with new factory settings." Transmitting "know-how" requires personal interaction which is difficult over long distances. Fischer concluded that "successful globalization is much too difficult a journey without the assurance of having some knowledge that gives your organization a basis for advantage. . . . To do otherwise is to risk following on the wrong Toyota path to success."[12] In other words, Toyota made a strategic error in its global expansion.

Johnson, Lim, and Padmanabhan offered further explanation on this idea: "When Toyota focused on the Kaizen culture, it was able to maintain closer links with its suppliers, and ensure the quality of its components primarily because they were located in close proximity to Toyota's plants. However, when their expansion and growth strategies required them to build production facilities overseas, and given intense competition in the auto industry, Toyota had to resort to a strategy where they forced suppliers to compete on price. Since it is difficult to pursue Kaizen because of geographic distance, Toyota may have inadvertently sacrificed quality for cost considerations. Mr. Toyoda admitted as much himself when he recently told Congress that his company's focus on growth replaced its traditional priorities of improvements in safety and quality."[13]

未来
Going Forward

With an understanding of what caused Toyota's crisis, what steps should Toyota take going forward? Kingston recommended that Toyota become more focused on the customer and improve corporate governance by appointing independent outside directors. Johnson, Lim, and Padmanabhan suggest that Toyota use this crisis as an opportunity "to adapt its management style to become more decentralized and responsive." Toyota managers need to keep their key cultural strength (Kaizen) while mitigating the negative aspects of their culture which have contributed to the company's present problems. With good managerial oversight, Toyota may once again regain its status as a worldwide symbol of quality.

Our opening discussion in The World of International Management about Toyota shows how culture can have a great impact on business practices. National cultural characteristics can strengthen, empower, and enrich management effectiveness and success. Some cultural qualities, however, may interfere with or constrain managerial decision making and efficacy. Japan's culture has often been credited with creating high-quality products that are the envy of the world. Canon, SONY, Toyota, and others are cited as exemplars in their respective industries, partly because they have leveraged some of the most productive aspects of Japanese culture. At the same time, these same cultural characteristics may retard communication and openness, which may be critical in times of crisis. MNCs that are aware of the potential positives and negatives of different cultural characteristics will be better equipped to manage under both smooth and trying times and environments.

文化的特性
The Nature of Culture

The word *culture* comes from the Latin *cultura,* which is related to cult or worship. In its broadest sense, the term refers to the result of human interaction.[14] For the purposes of the study of international management, **culture** is acquired knowledge that people use to interpret experience and generate social behavior.[15] This knowledge forms values, creates attitudes, and influences behavior. Most scholars of culture would agree on the following characteristics of culture:

culture
Acquired knowledge that people use to interpret experience and generate social behavior. This knowledge forms values, creates attitudes, and influences behavior.

1. *Learned.* Culture is not inherited or biologically based; it is acquired by learning and experience.
2. *Shared.* People as members of a group, organization, or society share culture; it is not specific to single individuals.
3. *Transgenerational.* Culture is cumulative, passed down from one generation to the next.
4. *Symbolic.* Culture is based on the human capacity to symbolize or use one thing to represent another.
5. *Patterned.* Culture has structure and is integrated; a change in one part will bring changes in another.
6. *Adaptive.* Culture is based on the human capacity to change or adapt, as opposed to the more genetically driven adaptive process of animals.[16]

Because different cultures exist in the world, an understanding of the impact of culture on behavior is critical to the study of international management.[17] If international managers do not know something about the cultures of the countries they deal with, the results can be quite disastrous. For example, a partner in one of New York's leading private banking firms tells the following story:

> I traveled nine thousand miles to meet a client and arrived with my foot in my mouth. Determined to do things right, I'd memorized the names of the key men I was to see in Singapore. No easy job, inasmuch as the names all came in threes. So, of course, I couldn't resist showing off that I'd done my homework. I began by addressing top man Lo Win Hao with plenty of well-placed Mr. Hao's—sprinkled the rest of my remarks with a Mr. Chee this and a Mr. Woon that. Great show. Until a note was passed to me from one man I'd met before, in New York. Bad news. "Too friendly too soon, Mr. Long," it said. Where diffidence is next to godliness, there I was, calling a room of VIPs, in effect, Mr. Ed and Mr. Charlie. I'd remembered everybody's name—but forgot that in Chinese the surname comes first and the given name last.[18]

文化多样性

Cultural Diversity

There are many ways of examining cultural differences and their impact on international management. Culture can affect technology transfer, managerial attitudes, managerial ideology, and even business-government relations. Perhaps most important, culture affects how people think and behave. Table 1–1, for example, compares the most important cultural values of the United States, Japan, and Arab countries. A close look at this table shows a great deal of difference among these three cultures. Culture affects a host of business-related activities, even including the common handshake. Here are some contrasting examples:

Culture	Type of Handshake
United States	Firm
Asian	Gentle (shaking hands is unfamiliar and uncomfortable for some; the exception is the Korean, who usually has a firm handshake)
British	Soft
French	Light and quick (not offered to superiors); repeated on arrival and departure
German	Brusque and firm; repeated on arrival and departure
Latin American	Moderate grasp; repeated frequently
Middle Eastern	Gentle; repeated frequently
South Africa	Light/soft; long and involved[19]

Table 1–1
Priorities of Cultural Values: United States, Japan, and Arab Countries

United States	Japan	Arab Countries
1. Freedom	1. Belonging	1. Family security
2. Independence	2. Group harmony	2. Family harmony
3. Self-reliance	3. Collectiveness	3. Parental guidance
4. Equality	4. Age/seniority	4. Age
5. Individualism	5. Group consensus	5. Authority
6. Competition	6. Cooperation	6. Compromise
7. Efficiency	7. Quality	7. Devotion
8. Time	8. Patience	8. Patience
9. Directness	9. Indirectness	9. Indirectness
10. Openness	10. Go-between	10. Hospitality

Note: "1" represents the most important cultural value. "10" the least.

Source: Adapted from information found in F. Elashmawi and Philip R. Harris, *Multicultural Management* (Houston: Gulf Publishing, 1993), p. 63.

In overall terms, the cultural impact on international management is reflected by basic beliefs and behaviors. Here are some specific examples where the culture of a society can directly affect management approaches:

- *Centralized vs. decentralized decision making.* In some societies, top managers make all important organizational decisions. In others, these decisions are diffused throughout the enterprise, and middle- and lower-level managers actively participate in, and make, key decisions.
- *Safety vs. risk.* In some societies, organizational decision makers are risk-averse and have great difficulty with conditions of uncertainty. In others, risk taking is encouraged, and decision making under uncertainty is common.
- *Individual vs. group rewards.* In some countries, personnel who do outstanding work are given individual rewards in the form of bonuses and commissions. In others, cultural norms require group rewards, and individual rewards are frowned on.
- *Informal vs. formal procedures.* In some societies, much is accomplished through informal means. In others, formal procedures are set forth and followed rigidly.
- *High vs. low organizational loyalty.* In some societies, people identify very strongly with their organization or employer. In others, people identify with their occupational group, such as engineer or mechanic.
- *Cooperation vs. competition.* Some societies encourage cooperation between their people. Others encourage competition between their people.
- *Short-term vs. long-term horizons.* Some cultures focus most heavily on short-term horizons, such as short-range goals of profit and efficiency. Others are more interested in long-range goals, such as market share and technological development.
- *Stability vs. innovation.* The culture of some countries encourages stability and resistance to change. The culture of others puts high value on innovation and change.

These cultural differences influence the way that international management should be conducted. The International Management in Action, "Business Customs in South Africa," provides some examples from a country where many international managers are unfamiliar with day-to-day business protocol.

Another way of depicting cultural diversity is through visually separating its components. Figure 1–1 provides an example by using concentric circles. The outer ring consists

Figure 1–1
A Model of Culture

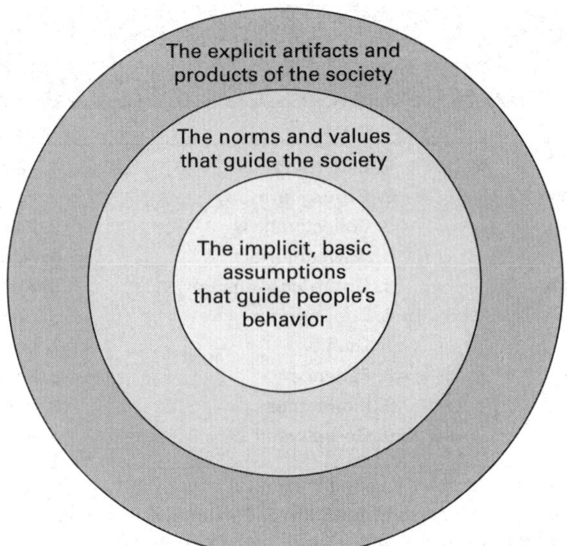

Business Customs in South Africa

The proper methods for conducting business in Africa can vary greatly depending on the region. Africa consists of many traditions often within the same area. Adding further complication is the propensity for northern regions of Africa to mirror Islamic fundamentals. For simplicity, we will focus on some suggestions with regard to business customs in one country, South Africa:

1. Arrange a meeting before discussing business over the phone. Most South Africans prefer face-to-face interactions. Be prepared for informal small talk before and during the meeting to be better acquainted. In most cases, first meetings are less about business and more about establishing a relationship. Sincere inquiries about family or discussion of topics such as sports (e.g., rugby, cricket, or soccer) are encouraged to avoid talking about racial politics as it is viewed as taboo.
2. Appointments should be made as far in advance as possible. There is a chance that senior-level managers may be unavailable on short notice, but last-minute arrangements occur often. South Africans are early risers, so breakfast and lunch meetings are quite common. If you have a few meetings scheduled, be sure to allow ample time between them as the view of time is more lax in this area and meetings are prone to being postponed.
3. When introduced, maintain eye contact, shake hands, and provide business cards to everyone. Do not sit until invited to do so. Men and women do not shake hands as often in South Africa, so wait for women to initiate handshakes. Women visiting the country who extend their hand may not have it taken by a South African male, so do not take this as a rude response.
4. Since women are not yet in senior level positions in South Africa, female representatives may encounter condescending behavior or "tests" that would not be extended to male counterparts. Men are expected to leave a room before the women as a "protective" measure, and when a woman or elder enters the room, men are expected to stand.
5. After establishing a trustworthy relationship, make business plans clear, including deadlines, since these are seen as more fluid than contractual. Be sure to keep a tone of negotiation while keeping figures manageable. Negotiation is not their strong point, and an aggressive approach will not prove to be successful. Maintain a win-win strategy.
6. Patience is very important when dealing with business. Never interrupt a South African. Be prepared for a long lag-time between business proposition and acceptance or rejection. Decision-making procedures include a lot of discussion between top managers and subordinates, resulting in slow processes.
7. Keep presentations short, and do away with flashy visuals. Follow up and be clear that you intend to continue relations with the business or individual; a long-term business relationship is valued with South Africans.

Source: www.kwintessential.co.uk/resources/global-etiquette/south-africa-country-profile.html; Going Global Inc., "Cultural Advice," *South Africa Career Guide, 2006,* content.epnet.com.ps2.villanova.edu/pdf18_21/pdf/2006/ONI/01Jan06/22291722.pdf; Fons Trompenaars and Charles Hampden-Turner, *Riding the Waves of Culture: Understanding Diversity in Global Business,* 2nd ed. (New York: McGraw-Hill, 1998), p. 25.

of the explicit artifacts and products of the culture. This level is observable and consists of such things as language, food, buildings, and art. The middle ring contains the norms and values of the society. These can be both formal and informal, and they are designed to help people understand how they should behave. The inner circle contains the implicit, basic assumptions that govern behavior. By understanding these assumptions, members of a culture are able to organize themselves in a way that helps them increase the effectiveness of their problem-solving processes and interact well with each other. In explaining the nature of the inner circle, Trompenaars and Hampden-Turner have noted that:

> The best way to test if something is a basic assumption is when the [situation] provokes confusion or irritation. You might, for example, observe that some Japanese bow deeper than others. . . . If you ask why they do it the answer might be that they don't know but that the other person

Figure 1–2

Comparing Cultures as Overlapping Normal Distributions

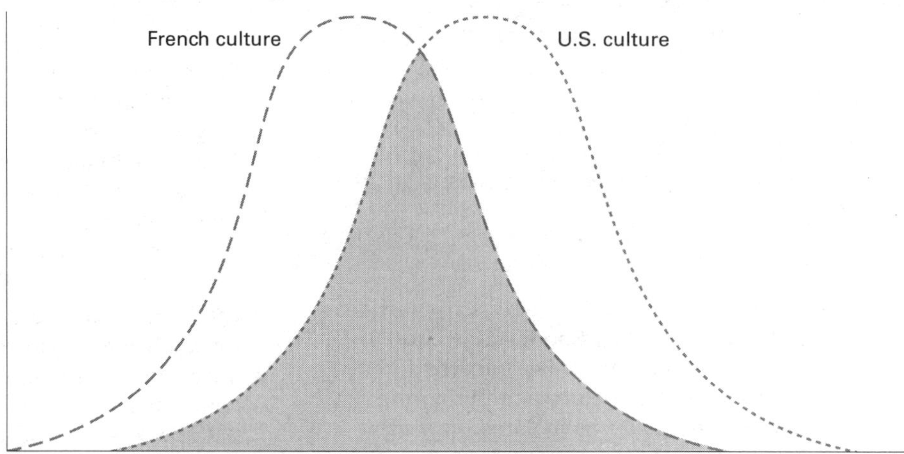

Source: Adapted from Fons Trompenaars and Charles Hampden-Turner, *Riding the Waves of Culture: Understanding Diversity in Global Business,* 2nd ed. (New York: McGraw-Hill, 1998), p. 25.

> does it too (norm) or that they want to show respect for authority (value). A typical Dutch question that might follow is: "Why do you respect authority?" The most likely Japanese reaction would be either puzzlement or a smile (which might be hiding their irritation). When you question basic assumptions you are asking questions that have never been asked before. It might lead others to deeper insights, but it also might provoke annoyance. Try in the USA or the Netherlands to raise the question of why people are equal and you will see what we mean.[20]

A supplemental way of understanding cultural differences is to compare culture as a normal distribution, as in Figure 1–2, and then to examine it in terms of stereotyping, as in Figure 1–3. French culture and American culture, for example, have quite different norms and values. So the normal distribution curves for the two cultures have only limited overlap. However, when one looks at the tail-ends of the two curves, it is possible to identify stereotypical views held by members of one culture about the other. The stereotypes

Figure 1–3

Stereotyping from the Cultural Extremes

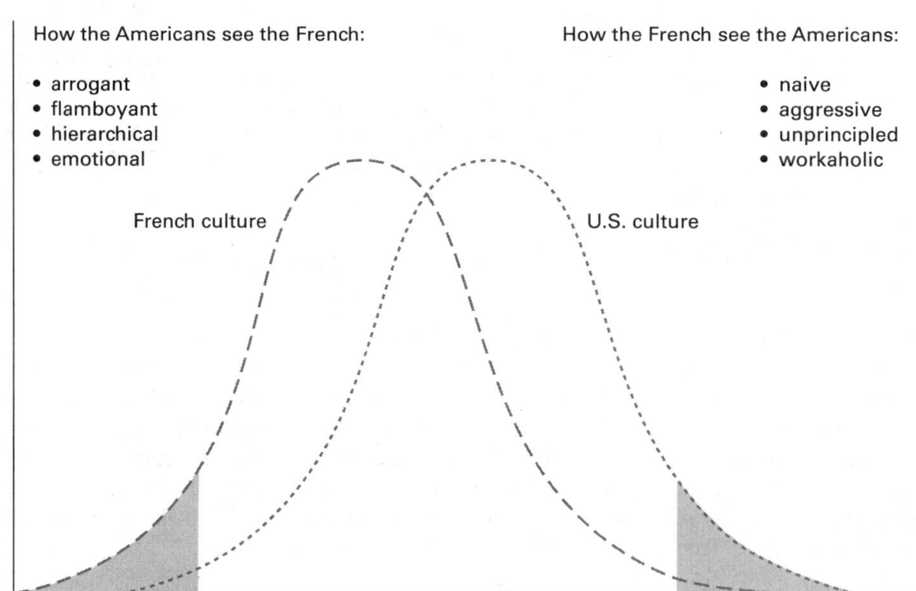

Source: Adapted from Fons Trompenaars and Charles Hampden-Turner, *Riding the Waves of Culture: Understanding Diversity in Global Business,* 2nd ed. (New York: McGraw-Hill, 1998), p. 23.

are often exaggerated and used by members of one culture in describing the other, thus helping reinforce the differences between the two while reducing the likelihood of achieving cooperation and communication. This is one reason why an understanding of national culture is so important in the study of international management.

文化中的价值观
Values in Culture

A major dimension in the study of culture is values. **Values** are basic convictions that people have regarding what is right and wrong, good and bad, and important and unimportant. These values are learned from the culture in which the individual is reared, and they help direct the person's behavior. Differences in cultural values often result in varying management practices. Table 1–2 provides an example. Note that U.S. values can result in one set of business responses and that alternative values can bring about different responses.

values
Basic convictions that people have regarding what is right and wrong, good and bad, and important and unimportant.

不同文化的价值观差异和相似性
Value Differences and Similarities across Cultures

Personal values have been the focus of numerous intercultural studies. In general, the findings show both differences and similarities between the work values and managerial values of different cultural groups. For example, one study found differences in work values between Western-oriented and tribal-oriented black employees in South Africa.[21] The Western-oriented group accepted most of the tenets of the Protestant work ethic, but the tribal-oriented group did not. The results were explained in terms of the differences of the cultural backgrounds of the two groups.

Differences in work values also have been found to reflect culture and industrialization. Researchers gave a personal-values questionnaire (PVQ) to over 2,000 managers in five countries: Australia (n = 281), India (n = 485), Japan (n = 301), South Korea

Table 1–2
U.S. Values and Possible Alternatives

U.S. Cultural Values	Alternative Values	Examples of Management Function Affected
Individuals can influence the future (where there is a will there is a way).	Life follows a preordained course, and human action is determined by the will of God.	Planning and scheduling.
Individuals should be realistic in their aspirations.	Ideals are to be pursued regardless of what is "reasonable."	Goal setting and career development.
We must work hard to accomplish our objectives (Puritan ethic).	Hard work is not the only prerequisite for success. Wisdom, luck, and time are also required.	Motivation and reward system.
A primary obligation of an employee is to the organization.	Individual employees have a primary obligation to their family and friends.	Loyalty, commitment, and motivation.
Employees can be removed if they do not perform well.	The removal of an employee from a position involves a great loss of prestige and will rarely be done.	Promotion.
Company information should be available to anyone who needs it within the organization.	Withholding information to gain or maintain power is acceptable.	Organization, communication, and managerial style.
Competition stimulates high performance.	Competition leads to imbalances and disharmony.	Career development and marketing.
What works is important.	Symbols and the process are more important than the end point.	Communication, planning, and quality control.

Source: Adapted from information found in Philip R. Harris and Robert T. Moran, *Managing Cultural Differences* (Houston: Gulf Publishing, 1991), pp. 79–80.

($n = 161$), and the United States ($n = 833$).[22] The PVQ consisted of 66 concepts related to business goals, personal goals, ideas associated with people and groups of people, and ideas about general topics. Ideologic and philosophic concepts were included to represent major value systems of all groups. The results showed some significant differences between the managers in each group. U.S. managers placed high value on the tactful acquisition of influence and on regard for others. Japanese managers placed high value on deference to superiors, company commitment, and the cautious use of aggressiveness and control. Korean managers placed high value on personal forcefulness and aggressiveness and low value on recognition of others. Indian managers put high value on the nonaggressive pursuit of objectives. Australian managers placed major importance on values reflecting a low-key approach to management and a high concern for others.[23] In short, value systems across national boundaries often are different.

At the same time, value similarities exist between cultures. In fact, research shows that managers from different countries often have similar personal values that relate to success. England and Lee examined the managerial values of a diverse sample of U.S. ($n = 878$), Japanese ($n = 312$), Australian ($n = 301$), and Indian ($n = 500$) managers. They found that:

1. There is a reasonably strong relationship between the level of success achieved by managers and their personal values.
2. It is evident that value patterns predict managerial success and could be used in selection and placement decisions.
3. Although there are country differences in the relationships between values and success, findings across the four countries are quite similar.
4. The general pattern indicates that more successful managers appear to favor pragmatic, dynamic, achievement-oriented values, while less successful managers prefer more static and passive values. More successful managers favor an achievement orientation and prefer an active role in interaction with other individuals who are instrumental to achieving the managers' organizational goals. Less successful managers have values associated with a static and protected environment in which they take relatively passive roles.[24]

The International Management in Action box, "Common Personal Values," on page 119 discusses these findings in more depth.

价值观转变
Values in Transition

Do values change over time? George England found that personal value systems are relatively stable and do not change rapidly.[25] However, changes are taking place in managerial values as a result of both culture and technology. A good example is the Japanese. Reichel and Flynn examined the effects of the U.S. environment on the cultural values of Japanese managers working for Japanese firms in the United States. In particular, they focused attention on such key organizational values as lifetime employment, formal authority, group orientation, seniority, and paternalism. Here is what they found:

1. Lifetime employment is widely accepted in Japanese culture, but the stateside Japanese managers did not believe that unconditional tenure in one organization was of major importance. They did believe, however, that job security was important.
2. Formal authority, obedience, and conformance to hierarchic position are very important in Japan, but the stateside managers did not perceive obedience and conformity to be very important and rejected the idea that one should not question a superior. However, they did support the concept of formal authority.
3. Group orientation, cooperation, conformity, and compromise are important organizational values in Japan. The stateside managers supported these values but also believed it was important to be an individual, thus maintaining a balance between a group and a personal orientation.

International Management in Action

Common Personal Values

One of the most interesting findings about successful managers around the world is that while they come from different cultures, many have similar personal values. Of course, there are large differences in values within each national group. For example, some managers are very pragmatic and judge ideas in terms of whether they will work; others are highly ethical and moral and view ideas in terms of right or wrong; still others have a "feeling" orientation and judge ideas in terms of whether they are pleasant. Some managers have a very small set of values; others have a large set. Some have values that are related heavily to organization life; others include a wide range of personal values; others have highly group-oriented values. There are many different value patterns; however, overall value profiles have been found within successful managers in each group. Here are some of the most significant:

U.S. managers

- Highly pragmatic
- High achievement and competence orientation
- Emphasis on profit maximization, organizational efficiency, and high productivity

Japanese managers

- Highly pragmatic
- Strong emphasis on size and growth
- High value on competence and achievement

Korean managers

- Highly pragmatic
- Highly individualistic
- Strong achievement and competence orientation

Australian managers

- High moral orientation
- High humanistic orientation
- Low value on achievement, success, competition, and risk

Indian managers

- High moral orientation
- Highly individualistic
- Strong focus on organization compliance and competence

The findings listed here show important similarities and differences. Most of the profiles are similar in nature; however, note that successful Indian and Australian managers have values that are distinctly different. In short, although values of successful managers within countries often are similar, there are intercountry differences. This is why the successful managerial value systems of one country often are not ideal in another country.

4. In Japan, organizational personnel often are rewarded based on seniority, not merit. Support for this value was directly influenced by the length of time the Japanese managers had been in the United States. The longer they had been there, the lower their support for this value.
5. Paternalism, often measured by a manager's involvement in both personal and off-the-job problems of subordinates, is very important in Japan. Stateside Japanese managers disagreed, and this resistance was positively associated with the number of years they had been in the United States.[26]

There is increasing evidence that individualism in Japan is on the rise, indicating that Japanese values are changing—and not just among managers outside the country. The country's long economic slump has convinced many Japanese that they cannot rely on the large corporations or the government to ensure their future. They have to do it for themselves. As a result, today a growing number of Japanese are starting to embrace what is being called the "era of personal responsibility." Instead of denouncing individualism as a threat to society, they are proposing it as a necessary solution to many of the country's economic ills. A vice chairman of the nation's largest business lobby summed up this thinking at the opening of a recent conference on economic change when he said, "By establishing personal responsibility, we must return dynamism to the economy and revitalize society."[27] This thinking is supported by Lee and Peterson's research which reveals that a culture with a strong entrepreneurial orientation is important to global competitiveness, especially in the small business sector of an economy. So this current trend may well be helpful to the Japanese economy in helping it meet foreign competition at home.[28]

The focus here has been on Japan due to the concrete experiential and experimental evidence. While Japanese cultures and values continue to evolve, other countries such as China are just beginning to undergo a new era. We know how China is moving away from a collectivist culture, and it appears as though even China is not sure what cultural values it will adhere to. Confucianism was worshipped for over 2,000 years, but the powerful messages through Confucius's teachings were overshadowed in a world where profit became a priority. Now, Confucianism is slowly gaining popularity once again, emphasizing respect for authority, concern for others, balance, harmony, and overall order. While this may provide sanctuary for some, it poses problems within the government, since it will have to prove its worthiness to remain in power. As long as China continues to prosper, hope for a unified culture may be on the horizon. Many are still concerned with the lack of an alternative if China's growth is stunted, creating even more confusion in the journey to maintain cultural values.[29]

文化维度
Cultural Dimensions

Understanding the cultural context of a society, and being able to respond and react appropriately to cultural differences, is becoming increasingly important as the global environment becomes more interconnected. Over the past several decades, researchers have attempted to provide a composite picture of culture by examining its subparts, or dimensions.

霍夫斯泰德
Hofstede

In 1980, Dutch researcher Geert Hofstede identified four original, and later two additional, dimensions of culture that help explain how and why people from various cultures behave as they do.[30] His initial data were gathered from two questionnaire surveys with over 116,000 respondents from over 70 different countries around the world—making it the largest organizationally based study ever conducted. The individuals in these studies all worked in the local subsidiaries of IBM. As a result, Hofstede's research has been criticized because of its focus on just one company; however, he has countered this criticism. Hofstede is well aware of the amazement of some people about how employees of a very specific corporation like IBM can serve as a sample for discovering something about the culture of their countries at large. "We know IBMers," they say. "They are very special people, always in a white shirt and tie, and not at all representative of our country." The people who say this are quite right. IBMers do not form representative samples from national populations. However, samples for cross-national comparison need not be representative, as long as they are functionally equivalent. IBM employees are a narrow sample, but very well matched. Employees of multinational companies in general and of IBM in particular form attractive sources of information for comparing national traits, because they are so similar in respects other than nationality: their employers, their kind of work, and—for matched occupations—their level of education. The only thing that can account for systematic and consistent differences between national groups within such a homogenous multinational population is nationality itself; the national environment in which people were brought up before they joined this employer. Comparing IBM subsidiaries therefore shows national culture differences with unusual clarity.[31] Hofstede's massive study continues to be a focal point for additional research, including the most recent GLOBE project, discussed at the end of this chapter.

power distance
The extent to which less powerful members of institutions and organizations accept that power is distributed unequally.

The original four dimensions that Hofstede examined were (1) power distance, (2) uncertainty avoidance, (3) individualism, and (4) masculinity.[32]

权力距

Power Distance **Power distance** is "the extent to which less powerful members of institutions and organizations accept that power is distributed unequally."[33] Countries in which people blindly obey the orders of their superiors have high power distance. In many societies, lower-level employees tend to follow orders as a matter of procedure. In societies with high power distance, however, strict obedience is found even at the upper levels; examples include Mexico, South Korea, and India. For example, a senior Indian executive with a PhD from a prestigious U.S. university related the following story:

> What is most important for me and my department is not what I do or achieve for the company, but whether the [owner's] favor is bestowed on me. . . . This I have achieved by saying "yes" to everything [the owner] says or does. . . . To contradict him is to look for another job. . . . I left my freedom of thought in Boston.[34]

The effect of this dimension can be measured in a number of ways. For example, organizations in low-power-distance countries generally will be decentralized and have flatter organization structures. These organizations also will have a smaller proportion of supervisory personnel, and the lower strata of the workforce often will consist of highly qualified people. By contrast, organizations in high-power-distance countries will tend to be centralized and have tall organization structures. Organizations in high-power-distance countries will have a large proportion of supervisory personnel, and the people at the lower levels of the structure often will have low job qualifications. This latter structure encourages and promotes inequality between people at different levels.[35]

规避不确定性

Uncertainty Avoidance **Uncertainty avoidance** is "the extent to which people feel threatened by ambiguous situations and have created beliefs and institutions that try to avoid these."[36] Countries populated with people who do not like uncertainty tend to have a high need for security and a strong belief in experts and their knowledge; examples include Germany, Japan, and Spain. Cultures with low uncertainty avoidance have people who are more willing to accept that risks are associated with the unknown, and that life must go on in spite of this. Examples include Denmark and Great Britain.

uncertainty avoidance
The extent to which people feel threatened by ambiguous situations and have created beliefs and institutions that try to avoid these.

The effect of this dimension can be measured in a number of ways. Countries with high-uncertainty-avoidance cultures have a great deal of structuring of organizational activities, more written rules, less risk taking by managers, lower labor turnover, and less ambitious employees.

Low-uncertainty-avoidance societies have organization settings with less structuring of activities, fewer written rules, more risk taking by managers, higher labor turnover, and more ambitious employees. The organization encourages personnel to use their own initiative and assume responsibility for their actions.

个人主义

Individualism **Individualism** is the tendency of people to look after themselves and their immediate family only.[37] Hofstede measured this cultural difference on a bipolar continuum with individualism at one end and collectivism at the other. **Collectivism** is the tendency of people to belong to groups or collectives and to look after each other in exchange for loyalty.[38]

individualism
The tendency of people to look after themselves and their immediate family only.

collectivism
The tendency of people to belong to groups or collectives and to look after each other in exchange for loyalty.

Like the effects of the other cultural dimensions, the effects of individualism and collectivism can be measured in a number of different ways.[39] Hofstede found that wealthy countries have higher individualism scores and poorer countries higher collectivism scores (see Table 1–3 for the 74 countries used in Figure 1–4 and subsequent figures). Note that in Figure 1–4, shown on page 15, the United States, Canada, Australia, Denmark, and Sweden, among others, have high individualism and high GNP. Conversely, Indonesia, Pakistan, and a number of South American countries have low individualism (high collectivism) and low GNP. Countries with high individualism also tend to have greater support for the Protestant work ethic, greater individual initiative, and promotions based on market value. Countries with low individualism tend to have less support for the Protestant work ethic, less individual initiative, and promotions based on seniority.

Table 1–3
Countries and Regions Used in Hofstede's Research

Arabic-speaking countries (Egypt, Iraq, Kuwait, Lebanon, Libya, Saudi Arabia, United Arab Emirates)	Ecuador	Panama
	Estonia	Peru
	Finland	Philippines
	France	Poland
	Germany	Portugal
	Great Britain	Romania
	Greece	Russia
Argentina	Guatemala	Salvador
Australia	Hong Kong (China)	Serbia
Austria		Singapore
Bangladesh	Hungary	Slovakia
Belgium Flemish (Dutch speaking)	India	Slovenia
	Indonesia	South Africa
Belgium Walloon (French speaking)	Iran	Spain
	Ireland	Suriname
Brazil	Israel	Sweden
Bulgaria	Italy	Switzerland French
Canada Quebec	Jamaica	Switzerland German
Canada total	Japan	Taiwan(China)
Chile	Korea (South)	Thailand
China	Luxembourg	Trinidad
Colombia	Malaysia	Turkey
Costa Rica	Malta	United States
Croatia	Mexico	Uruguay
Czech Republic	Morocco	Venezuela
Denmark	Netherlands	Vietnam
East Africa (Ethiopia, Kenya, Tanzania, Zambia)	New Zealand	West Africa (Ghana, Nigeria, Sierra Leone)
	Norway	
	Pakistan	

Source: From Hofstede and Hofstede, *Cultures and Organizations: Software of the Mind.* Copyright © 2005 The McGraw-Hill Companies, Inc. Reprinted with permission.

masculinity
A cultural characteristic in which the dominant values in society are success, money, and things.

femininity
A cultural characteristic in which the dominant values in society are caring for others and the quality of life.

男性气质

Masculinity **Masculinity** is defined by Hofstede as "a situation in which the dominant values in society are success, money, and things."[40] Hofstede measured this dimension on a continuum ranging from masculinity to femininity. Contrary to some stereotypes and connotations, **femininity** is the term used by Hofstede to describe "a situation in which the dominant values in society are caring for others and the quality of life."[41]

Countries with a high masculinity index, such as the Germanic countries, place great importance on earnings, recognition, advancement, and challenge. Individuals are encouraged to be independent decision makers, and achievement is defined in terms of recognition and wealth. The workplace is often characterized by high job stress, and many managers believe that their employees dislike work and must be kept under some degree of control. The school system is geared toward encouraging high performance. Young men expect to have careers, and those who do not often view themselves as failures. Historically, fewer women hold higher-level jobs, although this is changing. The school system is geared toward encouraging high performance.

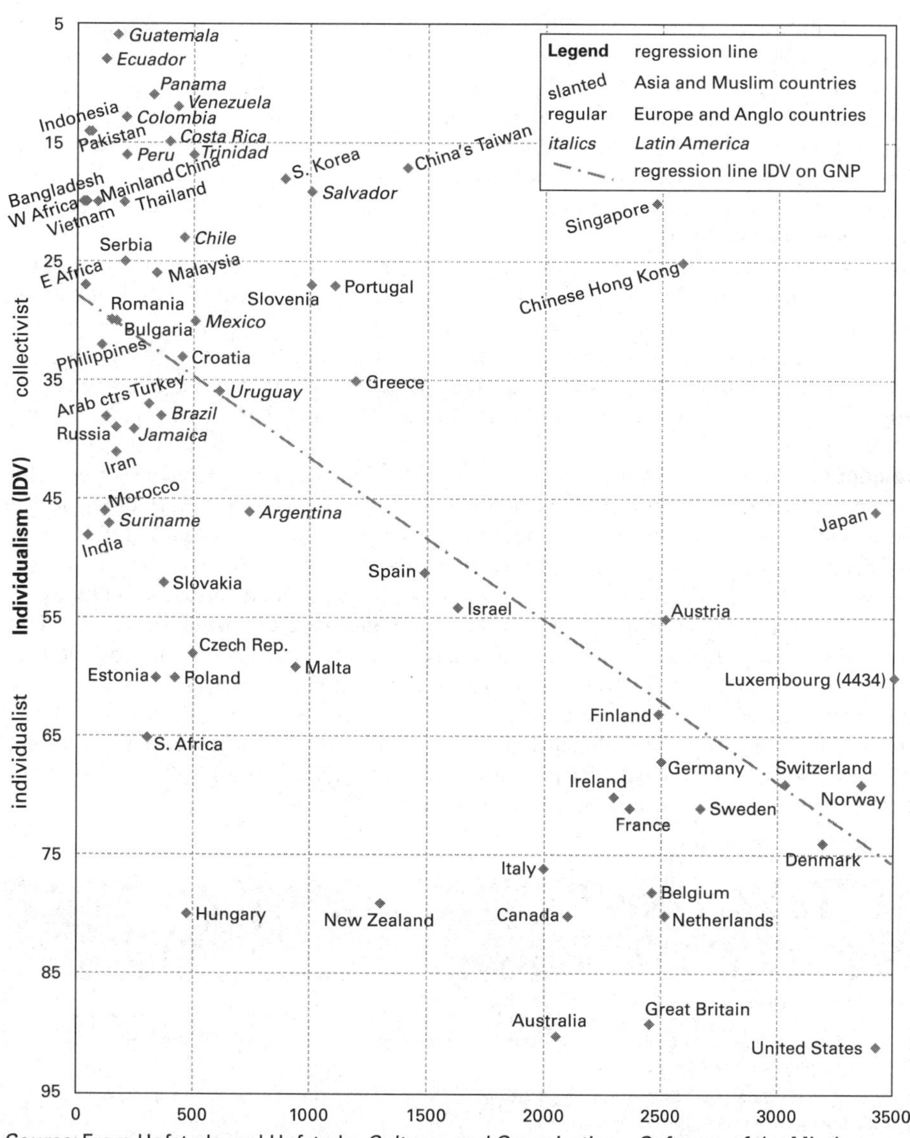

Source: From Hofstede and Hofstede, *Cultures and Organizations: Software of the Mind.* Copyright © 2005 The McGraw-Hill Companies, Inc. Reprinted with permission.

Figure 1–4

GNP per Capita in 2000 versus Individualism

Countries with a low masculinity index (Hofstede's femininity dimension), such as Norway, tend to place great importance on cooperation, a friendly atmosphere, and employment security. Individuals are encouraged to be group decision makers, and achievement is defined in terms of layman contacts and the living environment. The workplace tends to be characterized by low stress, and managers give their employees more credit for being responsible and allow them more freedom. Culturally, this group prefers small-scale enterprises, and they place greater importance on conservation of the environment. The school system is designed to teach social adaptation. Some young men and women want careers; others do not. Many women hold higher-level jobs, and they do not find it necessary to be assertive.

Further research by Hofstede led to the recent identification of the fifth and sixth cultural dimensions: (5) time orientation, identified in 1988, and (6) indulgence versus restraint, identified in 2010.[42]

时间取向

Time Orientation Originally called Confucian Work Dynamism, time orientation is defined by Hofstede as "dealing with society's search for virtue." Long-term oriented societies tend to focus on the future. They have the ability to adapt their traditions when conditions change, have a tendency to save and invest for the future, and focus on achieving long-term results. Short-term oriented cultures focus more on the past and present than on the future. These societies have a deep respect for tradition, focus on achieving quick results, and do not tend to save for the future.[43] Table 1–4 highlights ten differences between long- and short-term oriented cultures.

Asian cultures primarily exhibit long-term orientation. Countries with a high long-term orientation index include China, Japan, and Brazil. In these cultures, individuals are persistent, thrifty with their money, and highly adaptable to unexpected circumstances. Spain, the USA, and the UK were identified as having a low long-term orientation index (Hofstede's short-term orientation). Individuals in short-term oriented societies believe in absolutes (good and evil), value stability and leisure time, and spend money more freely.[44]

放纵和约束

Indulgence versus Restraint Based on research related to relative happiness around the world, Hofstede's most recent dimension measures the freedom to satisfy one's natural needs and desires within a society. Indulgent societies encourage instant gratification of natural human needs, while restrained cultures regulate and control behavior based on social norms.[45] Table 1–5 highlights ten differences between indulgent and restrained cultures.

Countries that show a high indulgence index include the USA, Australia, the UK, and Chile. Freely able to satisfy their basic human desires, individuals in these societies tend to live in the moment. They participate in more activities, express happiness freely, and view themselves as being in control of their own destiny. Countries that show a low indulgence index (Hofstede's dimension of restraint) include Egypt, Romania, and China. In these societies, individuals participate in fewer activities, express less happiness, and believe that their own destiny is not in their control.[46]

Table 1–4
Ten Differences between Short- and Long-Term Oriented Societies

Short-Term Orientation	Long-Term Orientation
Most important events in life occurred in the past or take place now	Most important events in life will occur in the future
Personal steadiness and stability: a good person is always the same	A good person adapts to the circumstances
There are universal guidelines about what is good and evil	What is good and evil depends on the circumstances
Traditions are sacrosanct	Traditions are adaptable to changed circumstances
Family life guided by imperatives	Family life guided by shared tasks
Supposed to proud of one's country	Trying to learn from other countries
Service to others is an important goal	Thrift and perseverance are important goals
Social spending and consumption	Large savings quote, funds available for investment
Students attribute success and failure to luck	Students attribute success to effort and failure to lack of effort
Slow or no economic growth of poor countries	Fast economic growth of countries up till a level of prosperity

Source: From Hofstede, G. (2011). "Dimensionalizing Cultures: The Hofstede Model in Context," *Online readings in Psychology and Culture, Unit 2. http://scholarworks.gvsu.edu/orpc/vol2/iss1/8.* © 2011 IACCP.

Table 1–5
Ten Differences between Indulgent and Restrained Societies

Indulgent	Restrained
Higher percentage of people declaring themselves very happy	Fewer very happy people
A perception of personal life control	A perception of helplessness: what happens to me is not my own doing
Freedom of speech seen as important	Freedom of speech is not a primary concern
Higher importance of leisure	Lower importance of leisure
More likely to remember positive emotions	Less likely to remember positive emotions
In countries with educated populations, higher birthrates	In countries with educated populations, lower birthrates
More people actively involved in sports	Fewer people actively involved in sports
In countries with enough food, higher percentages of obese people	In countries with enough food, fewer obese people
In wealthy countries, lenient sexual norms	In wealthy countries, stricter sexual norms
Maintaining order in the nation is not given a high priority	Higher number of police officers per 100,000 population

Source: From Hofstede, G. (2011). "Dimensionalizing Cultures: The Hofstede Model in Context," *Online readings in Psychology and Culture, Unit 2. http://scholarworks.gvsu.edu/orpc/vol2/iss1/8.* © 2011 IACCP.

综合维度

Integrating the Dimensions A description of the four original and two additional dimensions of culture is useful in helping to explain the differences between various countries, and Hofstede's research has extended beyond this focus and shown how countries can be described in terms of pairs of dimensions. In Hofstede's and later research, pairings and clusters can provide useful summaries for international managers. It is always best to have an in-depth understanding of the multicultural environment, but the general groupings outline common ground that one can use as a starting point. Figure 1–5, which incorporates power distance and individualism, provides an example.

Upon first examination of the cluster distribution, the data may appear confusing. However, they are very useful in depicting what countries appear similar in values, and to what extent they differ with other country clusters. The same countries are not always clustered together in subsequent dimension comparisons. This indicates that while some beliefs overlap between cultures, it is where they diverge that makes groups unique to manage.

In Figure 1–5, the United States, Australia, Canada, Britain, Denmark, and New Zealand are located in the lower-left-hand quadrant. Americans, for example, have very high individualism and relatively low power distance. They prefer to do things for themselves and are not upset when others have more power than they do. The other countries, while they may not be a part of the same cluster, share similar values. Conversely, many of the underdeveloped or newly industrialized countries and regions, such as Colombia, Chinese Hong Kong, Portugal, and Singapore, are characterized by large power distance and low individualism. These nations and regions tend to be collectivist in their approach.

Similarly, Figure 1–6 plots the uncertainty-avoidance index against the power-distance index. Once again, there are clusters of countries. Many of the Anglo nations tend to be in the upper-left-hand quadrant, which is characterized by small power distance and weak uncertainty avoidance, while, in contrast, many Latin, Mediterranean, and Asian nations are characterized by high power distance and strong uncertainty avoidance.

Figure 1–5

Power Distance versus Individualism

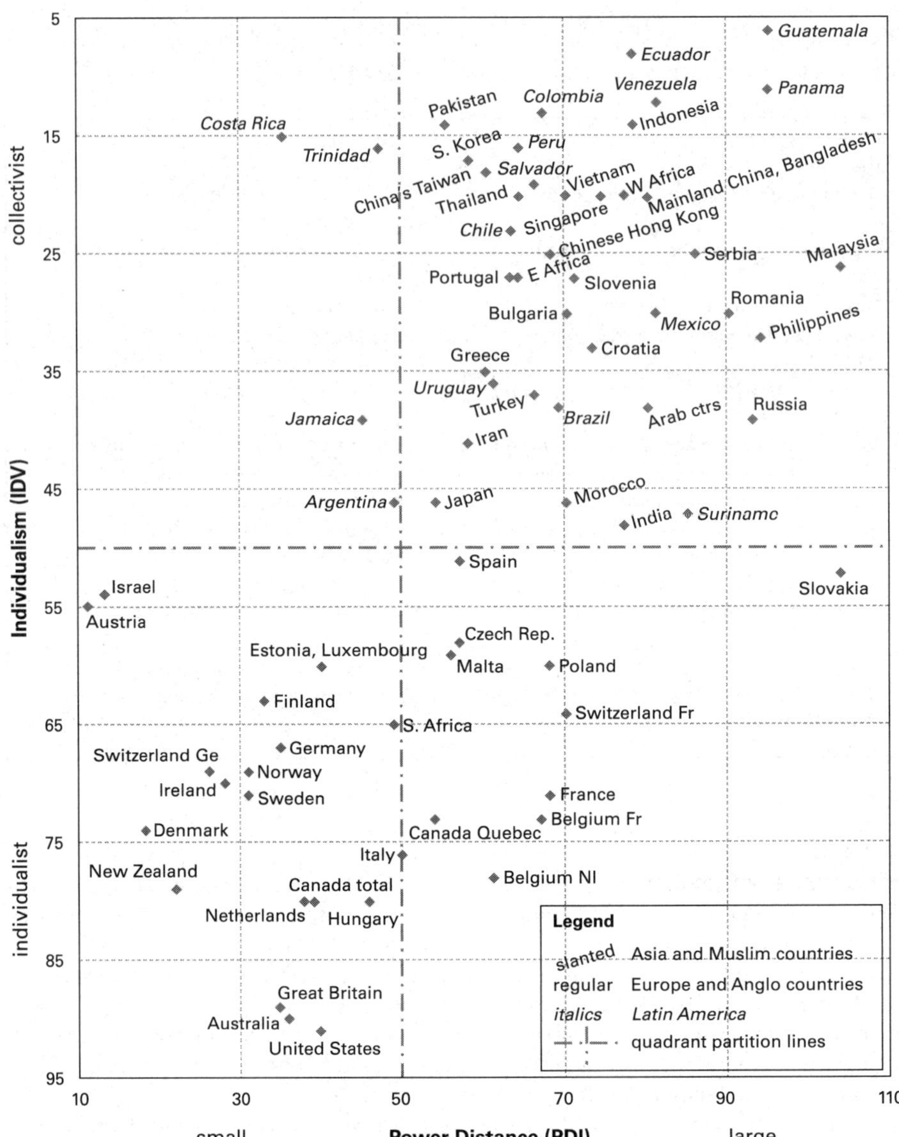

Source: From Hofstede and Hofstede, *Cultures and Organizations: Software of the Mind.* Copyright © 2005 The McGraw-Hill Companies, Inc. Reprinted with permission.

The integration of these cultural factors into two-dimensional plots helps illustrate the complexity of understanding culture's effect on behavior. A number of dimensions are at work, and sometimes they do not all move in the anticipated direction. For example, at first glance, a nation with high power distance would appear to be low in individualism, and vice versa, and Hofstede found exactly that (see Figure 1–5). However, low uncertainty avoidance does not always go hand in hand with high masculinity, even though those who are willing to live with uncertainty will want rewards such as money and power and accord low value to the quality of work life and caring for others (see Figure 1–7). Simply put, empirical evidence on the impact of cultural dimensions may differ from commonly held beliefs or stereotypes. Research-based data are needed to determine the full impact of differing cultures.

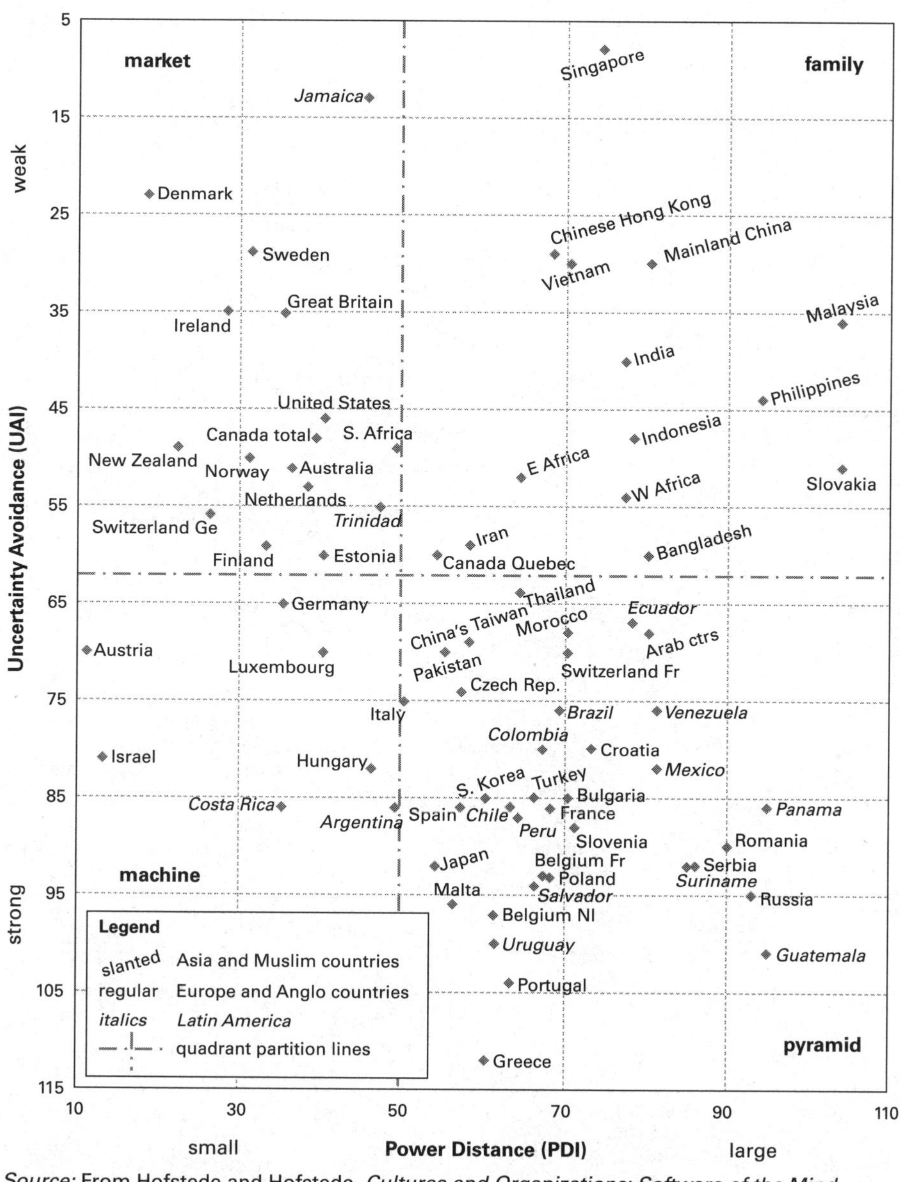

Figure 1–6
Power Distance versus Uncertainty Avoidance

Source: From Hofstede and Hofstede, *Cultures and Organizations: Software of the Mind.* Copyright © 2005 The McGraw-Hill Companies, Inc. Reprinted with permission.

The Hofstede cultural dimensions and country clusters are widely recognized and accepted in the study of international management. His work has served as a springboard to numerous recent cultural studies and research projects.

特朗皮纳斯
Trompenaars

In 1994, another Dutch researcher, Fons Trompenaars, expanded on the research of Hofstede and published the results of his own 10-year study on cultural dimensions.[47] He administered research questionnaires to over 15,000 managers from 28 countries and received usable responses from at least 500 in each nation; the 23 countries in his

Figure 1–7
Masculinity versus Uncertainty Avoidance

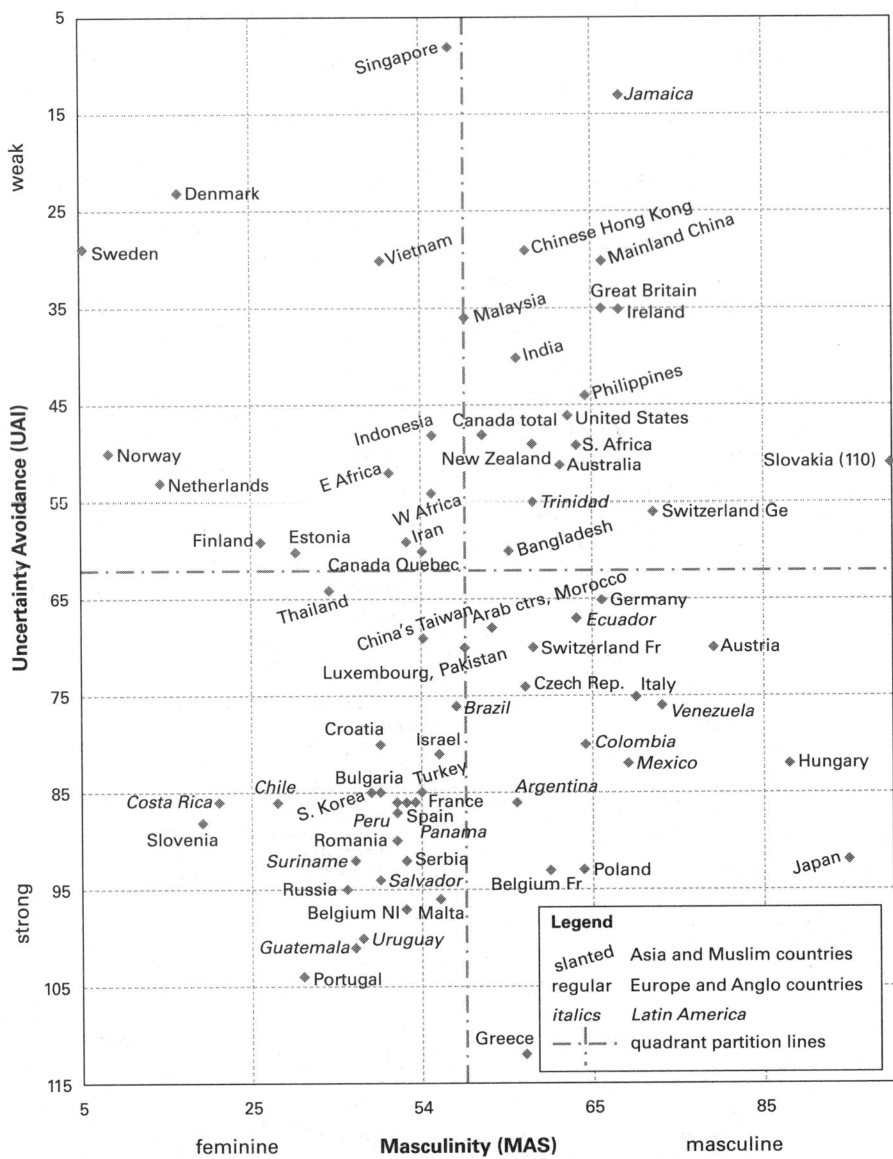

Source: From Hofstede and Hofstede, *Cultures and Organizations: Software of the Mind.* Copyright © 2005 The McGraw-Hill Companies, Inc. Reprinted with permission.

research are presented in Table 1–6. Building heavily on value orientations and the relational orientations of well-known sociologist Talcott Parsons,[48] Trompenaars derived five relationship orientations that address the ways in which people deal with each other; these can be considered to be cultural dimensions that are analogous to Hofstede's dimensions. Trompenaars also looked at attitudes toward both time and the environment, and the result of his research is a wealth of information helping explain how cultures differ and offering practical ways in which MNCs can do business in various countries. The following discussion examines each of the five relationship orientations as well as attitudes toward time and the environment.[49]

Table 1–6
Trompenaars's Country and Region Abbreviations

Abbreviation	Country
ARG	Argentina
AUS	Austria
BEL	Belgium
BRZ	Brazil
CHI	Mainland China
CIS	Former Soviet Union
CZH	Former Czechoslovakia
FRA	France
GER	Germany (excluding former East Germany)
HK	Chinese Hong Kong
IDO	Indonesia
ITA	Italy
JPN	Japan
MEX	Mexico
NL	Netherlands
SIN	Singapore
SPA	Spain
SWE	Sweden
SWI	Switzerland
THA	Thailand
UK	United Kingdom
USA	United States
VEN	Venezuela

普遍主义和特殊主义

Universalism vs. Particularism **Universalism** is the belief that ideas and practices can be applied everywhere without modification. **Particularism** is the belief that circumstances dictate how ideas and practices should be applied. In cultures with high universalism, the focus is more on formal rules than on relationships, business contracts are adhered to very closely, and people believe that "a deal is a deal." In cultures with high particularism, the focus is more on relationships and trust than on formal rules. In a particularist culture, legal contracts often are modified, and as people get to know each other better, they often change the way in which deals are executed. In his early research, Trompenaars found that in countries such as the United States, Australia, Germany, Sweden, and the United Kingdom, there was high universalism, while countries such as Venezuela, the former Soviet Union, Indonesia, and China were high on particularism. Figure 1–8 shows the continuum.

universalism
The belief that ideas and practices can be applied everywhere in the world without modification.

particularism
The belief that circumstances dictate how ideas and practices should be applied and that something cannot be done the same everywhere.

In follow-up research, Trompenaars and Hampden-Turner presented the respondents with a dilemma and asked them to make a decision. Here is one of these dilemmas along with the national scores of the respondents:[50]

> You are riding in a car driven by a close friend. He hits a pedestrian. You know he was going at least 35 miles per hour in an area of the city where the maximum allowed speed is 20 miles per hour. There are no witnesses. His lawyer says that if you testify under oath that he was driving 20 miles per hour it may save him from serious consequences. What right has your friend to expect you to protect him?
>
> (*a*) My friend has a definite right as a friend to expect me to testify to the lower figure.
> (*b*) He has some right as a friend to expect me to testify to the lower figure.
> (*c*) He has no right as a friend to expect me to testify to the lower figure.

Figure 1–8

Trompenaars's Relationship Orientations on Cultural Dimensions

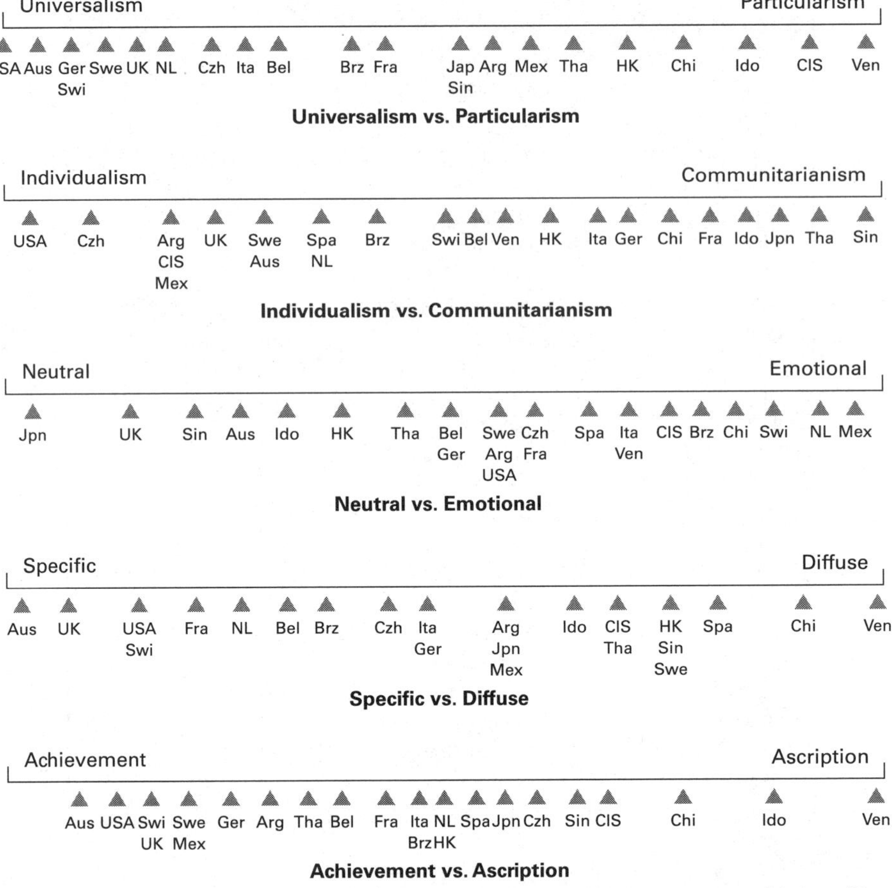

Source: Adapted from information found in Fons Trompenaars, *Riding the Waves of Culture* (New York: Irwin, 1994); Charles M. Hampden-Turner and Fons Trompenaars, "A World Turned Upside Down: Doing Business in Asia," in *Managing Across Cultures: Issues and Perspectives,* ed. Pat Joynt and Malcolm Warner (London: International Thomson Business Press, 1996), pp. 275–305.

With a high score indicating strong universalism (choice c) and a low score indicating strong particularism (choice a), here is how the different nations scored:

Universalism (no right)	
Canada	96
United States	95
Germany	90
United Kingdom	90
Netherlands	88
France	68
Japan	67
Singapore	67
Thailand	63
Chinese Hong Kong	56
Particularism (some or definite right)	
Mainland China	48
South Korea	26

As noted earlier, respondents from universalist cultures (e.g., North America and Western Europe) felt that the rules applied regardless of the situation, while respondents from particularist cultures were much more willing to bend the rules and help their friend.

Based on these types of findings, Trompenaars recommends that when individuals from particularist cultures do business in a universalistic culture, they should be prepared for rational, professional arguments and a "let's get down to business" attitude. Conversely, when individuals from universalist cultures do business in a particularist environment, they should be prepared for personal meandering or irrelevancies that seem to go nowhere and should not regard personal, get-to-know-you attitudes as mere small talk.

个人主义和社群主义

Individualism vs. Communitarianism Individualism and communitarianism are key dimensions in Hofstede's earlier research. Although Trompenaars derived these two relationships differently than Hofstede does, they still have the same basic meaning, although in his more recent work Trompenaars has used the word **communitarianism** rather than collectivism. For him, individualism refers to people regarding themselves as individuals, while communitarianism refers to people regarding themselves as part of a group. As shown in Figure 1–8, the United States, former Czechoslovakia, Argentina, the former Soviet Union (CIS), and Mexico have high individualism.

communitarianism Refers to people regarding themselves as part of a group.

In his most recent research, Trompenaars posed the following situation. If you were to be promoted, which of the two following issues would you emphasize most: (a) the new group of people with whom you will be working or (b) the greater responsibility of the work you are undertaking and the higher income you will be earning? The following reports the scores associated with the individualism of option b—greater responsibility and more money.[51]

Individualism (emphasis on larger responsibilities and more income)	
Canada	77
Thailand	71
United Kingdom	69
United States	67
Netherlands	64
France	61
Japan	61
Mainland China	54
Singapore	50
Chinese Hong Kong	47
Communitarianism (emphasis on the new group of people)	
Malaysia	38
Korea	32

These findings are somewhat different from those presented in Figure 1–8 and show that cultural changes may be occurring more rapidly than many people realize. For example, findings show Thailand very high on individualism (possibly indicating an increasing entrepreneurial spirit/cultural value), whereas the Thais were found to be low on individualism a few years before, as shown in Figure 1–8. At the same time, it is important to remember that there are major differences between people in high-individualism societies and those in high-communitarianism societies. The former stress personal and individual matters; the latter value group-related issues. Negotiations in cultures with high individualism typically are made on the spot by a representative, people ideally achieve things alone, and they assume a great deal of personal responsibility. In cultures with high communitarianism, decisions typically are referred to committees, people ideally achieve things in groups, and they jointly assume responsibility.

Trompenaars recommends that when people from cultures with high individualism deal with those from communitarianistic cultures, they should have patience for the time taken to consent and to consult, and they should aim to build lasting relationships. When people from cultures with high communitarianism deal with those from individualistic cultures, they should be prepared to make quick decisions and commit their organization to these decisions. Also, communitarianists dealing with individualists should realize that the reason they are dealing with only one negotiator (as opposed to a group) is that this person is respected by his or her organization and has its authority and esteem.

neutral culture
A culture in which emotions are held in check.

emotional culture
A culture in which emotions are expressed openly and naturally.

中立文化和情感文化

Neutral vs. Emotional A **neutral culture** is one in which emotions are held in check. As seen in Figure 1–8, both Japan and the United Kingdom are high-neutral cultures. People in these countries try not to show their feelings; they act stoically and maintain their composure. An **emotional culture** is one in which emotions are openly and naturally expressed. People in emotional cultures often smile a great deal, talk loudly when they are excited, and greet each other with a great deal of enthusiasm. Mexico, the Netherlands, and Switzerland are examples of high emotional cultures.

Trompenaars recommends that when individuals from emotional cultures do business in neutral cultures, they should put as much as they can on paper and submit it to the other side. They should realize that lack of emotion does not mean a lack of interest or boredom, but rather that people from neutral cultures do not like to show their hand. Conversely, when those from neutral cultures do business in emotional cultures, they should not be put off stride when the other side creates scenes or grows animated and boisterous, and they should try to respond warmly to the emotional affections of the other group.

specific culture
A culture in which individuals have a large public space they readily share with others and a small private space they guard closely and share with only close friends and associates.

diffuse culture
A culture in which public space and private space are similar in size and individuals guard their public space carefully, because entry into public space affords entry into private space as well.

特定文化和扩散文化

Specific vs. Diffuse A **specific culture** is one in which individuals have a large public space they readily let others enter and share and a small private space they guard closely and share with only close friends and associates. A **diffuse culture** is one in which public space and private space are similar in size and individuals guard their public space carefully, because entry into public space affords entry into private space as well. As shown in Figure 1–8, Austria, the United Kingdom, the United States, and Switzerland all are specific cultures, while Venezuela, China, and Spain are diffuse cultures. In specific cultures, people often are invited into a person's open, public space; individuals in these cultures often are open and extroverted; and there is a strong separation of work and private life. In diffuse cultures, people are not quickly invited into a person's open, public space, because once they are in, there is easy entry into the private space as well. Individuals in these cultures often appear to be indirect and introverted, and work and private life often are closely linked.

An example of these specific and diffuse cultural dimensions is provided by the United States and Germany. A U.S. professor, such as Robert Smith, PhD, generally would be called "Doctor Smith" by students when at his U.S. university. When shopping, however, he might be referred to by the store clerk as "Bob," and when golfing, Bob might just be one of the guys, even to a golf partner who happens to be a graduate student in his department. The reason for these changes in status is that, with the specific U.S. cultural values, people have large public spaces and often conduct themselves differently depending on their public role. In high-diffuse cultures, on the other hand, a person's public life and private life often are similar. Therefore, in Germany, Herr Professor Doktor Schmidt would be referred to that way at the university, local market, and bowling alley—and even his wife might address him formally in public. A great deal of formality is maintained, often giving the impression that Germans are stuffy or aloof.

Trompenaars recommends that when those from specific cultures do business in diffuse cultures, they should respect a person's title, age, and background connections, and they should not get impatient when people are being indirect or circuitous. Conversely, when individuals from diffuse cultures do business in specific cultures, they should try to get to the point and be efficient, learn to structure meetings with the judicious use of agendas, and not use their titles or acknowledge achievements or skills that are irrelevant to the issues being discussed.

成就文化和归属文化

Achievement vs. Ascription An **achievement culture** is one in which people are accorded status based on how well they perform their functions. An **ascription culture** is one in which status is attributed based on who or what a person is. Achievement cultures give high status to high achievers, such as the company's number-one salesperson or the medical researcher who has found a cure for a rare form of bone cancer. Ascription cultures accord status based on age, gender, or social connections. For example, in an ascription culture, a person who has been with the company for 40 years may be listened to carefully because of the respect that others have for the individual's age and longevity with the firm, and an individual who has friends in high places may be afforded status because of whom she knows. As shown in Figure 1–8, Austria, the United States, Switzerland, and the United Kingdom are achievement cultures, while Venezuela, Indonesia, and China are ascription cultures.

achievement culture
A culture in which people are accorded status based on how well they perform their functions.

ascription culture
A culture in which status is attributed based on who or what a person is.

Trompenaars recommends that when individuals from achievement cultures do business in ascription cultures, they should make sure that their group has older, senior, and formal position holders who can impress the other side, and they should respect the status and influence of their counterparts in the other group. Conversely, he recommends that when individuals from ascription cultures do business in achievement cultures, they should make sure that their group has sufficient data, technical advisers, and knowledgeable people to convince the other group that they are proficient, and they should respect the knowledge and information of their counterparts on the other team.

时间

Time Aside from the five relationship orientations, another major cultural difference is the way in which people deal with the concept of time. Trompenaars has identified two different approaches: sequential and synchronous. In cultures where sequential approaches are prevalent, people tend to do only one activity at a time, keep appointments strictly, and show a strong preference for following plans as they are laid out and not deviating from them. In cultures where synchronous approaches are common, people tend to do more than one activity at a time, appointments are approximate and may be changed at a moment's notice, and schedules generally are subordinate to relationships. People in synchronous-time cultures often will stop what they are doing to meet and greet individuals coming into their office.

A good contrast is provided by the United States, Mexico, and France. In the United States, people tend to be guided by sequential-time orientation and thus set a schedule and stick to it. Mexicans operate under more of a synchronous-time orientation and thus tend to be much more flexible, often building slack into their schedules to allow for interruptions. The French are similar to the Mexicans and, when making plans, often determine the objectives they want to accomplish but leave open the timing and other factors that are beyond their control; this way, they can adjust and modify their approach as they go along. As Trompenaars noted, "For the French and Mexicans, what was important was that they get to the end, not the particular path or sequence by which that end was reached."[52]

Another interesting time-related contrast is the degree to which cultures are past- or present-oriented as opposed to future-oriented. In countries such as the United States, Italy, and Germany, the future is more important than the past or the present. In countries such as Venezuela, Indonesia, and Spain, the present is most important. In France and Belgium, all three time periods are of approximately equal importance. Because different emphases are given to different time periods, adjusting to these cultural differences can create challenges.

Trompenaars recommends that when doing business with future-oriented cultures, effective international managers should emphasize the opportunities and limitless scope that any agreement can have, agree to specific deadlines for getting things done, and be aware of the core competence or continuity that the other party intends to carry with it into the future. When doing business with past- or present-oriented cultures, he recommends that managers emphasize the history and tradition of the culture, find out whether internal relationships will sanction the types of changes that need to be made, and agree to future meetings in principle but fix no deadlines for completions.

环境

The Environment Trompenaars also examined the ways in which people deal with their environment. Specific attention should be given to whether they believe in controlling outcomes (inner-directed) or letting things take their own course (outer-directed). One of the things he asked managers to do was choose between the following statements:

1. What happens to me is my own doing.
2. Sometimes I feel that I do not have enough control over the directions my life is taking.

Managers who believe in controlling their own environment would opt for the first choice; those who believe that they are controlled by their environment and cannot do much about it would opt for the second.

Here is an`example by country and region of the sample respondents who believe that what happens to them is their own doing: [53]

United States	89%
Switzerland	84%
Australia	81%
Belgium	76%
Indonesia	73%
Chinese Hong Kong	69%
Greece	63%
Singapore	58%
Japan	56%
Mainland China	35%

In the United States, managers feel strongly that they are masters of their own fate. This helps account for their dominant attitude (sometimes bordering on aggressiveness) toward the environment and discomfort when things seem to get out of control. Many Asian cultures do not share these views. They believe that things move in waves or natural shifts and one must "go with the flow," so a flexible attitude, characterized by a willingness to compromise and maintain harmony with nature, is important.

Trompenaars recommends that when dealing with those from cultures that believe in dominating the environment, it is important to play hardball, test the resilience of the opponent, win some objectives, and always lose from time to time. For example, representatives of the U.S. government have repeatedly urged Japanese automobile companies to purchase more component parts from U.S. suppliers to partially offset the large volume of U.S. imports of finished autos from Japan. Instead of enacting trade barriers, the United States was asking for a quid pro quo. When dealing with those from cultures that believe in letting things take their natural course, it is important to be persistent and polite, maintain good relationships with the other party, and try to win together and lose apart.

文化模式和文化聚落

Cultural Patterns or Clusters Like Hofstede's work, Trompenaars's research lends itself to cultural patterns or clusters. Table 1–7 relates his findings to the five relational orientations. It is useful to compare Hofstede and Trompenaars, because of the overlapping information. For example, Hofstede's country assessments included India but not China. Trompenaars, conversely, shows results for China but not India. Today, international managers must become familiar with beliefs and traditions in both areas, since they play a significant role in the new

Table 1–7
Cultural Groups Based on Trompenaars's Research

	Anglo Cluster	
Relationship	**United States**	**United Kingdom**
Individualism (I) / Communitarianism (C)	I	I
Specific relationship (S) / Diffuse relationship (D)	S	S
Universalism (U) / Particularism (P)	U	U
Neutral relationship (N) / Emotional relationship (E)	E	N
Achievement (Ach) / Ascription (As)	Ach	Ach

	Asian Cluster				
Relationship	**Japan**	**Mainland China**	**Indonesia**	**Chinese Hong Kong**	**Singapore**
Individualism (I) / Communitarianism (C)	C	C	C	C	C
Specific relationship (S) / Diffuse relationship (D)	D	D	D	D	D
Universalism (U) / Particularism (P)	P	P	P	P	P
Neutral relationship (N) / Emotional relationship (E)	N	E	N	N	N
Achievement (Ach) / Ascription (As)	As	As	As	As	As

	Latin American Cluster			
Relationship	**Argentina**	**Mexico**	**Venezuela**	**Brazil**
Individualism (I) / Communitarianism (C)	I	I	C	I
Specific relationship (S) / Diffuse relationship (D)	D	D	D	S
Universalism (U) / Particularism (P)	P	P	P	U
Neutral relationship (N) / Emotional relationship (E)	N	N	N	E
Achievement (Ach) / Ascription (As)	Ach	Ach	As	As

	Latin European Cluster			
Relationship	**France**	**Belgium**	**Spain**	**Italy**
Individualism (I) / Communitarianism (C)	C	C	I	C
Specific relationship (S) / Diffuse relationship (D)	S	S	D	S
Universalism (U) / Particularism (P)	U	U	P	U
Neutral relationship (N) / Emotional relationship (E)	E	E	N	E
Achievement (Ach) / Ascription (As)	As	As	Ach	As

(continued)

Table 1–7 *(continued)*
Cultural Groups Based on Trompenaars's Research

Relationship	Germanic Cluster			
	Austria	Germany	Switzerland	Czechoslovakia
Individualism (I) Communitarianism (C)	I	C	C	C
Specific relationship (S) Diffuse relationship (D)	S	D	S	S
Universalism (U) Particularism (P)	U	U	U	U
Neutral relationship (N) Emotional relationship (E)	N	E	E	N
Achievement (Ach) Ascription (As)	Ach	Ach	As	Ach

Source: Fons Trompenaars, *Riding the Waves of Culture.* Copyright © 1994 McGraw-Hill Education. Reprinted by permission of McGraw-Hill Education.

world economy. Further examination of Table 1–7 shows that while general clusters can be formed, there still exist inherent, significant differences within. For example, Brazil is considered to be a part of the Latin American cluster, though some of the unique findings suggest that Brazil is more independent than strictly "Latin American." The Latin European grouping mirrors similar results, with Italy showing some preferences that are different from both France and Belgium, and with Spain displaying distinguishing characteristics as compared to the other three in the cluster.

Overall, Table 1–7 shows that a case can be made for cultural similarities between clusters of countries. With only small differences, Trompenaars's research helps support and, more importantly, extend the work of Hofstede. Such research provides a useful point of departure for recognizing cultural differences, and it provides guidelines for doing business effectively around the world.

整合文化和管理：GLOBE项目

Integrating Culture and Management: The GLOBE Project

GLOBE
A multicountry study and evaluation of cultural attributes and leadership behaviors among more than 17,000 managers from 951 organizations in 62 countries.

Most recently, the **GLOBE** (Global Leadership and Organizational Behavior Effectiveness) research program reflects an additional approach to measuring cultural differences. Conceived in 1991, the GLOBE project is an ongoing research project, currently consisting of three major interrelated phases. GLOBE extends and integrates the previous analyses of cultural attributes and variables published by Hofstede and Trompenaars. The three completed GLOBE phases explore the various elements of the dynamic relationship between the culture and organizational behavior.[54]

At the heart of phases one and two, first published in 2004 and 2007, is the study and evaluation of nine different cultural attributes using middle managers from 951 organizations in 62 countries.[55,56] A team of 170 scholars worked together to survey over 17,000 managers in three industries: financial services, food processing, and telecommunications. When developing the measures and conducting the analysis, they also used archival measures of country economic prosperity and of the physical and psychological well-being of the cultures studied. Countries were selected so that every major geographic location in the world was represented. Additional countries, including those with unique types of political and economic systems, were selected to create a complete and comprehensive database upon which to build the analysis.[57] This research has been considered among the most sophisticated in the field to date, and a collaboration of the work of Hofstede and GLOBE researchers could provide an influential outlook on the major factors characterizing global cultures.[58]

While phases one and two focus on middle management, phase three, first published in 2012, examines the interactions of culture and leadership in upper-level management positions. More than 1,000 CEOs, and more than 5,000 of their direct reports, were surveyed by 40 researchers across 24 countries. To provide compatibility across all phases of the GLOBE project, 17 of the 24 countries surveyed in phase 3 were also included in the initial study performed for phases one and two.[59] A further explanation of phase three, which deals primarily with leadership. Table 1–8
also provides an overview of the purposes and results of the different phases.

The GLOBE study is interesting because its nine constructs were defined, conceptualized, and operationalized by a multicultural team of over 100 researchers. In addition, the data in each country were collected by investigators who were either natives of the cultures studied or had extensive knowledge and experience in those cultures.

文化和管理
Culture and Management

GLOBE researchers adhere to the belief that certain attributes that distinguish one culture from others can be used to predict the most suitable, effective, and acceptable organizational and leader practices within that culture. In addition, they contend that societal culture has a direct impact on organizational culture and that leader acceptance stems from tying leader attributes and behaviors to subordinate norms.[60]

The GLOBE project set out to answer many fundamental questions about cultural variables shaping leadership and organizational processes. The meta-goal of GLOBE was to develop an empirically based theory to describe, understand, and predict the impact of specific cultural variables on leadership and organizational processes and the effectiveness of these processes. Overall, GLOBE hopes to provide a global standard guideline that allows managers to focus on local specialization. Specific objectives include answering these fundamental questions:[61]

- Are there leader behaviors, attributes, and organizational practices that are universally accepted and effective across cultures?
- Are there leader behaviors, attributes, and organizational practices that are accepted and effective in only some cultures?
- How do attributes of societal and organizational cultures affect the kinds of leader behaviors and organizational practices that are accepted and effective?

Table 1–8
GLOBE Cultural Variable Results

Variable	Highest Ranking	Medium Ranking	Lowest Ranking
Assertiveness	Spain, U.S.	Egypt, Ireland	Sweden, New Zealand
Future orientation	Denmark, Canada	Slovenia, Egypt	Russia, Argentina
Gender differentiation	South Korea, Egypt	Italy, Brazil	Sweden, Denmark
Uncertainty avoidance	Austria, Denmark	Israel, U.S.	Russia, Hungary
Power distance	Russia, Spain	England, France	Denmark, Netherlands
Collectivism/societal	Denmark, Singapore	Chinese Hong Kong, U.S.	Greece, Hungary
In-group collectivism	Egypt, Mainland China	England, France	Denmark, Netherlands
Performance orientation	U.S., China's Taiwan	Sweden, Israel	Russia, Argentina
Humane orientation	Indonesia, Egypt	Chinese Hong Kong, Sweden	Germany, Spain

Source: From Mansour Javidan, Peter W. Dorfman et al., "In the Eye of the Beholder: Cross Cultural Lessons in Leadership from Project GLOBE," *Perspectives—Academy of Management* 20, no. 1 (2006), p. 76. Reproduced with permission of Academy of Management via Copyright Clearance Center.

- What is the effect of violating cultural norms that are relevant to leadership and organizational practices?
- What is the relative standing of each of the cultures studied on each of the nine core dimensions of culture?
- Can the universal and culture-specific aspects of leader behaviors, attributes, and organizational practices be explained in terms of an underlying theory that accounts for systematic differences across cultures?

GLOBE的文化维度
GLOBE's Cultural Dimensions

Phase one of the GLOBE project identified the nine cultural dimensions:[62]

1. *Uncertainty avoidance* is defined as the extent to which members of an organization or society strive to avoid uncertainty by reliance on social norms, rituals, and bureaucratic practices to alleviate the unpredictability of future events.
2. *Power distance* is defined as the degree to which members of an organization or society expect and agree that power should be unequally shared.
3. *Collectivism I: Societal collectivism* refers to the degree to which organizational and societal institutional practices encourage and reward collective distribution of resources and collective action.
4. *Collectivism II: In-group collectivism* refers to the degree to which individuals express pride, loyalty, and cohesiveness in their organizations or families.
5. *Gender egalitarianism* is defined as the extent to which an organization or a society minimizes gender role differences and gender discrimination.
6. *Assertiveness* is defined as the degree to which individuals in organizations or societies are assertive, confrontational, and aggressive in social relationships.
7. *Future orientation* is defined as the degree to which individuals in organizations or societies engage in future-oriented behaviors such as planning, investing in the future, and delaying gratification.
8. *Performance orientation* refers to the extent to which an organization or society encourages and rewards group members for performance improvement and excellence.
9. *Humane orientation* is defined as the degree to which individuals in organizations or societies encourage and reward individuals for being fair, altruistic, friendly, generous, caring, and kind to others.

The first six dimensions have their origins in Hofstede's cultural dimensions. The collectivism I dimension measures societal emphasis on collectivism; low scores reflect individualistic emphasis, and high scores reflect collectivistic emphasis by means of laws, social programs, or institutional practices. The collectivism II scale measures in-group (family or organization) collectivism such as pride in and loyalty to family or organization and family or organizational cohesiveness. In lieu of Hofstede's masculinity dimension, the GLOBE researchers developed the two dimensions they labeled gender egalitarianism and assertiveness. Likewise, the future orientation, performance orientation, and humane orientation measures have their origin in past research.[63] These measures are therefore integrative and combine a number of insights from previous studies. Recently, further analysis has been conducted with regard to corporate social responsibility (CSR).[64]

GLOBE国家分析
GLOBE Country Analysis

The initial results of the GLOBE analysis are presented in Table 1–9. The GLOBE analysis corresponds generally with those of Hofstede and Trompenaars, although with some

Table 1–9
Globe Phases 1, 2, & 3

Purpose	Method	Design strategy	Major results
GLOBE phases 1 & 2 • Design and implement multi-phase and multi-method program to examine the relationship between national culture, leadership effectiveness and societal phenomena • Identify leadership attributes critical for outstanding leadership • Develop societal culture questionnaire • Develop leadership questionnaire	• Involve a total of over 160 researchers from 62 national societies in the research project • Conduct individual and focus group interviews with mid-level managers in domestic organizations • Check items for relevance and understandability • Survey over 17,000 managers representing 951 organizations in 62 cultures	• Employ rigorous psychometric assessment procedures for scale items • Translate and back translate survey instruments in each country • Conduct pilot tests in several countries • Control for common source error in research design • Use rigorous statistical procedures to ensure scales can be aggregated and reliable • Assess cultures and organizations on practices (i.e., as is) and values (should be) • HLM used to test hypotheses (culture to leadership at organizational and societal level)	• Validation of culture and leadership scales • Ranking of 62 societal cultures on 9 culture dimensions • Grouping of 62 cultures into 10 culture clusters • Creation of 21 primary leadership and 6 global leadership scales • Determining relationships between culture dimensions and leadership dimensions • Determination of universally desirable and culturally specific leadership qualities (i.e., CLTs)
GLOBE phase 3 • Determine the manner in which national culture influences executive leadership processes • Examine the relationship between leadership expectations (CLTs) and CEO behavior • Examine the relationship between CEO leadership behavior and effectiveness • Determine which CEO leadership behaviors are most effective	• Involvement of more than 40 researchers in 24 countries • 17 of the 24 countries completed phases 1 and 2 in addition to phase 3 • Interviews and surveys were conducted for 40 CEOs within each country • A total of more than 1000 CEOs and 5000 of their direct reports were respondents in the project • Previously defined leadership qualities from phases 1 and 2 (i.e., CLTs) were converted into behavioral leadership items and combined into scales for phase 3	• Between 6 and 9 direct reports of each CEO assessed the CEOs leadership behaviors, their personal reactions, and firm performance • Common method and response variance eliminated through research design • Internally oriented top management team (TMT) outcomes included commitment, effort, and team solidarity • Externally oriented firm outcomes included competitive sales performance, competitive ROI and competitive domination of the industry	• Leaders tend to behave in a manner expected within their country • Cultural values do NOT have a direct effect on CEO behavior, rather the effect is indirect through CLTs (culturally endorsed theory – i.e., leadership expectations) • Both the fit of CEO behaviors (to expectations) and degree of leadership behavior predict effectiveness • Superior and inferior CEOs exhibit different patterns of behavior within their country

Source: From Peter Dorfman, Mansour Javidan, Paul Hanges, Ali Dastmalchian, and Robert House, "GLOBE: A twenty year journey into the intriguing world of culture and leadership," *Journal of World Business* 47, (2012), p. 505.

variations resulting from the variable definitions and methodology. Hofstede critiqued the GLOBE analysis, pointing out key differences between the research methods; Hofstede was the sole researcher and writer of his findings, while GLOBE consisted of a team of perspectives; Hofstede focused on one institution and surveyed employees, while GLOBE interviewed managers across many corporations, and so on. The disparity of the terminology between these two, coupled with the complex research, makes it challenging to compare and fully reconcile these two approches.[65] Other assessments have pointed out that Hofstede may have provided an introduction into the psychology of culture, but further research is necessary in this changing world. The GLOBE analysis is sometimes seen as complicated, but so are cultures and perceptions. An in-depth understanding of all facets of culture is difficult, if not impossible, to attain, but GLOBE provides a current comprehensive overview of general stereotypes that can be further analyzed for greater insight.[66]

Examination of the GLOBE project has resulted in an extensive breakdown of how managers behave and how different cultures can yield managers with similar perspectives in some realms, with quite divergent opinions in other sectors. One example, as illustrated in Figure 1–9, shows how managers in Brazil compare to managers in the United States in a web structure, based on factors such as individualism, consciousness of social and professional status, and risky behaviors. Brazilian managers are typically class and status conscious, rarely conversing with subordinates on a personal level within or outside of work. They are known for avoiding conflict within groups and risky endeavors and tend to exhibit group dynamics with regard to decision-making processes. Managers in the United States, on the other hand, do not focus intensely on different class or status levels. They are more likely to take risks, and while it appears as though they are more individualistic, the graph

Figure 1–9

GLOBE Analysis: Managerial Perspectives in the United States and Brazil

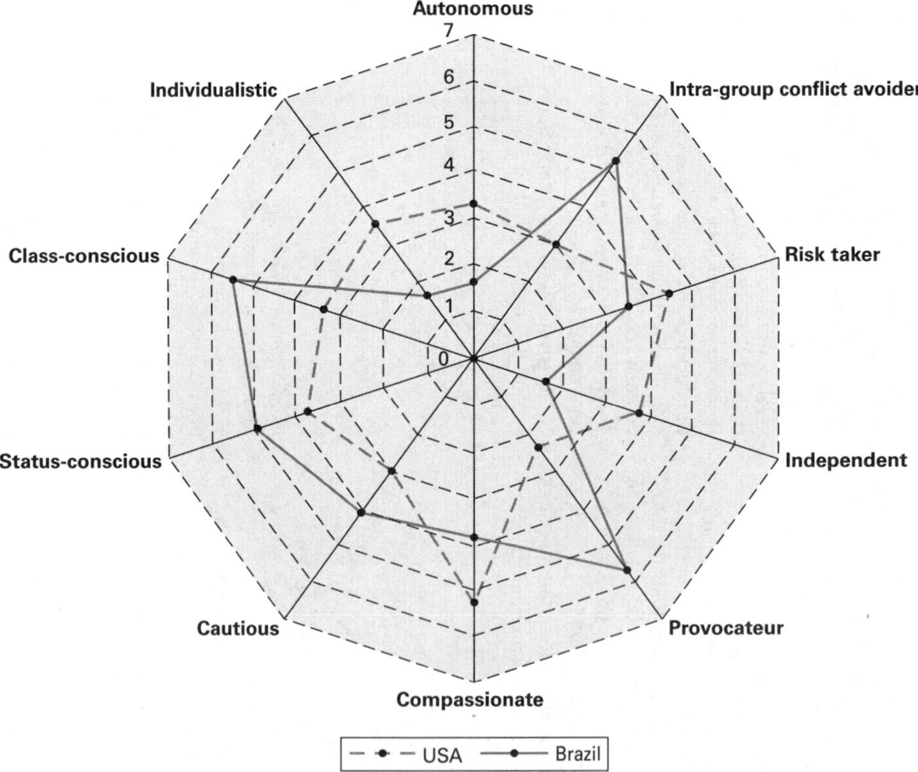

Source: From Mansour Javidan, Peter W. Dorfman et al., "In the Eye of the Beholder: Cross Cultural Lessons in Leadership from Project GLOBE," *Perspectives—Academy of Management 20,* no. 1 (2006), p. 76. Reproduced with permission of Academy of Management via Copyright Clearance Center.

implies a more tolerant attitude than direct single-person-decision-making structure. Here, both Brazil and the United States show how it is important to have group communication on some level. While Americans value mutual respect and open dialogue, Brazilians may see this behavior as unacceptable, even aggressive, if discussion discloses a large amount of information and includes members from different groups; subordinate and managerial positions.[67]

It has been suggested that if Americans are preparing to do business in Brazil, the representatives should spend an ample amount of time getting to know the Brazilian executives. Be sure to show respect for top managers, and inform subordinates of any plans or changes, encouraging feedback. Managers still make the final decisions, and it is very unlikely that workers will provide any suggestions, but they also do not appreciate simply being told what to do. In other words, family structures, including in-group structures, are very important to Brazilians, but the head of the household still has the last word. Finally, stress short-term, risk-aversive goals to maintain vision and interest in business proposals.[68]

We will explore additional implications of the GLOBE findings as they relate to managerial leadership.

再看国际化管理的世界

■ The World of International Management—Revisited

The discussion of Toyota's problems in the World of International Management that opened this chapter illustrates the importance of culture and how cultural differences may contribute to global management challenges. Cultural distance can influence both positively and negatively how decisions are made, reported, and resolved. Having read this chapter, you should understand the impact culture has on the actions of MNCs, including general management practices and relations with employees and customers, and on maintaining overall reputation.

Recall the chapter opening discussion about Toyota and then draw on your understanding of Hofstede's and Trompenaars's cultural dimensions to answer the following questions: (1) What dimensions contribute to the differences between how Americans and Japanese workers address management problems, including operational or product flaws? (2) What are some ways that Japanese culture may affect operational excellence in a positive way? How might it hurt quality, especially when things go wrong? (3) How could managers from Japan or other Asian cultures adopt practices from U.S. and European cultures when investing in those regions?

SUMMARY OF KEY POINTS

1. Culture is acquired knowledge that people use to interpret experience and generate social behavior. Culture also has the characteristics of being learned, shared, transgenerational, symbolic, patterned, and adaptive. There are many dimensions of cultural diversity, including centralized vs. decentralized decision making, safety vs. risk, individual vs. group rewards, informal vs. formal procedures, high vs. low organizational loyalty, cooperation vs. competition, short-term vs. long-term horizons, and stability vs. innovation.
2. Values are basic convictions that people have regarding what is right and wrong, good and bad, important and unimportant. Research shows that there are both differences and similarities between the work values and managerial values of different cultural groups. Work values often reflect culture and industrialization, and managerial values are highly related to success. Research shows that values tend to change over time and often reflect age and experience.
3. Hofstede has identified and researched four major dimensions of culture: power distance, uncertainty avoidance, individualism, and masculinity. Recently, he has added a fifth dimension, time orientation and more recently yet, a sixth dimension indulgence vs. restraint: Each will affect a country's political and social system. The integration of these factors into

two-dimensional figures can illustrate the complexity of culture's effect on behavior.

4. In recent years, researchers have attempted to cluster countries into similar cultural groupings to study similarities and differences. Through analyzing the relationship between two dimensions, as Hofstede illustrated, two-dimensional maps can be created to show how countries differ and where they overlap.
5. Research by Trompenaars has examined five relationship orientations: universalism vs. particularism, individualism vs. communitarianism, affective vs. neutral, specific vs. diffuse, and achievement vs. ascription. Trompenaars also looked at attitudes toward time and toward the environment. The result is a wealth of information helping to explain how cultures differ as well as practical ways in which MNCs can do business effectively in these environments. In particular, his findings update those of Hofstede while helping support the previous work by Hofstede on clustering countries.
6. Recent research undertaken by the GLOBE project has attempted to extend and integrate cultural attributes and variables as they relate to managerial leadership and practice. These analyses confirm much of the Hofstede and Trompenaars research, with greater emphasis on differences in managerial leadership styles.

KEY TERMS

achievement culture
ascription culture
collectivism
communitarianism
culture
diffuse culture
emotional culture
femininity
GLOBE
individualism
masculinity
neutral culture
particularism
power distance
specific culture
uncertainty avoidance
universalism
values

REVIEW AND DISCUSSION QUESTIONS

1. What is meant by the term *culture?* In what way can measuring attitudes about the following help differentiate between cultures: centralized or decentralized decision making, safety or risk, individual or group rewards, high or low organizational loyalty, cooperation or competition? Use these attitudes to compare the United States, Germany, and Japan. Based on your comparisons, what conclusions can you draw regarding the impact of culture on behavior?
2. What is meant by the term *value?* Are cultural values the same worldwide, or are there marked differences? Are these values changing over time, or are they fairly constant? How does your answer relate to the role of values in a culture?
3. What are the four major dimensions of culture studied by Geert Hofstede? Identify and describe each. What is the cultural profile of the United States? Of Asian countries? Of Latin American countries? Of Latin European countries? Based on your comparisons of these four profiles, what conclusions can you draw regarding cultural challenges facing individuals in one group when they interact with individuals in one of the other groups? Why do you think Hofstede added the fifth dimension of time orientation and the sixth dimension related to indulgence versus restraint?
4. As people engage in more international travel and become more familiar with other countries, will cultural differences decline as a roadblock to international understanding, or will they continue to be a major barrier? Defend your answer.
5. What are the characteristics of each of the following pairs of cultural characteristics derived from Trompenaars's research: universalism vs. particularism, neutral vs. emotional, specific vs. diffuse, achievement vs. ascription? Compare and contrast each pair.
6. How did project GLOBE build on and extend Hofstede's analysis? What unique contributions are associated with project GLOBE?
7. In what way is time a cultural factor? In what way is the need to control the environment a cultural factor? Give an example for each.

INTERNET EXERCISE: RENAULT-NISSAN IN SOUTH AFRICA

The Renault-Nissan alliance, established in March 1999, is the first industrial and commercial partnership of its kind involving a French company and a Japanese company. The Alliance invested more than 1 billion rand in upgrading Nissan's manufacturing plant in Rosslyn, outside Pretoria, to increase output and produce the Nissan NP200 pickup and the Renault Sandero for the South African market. Visit the Renault-Nissan website at http://www.renault.com to see where factories reside for each car group. Compare and contrast the similarities and differences in these markets. Then answer these three questions: (1) How do you think cultural differences affect the way the firm operates in South Africa versus France versus Japan? (2) In what way is culture a factor in auto sales? (3) Is it possible for a car company to transcend national culture and produce a global automobile that is accepted by people in every culture? Why or why not?

South Africa

South Africa, as the name reflects, is located on the far southern tip of the African continent. It is surrounded by water on three sides: in the south and in the west by the Atlantic Ocean, and in the east by the Indian Ocean. Neighboring countries are Zimbabwe, Swaziland, Botswana, Namibia, and Lesotho. The form of government is a presidential democracy. South Africa has three capitals: Pretoria, Cape Town, and Bloemfontein. The country is 1,219,080 square kilometers. The population (in 2011) was 50.6 million people. GDP in 2011 was $408.2 billion, with per capita income at $8,070.

South Africa is known as the "Rainbow Nation," a title that reflects its cultural diversity and the fact that the country's population is one of the most diverse and complex in the world. Of the total population, about 31 million are Black, 5 million White, 3 million Coloured, and 1 million Indian. The Black population covers four major ethnic groups consisting of Nguni, Sotho, Shangaan-Tsonga, and Venda. There are a number of subgroups; the Zulu and Xhosa are the largest subgroups of the Nguni. The majority of the White population has Afrikaans roots, and 40 percent are of British descent. In South Africa eleven official languages are spoken.

The most significant characteristic of South Africa's modern history was apartheid, a system of legal racial segregation enforced by the Nationalist Party between 1948 and 1994, under which the rights of the majority nonwhite population were curtailed in all avenues of life. Apartheid sparked significant tension and violence internally as well as a UN trade embargo against South Africa. A series of popular uprisings and protests were met with the banning of opposition and imprisonment of anti-apartheid leaders, including Nobel Peace Prize winner Nelson Mandela. Reforms to apartheid in the 1980s failed to quell the mounting opposition, and in 1990 President Frederik Willem de Klerk began negotiations to end apartheid, culminating in multiracial democratic elections in 1994, which were won by the African National Congress under Nelson Mandela.

One feature of post-apartheid South Africa was the program Black Economic Empowerment (BEE) designed to redress the inequalities of apartheid by giving previously disadvantaged groups (Black Africans, Coloureds, Indians, and Chinese) economic opportunities previously not available to them. It has included measures such as employment equity; skills development; ownership, management, and socioeconomic development; and preferential procurement. The BEE is not free of criticism; many claim the program has caused qualified white expertise to leave for areas where they would not be discriminated against. Inkatha Freedom Party leader Mangosu-thu Buthelezi has stated that "the government's reckless implementation of the affirmative action policy is forcing many white people to leave the country in search of work, creating a skills shortage crisis." Archbishop Desmond Tutu has warned that South Africa is sitting on a "powder keg" because millions are living in "dehumanising poverty" stating that Black Economic Empowerment only serves an elite few.

The 2010 World Cup Soccer tournament put South Africa on the international stage and provided significant economic stimulus, with more than 160,000 new jobs created. An economist of the German Standard Bank said: "The World Championship 2010 is an important impulse for the South African people. Many people doubted that South Africa would be able to host an event of such international attention, but its stable political situation under the government of the African National Congress, which Nelson Mandela was a member of, is a good sign for potential investors and the finance market." In advance of the games, South Africa invested heavily in transportation infrastructure. South Africa finished most of the first section of their new high-speed Gautrain passenger railway and installed new bus lines. Highways have been upgraded, and the city of Durban managed to complete South Africa's first new greenfield airport in 50 years. The infrastructure projects are creating employment opportunities and are providing workers long-term skills and training. One of many challenges in building the infrastructure for the World Championship was generating power without an unduly adverse environmental impact. Environmentally friendly features such as natural ventilation and rain water capture systems were used in the new stadium facilities.

Despite these developments and improvements, South Africa is still plagued by severe social problems such as pervasive poverty, lack of infrastructure in Black African areas, AIDS, crime, and corruption.

Although South Africa is a transactional culture, meaning they do not require a history with people in order to do business, they are a personable people that have deeply rooted traditions. This means it is a good idea to build a rapport with them before doing business as well as furnish counterparts with some background information about oneself or company. South Africans follow the European approach to personal space, meaning people keep their distance when speaking and interacting in the public space.

www.southafrica.info, www.kwintessential.co.uk, www.infoplease.com, data.worldbank.org

Questions

1. In what way could the huge cultural diversity in South Africa pose challenges for MNCs seeking to set up a business there?
2. How is South African culture different from or similar to U.S. culture?
3. In what ways could South Africa benefit from hosting the World Cup in the long term?
4. What do you think are the most pressing social issues in South Africa and how is the country doing in resolving them?

Chapter 2
跨文化管理
MANAGING ACROSS CULTURES

OBJECTIVES OF THE CHAPTER

Traditionally, both scholars and practitioners assumed the universality of management. There was a tendency to take the management concepts and techniques that worked at home into other countries and cultures. It is now clear, from both practice and cross-cultural research, that this universality assumption, at least across cultures, does not hold up. Although there is a tendency in a borderless economy to promote a universalist approach, there is enough evidence from many cross-cultural researchers to conclude that the universalist assumption that may have held for U.S. organizations and employees is not generally true in other cultures.[1]

The overriding purpose of this chapter is to examine how MNCs can and should manage across cultures. This chapter puts into practice Chapter 1's discussion on the meaning and dimensions of culture.

The first part of this chapter addresses the traditional tendency to attempt to replicate successful home-country operations overseas without taking into account cultural differences. Next, attention is given to cross-cultural challenges, focusing on how differences can impact multinational management strategies. Finally, the cultures in specific countries and geographic regions are examined. The specific objectives of this chapter are:

1. **EXAMINE** the strategic dispositions that characterize responses to different cultures.
2. **DISCUSS** cross-cultural differences and similarities.
3. **REVIEW** cultural differences in select countries and regions, and note some of the important strategic guidelines for doing business in each.

国际化管理的世界
The World of *International Management*
苹果和三星：公司文化比较
Apple v. Samsung: Comparing Corporate Culture

Constituting 50 percent of the global market share, Samsung and Apple have achieved unmatched success in the smartphone industry. Culturally, however, these two companies could not be more different. Their approach to innovation, the supply chain, product lines, and even their ideas about intellectual property rights are diametrically opposed. How have these two incredibly different companies achieved such similar levels of success, and which corporate culture will ultimately win the smartphone battle?

个人主义和集体主义
Individual versus the Collective

At Apple, individual achievement is highly regarded. Innovating for the company, as an individual, is expected and required. In fact, according to an urban legend, Steve Jobs once fired an employee in the elevator for not having an answer to the question, "So what have you done for Apple lately?" Personal excellence is required by every employee, with an overall focus on end results and exceeding corporate goals.[2] Internal competition, and challenging others, is strongly encouraged. Hierarchy exists, but individuals are encouraged to speak up if it means achieving a better, more innovative product. According to a former employee, "There's a mentality that it's okay to shred somebody in the spirit of making the best products."[3]

Collectivism and group achievement, on the other hand, permeate Samsung's corporate culture. At Samsung, employees are expected "to fall in line."[4] Working together to achieve the corporate goals is valued above individual innovation. With a strong hierarchy that sets the direction of the company, product innovation is often overruled by managers. Creativity is secondary to achieving the preset corporate goals. This focus on group achievement has enabled Samsung to quickly respond to new Apple products and counter with changes to its product line. With the collective group working together, new products can be designed and produced within months.[5] For many at Samsung, the "group" identity has even spread beyond the work environment. The personal and professional lives of employees often blend together, with some employees choosing to live in dormitories right on the factory campuses.[6]

供应链管理

Supply Chain Management

The approach to the supply chain and manufacturing processes at Samsung and Apple could not be more different. Apple has been able to maximize profits through its complex, yet carefully doctored, supply chain. To minimize costs, Apple outsources the majority of its production processes. Nearly a thousand factories produce components for Apple across the globe, with over 600 in Southeast Asia alone.[7] As a result of its low manufacturing costs, Apple is able to sell the majority of its products with a 70 percent gross profit margin. Relinquishing its control over the manufacturing process, however, has led to some major negative consequences for Apple. In 2012, Apple was unable to meet customer demand for the iPad Mini due to supply chain issues that resulted in lower-than-expected production numbers.[8] Furthermore, the lack of control over its suppliers' actions has exposed Apple to criticism over human rights violations. Highly publicized worker suicides and alleged underage labor have tarnished Apple's image, even though the abuses occurred at the suppliers' facilities.

Samsung, on the contrary, maintains direct control over most of its supply chain processes. Over 90 percent of its products are manufactured within its own factories across South Korea and China. As a result, Samsung's workforce has swelled to over 200,000 employees. This internal manufacturing system results in smaller profit margins and higher overhead costs. However, organizationally, Samsung is able to retain some key advantages by maintaining control over manufacturing. For example, the company can quickly adapt production to meet demand, cutting some costs and avoiding time-sensitive errors. Manufacturing internally has also given Samsung the ability to maintain oversight of its employee's wages and hours, allowing the company to largely avoid the public relations nightmares and accusations of human rights violations that have plagued Apple's supply chain. Additionally, when Samsung has excess capacity, the company has the ability to manufacture for its competition—including Apple.[9]

关注产品

Product Focus

Apple is dedicated to maintaining first-mover advantage. As a result, Apple focuses narrowly on a few key products, with little variation in features and price. The iPhone, for example, is the only phone offered by Apple. When purchasing the latest Apple product, customers know that they are buying the most current technology on the market. By continually being the first to market with new technology, Apple is able to maintain a loyal customer base that is willing to put up with minor defects and flaws in design. This narrow product focus has created a trendy "brand" image for the company. However, by only offering one product line, Apple sacrifices sales to potential customers who are less concerned with the latest technology.

Unlike Apple, Samsung offers a wide array of products at multiple price points. With over a dozen different phone products, for example, customers can sacrifice features and the most current technology for a phone within their budget. Samsung is willing to quickly try multiple products, altering production as customers trend toward specific phones.[10] Knowing that it cannot compete for the first-mover customers who want the newest technology fastest, Samsung focuses on being "first to follow" Apple, rather than first to market. For example, Samsung's Galaxy offers many of the same features as the Apple iPhone. Though released several months after the iPhone, Samsung's Galaxy was able to sell to customers who valued technology but were not as brand focused or time-sensitive as the typical Apple customer.

知识产权

Intellectual Property

Differences in product development have led directly to recent legal conflicts between the two companies. Cultural differences regarding intellectual property rights have perhaps been the most publicized. Apple, having spent millions in research and development for new technology and improved designs, has accused Samsung of essentially stealing patent-protected technology. Samsung claims that it is developing its own technology, and that Apple has infringed its technology as well.

As a component manufacturer for Apple products, Samsung has benefited from getting a direct look at Apple's newest innovations before they hit the market. Furthermore, by knowing what technology Apple is launching in its latest round of products, Samsung has basically been given Apple's strategic roadmap. This has undoubtedly given Samsung the ability to respond more rapidly to Apple's innovation.[11]

In 2012 alone, Apple and Samsung launched over a dozen lawsuits against each other, primarily over patent infringements. Contested issues range from component technology to software design. The South Korean and Japanese rulings largely favored Samsung, while the U.S. lawsuits ended in wins for Apple. According to Apple, protecting its patents allows it to provide "distinctive products that stand apart from the masses," while Samsung claims that these patents result in "fewer choices, less innovation, and potentially higher prices" for customers.[12]

展望未来：哪一种战略会起作用

Looking Forward—Which Strategy Is Working?

Whether Apple or Samsung ultimately wins the smartphone battle is yet to be seen. The first-mover advantage that Apple has leveraged since 2007 has all but disappeared. In 2011, Samsung surpassed Apple in smartphone sales for the first time.[13] Samsung achieved 21.8 percent of the global smartphone market share in 2012, while Apple took 15.1 percent. Samsung's growth rate is also escalating; shipments of new smartphones grew by 97.5 percent in 2012, far eclipsing the 38.3 percent growth of Apple. And in 2013, Samsung ranked first for smartphone brand loyalty, knocking Apple off of the number one position for the first time.[14]

Despite Samsung's gains, Apple maintains one huge advantage—profits. In 2012, despite selling 20 million fewer phones than Samsung, Apple posted profits that were 43 percent greater.[15] Whether or not Apple will be able to maintain its finely-tuned supply chain and high profit margin is yet to be seen.

The cultural differences of Samsung and Apple highlight how, within the same industry, two companies can achieve similar levels of success despite opposing strategies. This chapter provides insight into uncovering similarities and differences across cultures and using those insights to develop international management approaches that are effective and responsive to local cultures.

跨文化管理战略

The Strategy for Managing across Cultures

As MNCs become more transnational, their strategies must address the cultural similarities and differences in their varied markets. A good example is provided by Renault, the French auto giant. For years Renault manufactured a narrow product line that it sold primarily in France. Because of this limited geographic market and the fact that its cars continued to have quality-related problems, the company's performance was at best mediocre. Several years ago, however, Renault made a number of strategic decisions that dramatically changed the way it did business. Among other things, it bought controlling stakes in Nissan Motors of Japan, Samsung Motors of South Korea, and Dacia, the Romanian automaker. The company also built a $1 billion factory in Brazil to produce its successful Mégane sedan and acquired an idle factory near Moscow to manufacture Renaults for the Eastern European market.

Today, Renault is a multinational automaker with operations on four continents. The challenge the company now faces is to make all these operations profitable. This has not been easy. Nissan's profits are unpredictable, and while it has had a good run since 1999, profits plummeted in 2007. Experiencing a net income loss of 234 billion yen in 2009, Nissan has since rebounded with net incomes of 42 billion yen in 2010, 319 billion yen in 2011, and 341 billion yen in 2012. Similarly, Renault, experiencing a net loss of 3.13 billion euros in 2009, has rebounded to net incomes of 3.55 billion euros and 2.65 billion euros in 2010 and 2011, respectively.[16] In a world market that contracted 4.7 percent in 2009, the Renault Group was down just 3.1 percent, with sales of 2.309 million vehicles. Renault's quest for greater global market share continues to progress, with world market share up to 3.6 percent in 2011. In the passenger car market, the Renault Group reported market share of 4.0 percent.[17] The Renault brand reclaimed the position of third-ranked brand in Western Europe mainly owing to the success of the Mégane family and Twingo. In the light commercial vehicle (LCV) market, the Renault brand has been the number-one brand in Western Europe since 1998.

Dacia has manufactured what some call a genuine world car, known as the Logan. Now sold in 36 countries, this simple, compact vehicle is sold at an affordable price in European markets and has recently been introduced in India. Renault maintains innovative strategies by offering the Logan under either the Dacia, Renault, or Nissan name, depending on the market. Constituting 17 percent of Renault's total sales volume in Western Europe in 2012, Dacia's healthy 9.0 percent operating margin far exceeded the 0.4 percent operating margin of Renault as a whole. The decision to integrate its sales organizations with those of Nissan in Europe, thus creating one well-integrated, efficient sales force on the continent, and the decision to start producing Nissan models in its Brazilian plant, so that it can expand its South American offerings by more efficiently using current facilities, have led to continual growth year-over-year.[18]

In 2012, Renault announced plans for an ultra-low-cost compact car for India. Scheduled to enter production in 2014, the new low-cost car will be priced to compete directly with Hyundai's Eon, currently priced at US$5,500.[19] On the 10th year of the Renault-Nissan alliance, the Group called attention to a number of milestones achieved over that period:

- Growth in sales from 4,989,709 units in 1999 to 6,090,304 in 2008.
- Common platforms and common parts: sales of cars using common platforms among the two firms represented more than 50 percent of the vehicles sold by Renault and Nissan globally in 2008.
- Achievement of the Renault-Nissan Purchasing Organization (RNPO); RNPO is the Alliance's largest common organization, negotiating with parts suppliers on behalf of Renault and Nissan.
- Exchanges of powertrains and common powertrains; in total, eight engines are commonly used.
- Expansion of the portfolio of advanced technologies.
- Manufacturing standardization.
- Cross production.
- Global footprint—Renault and Nissan cover key markets on all continents.
- Expansion of product line-ups.
- Cross-cultural management.[20]

Regarding this last issue (cross-cultural management), the Renault-Nissan Alliance has sought to foster multicultural management at all levels. Each year, more than 30 teams with Renault and Nissan employees from all regions and functions work together to identify synergies and best practices. Thousands of people with cross-cultural experience have been in collaboration since the beginning of the Alliance. Renault's chief Carlos Ghoshen, who also serves as CEO of Nissan Motor Co., is widely credited with both the operational and strategic improvements at both Renault and Nissan. His multicultural and multinational upbringing and career have convinced him of the value of cultural diversity and the creativity they generate.

Renault's recent experiences underscore the need to carefully consider different national cultures and practices when developing international strategies.

战略倾向
Strategic Predispositions

Most MNCs have a cultural strategic predisposition toward doing things in a particular way. Four distinct predispositions have been identified: ethnocentric, polycentric, regiocentric, and geocentric.

A company with an **ethnocentric predisposition** allows the values and interests of the parent company to guide strategic decisions. Firms with a **polycentric predisposition** make strategic decisions tailored to suit the cultures of the countries where the MNC operates. A **regiocentric predisposition** leads a firm to try to blend its own interests with those of its subsidiaries on a regional basis. A company with a **geocentric predisposition**

ethnocentric predisposition
A nationalistic philosophy of management whereby the values and interests of the parent company guide strategic decisions.

polycentric predisposition
A philosophy of management whereby strategic decisions are tailored to suit the cultures of the countries where the MNC operates.

regiocentric predisposition
A philosophy of management whereby the firm tries to blend its own interests with those of its subsidiaries on a regional basis.

geocentric predisposition
A philosophy of management whereby the company tries to integrate a global systems approach to decision making.

Table 2–1
Orientation of an MNC Under Different Profiles

	Orientation of the Firm			
	Ethnocentric	**Polycentric**	**Regiocentric**	**Geocentric**
Mission	Profitability (viability)	Public acceptance (legitimacy)	Both profitability and public acceptance (viability and legitimacy)	Same as regiocentric
Governance	Top-down	Bottom-up (each subsidiary decides on local objectives)	Mutually negotiated between region and its subsidiaries	Mutually negotiated at all levels of the corporation
Strategy	Global integration	National responsiveness	Regional integration and national responsiveness	Global integration and national responsiveness
Structure	Hierarchical product divisions	Hierarchical area divisions, with autonomous national units	Product and regional organization tied through a matrix	A network of organizations (including some stakeholders and competitor organizations)
Culture	Home country	Host country	Regional	Global
Technology	Mass production	Batch production	Flexible manufacturing	Flexible manufacturing
Marketing	Product development determined primarily by the needs of home country customers	Local product development based on local needs	Standardize within region, but not across regions	Global product, with local variations
Finance	Repatriation of profits to home country	Retention of profits in host country	Redistribution within region	Redistribution globally
Personnel practices	People of home country developed for key positions everywhere in the world	People of local nationality developed for key positions in their own country	Regional people developed for key positions anywhere in the region	Best people everywhere in the world developed for key positions everywhere in the world

Source: From Balaji S. Chakravarthy and Howard V. Perlmutter, "Strategic Planning for a Global Business," *Columbia Journal of World Business,* Summer 1985, pp. 5–6. Copyright © 1985 Elsevier. Reprinted with permission.

tries to integrate a global systems approach to decision making. Table 2–1 provides details of each of these orientations.

If an MNC relies on one of these profiles over an extended time, the approach may become institutionalized and greatly influence strategic planning. By the same token, a predisposition toward any of these profiles can provide problems for a firm if it is out of step with the economic or political environment. For example, a firm with an ethnocentric predisposition may find it difficult to implement a geocentric strategy, because it is unaccustomed to using global integration. Commonly, successful MNCs use a mix of these predispositions based on the demands of the current environment.

迎接挑战
Meeting the Challenge

globalization imperative A belief that one worldwide approach to doing business is the key to both efficiency and effectiveness.

Despite the need for and, in general, the tendency of MNCs to address regional differentiation issues, many MNCs remain committed to a **globalization imperative**, which is a belief that one worldwide approach to doing business is the key to both efficiency and effectiveness. However, despite this predilection to use home strategies, effective MNCs are continuing their efforts to address local needs. A number of factors are moving companies to facilitate the development of unique strategies for different cultures, including:

1. The diversity of worldwide industry standards such as those in broadcasting, where television sets must be manufactured on a country-by-country basis.

2. A continual demand by local customers for differentiated products, as in the case of consumer goods that must meet local tastes.
3. The importance of being an insider, as in the case of customers who prefer to "buy local."
4. The difficulty of managing global organizations, as in the case of some local subsidiaries that want more decentralization and others that want less.
5. The need to allow subsidiaries to use their own abilities and talents and not be restrained by headquarters, as in the case of local units that know how to customize products for their market and generate high returns on investment with limited production output.

Responding to the cultural needs of local operations and customers, MNCs find that regional strategies can be used effectively in capturing and maintaining worldwide market niches. One example is Haier, which you may become more familiar with after completing the Internet Exercise at the end of the chapter. One of the best examples is Warner-Lambert, which has manufacturing facilities in Belgium, France, Germany, Italy, Ireland, Spain, and the United Kingdom. Each plant is specialized and produces a small number of products for the entire European market; in this way, each can focus on tailoring products for the unique demands of the various markets.

The globalization versus national responsiveness challenge is even more acute when marketing cosmetics and other products that vary greatly in consumer use. For example, marketers sell toothpaste as a cosmetic product in Spain and Greece but as a cavity fighter in the Netherlands and United States. Soap manufacturers market their product as a cosmetic item in Spain but as a functional commodity in Germany. Moreover, the way in which the marketing message is delivered also is important. For example:

- Germans want advertising that is factual and rational; they fear being manipulated by "the hidden persuader." The typical German spot features the standard family of two parents, two children, and grandmother.
- The French avoid reasoning or logic. Their advertising is predominantly emotional, dramatic, and symbolic. Spots are viewed as cultural events—art for the sake of money—and are reviewed as if they were literature or films.
- The British value laughter above all else. The typical broad, self-deprecating British commercial amuses by mocking both the advertiser and consumer.[21]

In some cases, however, both the product and the marketing message are similar worldwide. This is particularly true for high-end products, where the lifestyles and expectations of the market niche are similar regardless of the country. Heineken beer, Hennessey brandy, Porsche cars, and the Financial Times all appeal to consumer niches that are fairly homogeneous, regardless of geographic locale. The same is true at the lower end of the market for goods that are impulse purchases, novel products, or fast foods, such as Coca-Cola's soft drinks, Levi's jeans, pop music, and ice-cream bars. In most cases, however, it is necessary to modify products as well as the market approach for the regional or local market. One analysis noted that the more marketers understand about the way in which a particular culture tends to view emotion, enjoyment, friendship, humor, rules, status, and other culturally based behaviors, the more control they have over creating marketing messages that will be interpreted in the desired way.

Figure 2–1 provides an example of the role that culture should play in advertising by recapping the five relationship orientations identified through Trompenaars's research (see Chapter 1). Figure 2–1 shows how value can be added to the marketing approach by carefully tailoring the advertising message to the particular culture. For example, advertising in the United States should target individual achievement, be expressive and direct, and appeal to U.S. values of success through personal hard work. On the other hand, the focus in China and other Asian countries should be much more indirect and subtle, emphasizing group references, shared responsibility, and interpersonal trust.

Figure 2–1

Trompenaar's Cultural Dimensions and Advertising: Adjusting the Message for Local Meaning

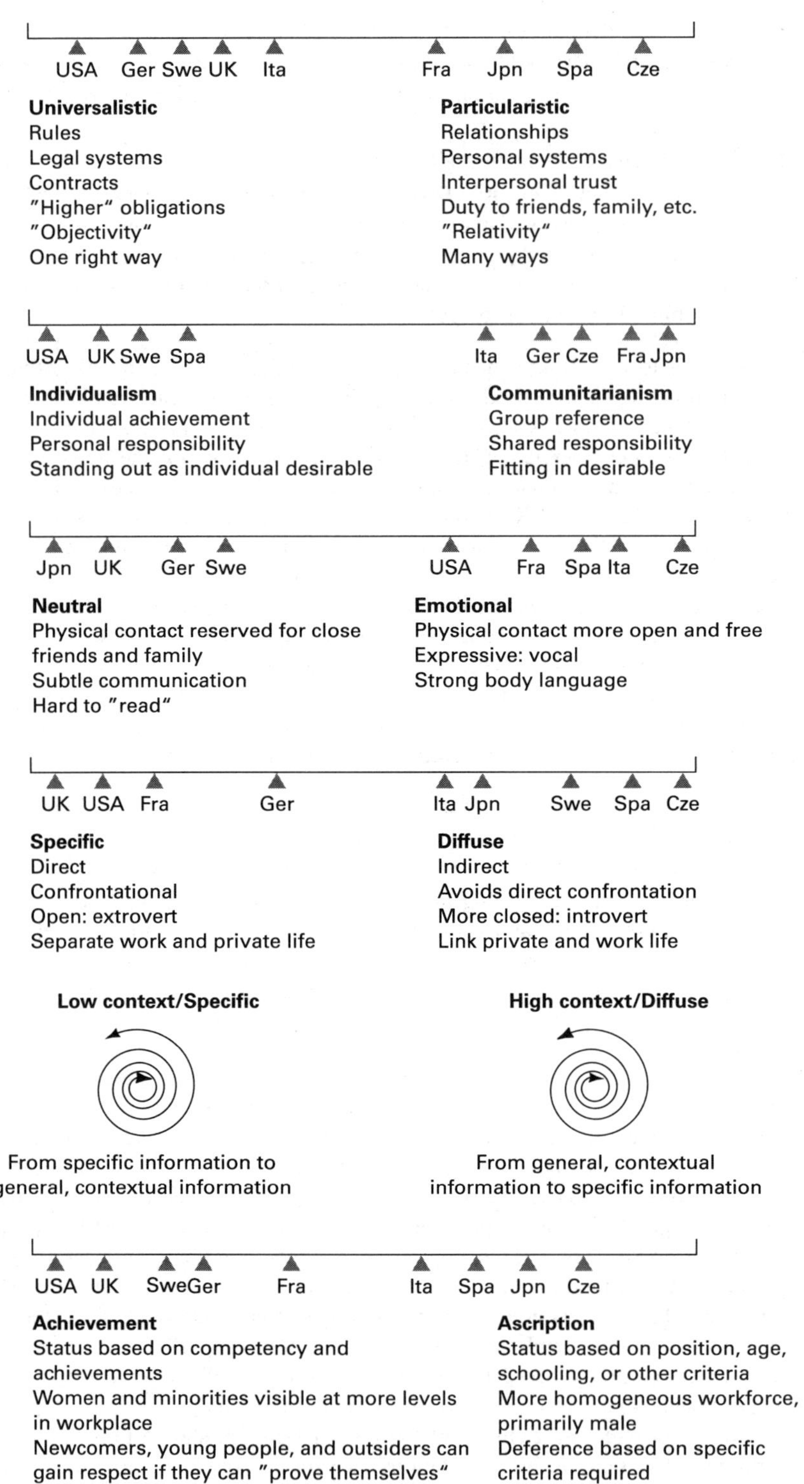

Source: Lisa Hoecklin, *Managing Cultural Differences: Strategies for Competitive Advantage* (Workingham, England: Addison-Wesley, 1995), p. 107, which is drawn from information found in Fons Trompenaars, *Riding the Waves of Culture.* Copyright © 1994 McGraw-Hill Education. Reprinted by permission of McGraw-Hill Education.

International Management in Action

Ten Key Factors for MNC Success

Why are some international firms successful while others are not? Some of the main reasons are that successful multinational firms take a worldwide view of operations, support their overseas activities, pay close attention to political winds, and use local nationals whenever possible. These are the overall findings of a report that looked into the development of customized executive education programs. Specifically, there are 10 factors or guidelines that successful global firms seem to employ. Successful global competitors:

1. See themselves as multinational enterprises and are led by a management team that is comfortable in the world arena.
2. Develop integrated and innovative strategies that make it difficult and costly for other firms to compete.
3. Aggressively and effectively implement their worldwide strategy and back it with large investments.
4. Understand that innovation no longer is confined to the United States and develop systems for tapping innovation abroad.
5. Operate as if the world were one large market rather than a series of individual, small markets.
6. Have organization structures that are designed to handle their unique problems and challenges and thus provide them the greatest efficiency.
7. Develop a system that keeps them informed about political changes around the world and the implications of these changes on the firm.
8. Have management teams that are international in composition and thus better able to respond to the various demands of their respective markets.
9. Allow their outside directors to play an active role in the operation of the enterprise.
10. Are well managed and tend to follow such important guidelines as sticking close to the customer, having lean organization structures, and encouraging autonomy and entrepreneurial activity among the personnel.

The need to adjust global strategies for regional markets presents three major challenges for most MNCs. First, the MNC must stay abreast of local market conditions and sidestep the temptation to assume that all markets are basically the same. Second, the MNC must know the strengths and weaknesses of its subsidiaries so that it can provide these units with the assistance needed in addressing local demands. Third, the multinational must give the subsidiary more autonomy so that it can respond to changes in local demands. The International Management in Action, "Ten Key Factors for MNC Success," provides additional insights into the ways that successful MNCs address these challenges.

跨文化差异性和相似性
Cross-Cultural Differences and Similarities

As you saw in Chapter 1, cultures can be similar or quite different across countries. The challenge for MNCs is to recognize and effectively manage the similarities and differences. Generally, the way in which MNCs manage their home businesses often should be different from the way they manage their overseas operations.[22] After recognizing the danger for MNCs of drifting toward parochialism and simplification in spite of cultural differences, the discussion in this section shifts to some examples of cultural similarities and differences and how to effectively manage across cultures by a *contingency approach.*

狭隘主义和专一化
Parochialism and Simplification

Parochialism is the tendency to view the world through one's own eyes and perspectives. This can be a strong temptation for many international managers, who often come from advanced economies and believe that their state-of-the-art knowledge is more than adequate to handle the challenges of doing business in less developed countries. In addition,

parochialism
The tendency to view the world through one's own eyes and perspectives.

many of these managers have a parochial point of view fostered by their background.[23] A good example is provided by Randall and Coakley, who studied the impact of culture on successful partnerships in the former Soviet Union. Initially after the breakup of the Soviet Union, the republics called themselves the Commonwealth of Independent States (CIS). Randall and Coakley found that while outside MNC managers typically entered into partnerships with CIS enterprises with a view toward making them efficient and profitable, the CIS managers often brought a different set of priorities to the table.

Commenting on their research, Randall and Coakley noted that the way CIS managers do business is sharply different from that of their American counterparts. CIS managers are still emerging from socially focused cultural norms embedded in their history, past training, and work experiences which emphasize strategic values unlike those that exist in an international market-driven environment. For example, while an excess of unproductive workers may lead American managers to lay off some individuals for the good of the company, CIS managers would focus on the good of the working community and allow the company to accept significant profit losses as a consequence. This led the researchers to conclude:

> As behavioral change continues to lag behind structural change, it becomes imperative to understand that this inconsistency between what economic demands and cultural norms require manifests problems and complexities far beyond mere structural change. In short, the implications of the different perspectives on technology, labor, and production . . . for potential partnerships between U.S. and CIS companies need to be fully grasped by all parties entering into any form of relationship.[24]

simplification
The process of exhibiting the same orientation toward different cultural groups.

Simplification is the process of exhibiting the same orientation toward different cultural groups. For example, the way in which a U.S. manager interacts with a British manager is the same way in which he or she behaves when doing business with an Asian executive. Moreover, this orientation reflects one's basic culture. Table 2–2 provides an example, showing several widely agreed-on, basic cultural orientations and the range of variations for each. Asterisks indicate the dominant U.S. orientation. Quite obviously, U.S. cultural values are not the same as those of managers from other cultures; as a result, a U.S. manager's attempt to simplify things can result in erroneous behavior. Here is an example of a member of the purchasing department of a large European oil company who was negotiating an order with a Korean supplier:

> At the first meeting, the Korean partner offered a silver pen to the European manager. The latter, however, politely refused the present for fear of being bribed (even though he knew about the Korean custom of giving presents). Much to our manager's surprise, the second meeting began with the offer of a stereo system. Again the manager refused, his fear of being bribed probably heightened. When he gazed at a piece of Korean china on the third meeting, he finally realized what was going on. His refusal had not been taken to mean "let's get on with business right away," but rather "If you want to get into business with me, you had better come up with something bigger."[25]

Understanding the culture in which they do business can make international managers more effective.[26] Unfortunately, when placed in a culture with which they are unfamiliar, most international managers are not culturally knowledgeable, so they often misinterpret what is happening. This is particularly true when the environment is markedly different from the one from which they come. Consider, for example, the difference between the cultures in Malaysia and the United States. Malaysia has what could be called a high-context culture, which possesses characteristics such as:

1. Relationships between people are relatively long lasting, and individuals feel deep personal involvement with each other.
2. Communication often is implicit, and individuals are taught from an early age to interpret these messages accurately.
3. People in authority are personally responsible for the actions of their subordinates, and this places a premium on loyalty to both superiors and subordinates.

Table 2–2
Six Basic Cultural Variations

Orientations	Range of Variations
What is the nature of people?	Good (changeable/unchangeable)
	A mixture of good and evil*
	Evil (changeable/unchangeable)
What is the person's relationship to nature?	Dominant*
	In harmony with nature
	Subjugation
What is the person's relationship to other people?	Lineal (hierarchic)
	Collateral (collectivist)
	Individualist*
What is the modality of human activity?	Doing*
	Being and becoming
	Being
What is the temporal focus of human activity?	Future*
	Present
	Past
What is the conception of space?	Private*
	Mixed
	Public

Note: *Indicates the dominant U.S. orientation.
Source: Adapted from the work of Florence Rockwood Kluckhohn and Fred L. Stodtbeck.

4. Agreements tend to be spoken rather than written.
5. Insiders and outsiders are easily distinguishable, and outsiders typically do not gain entrance to the inner group.

These Malaysian cultural characteristics are markedly different from those of low-context cultures such as the United States, which possess the following characteristics:

1. Relationships between individuals are relatively short in duration, and in general, deep personal involvement with others is not valued greatly.
2. Messages are explicit, and individuals are taught from a very early age to say exactly what they mean.
3. Authority is diffused throughout the bureaucratic system, and personal responsibility is hard to pin down.
4. Agreements tend to be in writing rather than spoken.
5. Insiders and outsiders are not readily distinguished, and the latter are encouraged to join the inner circle.[27]

These differences are exacerbated by the fact that Malaysian culture is based on an amalgamation of diverse religions, including Hinduism, Buddhism, and Islam. The belief is pervasive that success and failure are the will of God, which may create issues with American managers attempting to make deals, as Malaysians will focus less on facts and more on intuitive feelings.[28]

At the same time, it is important to realize that while there are cultural differences, there also are similarities. Therefore, in managing across cultures, not everything is totally different. Some approaches that work at home also work well in other cultural settings.

跨文化相似性
Similarities across Cultures

When internationalization began to take off in the 1970s, many companies quickly admitted that it would not be possible to do business in the same way in every corner of the globe. There was a secret hope, however, that many of the procedures and strategies that worked so well at home could be adopted overseas without modification. This has proved to be a false hope. At the same time, some similarities across cultures have been uncovered by researchers. For example, a co-author of this text (Luthans) and his associates studied through direct observation a sample of managers in the largest textile factory in Russia to determine their activities. Like U.S. managers studied earlier, Russian managers carried out traditional management, communication, human resources, and networking activities. The study also found that, as in the United States, the relative attention given to the networking activity increased the Russian managers' opportunities for promotion, and that communication activity was a significant predictor of effective performance in both Russia and the United States.[29]

Besides the similarities of managerial activities, another study at the same Russian factory tested whether organizational behavior modification (O.B.Mod.) interventions that led to performance improvements in U.S. organizations would do so in Russia.[30] As with the applications of O.B.Mod. in the United States, Russian supervisors were trained to administer social rewards (attention and recognition) and positive feedback when they observed workers engaging in behaviors that contributed to the production of quality fabric. In addition, Russian supervisors were taught to give corrective feedback for behaviors that reduced product quality. The researchers found that this O.B.Mod. approach, which had worked so well in the United States, produced positive results in the Russian factory. They concluded that the hypothesis that "the class of interventions associated with organizational behavior modification are likely to be useful in meeting the challenges faced by Russian workers and managers [is] given initial support by the results of this study."[31]

In another cross-cultural study, this time using a large Korean sample, Luthans and colleagues analyzed whether demographic and situational factors identified in the U.S.-based literature had the same antecedent influence on the commitment of Korean employees.[32] As in the U.S. studies, Korean employees' position in the hierarchy, tenure in their current position, and age all related to organizational commitment. Other similarities with U.S. firms included (1) as organizational size increased, commitment declined; (2) as structure became more employee-focused, commitment increased; and (3) the more positive the perceptions of organizational climate, the greater the employee commitment. The following conclusion was drawn:

> This study provides beginning evidence that popular constructs in the U.S. management and organizational behavior literature should not be automatically dismissed as culture bound. Whereas some organizational behavior concepts and techniques do indeed seem to be culture specific . . . a growing body of literature is demonstrating the ability to cross-culturally validate other concepts and techniques, such as behavior management. . . . This study contributed to this cross-cultural evidence for the antecedents to organizational commitment. The antecedents for Korean employees' organizational commitment were found to be similar to their American counterparts.[33]

跨文化差异性
Many Differences across Cultures

We have stressed throughout the text how different cultures can be from one another and how important it is for MNCs to understand the points of disparity. Here, we look at some differences from a human resources perspective. We introduce human resource management (HRM) here as a way to illustrate that the cultural foundations utilized in the selection of employees can further form the culture that international managers will oversee. In other words, understanding the HRM strategies before becoming a manager in the industry can aid in effective performance. The focus here is more from a socially cultural perspective.

Despite similarities between cultures in some studies, far more differences than similarities have been found. MNCs are discovering that they must carefully investigate and understand the culture where they intend to do business and modify their approaches appropriately. Sometimes these cultures are quite different from the United States—as well as from each other! One human resource management example has been offered by Trompenaars, who examined the ways in which personnel in international subsidiaries were appraised by their managers. The head office had established the criteria to be used in these evaluations but left the prioritization of the criteria to the national operating company. As a result, the outcome of the evaluations could be quite different from country to country because what was regarded as the most important criterion in one subsidiary might be ranked much lower on the evaluation list of another subsidiary. In the case of Shell Oil, for example, Trompenaars found that the firm was using a HAIRL system of appraisal. The five criteria in this acronym stood for (a) helicopter—the capacity to take a broad view from above; (b) analysis—the ability to evaluate situations logically and completely; (c) imagination—the ability to be creative and think outside the box; (d) reality—the ability to use information realistically; and (e) leadership—the ability to effectively galvanize and inspire personnel. When staff in Shell's operating companies in four countries were asked to prioritize these five criteria from top to bottom, the results were as follows:

Netherlands	France	Germany	Britain
Reality	Imagination	Leadership	Helicopter
Analysis	Analysis	Analysis	Imagination
Helicopter	Leadership	Reality	Reality
Leadership	Helicopter	Imagination	Analysis
Imagination	Reality	Helicopter	Leadership

Quite obviously, personnel in different operating companies were being evaluated differently. In fact, no two of the operating companies in the four countries had the same criterion at the top of their lists. Moreover, the criterion at the top of the list for operating companies in the Netherlands—reality—was at the bottom of the list for those in France; and the one at the top of the list in French operating companies—imagination—was at the bottom of the list of the Dutch firms. Similarly, the German operating companies put leadership at the top of the list and helicopter at the bottom, while the British companies did the opposite! In fact, the whole list for the Germans is in the exact reverse order of the British list.[34]

Other HRM differences can be found in areas such as wages, compensation, pay equity, and maternity leave. Here are some representative examples.

1. The concept of an hourly wage plays a minor role in Mexico. Labor law requires that employees receive full pay 365 days a year.
2. In Austria and Brazil, employees with one year of service are automatically given 30 days of paid vacation.
3. Some jurisdictions in Canada have legislated pay equity—known in the United States as comparable worth—between male- and female-intensive jobs.
4. In Japan, compensation levels are determined by using the objective factors of age, length of service, and educational background rather than skill, ability, and performance. Performance does not count until after an employee reaches age 45.
5. In the United Kingdom, employees are allowed up to 40 weeks of maternity leave, and employers must provide a government-mandated amount of pay for 18 of those weeks.
6. In 87 percent of large Swedish companies, the head of human resources is on the board of directors.[35]

These HRM practices certainly are quite different from those in the United States, and U.S. MNCs need to modify their approaches when they go into these countries if they hope to be successful. Compensation plans, in particular, provide an interesting area of contrast across different cultures.

Drawing on the work of Hofstede (see Chapter 1), it is possible to link cultural clusters and compensation strategies. Table 2–3 shows a host of different cultural groupings, including some in Asia, the EU, and Anglo countries. Each cluster requires a different approach to formulating an effective compensation strategy, and after analyzing each such cluster, we suggest that:

1. In Pacific Rim countries and regions, incentive plans should be group-based. In high-masculinity cultures (Japan, Chinese Hong Kong, Malaysia, the Philippines, Singapore), high salaries should be paid to senior-level managers.
2. In EU nations such as France, Spain, Italy, and Belgium, compensation strategies should be similar. In the latter two nations, however, significantly higher salaries should be paid to local senior-level managers because of the high masculinity index. In Portugal and Greece, both of which have a low individualism index, profit-sharing plans would be more effective than individual incentive plans, while in Denmark, the Netherlands, and Germany, personal-incentive plans would be highly useful because of the high individualism in these cultures.
3. In Great Britain, Ireland, and the United States, managers value their individualism and are motivated by the opportunity for earnings, recognition, advancement, and challenge. Compensation plans should reflect these needs.[36]

Figure 2–2 shows how specific HRM areas can be analyzed contingently on a country-by-country basis. Take, for example, the information on Japan. When it is contrasted with U.S. approaches, a significant number of differences are found. Recruitment

Table 2–3
Cultural Clusters in the Pacific Rim, EU, and United States

	Power Distance	Individualism	Masculinity	Uncertainty Avoidance
Pacific Rim				
Chinese Hong Kong, Malaysia, Philippines, Singapore	+	−	+	−
Japan	+	−	+	+
South Korea, China's Taiwan	+	−	−	+
EU and United States				
France, Spain	+	+	−	+
Italy, Belgium	+	+	+	+
Portugal	+	−	−	+
Greece	+	−	+	+
Denmark, Netherlands	−	+	+	−
Germany	−	+	+	+
Great Britain, Ireland, United States	−	−	+	+

Note: + indicates high or strong; − indicates low or weak.

Source: Based on research by Hofstede and presented in Richard M. Hodgetts and Fred Luthans, "U.S. Multinationals' Compensation Strategies for Local Management: Cross-Cultural Implications," *Compensation and Benefits Review,* March–April 1993, p. 47. Reproduced with permission of Sage Publications, Inc. via Copyright Clearance Center.

Figure 2–2 **A Partially Completed Contingency Matrix for International Human Resource Management**

	Japan	Germany	Mexico	China
Recruitment and selection	• Prepare for long process • Ensure that your firm is "here to stay" • Develop trusting relationship with recruit	• Obtain skilled labor from government subsidized apprenticeship program	• Use expatriates sparingly • Recruit Mexican nationals at U.S. colleges	• Recent public policy shifts encourage use of sophisticated selection procedures
Training	• Make substantial investment in training • Use general training and cross-training • Training is everyone's responsibility	• Reorganize and utilize apprenticeship programs • Be aware of government regulations on training	• Use bilingual trainers	• Careful observations of existing training programs • Utilize team training
Compensation	• Use recognition and praise as motivator • Avoid pay for performance	• Note high labor costs for manufacturing	• Consider all aspects of labor cost	• Use technical training as reward • Recognize egalitarian values • Use "more work more pay" with caution
Labor relations	• Treat unions as partners • Allow time for negotiations	• Be prepared for high wages and short work week • Expect high productivity from unionized workers	• Understand changing Mexican labor law • Prepare for increasing unionization of labor	• Tap large pool of labor cities • Lax labor laws may become more stringent
Job design	• Include participation • Incorporate group goal setting • Use autonomous work teams • Use uniform, formal approaches • Encourage co-worker input • Empower teams to make decision	• Utilize works councils to enhance worker participation	• Approach participation cautiously	• Determine employee's motives before implementing participation

Source: From Fred Luthans, Paul A. Marsnik, and Kyle W. Luthans, "A Contingency Matrix Approach to IHRM," *Human Resource Management Journal* 36, no. 2, 1997. Reprinted with permission of John Wiley & Sons, Inc.

and selection in Japanese firms often are designed to help identify those individuals who will do the best job over the long run. In the United States, people often are hired based on what they can do for the firm in the short run, because many of them eventually will quit or be downsized. Similarly, the Japanese use a great deal of cross-training, while the Americans tend to favor specialized training. The Japanese use group performance appraisal and reward people as a group; at least traditionally, Americans use manager-subordinate performance appraisal and reward people as individuals. In Japan, unions are regarded as partners; in the United States, management and unions view each other in a much more adversarial way. Only in the area of job design, where the Japanese use a great deal of participative management and autonomous work teams, are the Americans beginning to employ a similar approach. The same types of differences can be seen in the matrix of Figure 2–2 among Japan, Germany, Mexico, and China.

These differences should not be interpreted to mean that one set of HRM practices is superior to another. In fact, recent research from Japan and Europe shows these firms often have a higher incidence of personnel-related problems than do U.S. companies. Figure 2–2 clearly indicates the importance of MNCs' using a contingency approach to HRM across cultures. Not only are there different HRM practices in different cultures, but there also are different practices within the same cultures. For instance, one study involving 249 U.S. affiliates of foreign-based MNCs found that in general, affiliate HRM practices closely follow local practices when dealing with the rank and file but even more closely approximate parent-company practices when dealing with upper-level management.[37] In other words, this study found that a hybrid approach to HRM was being used by these MNCs.

Aside from the different approaches used in different countries, it is becoming clear that common assumptions and conventional wisdom about HRM practices in certain countries no longer are valid. For example, for many years, it has been assumed that Japanese employees do not leave their jobs for work with other firms, that they are loyal to their first employer, and that it would be virtually impossible for MNCs operating in Japan to recruit talent from Japanese firms. Recent evidence, however, reveals that job-hopping among Japanese employees is increasingly common. One report concluded:

> While American workers, both the laid-off and the survivors, grapple with cutbacks, one in three Japanese workers willingly walks away from his job within the first 10 years of his career, according to the Japanese Institute of Labor, a private research organization. And many more are thinking about it. More than half of salaried Japanese workers say they would switch jobs or start their own business if a favorable opportunity arose, according to a survey by the Recruit Research Corporation.[38]

These findings clearly illustrate one important point: Managing across cultures requires careful understanding of the local environment, because common assumptions and stereotypes may not be valid. Cultural differences must be addressed, and this is why cross-cultural research will continue to be critical in helping firms learn how to manage across cultures.[39]

挑选出的国家和地区的文化差异

Cultural Differences in Selected Countries and Regions

As noted in Chapter 1, MNCs are increasingly active in all parts of the world, including the developing and emerging regions because of their recent growth and future potential. Chapter 1 introduced the concept of country clusters, which is the idea that certain regions of the world have similar cultures. For example, the way that Americans do business in the United States is very similar to the way that British do business in England. Even in this Anglo culture, however, there are pronounced differences, and in other clusters, such as in Asia, these differences become even more pronounced. The International Management in Action, "Managing in Hong Kong," depicts such differences. The next sections focus on cultural highlights and differences in selected countries and regions that provide the necessary understanding and perspective for effective management across cultures.

One interesting development is the increasing frequency of managers and executives from one part of the world assuming leadership roles in another. For example, in 2008 Aozora Bank hired Brian Prince as their new CEO, becoming one of only a few—but an increasing number—of foreign heads of Japanese firms who now include Eva Chen of Trend Micro and Carlos Ghoshen of Nissan Motor Co. Foreign CEOs still face cultural difficulties, however. At Nippon Sheet Glass, for example, American Craig Naylor resigned suddenly in 2012 after just two years as CEO. Naylor cited "fundamental disagreements

International Management in Action

Managing in Hong Kong

www.asiapages.com.sg/vgt/welcome.htm

Managing across cultures has long been recognized as a potential problem for multinationals. To help expatriates who are posted overseas deal with a new culture, many MNCs offer special training and coaching. Often, however, little is done to change expatriates' basic cultural values or specific managerial behaviors. Simply put, this traditional approach could be called the *practical school of management thought,* which holds that effective managerial behavior is universal and a good manager in the United States also will be effective in Hong Kong or any other location around the world. In recent years, it generally has been recognized that such an approach no longer is sufficient, and there is growing support for what is called the *cross-cultural school of management thought,* which holds that effective managerial behavior is a function of the specific culture. As Black and Porter pointed out, successful managerial action in Los Angeles may not be effective in Hong Kong.

Black and Porter investigated the validity of these two schools of thought by surveying U.S. managers working in Hong Kong, U.S. managers working in the United States, and Hong Kong managers working in Hong Kong. Their findings revealed some interesting differences. The U.S. managers in Hong Kong exhibited managerial behaviors similar to those of their counterparts back in the United States; however, Hong Kong managers had managerial behaviors different from either group of U.S. managers. Commenting on these results, the researchers noted:

> This study . . . points to some important practical implications. It suggests that American firms and the practical school of thought may be mistaken in the assumption that a good manager in Los Angeles will necessarily do fine in Hong Kong or some other foreign country. It may be that because firms do not include in their selection criteria individual characteristics such as cognitive flexibility, cultural flexibility, degree of ethnocentricity, etc., they end up sending a number of individuals on international assignments who have a tendency to keep the same set of managerial behaviors they used in the U.S. and not adjust or adapt to the local norms and practices. Including the measurement of these characteristics in the selection process, as well as providing cross-cultural training before departure, may be a means of obtaining more effective adaptation of managerial behaviors and more effective performance in overseas assignments.

Certainly the study shows that simplistic assumptions about culture are erroneous and that what works in one country will not necessarily produce the desired results in another. If MNCs are going to manage effectively throughout the world, they are going to have to give more attention to training their people about intercultural differences.

with the board on company strategy" as the key reason for his departure.[40]

Because of the increasing importance of developing and emerging regions and countries in the global economy, knowledge of these contexts is more and more important for global managers. In a study by the China Europe International Business School's Leadership Behavioral Laboratory and the Center for Creative Leadership, executives identified critical characteristics in their careers that contributed to their development as managers in emerging markets settings. These included setting an example for junior employees and learning to thrive in unstable environments.[41] In addition, managers emphasized the importance of learning about their business and the emerging markets environment, through formal classes, mentoring, and direct experience.

在中国做生意
Doing Business in China

The People's Republic of China (PRC or China, for short) has had a long tradition of isolation. In 1979, Deng Xiaoping opened this country to the world.

China is rapidly trying to close the gap between itself and economically advanced nations and to establish itself as a power in the world economy. China is actively trading in world markets, is a member of the WTO, and is a major trading partner of the United States. Despite this global presence, many U.S. and European multinationals still find that doing business in the PRC can be a long, grueling process.[42] Very few outside firms have yet to make a profit in China. One primary reason is that Western-based MNCs do not appreciate the important role and impact of Chinese culture.

Experienced executives report that the primary criterion for doing business in China is technical competence. For example, in the case of MNCs selling machinery, the Chinese want to know exactly how the machine works, what its capabilities are, and how repairs and maintenance must be handled. Sellers must be prepared to answer these questions in precise detail. This is why successful multinationals send only seasoned engineers and technical people to the PRC. They know that the questions to be answered will require both knowledge and experience, and young, fresh-out-of-school engineers will not be able to answer them.

A major cultural difference between the PRC and many Western countries is the issue of time. The Chinese tend to be punctual, so it is important that those who do business with them arrive on time. During meetings, such as those held when negotiating a contract, the Chinese may ask many questions and nod their assent at the answers. This nodding usually means that they understand or are being polite; it seldom means that they like what they are hearing and want to enter into a contract. For this reason, when dealing with the Chinese, one must keep in mind that patience is critically important. The Chinese will make a decision in their own good time, and it is common for outside businesspeople to make several trips to China before a deal is finally concluded. Moreover, not only are there numerous meetings, but sometimes these are unilaterally cancelled at the last minute and rescheduled. This often tries the patience of outsiders and is inconvenient in terms of rearranging travel plans and other problems.

guanxi
Chinese for "good connections."

Another important dimension of Chinese culture is **guanxi**, which means "good connections."[43] In turn, these connections can result in such things as lower costs for doing business.[44] Yet guanxi goes beyond just lower costs. Yi and Ellis surveyed Chinese mainland and Hong Kong managers and found that both groups agreed that guanxi networking offered a number of potential benefits, including increased business, higher sales revenue, more sources of information, greater prospecting opportunities, and the facilitation[45] of future transactions. In practice, guanxi resembles nepotism, where individuals in authority make decisions on the basis of family ties or social connections rather than objective indices. Tung has reported:

> In a survey of 2,000 Chinese from Shanghai and its surrounding rural community, 92 percent of the respondents confirmed that guanxi played a significant role in their daily lives. Furthermore, the younger generation tended to place greater emphasis on guanxi. In fact, guanxi has become more widespread in the recent past. . . . Most business practitioners who have experience in doing business with East Asians will readily agree that in order to succeed in these countries "who you know is more important than what you know." In other words, having connections with the appropriate individuals and authorities is often more crucial than having the right product and/or price.[46]

Additionally, outsiders doing business in China must be aware that Chinese people will typically argue that they have the guanxi to get a job done, when in reality they may or may not have the necessary connections.

In China, it is important to be a good listener. This may mean having to listen to the same stories about the great progress that has been made by the PRC over the past decade. The Chinese are very proud of their economic accomplishments and want to share these feelings with outsiders.

When dealing with the Chinese, one must realize they are a collective society in which people pride themselves on being members of a group. This is in sharp contrast to the situation in the United States and other Western countries, where individualism is highly prized. For this reason, one must never single out a Chinese and praise him or her for a particular quality, such as intelligence or kindness, because doing so may embarrass the individual in the presence of his or her peers. It is equally important to avoid using self-centered conversation, such as excessive use of the word "I," because it appears that the speaker is trying to single him- or herself out for special consideration.

The Chinese also are much less animated than Westerners. They avoid open displays of affection, do not slap each other on the back, and are more reticent, retiring, and reserved than North or South Americans. They do not appreciate loud, boisterous behavior, and when speaking to each other, they maintain a greater physical distance than is typical in the West.

Cultural highlights that affect doing business in China can be summarized and put into some specific guidelines as follows:

1. The Chinese place values and principles above money and expediency.[47]
2. Business meetings typically start with pleasantries such as tea and general conversation about the guest's trip to the country, local accommodations, and family. In most cases, the host already has been briefed on the background of the visitor.
3. When a meeting is ready to begin, the Chinese host will give the appropriate indication. Similarly, when the meeting is over, the host will indicate that it is time for the guest to leave.
4. Once the Chinese decide who and what are best, they tend to stick with these decisions. Therefore, they may be slow in formulating a plan of action, but once they get started, they make fairly good progress.
5. In negotiations, reciprocity is important. If the Chinese give concessions, they expect some in return. Additionally, it is common to find them slowing down negotiations to take advantage of Westerners' desire to conclude arrangements as quickly as possible. The objective of this tactic is to extract further concessions. Another common ploy used by the Chinese is to pressure the other party during final arrangements by suggesting that this counterpart has broken the spirit of friendship in which the business relationship originally was established. Again, through this ploy, the Chinese are trying to gain additional concessions.
6. Because negotiating can involve a loss of face, it is common to find Chinese carrying out the whole process through intermediaries. This allows them to convey their ideas without fear of embarrassment.[48]
7. During negotiations, it is important not to show excessive emotion of any kind. Anger or frustration, for example, is viewed as antisocial and unseemly.
8. Negotiations should be viewed with a long-term perspective. Those who will do best are the ones who realize they are investing in a long-term relationship.[49]

While these are the traditional behaviors of Chinese businesspeople, the transitioning economy has also caused a shift in business culture, which has affected working professionals' private lives. Performance, which was once based on effort, is now being evaluated from the angle of results as the country continues to maintain its flourishing profits. While traditional Chinese culture focused on family first, financial and material well-being has become a top priority. This performance orientation has increased stress and contributed to growing incidence of burnout, depression, substance abuse, and other ailments. Some U.S. companies have attempted to curb these psychological ailments by offering counseling; however, this service is not as readily accepted by the Chinese. Instead of bringing attention to the "counseling" aspect, firms instead promote "workplace harmony" and "personal well-being services."[50] This suggests that while some aspects of Chinese culture are changing, international managers must recognize the foundational culture of the country and try to deal with such issues according to local beliefs.

在俄罗斯做生意
Doing Business in Russia

As pointed out in Chapter 1, the Russian economy has experienced severe problems, and the risks of doing business there cannot be overstated. At the same time, however, by following certain guidelines, MNCs can begin to tap the potential opportunities. Here are some suggestions for being successful in Russia:

1. Build personal relationships with partners. Business laws and contracts do not mean as much in Russia as they do in the West. When there are

contract disputes, there is little protection for the aggrieved party because of the time and effort needed to legally enforce the agreement. Detailed contracts can be hammered out later on; in the beginning, all that counts is friendship.

2. Use local consultants. Because the rules of business have changed so much in recent years, it pays to have a local Russian consultant working with the company. Russian expatriates often are not up to date on what is going on and, quite often, are not trusted by local businesspeople who have stayed in the country. So the consultant should be someone who has been in Russia all the time and understands the local business climate.
3. Consider business ethics. Ethical behavior in the United States is not always the same as in Russia. For example, it is traditional in Russia to give gifts to those with whom one wants to transact business, an approach that may be regarded as bribery in the United States.
4. Be patient. In order to get something done in Russia, it often takes months of waiting. Those who are in a hurry to make a quick deal are often sorely disappointed.
5. Stress exclusivity. Russians like exclusive arrangements and often negotiate with just one firm at a time. This is in contrast to Western businesspeople who often "shop" their deals and may negotiate with a half-dozen firms at the same time before settling on one.
6. Remember that personal relations are important. Russians like to do business face to face. So when they receive letters or faxes, they often put them on their desk but do not respond to them. They are waiting for the businessperson to contact them and set up a personal meeting.
7. Keep financial information personal. When Westerners enter into business dealings with partners, it is common for them to share financial information with these individuals and to expect the same from the latter. However, Russians wait until they know their partner well enough to feel comfortable before sharing financial data. Once trust is established, then this information is provided.
8. Research the company. In dealing effectively with Russian partners, it is helpful to get information about this company, its management hierarchy, and how it typically does business. This information helps ensure the chances for good relations because it gives the Western partner a basis for establishing a meaningful relationship.
9. Stress mutual gain. The Western idea of "win-win" in negotiations also works well in Russia. Potential partners want to know what they stand to gain from entering into the venture.
10. Clarify terminology. For-profit business deals are new in Russia, so the language of business is just getting transplanted there. As a result, it is important to double-check and make sure that the other party clearly understands the proposal, knows what is expected and when, and is agreeable to the deal.[51]
11. Be careful about compromising or settling things too quickly, because this is often seen as a sign of weakness. During the Soviet Union days, everything was complex, and so Russians are suspicious of anything that is conceded easily. If agreements are not reached after a while, a preferred tactic on their part is to display patience and then wait it out. However, they will abandon this approach if the other side shows great patience because they will realize that their negotiating tactic is useless.

12. Written contracts are not as binding to Russians as they are to Westerners. Like Asians, Russians view contracts as binding only if they continue to be mutually beneficial. One of the best ways of dealing with this is to be able to continually show them the benefits associated with sticking to the deal.[52]

These 12 steps can be critical to the success of a business venture in Russia. They require careful consideration of cultural factors, and it often takes a lot longer than initially anticipated. However, the benefits may be worth the wait. And when everything is completed, there is a final cultural tradition that should be observed: Fix and reinforce the final agreements with a nice dinner together and an invitation to the Russians to visit your country and see your facilities.[53]

在印度做生意
Doing Business in India

In recent years, India has begun to attract the attention of large MNCs. Unsaturated consumer markets, coupled with cheap labor and production locations, have helped make India a desirable market for global firms. The government continues to play an important role in this process, although recently many of the bureaucratic restrictions have been lifted as India works to attract foreign investment and raise its economic growth rate.[54] In addition, although most Indian businesspeople speak English, many of their values and beliefs are markedly different from those in the West. Thus, understanding Indian culture is critical to successfully doing business in India.

Shaking hands with male business associates is almost always an acceptable practice. U.S. businesspeople in India are considered equals, however, and the universal method of greeting an equal is to press one's palms together in front of the chest and say namaste, which means "greetings to you." Therefore, if a handshake appears to be improper, it always is safe to use namaste.

Western food typically is available in all good hotels. Most Indians do not drink alcoholic beverages, or if they do, they tend to prefer liquor and avoid the popular Western choice of beer, and many are vegetarians or eat chicken but not beef. Therefore, when foreign businesspeople entertain in India, the menu often is quite different from that back home. Moreover, when a local businessperson invites an expatriate for dinner at home, it is not necessary to bring a gift, although it is acceptable to do so. The host's wife and children usually will provide help from the kitchen to ensure that the guest is well treated, but they will not be at the table. If they are, it is common to wait until everyone has been seated and the host begins to eat or asks everyone to begin. During the meal, the host will ask the guest to have more food. This is done to ensure that the person does not go away hungry; however, once one has eaten enough, it is acceptable to politely refuse more food.

For Western businesspeople in India, shirt, trousers, tie, and suit are proper attire. In the southern part of India, where the climate is very hot, a light suit is preferable. In the north during the winter, a light sweater and jacket are a good choice. Indian businesspeople, on the other hand, often will wear local dress. In many cases, this includes a dhoti, which is a single piece of white cloth (about five yards long and three feet wide) that is passed around the waist up to half its length and then the other half is drawn between the legs and tucked at the waist. Long shirts are worn on the upper part of the body. In some locales, such as Punjab, Sikhs will wear turbans, and well-to-do Hindus sometimes will wear long coats like the Rajahs. This coat, known as a sherwani, is the dress recognized by the government for official and ceremonial wear. Foreign businesspeople are not expected to dress like locals, and in fact, many Indian businesspeople will dress like Europeans. Therefore, it is unnecessary to adopt local dress codes.

When doing business in India, one will find a number of other customs useful to know, such as:

1. It is important to be on time for meetings.
2. Personal questions should not be asked unless the other individual is a friend or close associate.

3. Titles are important, so people who are doctors or professors should be addressed accordingly.
4. Public displays of affection are considered to be inappropriate, so one should refrain from backslapping or touching others.
5. Beckoning is done with the palm turned down; pointing often is done with the chin.
6. When eating or accepting things, use the right hand because the left is considered to be unclean.
7. The namaste gesture can be used to greet people; it also is used to convey other messages, including a signal that one has had enough food.
8. Bargaining for goods and services is common; this contrasts with Western traditions, where bargaining might be considered rude or abrasive.[55]

Finally, it is important to remember that Indians are very tolerant of outsiders and understand that many are unfamiliar with local customs and procedures. Therefore, there is no need to make a phony attempt to conform to Indian cultural traditions. Making an effort to be polite and courteous is sufficient.[56]

在法国做生意
Doing Business in France

Many in the United States believe that it is more difficult to get along with the French than with other Europeans. This feeling probably reflects the French culture, which is markedly different from that in the United States. In France, one's social class is very important, and these classes include the aristocracy, the upper bourgeoisie, the upper-middle bourgeoisie, the middle, the lower middle, and the lower. Social interactions are affected by class stereotypes, and during their lifetime, most French people do not encounter much change in social status. Unlike an American, who through hard work and success can move from the lowest economic strata to the highest, a successful French person might, at best, climb one or two rungs of the social ladder. Additionally, the French are very status conscious, and they like to provide signs of their status, such as knowledge of literature and the arts; a well-designed, tastefully decorated house; and a high level of education.

The French also tend to be friendly, humorous, and sardonic (sarcastic), in contrast to Americans, for example, who seldom are sardonic. The French may admire or be fascinated with people who disagree with them; in contrast, Americans are more attracted to those who agree with them. As a result, the French are accustomed to conflict and during negotiations accept that some positions are irreconcilable and must be accepted as such. Americans, on the other hand, believe that conflicts can be resolved and that if both parties make an extra effort and have a spirit of compromise, there will be no irreconcilable differences. Moreover, the French often determine a person's trustworthiness based on his or her firsthand evaluation of the individual's character. This is in marked contrast to Americans, who tend to evaluate a person's trustworthiness based on past achievements and other people's evaluations of this person.

In the workplace, many French people are not motivated by competition or the desire to emulate fellow workers. They often are accused of not having as intense a work ethic as, for example, Americans or Asians. Many French workers frown on overtime, and statistics show that on average, they have the longest vacations in the world (four to five weeks annually). On the other hand, few would disagree that they work extremely hard in their regularly scheduled time and have a reputation for high productivity. Part of this reputation results from the French tradition of craftsmanship. Part of it also is accounted for by a large percentage of the workforce being employed in small, independent businesses, where there is widespread respect for a job well done.

Most French organizations tend to be highly centralized and have rigid structures. As a result, it usually takes longer to carry out decisions. Because this arrangement is quite different from the more decentralized, flattened organizations in the United States, both middle- and lower-level U.S. expatriate managers who work in French subsidiaries often find bureaucratic red tape a source of considerable frustration. There also are marked differences at the upper levels of management. In French companies, top managers have far more authority than their U.S. counterparts, and they are less accountable for their actions. While top-level U.S. executives must continually defend their decisions to the CEO or board of directors, French executives are challenged only if the company has poor performance. As a result, those who have studied French management find that they take a more autocratic approach.[57]

In countries such as the United States, a great deal of motivation is derived from professional accomplishment. Americans realize there is limited job and social security in their country, so it is up to them to work hard and ensure their future. The French do not have the same view. While they admire Americans' industriousness and devotion to work, they believe that quality of life is what really matters. As a result, they attach a great deal of importance to leisure time, and many are unwilling to sacrifice the enjoyment of life for dedication to work.

The values and beliefs discussed here help to explain why French culture is so different from that in other countries. Some of the sharp contrasts with the United States, for example, provide insights regarding the difficulties of doing business in France. Additional cultural characteristics, such as the following, may act as guides in situations outsiders may encounter in France:

1. When shaking hands with a French person, use a quick shake with some pressure in the grip. A firm, pumping handshake, which is so common in the United States, is considered to be uncultured.
2. It is extremely important to be on time for meetings and social occasions. Being "fashionably late" is frowned on.
3. During a meal, it is acceptable to engage in pleasant conversation, but personal questions and the subject of money are never brought up.
4. Great importance is placed on neatness and taste. Therefore, visiting businesspeople should try very hard to be cultured and sophisticated.[58]
5. The French tend to be suspicious of early friendliness in the discussion and dislike first names, taking off jackets, or disclosure of personal or family details.
6. In negotiations the French try to find out what all of the other side's aims and demands are at the beginning, but they reveal their own hand only late in the negotiations.
7. The French do not like being rushed into making a decision, and they rarely make important decisions inside the meeting. In fact, the person who is ultimately responsible for making the decision is often not present.
8. The French tend to be very precise and logical in their approach to things, and will often not make concessions in negotiations unless their logic has been defeated. If a deadlock results, unlike Americans, who will try to break the impasse by suggesting a series of compromises by both sides, the French tend to remain firm and simply restate their position.[59]

在巴西做生意
Doing Business in Brazil

Brazil is considered a Latin American country, but it is important to highlight this nation since some characteristics make it markedly different to manage as compared to other Latin American countries.[60] Brazil was originally colonized by Portugal, and remained affiliated with its parent country until 1865. Even though today Brazil is extremely multicultural, the country still demonstrates many attributes derived from its Portuguese heritage, including its official language. For example, the Brazilian economy was once completely centrally controlled like many other Latin American countries, yet was motivated by such Portuguese influences as flexibility, tolerance, and commercialism.[61] This may be a significant reason behind its successful economic emergence.

Brazilians have a relaxed work ethic, often respecting those who inherit wealth and have strong familial roots over those seeking entrepreneurial opportunities. They view time in a very relaxed manner, so punctuality is not a strong suit in this country. Overall, the people are very good-natured and tend to avoid confrontation, yet they seek out risky endeavors.

Here are some factors to consider when pursuing business in Brazil:

1. Physical contact is acceptable as a form of communication. Brazilians tend to stand very close to others when having a conversation, and will touch the person's back, arm, or elbow as a greeting or sign of respect.
2. Face-to-face interaction is preferred as a way to communicate, so avoid simply e-mailing or calling. Do not be surprised if meetings begin anywhere from 10 to 30 minutes after the scheduled time, since Brazilians are not governed by the clock. Greet with a pleasant demeanor, and accept any offering of cafezinho, or small cups of Brazilian coffee, as it is one indication of a relaxed, social setting.
3. Brazilians tend not to trust others, so be sure to form a strong relationship before bringing up business issues. Be yourself, and be honest, since rigid exteriors or putting on a show is not revered. Close relationships are extremely important, since they will do anything for friends, hence the expression, "For friends, everything. For enemies, the law." Showing interest in their personal and professional life is greatly appreciated, especially if international representatives speak some Portuguese.
4. Appearance is very important, as it will reflect both you and your company. Be sure to have polished shoes. Men should wear conservative dark suits, shirts, and ties. Women should dress nicely, but avoid too conservative or formal attire. Think fashion. Brazilian managers often wonder, for example, if Americans make so much money, why do they dress like they are poor?
5. Patience is key. Many processes are long and drawn out, including negotiations. Expressing frustration or impatience and attempting to speed up procedures may lose the deal. It is worth waiting out, as Brazilians will be very committed and loyal once an agreement is reached.
6. The slow processes and relaxed atmosphere do not imply that it is acceptable to be ill-prepared. Presentations should be informative and expressive, as Brazilians respond to such emotional cues. Consistency is important. Be prepared to state your case multiple times. It is common for Brazilians to bring a lot of people to attend negotiations, mostly to observe and learn. Subsequent meetings may include members of higher management, requiring a rehashing of information.[62]

在阿拉伯国家做生意
Doing Business in Arab Countries

The intense media attention given to the Iraq War, terrorist actions, and continuing conflicts in the Middle East have perhaps revealed to everyone that Arab cultures are distinctly different from Anglo cultures.[63] Americans often find it extremely hard to do business in Arab countries, and a number of Arab cultural characteristics can be cited for this difficulty.

One is the Arab view of time. In the United States, it is common to use the cliché, "Time is money." In Arab countries, a favorite expression is *Bukra insha Allah,* which means "Tomorrow if God wills," an expression that explains the Arabs' fatalistic approach to time. Arabs believe that Allah controls time, in contrast to Westerners, who believe that they control their own time. As a result, if Arabs commit themselves to a date in the future and fail to show up, they feel no guilt or concern because they believe they have no control over time in the first place.

(This is perhaps a good point in our discussion to provide a word of caution on overgeneralizing about cultures, which is needed here and in all the examples in this chapter's discussion of cultural characteristics. There are many Arabs who are very particular about promises and appointments. There are also many Arabs who are very proactive and not fatalistic. The point is that there are always exceptions, and stereotyping in cross-cultural dealings is unwarranted. In this chapter we reviewed general cultural characteristics, but from your own experience you know the importance of an understanding of the particular individuals or situations you are dealing with.)

An Arab cultural belief that generally holds is that destiny depends more on the will of a supreme being than on the behavior of individuals. A higher power dictates the outcome of important events, so individual action is of little consequence. This thinking affects not only Arabs' aspirations but also their motivation. Also of importance is that the status of Arabs largely is determined by family position and social contact and connections, not necessarily by their own accomplishments. This view helps to explain why some Middle Easterners take great satisfaction in appearing to be helpless. In fact, helplessness can be used as a source of power, for in this area of the world, the strong are resented and the weak compensated. Here is an example:

> In one Arab country, several public administrators of equal rank would take turns meeting in each other's offices for their weekly conferences, and the host would serve as chairman. After several months, one of these men had a mild heart attack. Upon his recovery, it was decided to hold the meetings only in his office, in order not to inconvenience him. From then on, the man who had the heart attack became the permanent chairman of the conference. This individual appeared more helpless than the others, and his helplessness enabled him to increase his power.[64]

This approach is quite different from that in the United States, where the strong tend to be compensated and rewarded. If a person was ill, such as in this example, the individual would be relieved of his responsibility until he or she had regained full health. In the interim, the rest of the group would go on without the sick person, and he or she might lose power.

Another important cultural contrast between Arabs and Americans is that of emotion and logic. Arabs often act based on emotion; in contrast, those in an Anglo culture are taught to act on logic. Many Arabs live in unstable environments where things change constantly, so they do not develop trusting relationships with others. Americans, on the other hand, live in a much more predictable environment and develop trusting relationships with others.

Arabs also make wide use of elaborate and ritualized forms of greetings and leave-takings. A businessperson may wait past the assigned meeting time before being admitted to an Arab's office. Once there, the individual may find many others present; this situation is unlike the typical one-on-one meetings that are so common in the United States. Moreover, during the meeting, there may be continuous interruptions, visitors may arrive and begin talking to the host, and messengers may come in and go out on a regular basis. The businessperson is expected to take all this activity as perfectly normal and remain composed and ready to continue discussions as soon as the host is prepared to do so.

Business meetings typically conclude with an offer of coffee or tea. This is a sign that the meeting is over and that future meetings, if there are to be any, should now be arranged.

Unlike the case in many other countries, titles are not in general use on the Arabian Peninsula, except in the case of royal families, ministers, and high-level military officers. Additionally, initial meetings typically are used to get to know the other party. Business-related discussions may not occur until the third or fourth meeting. Also, in contrast to the common perception among many Western businesspeople who have never been to an Arab country, it is not necessary to bring the other party a gift. If this is done, however, it should be a modest gift. A good example is a novelty or souvenir item from the visitor's home country.

Arabs attach a great deal of importance to status and rank. When meeting with them, one should pay deference to the senior person first. It also is important never to criticize or berate anyone publicly. This causes the individual to lose face, and the same is true for the person who makes these comments. Mutual respect is required at all times.

Other useful guidelines for doing business in Arab cultures include:

1. It is important never to display feelings of superiority, because this makes the other party feel inferior. No matter how well someone does something, the individual should let the action speak for itself and not brag or put on a show of self-importance.
2. One should not take credit for joint efforts. A great deal of what is accomplished is a result of group work, and to indicate that one accomplished something alone is a mistake.
3. Much of what gets done is a result of going through administrative channels in the country. It often is difficult to sidestep a lot of this red tape, and efforts to do so can be regarded as disrespect for legal and governmental institutions.
4. Connections are extremely important in conducting business. Well-connected businesspeople can get things done much faster than their counterparts who do not know the ins and outs of the system.
5. Patience is critical to the success of business transactions. This time consideration should be built into all negotiations, thus preventing one from giving away too much in an effort to reach a quick settlement.
6. Important decisions usually are made in person, not by correspondence or telephone. This is why an MNC's representative's personal presence often is a prerequisite for success in the Arab world. Additionally, while there may be many people who provide input on the final decision, the ultimate power rests with the person at the top, and this individual will rely heavily on personal impressions, trust, and rapport.[65]

再看国际化管理的世界
The World of International Management—Revisited

Management at many companies and in many countries is becoming more and more multicultural, yet individual corporate cultures persist. Apple and Samsung are both examples of highly successful companies with radically different approaches to strategy and management. Apple prides itself on groundbreaking innovation, individual achievement, and excellence. At Samsung, the emphasis is on extending innovations and applications and on group achievement and collective responsibility, all geared toward company-wide success. The two companies even take a very different approach to their supply chains, with Apple outsourcing the entirety of its production, while Samsung manufactures more than 90 percent of its products in company-owned factories. In terms of products, Apple is a first-mover, while Samsung is a "fast follower." In some ways, these two companies epitomize the cultures from which they emanate, but both are now global players.

Cross-border investments by Chinese, Indian, and other developing-country firms have prompted investing firms especially in Europe and North America to more thoughtfully consider cultural issues as they seek to integrate local companies and employees into their global organizations. As we saw in Chapter 1, East Asian, U.S., and Western European cultures differ on many dimensions, which may pose challenges for companies seeking to operate across these geographical/cultural boundaries.

Now that you have read this chapter, you should have a good understanding of the importance and the difficulties of managing across cultures. Using this knowledge as a platform, answer the following questions: (1) Which aspects of Apple's culture have helped it succeed in its global growth and which may have impeded it? (2) Which aspects of Samsung's culture have helped it succeed in its global growth and which may have impeded it? (3) How would you characterize Apple and Samsung in terms of the four basic strategic predispositions? (4) What might Apple learn from Samsung and Samsung learn from Apple?

SUMMARY OF KEY POINTS

1. One major problem facing MNCs is that they sometimes attempt to manage across cultures in ways similar to those of their home country. MNC dispositions toward managing across cultures can be characterized as (1) ethnocentric, (2) polycentric, (3) regiocentric, and (4) geocentric. These different approaches shape how companies adapt and adjust to cultural pressures around the world.
2. One major challenge when dealing with cross-cultural problems is that of overcoming parochialism and simplification. Parochialism is the tendency to view the world through one's own eyes and perspectives. Simplification is the process of exhibiting the same orientation toward different cultural groups. Another problem is that of doing things the same way in foreign markets as they are done in domestic markets. Research shows that in some cases, this approach can be effective; however, effective cross-cultural management more commonly requires approaches different than those used at home. One area where this is particularly evident is human resource management. Recruitment, selection, training, and compensation often are carried out in different ways in different countries, and what works in the United States may have limited value in other countries and geographic regions.
3. Doing business in various parts of the world requires the recognition and understanding of cultural differences. Some of these differences revolve around the importance the society assigns to time, status, control of decision making, personal accomplishment, and work itself. These types of cultural differences help to explain why effective managers in China or Russia often are quite different from those in France, and why a successful style in the United States will not be ideal in Arab countries.

KEY TERMS

ethnocentric predisposition
geocentric predisposition
globalization imperative
guanxi
parochialism
polycentric predisposition
regiocentric predisposition
simplification

REVIEW AND DISCUSSION QUESTIONS

1. Define the four basic predispositions MNCs have toward their international operations.
2. If a locally based manufacturing firm with sales of $350 million decided to enter the EU market by setting up operations in France, which orientation would be the most effective: ethnocentric, polycentric, regiocentric, or geocentric? Why? Explain your choice.
3. In what way are parochialism and simplification barriers to effective cross-cultural management? In each case, give an example.
4. Many MNCs would like to do business overseas in the same way that they do business domestically. Do research findings show that any approaches that work well in the United States also work well in other cultures? If so, identify and describe two.
5. In most cases, local managerial approaches must be modified for doing business overseas. What are three specific examples that support this statement? Be complete in your answer.
6. What are some categories of cultural differences that help make one country or region of the world different from another? In each case, describe the value or norm and explain how it would result in different behavior in two or more countries. If you like, use the countries discussed in this chapter as your point of reference.

INTERNET EXERCISE: HAIER'S APPROACH

Haier is a China-based multinational corporation that sells a wide variety of commercial and household appliances in the international marketplace. These range from washers, dryers, refrigerators, and industrial heating and ventilations systems. Visit Haier.com and read about some of the latest developments in which the company is engaged: (1) What type of cultural challenges does Haier face when it attempts to market its products worldwide? Is demand universal for all these offerings, or is there a "national responsiveness" challenge, as discussed in the chapter, that must be addressed? (2) Investigate the way in which Haier has adapted its products in different countries and regions, especially emerging markets. What are some examples? (3) In managing its far-flung enterprise, what are two cultural challenges that the company is likely to face and what will it need to do to respond to these?

Mexico

Located directly south of the United States, Mexico covers an area of 756,000 square miles. The most recent estimates place the population at around 114 million, and this number is increasing at a rate of about 1.4 percent annually. As a result, with a median age of just 27.4, today Mexico is one of the "youngest" countries in the world. Approximately 25 percent of the population is under the age of 14, while a mere 6.6 percent is 65 years of age or older. Mexico's GDP in 2011 was US$1.2 trillion, or approximately US$10,064 per capita.

Although global economic uncertainty persists, Mexico has made itself attractive for foreign investment. Trade agreements with the United States and Canada (NAFTA), the EU, Japan, and dozens of Latin American countries have begun to fully integrate the Mexican economy into the global trading system. Multinationals in a wide variety of industries, from computers to electronics and from pharmaceuticals to manufacturing, have invested billions of dollars in the country. Telefonica, the giant Spanish telecommunications firm, is putting together a wireless network across Latin America, and Mexico is one of the countries that it has targeted for investment. Meanwhile, manufacturers not only from the United States but also from Asia to Europe have helped sustain Mexico's booming maquiladora assembly industry. In 2005 over 1.15 million people were employed in this industry.

Thomson SA, the French consumer electronics firm, has three plants in the border states that make export TVs and digital decoder boxes. And like a growing number of MNCs located in Mexico, the firm is now moving away from importing parts and materials from outside and producing everything within the country. One reason for this move is that under the terms of the North American Free Trade Agreement only parts and materials originating in one of the three NAFTA trading partners are now allowed to enter the processing zones duty-free. Anything originating outside these three countries is subject to tariffs of as much as 25 percent. So the French MNC Thomson is building a picture-tube factory in Baja California so that it will no longer have to import dutiable tubes from Italy. In many cases, imported items from the European Union, however, are allowed to enter duty-free because in 1999 Mexico signed a free-trade agreement with the EU. Over 90 percent of trade is under free trade agreements. As a result, a host of firms, including Philips Electronics and Siemens, have poured large amounts of investment into the country. At the same time Mexico also has begun negotiating another free-trade pact with the four Nordic countries. As a result firms such as Nokia, Ericsson, and Saab-Scania to this point invest heavily in the country.

While many European MNCs are now investing in Mexico, the United States still remains the largest investor and trading partner. Over 50 percent of all outside investment is by U.S. firms. Asian companies, in particular Japanese MNCs, also have large holdings in the country, although these firms have been scaling back in recent years because of the import duties and the fact that Mexican labor costs are rising, thus making it more cost-effective to produce some types of goods in Asia and export them to North America. The largest investments in Mexico are in the industrial sector (around 60 percent of the total) and services (around 30 percent).

One of the major benefits of locating in Mexico is the highly skilled labor force that can be hired at fairly low wages when compared with those paid elsewhere, especially in the United States. Additionally, manufacturing firms that have located there report high productivity growth rates and quality performance. A study by the Massachusetts Institute of Technology on auto assembly plants in Canada, the United States, and Mexico reported that Mexican plants performed well. Another by J. D. Power and Associates noted that Ford Motor's Hermosillo plant was the best in all of North America. In January of 2012, Renault-Nissan announced it would be investing more than $2 billion to build a new manufacturing plant in Aguascalientes to serve the entire Americas region. Computer and electronics firms are also finding Mexico to be an excellent choice for new expansion plants. Intel, for example, has invested more than $200 million in its Mexican plant. The technology industry must be very innovative to stay competitive. Intel operates out of many countries, but an investment of this size shows that Mexico is extremely valuable, and operations here will continue for years to come.

www.mexicool.com, www.state.gov/r/pa/prs/ps/2010/05/142020.htm, data.worldbank.org/country/mexico

Questions

1. Why would multinationals be interested in setting up operations in Mexico? Give two reasons.
2. Would cultural differences be a major stumbling block for U.S. MNCs doing business in Mexico? For European firms? For Japanese firms? Explain your answer.
3. Why might MNCs be interested in studying the organizational culture in Mexican firms before deciding whether to locate there? Explain your logic.

Chapter 3

组织文化与组织多样性

ORGANIZATIONAL CULTURES AND DIVERSITY

OBJECTIVES OF THE CHAPTER

The previous two chapters focused on national cultures. The overriding objective of this chapter is to examine the interaction of national culture (diversity) and organizational cultures and to discuss ways in which MNCs can manage the often inherent conflicts between national and organizational cultures. Many times, the cultural values and resulting behaviors that are common in a particular country are not the same as those in another. To be successful, MNCs must balance and integrate the national cultures of the countries in which they do business with their own organizational culture. Employee relations, which includes how organizational culture responds to national culture or diversity, deals with internal structures and defines how the company manages. Customer relations, associated with how national culture reacts to organizational cultures, reflects how the local community views the company from a customer service and employee satisfaction perspective.

Although the field of international management has long recognized the impact of national cultures, only recently has attention been given to the importance of managing organizational cultures and diversity. This chapter first examines common organizational cultures that exist in MNCs, and then presents and analyzes ways in which multiculturalism and diversity are being addressed by the best, world-class multinationals. The specific objectives of this chapter are:

1. **DEFINE** exactly what is meant by *organizational culture*, and discuss the interaction of national and MNC cultures.
2. **IDENTIFY** the four most common categories of organizational culture that have been found through research, and discuss the characteristics of each.
3. **PROVIDE** an overview of the nature and degree of multiculturalism and diversity in today's MNCs.
4. **DISCUSS** common guidelines and principles that are used in building multicultural effectiveness at the team and the organizational levels.

国际化管理的世界

The World of *International Management*

在全球团队中管理文化和多样性

Managing Culture and Diversity in Global Teams

According to many international consultants and managers, diverse and global teams are one of the most consistent sources of competitive advantage for any organization. Applied Materials, a global multinational manufacturer of nanotechnology, has a corporate culture that regards diversity as a competitive advantage. Its employees are located in Belgium, Canada, China, France, Germany, India, Ireland, Israel, Italy, Japan, Korea, Malaysia, the Netherlands, Singapore, Spain, Switzerland, the United Kingdom, and the United States.
According to the company, "understanding different perspectives, taking advantage of varied approaches and working together in cross-cultural teams are intrinsic to the company and have been integral to our success."[1]

Most global teams are also virtual teams. According to a study by Kirkman, Rosen, Gibson, and Tesluk, virtual teams are "groups of people who work interdependently with shared purpose across space, time, and organization boundaries using technology to communicate and collaborate."[2] These teams are often cross-cultural and cross-functional. Furthermore, Kirkman and colleagues explain that virtual teams allow "organizations to combine the best expertise regardless of geographic location."[3] To manage a global team, international managers must take into consideration three factors: culture, communication, and trust.

文化

Culture

A leader's management approach may vary based on his or her employees' culture. In his article "Culture Matters in Virtual Teams," Surinder Kahai explains how a manager's approach may differ based on whether the employees are part of an individualist or collectivist national culture. He first identifies four different possible management approaches:

- Outcome control—measure and regulate outcomes sought
- Behavior control—specify the procedures to be followed by employees
- Clan control—implement a set of values where employees are rewarded or punished according to their conformity with these values
- Self-control—allow individuals to set their own goals and then monitor their performance in achieving their goals[4]

Kahai cites the research of Ravi Narayanaswamy, who found that managers are most effective in using self-control and outcome control in virtual teams whose members come from a "high individualism culture, i.e., a culture in which ties between individuals are loose and people tend to achieve things individually and assume personal responsibility."[5] This culture is found in places such as the U.S., the U.K., and Australia. These individuals perform better when given freedom to do their work as they see fit. Outcome controls are needed to ensure that individuals' goals are aligned with the overall project's goals. In contrast, managers are most effective in using clan control and behavior control in virtual teams whose members come from a "high collectivistic culture, i.e., a culture characterized by strong interpersonal ties and by collective achievement and responsibility."[6] This culture is found in places such as China, the Philippines, and South Korea. These individuals perform better when their values are in harmony with their managers. Clan control can help create that harmony. Also, workers in these cultures tend to be motivated to follow procedures, so behavior control is recommended.[7]

沟通

Communication

Communicating without face-to-face interaction can have its drawbacks. Specifically, it is more likely that a message is misinterpreted. (See the figure below.) In her article, "Tips for Working in Global Teams," Melanie Doulton provides helpful suggestions for good communication in a global team:

- When starting a project with a new team, hold an initial meeting in which all members introduce themselves and describe the job each one is going to do.
- Hold regular meetings throughout the project to ensure everyone is "on the same page." Follow up conference calls with written minutes to reinforce what was discussed and what individual team members are responsible for.
- Put details of the project in writing, especially for a new team in which everyone speaks in different accents and uses different idioms and colloquialisms.
- Communicate using the most effective technology. For example, decide when e-mail is preferable to a phone call or instant messaging is preferable to a videoconference. In addition, try to understand everyone's communication style. For example, for a high-context culture such as India's, people tend to speak in the passive voice, whereas in North America, people use the active voice.[8]

Moreover, while acknowledging the challenges of communication in virtual teams, Steven R. Rayner also points out that written communication can have an advantage. He states, "The process of writing—where the sender must carefully examine how to communicate his/her message—provides the sender with the opportunity to create a more refined response than an 'off-the-cuff' verbal comment."[9]

Likelihood of Message Getting Interpreted Correctly

LOW				HIGH
Fax/Letter	E-mail	Telephone	Video Conferencing	Face-to-Face Interaction

←————————————————————→

Source: Adapted from Steven R. Rayner, "The Virtual Team Challenge," Rayner & Associates, Inc., 1997.

信任
Trust

Kirkman and colleagues emphasize that "a specific challenge for virtual teams, compared to face-to-face teams, is the difficulty of building trust between team members who rarely, or never, see each other."[10] Rayner notes that "by some estimates, as much as 30 percent of senior management time is spent in 'chance' encounters (such as unplanned hallway, parking lot, and lunch room conversations). . . . In a virtual team setting, these opportunities for relationship building and idea sharing are far more limited."[11]

How can managers build trust among virtual team members? From their research, Kirkman and colleagues discovered that "building trust requires rapid responses to electronic communications from team members, reliable performance, and consistent follow-through. Accordingly, team leaders should coach virtual team members to avoid long lags in responding, unilateral priority shifts, and failure to follow up on commitments."[12] In addition, Doulton recommends that virtual team members "exchange feedback early" and allow an extra day or two for responses due to time zone differences.[13]

Team building activities also build trust. According to Kirkman, as part of the virtual team launch, it is recommended that all members meet face-to-face to "set objectives, clarify roles, build personal relationships, develop team norms, and establish group identity."[14] Picking the right team members can help the teams become more cohesive as well. When Kirkman and colleagues interviewed 75 team leaders and members in virtual teams, people responded that skills in communication, teamwork, thinking outside the box, and taking initiative were more important than technical skills. This finding was surprising, considering most managers select virtual team members based on technical skills. Having people with the right skills is essential to bring together a successful virtual team.[15]

全球虚拟团队的优势
Advantages of Global Virtual Teams

In addition to its challenges of overcoming cultural and communication barriers, global virtual teams have certain advantages over face-to-face teams.

First, Kirkman concluded that "working virtually can reduce team process losses associated with stereotyping, personality conflicts, power politics, and cliques commonly experienced by face-to-face teams. Virtual team members may be unaffected by potentially divisive demographic differences when there is minimal face-to-face contact." Managers may even give fairer assessments of team members' work because managers are compelled to rely on objective data rather than being influenced by their perceptual biases.[16]

Second, Rayner observes that "having members span many different time zones can literally keep a project moving around the clock. . . . Work doesn't stop—it merely shifts to a different time zone."[17]

Third, according to Rayner, "The ability for an organization to bring people together from remote geography and form a cohesive team that is capable of quickly solving complex problems and making effective decisions is an enormous competitive advantage."[18]

For an international manager, this competitive advantage makes overcoming challenges of managing global teams worth the effort.

Clearly, there are both benefits and challenges inherent in multinational, multicultural teams. These teams, which almost always include a diverse group of members with varying functional, geographic, ethnic, and cultural backgrounds, can be an efficient and effective vehicle for tackling increasingly multidimensional business problems. At the same time, this very diversity brings challenges which are often exacerbated when the teams are primarily "virtual." Research has demonstrated the benefits of diversity and has also offered insight on how best to overcome the inherent challenges of global teams, including those that are "virtual."

In this chapter we will explore the nature and characteristics of organizational culture as it relates to doing business in today's global context. In addition, strategies and guidelines for establishing a strong organizational culture in the presence of diversity are presented.

组织文化的本质
The Nature of Organizational Culture

We knew the background on the external environment, and the chapters so far have been concerned with the external culture. Regardless of whether this environment or cultural context affects the MNC, when individuals join an MNC, not only do they bring their national culture, which greatly affects their learned beliefs, attitudes, values, and behaviors, but they also enter into an organizational culture. Employees of MNCs are expected to "fit in." For example, at PepsiCo, personnel are expected to be cheerful, positive, enthusiastic, and have committed optimism; at Ford, they are expected to show self-confidence, assertiveness, and machismo.[19] Regardless of the external environment or their national culture, managers and employees must understand and follow their organization's culture to be successful. In this section, after first defining organizational culture, we analyze the interaction between national and organizational cultures. An understanding of this interaction has become recognized as vital to effective international management.

定义和特点
Definition and Characteristics

organizational culture
Shared values and beliefs that enable members to understand their roles in and the norms of the organization.

Organizational culture has been defined in several different ways. In its most basic form, organizational culture can be defined as the shared values and beliefs that enable members to understand their roles in and the norms of the organization. A more detailed definition is offered by organizational cultural theorist Edgar Schein, who defines it as a pattern of shared basic assumptions that the group learned as it solved its problems of external adaptation and internal integration, and that has worked well enough to be considered valid and, therefore, to be taught to new members as the correct way to perceive, think, and feel in relation to those problems.[20]

Regardless of how the term is defined, a number of important characteristics are associated with an organization's culture. These have been summarized as:

1. Observed behavioral regularities, as typified by common language, terminology, and rituals.
2. Norms, as reflected by things such as the amount of work to be done and the degree of cooperation between management and employees.
3. Dominant values that the organization advocates and expects participants to share, such as high product and service quality, low absenteeism, and high efficiency.
4. A philosophy that is set forth in the MNC's beliefs regarding how employees and customers should be treated.
5. Rules that dictate the dos and don'ts of employee behavior relating to areas such as productivity, customer relations, and intergroup cooperation.
6. Organizational climate, or the overall atmosphere of the enterprise, as reflected by the way that participants interact with each other, conduct themselves with customers, and feel about the way they are treated by higher-level management.[21]

This list is not intended to be all-inclusive, but it does help illustrate the nature of organizational culture.[22] The major problem is that sometimes an MNC's organizational culture in one country's facility differs sharply from organizational cultures in other countries. For example, managers who do well in England may be ineffective in Germany, despite the fact that they work for the same MNC. In addition, the cultures of the English and German subsidiaries may differ sharply from those of the home U.S. location. Effectively dealing with multiculturalism within the various locations of an MNC is a major challenge for international management.

A good example is provided by the British-Swedish MNC AstraZeneca PLC, the fifth-largest pharmaceutical company in the world. With operations in over 100 countries on six continents, AstraZeneca's twelve-member senior executive team includes leaders from the United Kingdom, Sweden, France, the United States, and the Netherlands. Over 24 percent of the company's employees work in North America, and about 21 percent are employed in Asia.[23] To unite such a diverse set of employees under a common corporate culture, AstraZeneca's Global Steering Group has focused on three universal cultural pillars: "Leadership and Management Capability," "Transparency in Talent Management and Career Progression," and "Work/Life Challenges."[24] Furthermore, in 2012, the company introduced a new cross-cultural mentorship program, called Insight Exchange. By pairing senior- and junior-level employees from different cultural and professional backgrounds, AstraZeneca hopes to create a "more open culture."[25]

In some cases companies have deliberately maintained two different business cultures because they do not want one culture influencing the other. A good example is JCPenney, the giant department store chain. When this well-known retailer bought control of Renner, a Brazilian retail chain with 20 stores, it used a strategy that is not very common when one company controls another. Rather than impose its own culture on the chain, Penney's management took a back seat. Recognizing Renner's reputation for value and service among its middle-class customers, Penney let the Brazilian managers continue to run the stores while it provided assistance in the form of backroom operations, merchandise presentation, logistics, branding, and expansion funds. In a country where fashion is constantly evolving, Renner is able to keep up with the market by changing fashion lines seven to eight times a year. The company also provides rapid checkout service, credit cards to individuals who earn as little as $150 a month, and interest-free installment plans that allow people to pay as little as $5 a month toward their purchases. Thanks to Penney's infusion of capital, in the first two years Renner opened 30 more stores and sales jumped from $150 million to over $300 million. The company proved to be profitable for a while; however, the run did not last forever, and JCPenney sold its controlling interest in the company in 2005.

民族文化和组织文化的相互作用

Interaction between National and Organizational Cultures

There is a widely held belief that organizational culture tends to moderate or erase the impact of national culture. The logic of such conventional wisdom is that if a U.S. MNC set up operations in, say, France, it would not be long before the French employees began to "think like Americans." In fact, evidence is accumulating that just the opposite may be true. Hofstede's research found that the national cultural values of employees have a significant impact on their organizational performance, and that the cultural values employees bring to the workplace with them are not easily changed by the organization. So, for example, while some French employees would have a higher power distance than Swedes and some a lower power distance, chances are "that if a company hired locals in Paris, they would, on the whole, be less likely to challenge hierarchical power than would the same number of locals hired in Stockholm."[26]

Andre Laurent's research supports Hofstede's conclusions.[27] He found that cultural differences are actually more pronounced among foreign employees working within the same multinational organization than among personnel working for firms in their native lands. Nancy Adler summarized these research findings as follows:

> When they work for a multinational corporation, it appears that Germans become more German, Americans become more American, Swedes become more Swedish, and so on. Surprised by these results, Laurent replicated the research in two other multinational corporations, each with subsidiaries in the same nine Western European countries and the United States. Similar to the first company, corporate culture did not reduce or eliminate national differences in the second and third corporations. Far from reducing national differences, organization culture maintains and enhances them.[28]

There often are substantial differences between the organizational cultures of different subsidiaries, and of course, this can cause coordination problems. For example, when the Upjohn Company of Kalamazoo, Michigan, merged with Pharmacia AB of Sweden, which also has operations in Italy, the Americans failed to realize some of the cultural differences between themselves and their new European partners. As was reported in The Wall Street Journal, "Swedes take off the entire month of July for vacation, virtually en masse, and Italians take off August. Everyone in Europe knows, that is, but apparently hardly anyone in Kalamazoo, Michigan, does."[29] As a result, a linkup that was supposed to give a quick boost to the two companies, solving problems such as aging product lines and pressure from giant competitors, never got off the ground. Things had to be rescheduled, and both partners ended up having to meet and talk about their cultural differences, so that each side better understood the "dos and don'ts" of doing business with the other.

When the two firms first got together, they never expected these types of problems. Upjohn, with household names such as Rogaine and Motrin, had no likely breakthroughs in its product pipeline, so it was happy to merge with Pharmacia. The latter had developed a solid roster of allergy medicines, human-growth hormone, and other drugs, but its distribution in the United States was weak and its product line was aging. So a merger seemed ideal for both firms. The big question was how to bring the two companies together. Given that Pharmacia had recently acquired an Italian firm, there was a proposal by the European group that there be three major centers—Kalamazoo, Stockholm, and Milan—as well as a new headquarters in London. However, this arrangement had a number of built-in problems. For one, the executives in Italy and Sweden were accustomed to reporting to local bosses. Second, the people in London did not know a great deal about how to coordinate operations in Sweden and Italy. American cultural values added even more problems in that at Upjohn workers were tested for drug and alcohol abuse, but in Italy waiters pour wine freely every afternoon in the company dining room, and Pharmacia's boardrooms were stocked with humidors for executives who liked to light a cigar during long meetings. Quite obviously, there were cultural differences that had to be resolved by the companies. In the end, Pharmacia and Upjohn said they would meld the different cultures and attitudes and get on with their growth plans. However, one thing is certain: The different cultures of the merged firms created a major challenge.

In examining and addressing the differences between organizational cultures, Hofstede provided the early database of a set of proprietary cultural-analysis techniques and programs known as DOCSA (Diagnosing Organizational Culture for Strategic Application). This approach identifies the dimensions of organizational culture summarized in Table 3–1. It was found that when cultural comparisons were made between different subsidiaries of an MNC, different cultures often existed in each one. Such cultural differences within an MNC could reduce the ability of units to work well together. An example is provided in Figure 3–1, which shows the cultural dimensions of a California-based MNC and its European subsidiary as perceived by the Europeans. A close comparison of these perceptions reveals some startling differences.

The Europeans viewed the culture in the U.S. facilities as only slightly activities oriented (see Table 3–1 for a description of these dimensions), but they saw their own European operations as much more heavily activities oriented. The U.S. operation was viewed as moderately people oriented, but their own relationships were viewed as very job oriented. The Americans were seen as having a slight identification with their own organization, while the Europeans had a much stronger identification. The Americans were perceived as being very open in their communications; the Europeans saw themselves as moderately closed. The Americans were viewed as preferring very loose control, while the Europeans felt they preferred somewhat tight control. The Americans were seen as somewhat conventional in their conduct, while the Europeans saw themselves as somewhat pragmatic. If these perceptions are accurate, then it obviously would be necessary for both groups to discuss their cultural differences and carefully coordinate their activities to work well together.

This analysis is relevant to multinational alliances. It shows that even though an alliance may exist, the partners will bring different organizational cultures with them. Lessem and Neubauer, who have portrayed Europe as offering four distinct ways of dealing with multiculturalism (based on the United Kingdom, French, German, and Italian characteristics), provide an example in Table 3–2, which briefly describes each of these sets of cultural characteristics. A close examination of the differences highlights how difficult it can be to do business with two or more of these groups, because each

Table 3–1
Dimensions of Corporate Culture

Motivation	
Activities	**Outputs**
To be consistent and precise. To strive for accuracy and attention to detail. To refine and perfect. Get it right.	To be pioneers. To pursue clear aims and objectives. To innovate and progress. Go for it.
Relationship	
Job	**Person**
To put the demands of the job before the needs of the individual.	To put the needs of the individual before the needs of the job.
Identity	
Corporate	**Professional**
To identify with and uphold the expectations of the employing organizations.	To pursue the aims and ideals of each professional practice.
Communication	
Open	**Closed**
To stimulate and encourage a full and free exchange of information and opinion.	To monitor and control the exchange and accessibility of information and opinion.
Control	
Tight	**Loose**
To comply with clear and definite systems and procedures.	To work flexibly and adaptively according to the needs of the situation.
Conduct	
Conventional	**Pragmatic**
To put the expertise and standards of the employing organization first. To do what we know is right.	To put the demands and expectations of customers first. To do what they ask.

Source: Adapted from a study by the Diagnosing Organizational Culture for Strategic Application (DOCSA) group and reported in Lisa Hoecklin, *Managing Cultural Differences: Strategies for Competitive Advantage* (Workingham, England: Addison-Wesley), 1995, p. 146.

group perceives things differently from the others. Another example is the way in which negotiations occur between groups; here are some contrasts between French and Spanish negotiators:[30]

French	Spanish
Look for a meeting of minds.	Look for a meeting of people.
Intellectual competence is very important.	Social competence is very important.
Persuasion through carefully prepared and skilled rhetoric is employed.	Persuasion through emotional appeal is employed.
Strong emphasis is given to a logical presentation of one's position coupled with well-reasoned, detailed solutions.	Socialization always precedes negotiations, which are characterized by an exchange of grand ideas and general principles.
A contract is viewed as a well-reasoned transaction.	A contract is viewed as a long-lasting relationship.
Trust emerges slowly and is based on the evaluation of perceived status and intellect.	Trust is developed on the basis of frequent and warm interpersonal contact and transaction.

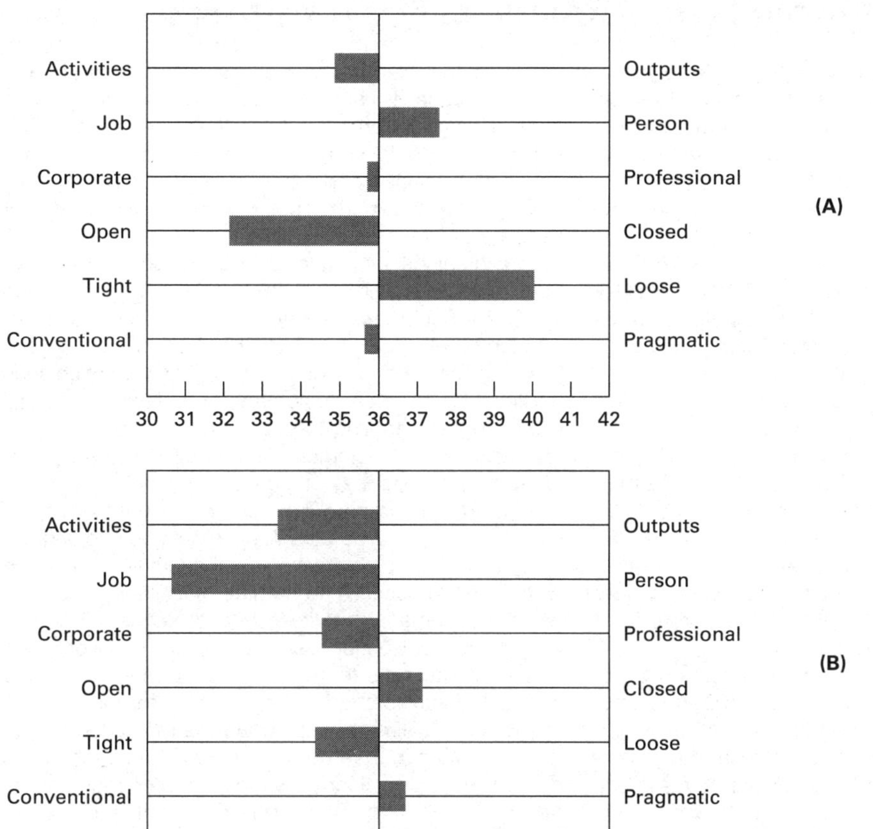

Figure 3–1
Europeans' Perception of the Cultural Dimensions of U.S. Operations (*A*) and European Operations (*B*) of the Same MNC

Source: Adapted from a study by the Diagnosing Organizational Culture for Strategic Application (DOCSA) group and reported in Lisa Hoecklin, *Managing Cultural Differences: Strategies for Competitive Advantage* (Workingham, England: Addison-Wesley), 1995, pp. 147–148.

Table 3–2
European Management Characteristics

	Characteristic			
Dimension	**Western (United Kingdom)**	**Northern (France)**	**Eastern (Germany)**	**Southern (Italy)**
Corporate	Commercial	Administrative	Industrial	Familial
Management attributes				
Behavior	Experiential	Professional	Developmental	Convivial
Attitude	Sensation	Thought	Intuition	Feeling
Institutional models				
Function	Salesmanship	Control	Production	Personnel
Structure	Transaction	Hierarchy	System	Network
Societal ideas				
Economics	Free market	Dirigiste	Social market	Communal
Philosophy	Pragmatic	Rational	Holistic	Humanistic
Cultural images				
Art	Theatre	Architecture	Music	Dance
Culture	(Anglo-Saxon)	(Gallic)	(Germanic)	(Latin)

Source: Adapted from Ronald Lessen and Fred Neubauer, European Management Systems (McGraw-Hill, London), 1994 and reported in Lisa Hoecklin, *Managing Cultural Differences: Strategies for Competitive Advantage* (Workingham, England: Addison-Wesley), 1995, p. 149.

International Management in Action

Doing Things the Walmart Way; Germans Say, "Nein, vielen Dank"

Across the globe, Walmart employees engage in the "Walmart cheer" to start their day. It is a way to show inclusivity and express their pride in the company, and can be heard in many different languages. Walmart not only operates in 27 countries but is also a leader in diversity in the workplace. In June 2007, Walmart was named one of the top 50 companies for diversity by *DiversityInc* magazine, and, in 2012, CEO Mike Duke was inducted into the CPG/Retail Diversity Hall of Fame. However, despite Walmart's multinational presence and representation, its internal culture proved to be less than satisfactory to the German market.

Walmart has experienced a fair share of negative PR over the years, so it is no surprise that some may have adverse reactions to news of Walmart moving into the neighborhood. Before the unflattering buzz, Walmart sometimes discovers that even the best intentions can fall flat. Walmart entered the German market in 1997 and stressed the idea of friendly service with a smile, where the customers always come first. Even before the employees walked onto the sales room floor, employee dissatisfaction became clear.

The pamphlet which outlined the workplace code of ethics was simply translated from English to German, but the message was not expressed the way Walmart had intended. It warned employees of potential supervisor-employee relationships, implying sexual harassment, and encouraged reports of "improper behavior," which spoke more to legal matters. The Germans interpreted this to mean that there was a ban on any romantic relationships in the workplace and saw the reporting methods as more of a way to rat out co-workers than benefit the company. Ethical values in one country may not be the same as in another, and Walmart experienced this firsthand. Another employee relations issue that arose dealt with local practices. Walmart has never been open to unionized employees, so when the German operations began dealing with workers' councils and adhering to co-determination rules, a common practice there, Walmart was less than willing to listen to suggestions as to how to improve employee working conditions. As if this was not enough, Walmart soon experienced problems with customer relations as well.

Doing things the Walmart way included smiling at customers and assisting them by bagging their groceries at the Supercenter locations. This policy presented problems in the German environment. Male employees who were ordered to smile at customers were often seen as flirtatious to male customers, and Germans do not like strangers handling their groceries. These are just a few reasons that customers did not enjoy their shopping experience. This does not mean that everything Walmart attempted was wrong. Products which are popular in Germany were available on the shelves in place of products that would be common in other countries. Enhanced distribution processes guaranteed availability of most requested items, and efficiency was pervasive.

Despite some successes and good intentions and numerous attempts to improve the German stores, the Walmart culture proved to be a poor fit for the German market, and Walmart vacated Germany in 2006. Unfortunately, Walmart learned the hard way that in the retail or service industry, local customs are often more important than a strong, unyielding organizational culture. The challenge to incorporate everyone into the Walmart family certainly fell short of expectations. If the Walmart culture does not become more flexible, or locally relevant, it may be chastised from numerous global markets, and the company could hear, "no, thank you" in even more languages than German as it continues to expand. (See the In-Depth Integrative Case at the end of Part Two for more detail on Walmart's experiences around the world.)

Such comparisons also help explain why it can be difficult for an MNC with a strong organizational culture to break into foreign markets where it is not completely familiar with divergent national cultures. The International Management in Action, "Doing Things the Walmart Way," provides an illustration. When dealing with these challenges, MNCs must work hard to understand the nature of the country and institutional practices to both moderate and adapt their operations in a way that accommodates the company and customer base.

跨国公司的组织文化

■ Organizational Cultures in MNCs

Organizational cultures of MNCs are shaped by a number of factors, including the cultural preferences of the leaders and employees. In the international arena, some MNCs have subsidiaries that, except for the company logo and reporting procedures, would not be easily recognizable as belonging to the same multinational.[31]

Given that many recent international expansions are a result of mergers or acquisition, the integration of these organizational cultures is a critical concern in international management. Numeroff and Abrahams have suggested that there are four steps that are critical in this process: (1) The two groups have to establish the purpose, goal, and focus of their merger. (2) Then they have to develop mechanisms to identify the most important organizational structures and management roles. (3) They have to determine who has authority over the resources needed for getting things done. (4) They have to identify the expectations of all involved parties and facilitate communication between both departments and individuals in the structure.

Companies all over the world are finding out firsthand that there is more to an international merger or acquisition than just sharing resources and capturing greater market share. Differences in workplace cultures sometimes temporarily overshadow the overall goal of long-term success of the newly formed entity. With the proper management framework and execution, successful integration of cultures is not only possible, but also the most preferable paradigm in which to operate. It is the role of the sponsors and managers to keep sight of the necessity to create, maintain, and support the notion of a united front. It is only when this assimilation has occurred that an international merger or acquisition can truly be labeled a success.[32]

In addition, there are three aspects of organizational functioning that seem to be especially important in determining MNC organizational culture: (1) the general relationship between the employees and their organization; (2) the hierarchical system of authority that defines the roles of managers and subordinates; and (3) the general views that employees hold about the MNC's purpose, destiny, goals, and their place in them.[33]

When examining these dimensions of organizational culture, Trompenaars suggested the use of two continua. One distinguishes between equity and hierarchy; the other examines orientation to the person and the task. Along these continua, which are shown in Figure 3–2, he identifies and describes four different types of organizational cultures: family, Eiffel Tower, guided missile, and incubator.[34]

In practice, of course, organizational cultures do not fit neatly into any of these four, but the groupings can be useful in helping examine the bases of how individuals relate to each other, think, learn, change, are motivated, and resolve conflict. The following discussion examines each of these cultural types.

Figure 3–2
Organizational Cultures

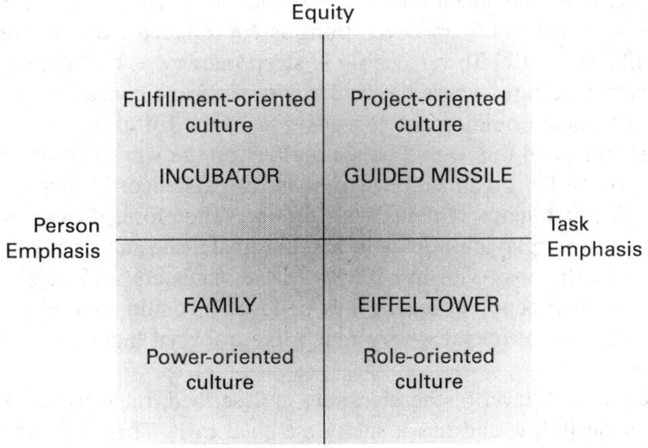

Source: Adapted from Fons Trompenaars, *Riding the Waves of Culture: Understanding Diversity in Global Business* (Burr Ridge, IL: Irwin, 1994), p. 154.

家族文化
Family Culture

family culture
A culture that is characterized by a strong emphasis on hierarchy and orientation to the person.

Family culture is characterized by a strong emphasis on hierarchy and orientation to the person. The result is a family-type environment that is power-oriented and headed by a leader who is regarded as a caring parent and one who knows what is best for the personnel. Trompenaars found that this organizational culture is common in countries and regions as Turkey, Pakistan, Venezuela, Singapore, Chinese mainland and Hong Kong.[35]

In this culture, personnel not only respect the individuals who are in charge but look to them for both guidance and approval as well. In turn, management assumes a paternal relationship with personnel, looks after employees, and tries to ensure that they are treated well and have continued employment. Family culture also is characterized by traditions, customs, and associations that bind together the personnel and make it difficult for outsiders to become members. When it works well, family culture can catalyze and multiply the energies of the personnel and appeal to their deepest feelings and aspirations. When it works poorly, members of the organization end up supporting a leader who is ineffective and drains their energies and loyalties.

This type of culture is foreign to most managers in the United States, who believe in valuing people based on their abilities and achievements, not on their age or position in the hierarchy. As a result, many managers in U.S.-based MNCs fail to understand why senior-level managers in overseas subsidiaries might appoint a relative to a high-level, sensitive position even though that individual might not appear to be the best qualified for the job. They fail to realize that family ties are so strong that the appointed relative would never do anything to embarrass or let down the family member who made the appointment. Here is an example:

> A Dutch delegation was shocked and surprised when the Brazilian owner of a large manufacturing company introduced his relatively junior accountant as the key coordinator of a $15 million joint venture. The Dutch were puzzled as to why a recently qualified accountant had been given such weighty responsibilities, including the receipt of their own money. The Brazilians pointed out that the young man was the best possible choice among 1,200 employees since he was the nephew of the owner. Who could be more trustworthy than that? Instead of complaining, the Dutch should consider themselves lucky that he was available.[36]

埃菲尔铁塔文化
Eiffel Tower Culture

Eiffel Tower culture
A culture that is characterized by strong emphasis on hierarchy and orientation to the task.

Eiffel Tower culture is characterized by strong emphasis on hierarchy and orientation to the task. Under this organizational culture, jobs are well defined, employees know what they are supposed to do, and everything is coordinated from the top. As a result, this culture—like the Eiffel Tower itself—is steep, narrow at the top, and broad at the base. Unlike family culture, where the leader is revered and considered to be the source of all power, the person holding the top position in the Eiffel Tower culture could be replaced at any time, and this would have no effect on the work that organization members are doing or on the organization's reasons for existence. In this culture, relationships are specific, and status remains with the job. Therefore, if the boss of an Eiffel Tower subsidiary were playing golf with a subordinate, the subordinate would not feel any pressure to let the boss win. In addition, these managers seldom create off-the-job relationships with their people, because they believe this could affect their rational judgment. In fact, this culture operates very much like a formal hierarchy—impersonal and efficient.

Each role at each level of the hierarchy is described, rated for its difficulty, complexity, and responsibility, and has a salary attached to it. Then follows a search for a person to fill it. In considering applicants for the role, the personnel department will treat everyone equally and neutrally, match the person's skills and aptitudes with the job requirements, and award the job to the best fit between role and person. The same procedure is followed in evaluations and promotions.[37]

Eiffel Tower culture most commonly is found in northwestern European countries. Examples include Denmark, Germany, and the Netherlands. The way that people in this culture learn and change differs sharply from that in the family culture. Learning involves the accumulation of skills necessary to fit a role, and organizations will use qualifications in deciding how to schedule, deploy, and reshuffle personnel to meet their needs. The organization also will employ such rational procedures as assessment centers, appraisal systems, training and development programs, and job rotation in managing its human resources. All these procedures help ensure that a formal hierarchic or bureaucracy-like approach works well. When changes need to be made, however, the Eiffel Tower culture often is ill-equipped to handle things. Manuals must be rewritten, procedures changed, job descriptions altered, promotions reconsidered, and qualifications reassessed.

Because the Eiffel Tower culture does not rely on values that are similar to those in most U.S. MNCs, U.S. expatriate managers often have difficulty initiating change in this culture. As Trompenaars notes:

> An American manager responsible for initiating change in a German company described to me the difficulties he had in making progress, although the German managers had discussed the new strategy in depth and made significant contributions to its formulation. Through informal channels, he had eventually discovered that his mistake was not having formalized the changes to structure or job descriptions. In the absence of a new organization chart, this Eiffel Tower company was unable to change.[38]

导弹文化
Guided Missile Culture

Guided missile culture is characterized by strong emphasis on equality in the workplace and orientation to the task. This organizational culture is oriented to work, which typically is undertaken by teams or project groups. Unlike the Eiffel Tower culture, where job assignments are fixed and limited, personnel in the guided missile culture do whatever it takes to get the job done. This culture gets its name from high-tech organizations such as the National Aeronautics and Space Administration (NASA), which pioneered the use of project groups working on space probes that resembled guided missiles. In these large project teams, more than a hundred different types of engineers often were responsible for building, say, a lunar landing module. The team member whose contribution would be crucial at any given time in the project typically could not be known in advance. Therefore, all types of engineers had to work in close harmony and cooperate with everyone on the team.

guided missile culture
A culture that is characterized by strong emphasis on equality in the workplace and orientation to the task.

To be successful, the best form of synthesis must be used in the course of working on the project. For example, in a guided missile project, formal hierarchical considerations are given low priority, and individual expertise is of greatest importance. Additionally, all team members are equal (or at least potentially equal), because their relative contributions to the project are not yet known. All teams treat each other with respect, because they may need the other for assistance. This egalitarian and task-driven organizational culture fits well with the national cultures of the United States and United Kingdom, which helps explain why high-tech MNCs commonly locate their operations in these countries.

Unlike family and Eiffel Tower cultures, change in guided missile culture comes quickly. Goals are accomplished, and teams are reconfigured and assigned new objectives. People move from group to group, and loyalties to one's profession and project often are greater than loyalties to the organization itself.

Trompenaars found that the motivation of those in guided missile cultures tends to be more intrinsic than just concern for money and benefits. Team members become enthusiastic about, and identify with, the struggle toward attaining their goal. For example, a project team that is designing and building a new computer for the Asian market may be highly motivated to create a machine that is at the leading edge of technology, user-friendly, and likely to sweep the market. Everything else is secondary to this overriding objective. Thus, both intragroup and intergroup conflicts are minimized and petty problems between team members set aside; everyone is so committed to the project's main goal that no one has time for petty disagreements. As Trompenaars notes:

> This culture tends to be individualistic since it allows for a wide variety of differently specialized persons to work with each other on a temporary basis. The scenery of faces keeps changing. Only the pursuit of chosen lines of personal development is constant. The team is a vehicle for the shared enthusiasm of its members, but is itself disposable and will be discarded when the project ends. Members are garrulous, idiosyncratic, and intelligent, but their mutuality is a means, not an end. It is a way of enjoying the journey. They do not need to know each other intimately, and may avoid doing so. Management by objectives is the language spoken, and people are paid for performance.[39]

孵化器文化
Incubator Culture

incubator culture
A culture that is characterized by strong emphasis on equality and orientation to the person.

Incubator culture is the fourth major type of organizational culture that Trompenaars identified, and it is characterized by strong emphasis on equality and personal orientation. This culture is based heavily on the existential idea that organizations per se are secondary to the fulfillment of the individuals within them. This culture is based on the premise that the role of organizations is to serve as incubators for the self-expression and self-fulfillment of their members; as a result, this culture often has little formal structure. Participants in an incubator culture are there primarily to perform roles such as confirming, criticizing, developing, finding resources for, or helping complete the development of an innovative product or service. These cultures often are found among start-up firms in Silicon Valley, California, or Silicon Glen, Scotland. These incubator-type organizations typically are entrepreneurial and often founded and made up by a creative team who left larger, Eiffel Tower–type employers. They want to be part of an organization where their creative talents will not be stifled.

Incubator cultures often create environments where participants thrive on an intense, emotional commitment to the nature of the work. For example, the group may be in the process of gene splitting that could lead to radical medical breakthroughs and extend life. Often, personnel in such cultures are overworked, and the enterprise typically is underfunded. As breakthroughs occur and the company gains stability, however, it starts moving down the road toward commercialization and profit. In turn, this engenders the need to hire more people and develop formalized procedures for ensuring the smooth flow of operations. In this process of growth and maturity, the unique characteristics of the incubator culture begin to wane and disappear, and the culture is replaced by one of the other types (family, Eiffel Tower, or guided missile).

As noted, change in the incubator culture often is fast and spontaneous. All participants are working toward the same objective. Because there may not yet be a customer who is using the final output, however, the problem itself often is open to redefinition, and the solution typically is generic, aimed at a universe of applications. Meanwhile, motivation of the personnel remains highly intrinsic and intense, and it is common to find employees working 70 hours a week—and loving it. The participants are more concerned with the unfolding creative process than they are in gathering power or ensuring personal monetary gain. In sharp contrast to the family culture, leadership in this incubator culture is achieved, not gained by position.

The four organizational cultures described by Trompenaars are "pure" types and seldom exist in practice. Rather the types are mixed and, as shown in Table 3–3, overlaid with one of the four major types of culture dominating the corporate scene. Recently, Trompenaars and his associates have created a questionnaire designed to identify national patterns of corporate culture as shown in Figure 3–3.

Table 3–3
Summary Characteristics of the Four Corporate Cultures

	Corporate Culture			
Characteristic	**Family**	**Eiffel Tower**	**Guided Missile**	**Incubator**
Relationships between employees	Diffuse relationships to organic whole to which one is bonded.	Specific role in mechanical system of required interaction.	Specific tasks in cybernetic system targeted on shared objectives.	Diffuse, spontaneous relationships growing out of shared creative process.
Attitude toward authority	Status is ascribed to parent figures who are close and powerful.	Status is ascribed to superior roles that are distant yet powerful.	Status is achieved by project group members who contribute to targeted goal.	Status is achieved by individuals exemplifying creativity and growth.
Ways of thinking and learning	Intuitive, holistic, lateral, and error correcting.	Logical, analytical, vertical, and rationally efficient.	Problem centered, professional, practical, cross-disciplinary.	Process oriented, creative, ad hoc, inspirational.
Attitudes toward people	Family members.	Human resources.	Specialists and experts.	Co-creators.
Ways of changing	"Father" changes course.	Change rules and procedures.	Shift aim as target moves.	Improvise and attune.
Ways of motivating and rewarding	Intrinsic satisfaction in being loved and respected.	Promotion to greater position, larger role.	Pay or credit for performance and problems solved.	Participation in the process of creating new realities.
	Management by subjectives.	Management by job description.	Management by objectives.	Management by enthusiasm.
Criticism and conflict resolution	Turn other cheek, save other's face, do not lose power game.	Criticism is accusation of irrationalism unless there are procedures to arbitrate conflicts.	Constructive task-related only, then admit error and correct fast.	Improve creative idea, not negate it.

Source: Adapted from Fons Trompenaars and Charles Hampden-Turner, *Riding the Waves of Culture: Understanding Diversity in Global Business,* 2nd ed. (New York: McGraw-Hill, 1998), p. 183.

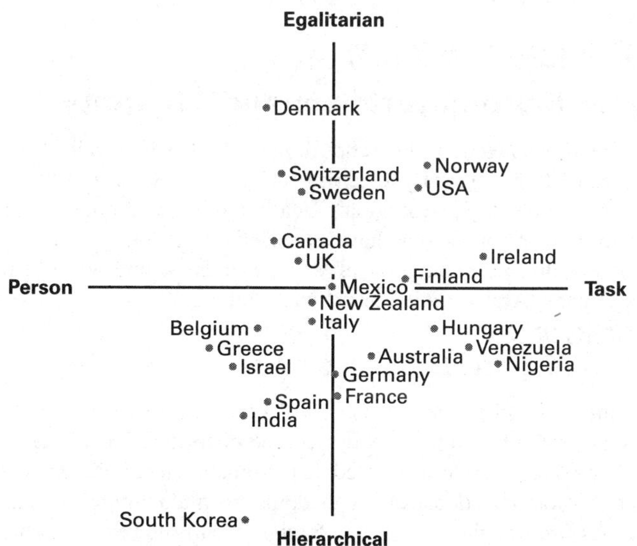

Figure 3–3
National Patterns of Corporate Culture

Source: Adapted from Fons Trompenaars and Charles Hampden-Turner, *Riding the Waves of Culture: Understanding Diversity in Global Business,* 2nd ed. (New York: McGraw-Hill, 1998), p. 184.

International Management in Action

Matsushita Goes Global www.panasonic.com

In recent years, growing numbers of multinationals have begun to expand their operations, realizing that if they do not increase their worldwide presence now, they likely will be left behind in the near future. In turn, this has created a number of different challenges for these MNCs, including making a fit between their home organizational culture and the organizational cultures at local levels in the different countries where the MNC operates. Matsushita provides an excellent example of how to handle this challenge with its macromicro approach. This huge, Japanese MNC has developed a number of guidelines that it uses in setting up and operating its more than 150 industrial units. At the same time, the company complements these macro guidelines with onsite micro techniques that help create the most appropriate organizational culture in the subsidiary.

At the macro level, Matsushita employs six overall guidelines that are followed in all locales: (1) Be a good corporate citizen in every country by, among other things, respecting cultures, customs, and languages. (2) Give overseas operations the best manufacturing technology the company has available. (3) Keep the expatriate head count down, and groom local management to take over. (4) Let operating plants set their own rules, fine-tuning manufacturing processes to match the skills of the workers. (5) Create local research and development to tailor products to markets. (6) Encourage competition between overseas outposts and plants back home. Working within these macro guidelines, Matsushita then allows each local unit to create its own culture. The Malaysian operations are a good example. Matsushita has erected 23 subsidiaries in Malaysia which collectively consist of about 30,000 employees. Less than 1 percent of the employee population, however, is Japanese. From these Malaysian operations, Matsushita has been producing more than 1.3 million televisions and 1.8 million air conditioners annually, and 75 percent of these units are shipped overseas. To produce this output, local plants reflect Malaysia's cultural mosaic of Muslim Malays, ethnic Chinese, and Indians. To accommodate this diversity, Matsushita cafeterias offer Malaysian, Chinese, and Indian food, and to accommodate Muslim religious customs, Matsushita provides special prayer rooms at each plant and allows two prayer sessions per shift.

How well does this Malaysian workforce perform for the Japanese MNC? In the past, the Malaysian plants' slogan was "Let's catch up with Japan." Today, however, these plants frequently outperform their Japanese counterparts in both quality and efficiency. The comparison with Japan no longer is used. Additionally, Matsushita has found that the Malaysian culture is very flexible, and the locals are able to work well with almost any employer. Commenting on Malaysia's multiculturalism, Matsushita's managing director notes, "They are used to accommodating other cultures, and so they think of us Japanese as just another culture. That makes it much easier for us to manage them than some other nationalities."

Today, Matsushita faces a number of important challenges, including remaining profitable in a slow-growth, high-cost Japanese economy. Fortunately, this MNC is doing extremely well overseas, which is buying it time to get its house in order back home. A great amount of this success results from the MNC's ability to nurture and manage overseas organizational cultures (such as in Malaysia) that are both diverse and highly productive.

管理多元文化主义和多样性

Managing Multiculturalism and Diversity

As the International Management in Action box on Matsushita indicates, success in the international arena often is greatly determined by an MNC's ability to manage both multiculturalism and diversity.[40] Both domestically and internationally, organizations find themselves leading workforces that have a variety of cultures (and subcultures) and consist of a largely diverse population of women, men, young and old people, blacks, whites, Latins, Asians, Arabs, Indians, and many others.

多元文化发展的阶段

Phases of Multicultural Development

The effect of multiculturalism and diversity will vary depending on the stage of the firm in its international evolution. Table 3–4 depicts the characteristics of the major phases in this evolution. For example, Adler has noted that international cultural diversity has minimal impact on domestic organizations, although domestic multiculturalism has a highly significant impact. As firms begin exporting to foreign clients, however, and become what she calls "international corporations" (Phase II in Table 3–4), they must adapt their approach and products to those of the local market. For these international firms, the impact of

Table 3–4
The Evolution of International Corporations

Characteristics/ Activities	Phase I (Domestic Corporations)	Phase II (International Corporations)	Phase III (Multinational Corporations)	Phase IV (Global Corporations)
Primary orientation	Product/service	Market	Price	Strategy
Competitive strategy	Domestic	Multidomestic	Multinational	Global
Importance of world business	Marginal	Important	Extremely important	Dominant
Product/service	New, unique	More standardized	Completely standardized (commodity)	Mass-customized
	Product engineering emphasized	Process engineering emphasized	Engineering not emphasized	Product and process engineering
Technology	Proprietary	Shared	Widely shared	Instantly and extensively shared
R&D/sales	High	Decreasing	Very low	Very high
Profit margin	High	Decreasing	Very low	High, yet immediately decreasing
Competitors	None	Few	Many	Significant (few or many)
Market	Small, domestic	Large, multidomestic	Larger, multinational	Largest, global
Production location	Domestic	Domestic and primary markets	Multinational, least cost	Imports and exports
Exports	None	Growing, high potential	Large, saturated	Imports and exports
Structure	Functional divisions	Functional with international division	Multinational lines of business	Global alliances, hierarchy
	Centralized	Decentralized	Centralized	Coordinated, decentralized
Primary orientation	Product/service	Market	Price	Strategy
Strategy	Domestic	Multidomestic	Multinational	Global
Perspective	Ethnocentric	Polycentric/ regiocentric	Multinational	Global/multicentric
Cultural sensitivity	Marginally important	Very important	Somewhat important	Critically important
With whom	No one	Clients	Employees	Employees and clients
Level	No one	Workers and clients	Managers	Executives
Strategic assumption	"One way"/ one best way	"Many good ways," equifinality	"One least-cost way" simultaneously	"Many good ways"

Source: From Adler. *International Dimensions of Organizational Behavior,* 5th ed. © 2008 South-Western, a part of Cengage Learning, Inc. Reproduced by permission. www.cengage.com/permissions.

multiculturalism is highly significant. As companies become what she calls "multinational corporations" (Phase III), they often find that price tends to dominate all other considerations, and the direct impact of culture may lessen slightly. For those who continue this international evolution and become full-blown "global corporations" (Phase IV), the impact of culture again becomes extremely important. Notes Adler:

> Global firms need an understanding of cultural dynamics to plan their strategy, to locate production facilities and suppliers worldwide, to design and market culturally appropriate products and services, as well as to manage cross-cultural interaction throughout the organization—from senior executive committees to the shop floor. As more firms today move from domestic, international, and multinational organizations to operating as truly global organizations and alliances, the importance of cultural diversity increases markedly. What once was "nice to understand" becomes imperative for survival, let alone success.[41]

Figure 3–4

Locations of International Cross-Cultural Interaction

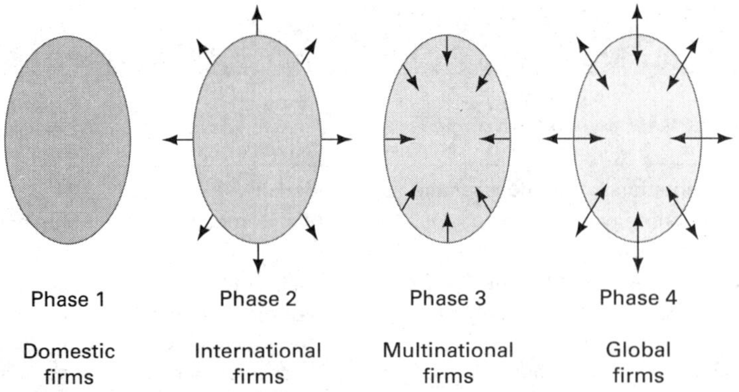

Source: From Adler. *International Dimensions of Organizational Behavior,* 5th ed. © 2008 South-Western, a part of Cengage Learning, Inc. Reproduced by permission. www.cengage.com/permissions.

As shown in Figure 3–4, international cultural diversity traditionally affects neither the domestic firm's organizational culture nor its relationship with its customers or clients. These firms work domestically, and only domestic multiculturalism has a direct impact on their dynamics as well as on their relationship to the external environment.

Conversely, among international firms, which focus on exporting and producing abroad, cultural diversity has a strong impact on their external relationships with potential buyers and foreign employees. In particular, these firms rely heavily on expatriate managers to help manage operations; as a result, the diversity focus is from the inside out. This is the reverse of what happens in multinational firms, where there is less emphasis on managing cultural differences outside the firm and more on managing cultural diversity within the company. This is because multinational firms hire personnel from all over the world. Adler notes that these multinational firms need to develop cross-cultural management skills up the levels of the hierarchy. As shown in Figure 3–4, this results in a diversity focus that is primarily internal.

Global firms need both an internal and an external diversity focus (again see Figure 3–4). To be effective, everyone in the global organization needs to develop cross-cultural skills that allow them to work effectively with internal personnel as well as external customers, clients, and suppliers.

多元文化主义的类型
Types of Multiculturalism

For the international management arena, there are several ways of examining multiculturalism and diversity. One is to focus on the domestic multicultural and diverse workforce that operates in the MNC's home country. In addition to domestic multiculturalism, there is the diverse workforce in other geographic locales, and increasingly common are the mix of domestic and overseas personnel found in today's MNCs. The following discussion examines both domestic and group multiculturalism and the potential problems and strengths.

本土的多元文化主义

Domestic Multiculturalism It is not necessary for today's organizations to do business in another country to encounter people with diverse cultural backgrounds. Culturally distinct populations can be found within organizations almost everywhere in the world. In Singapore, for example, there are four distinct cultural and linguistic groups: Chinese, Eurasian, Indian, and Malay. In Switzerland, there are four distinct ethnic communities: French, German, Italian, and Romansch. In Belgium, there are two linguistic groups: French and Flemish. In the United States, millions of first-generation immigrants have brought both their languages and their cultures. In Los Angeles, for example, there are more Samoans than on the island of Samoa, more Israelis than in any other city outside Israel, and more first- and second-generation Mexicans than in any other city except Mexico City. In Miami, over one-half the population is Latin, and most residents speak Spanish fluently. More Puerto Ricans live in New York City than in Puerto Rico.

It is even possible to examine domestic multiculturalism within the same ethnic groups. For example, Lee, after conducting research in Singapore among small Chinese family businesses, found that the viewpoints of the older generation differ sharply from those of the younger generation.[42] Older generations tend to stress hierarchies, ethics, group dynamics and the status quo, while the younger generations focus on worker responsibility, strategy, individual performance, and striving for new horizons. These differences can slow organizational processes as one generation considers the other to be ineffective in its methods. Managers, therefore, need to consider employees on an individual basis and try to compile techniques that convey a common message, ultimately maximizing productivity while satisfying everyone across the ages. In short, there is considerable multicultural diversity domestically in organizations throughout the world, and this trend will continue. For example, the U.S. civilian labor force of the next decade will change dramatically in ethnic composition. In particular, there will be a significantly lower percentage of white males in the workforce and a growing percentage of women, African Americans, Hispanics, and Asians.

群体多元文化主义

Group Multiculturalism There are a number of ways that diverse groups can be categorized. Four of the most common include:

1. **Homogeneous groups,** in which members have similar backgrounds and generally perceive, interpret, and evaluate events in similar ways. An example would be a group of male German bankers who are forecasting the economic outlook for a foreign investment.
2. **Token groups,** in which all members but one have the same background. An example would be a group of Japanese retailers and a British attorney who are looking into the benefits and shortcomings of setting up operations in Bermuda.
3. **Bicultural groups,** in which two or more members represent each of two distinct cultures. An example would be a group of four Mexicans and four Canadians who have formed a team to investigate the possibility of investing in Russia.
4. **Multicultural groups,** in which there are individuals from three or more different ethnic backgrounds. An example is a group of three American, three German, three Uruguayan, and three Chinese managers who are looking into mining operations in Chile.

As the diversity of a group increases, the likelihood of all members perceiving things in the same way decreases sharply. Attitudes, perceptions, and communication in general may be a problem. On the other hand, there also are significant advantages associated with the effective use of multicultural, diverse groups. Sometimes, local laws require a certain level of diversity in the workplace. More and more, people are moving to other countries to find the jobs that match their skills. International managers need to be cognizant of the likelihood that they will oversee a group that represents many cultures, not just the pervasive culture associated with that country. The following sections examine the potential problems and the advantages of workplace diversity.

homogeneous group
A group in which members have similar backgrounds and generally perceive, interpret, and evaluate events in similar ways.

token group
A group in which all members but one have the same background, such as a group of Japanese retailers and a British attorney.

bicultural group
A group in which two or more members represent each of two distinct cultures, such as four Mexicans and four prople from Taiwan who have formed a team to investigate the possibility of investing in a venture.

multicultural group
A group in which there are individuals from three or more different ethnic backgrounds, such as three U.S., three German, three Uruguayan, and three Chinese managers who are looking into mining operations in South Africa.

与多样性相关的潜在问题
Potential Problems Associated with Diversity

Overall, diversity may cause a lack of cohesion that results in the unit's inability to take concerted action, be productive, and create a work environment that is conducive to both efficiency and effectiveness. These potential problems are rooted in people's attitudes. An example of an attitudinal problem in a diverse group may be the mistrust of others. For example, many U.S. managers who work for Japanese operations in the United States complain that Japanese managers often huddle together and discuss matters in their native language. The U.S. managers wonder aloud why the Japanese do not speak English. What are they talking about that they do not want anyone else to hear? In fact, the Japanese often find it easier to communicate among themselves in their native language, and because no Americans are present, the Japanese managers ask why they should speak English. If there is no reason for anyone else to be privy to our conversation, why should we not opt for our own language? Nevertheless, such practices do tend to promote an atmosphere of mistrust.

Another potential problem may be perceptual. Unfortunately, when culturally diverse groups come together, they often bring preconceived stereotypes with them. In initial meetings, for example, engineers from economically advanced countries often are perceived as more knowledgeable than those from less advanced countries. In turn, this perception can result in status-related problems, because some of the group initially are regarded as more competent than others and likely are accorded status on this basis. As the diverse group works together, erroneous perceptions often are corrected, but this takes time. In one diverse group consisting of engineers from a major Japanese firm and a world-class U.S. firm, a Japanese engineer was assigned a technical task because of his stereotyped technical educational background. The group soon realized that this particular Japanese engineer was not capable of doing this job, because for the last four years, he had been responsible for coordinating routine quality and no longer was on the technological cutting edge. His engineering degree from the University of Tokyo had resulted in the other members perceiving him as technically competent and able to carry out the task; this perception proved to be incorrect.

A related problem is inaccurate biases. For example, it is well known that Japanese companies depend on groups to make decisions. Entrepreneurial behavior, individualism, and originality are typically downplayed.[43] However, in a growing number of Japanese firms this stereotype is proving to be incorrect.[44] Here is an example.

> Mr. Uchida, a 28-year-old executive in a small software company, dyes his hair brown, keeps a sleeping bag by his desk for late nights in the office and occasionally takes the day off to go windsurfing. "Sometimes I listen to soft music to soothe my feelings, and sometimes I listen to hard music to build my energy," said Mr. Uchida, who manages the technology development division of the Rimnet Corporation, an Internet access provider. "It's important that we always keep in touch with our sensibilities when we want to generate ideas." The creative whiz kid, a business personality often prized by corporate America, has come to Japan Inc. Unlikely as it might seem in a country renowned for its deference to authority and its devotion to group solidarity, freethinkers like Mr. Uchida are popping up all over the workplace. Nonconformity is suddenly in.[45]

Still another potential problem with diverse groups is miscommunication or inaccurate communication, which can occur for a number of reasons. Misunderstandings can be caused by a speaker using words that are not clear to other members. For example, in a diverse group in which one of the authors was working, a British manager told her U.S. colleagues, "I will fax you this report in a fortnight." When the author asked the Americans when they would be getting the report, most of them believed it would be arriving in four days. They did not know that the common British word fortnight (14 nights) means two weeks.

Another contribution to miscommunication may be the way in which situations are interpreted. Many Japanese nod their heads when others talk, but this does not mean that they agree with what is being said. They are merely being polite and attentive. In many societies, it is impolite to say no, and if the listener believes that the other person wants a positive answer, the listener will say yes even though this is incorrect. As a result, many U.S. managers find out that promises made by individuals from other cultures cannot be taken at face value—and in many instances, the other individual assumes that the American realizes this!

Diversity also may lead to communication problems because of different perceptions of time. For example, many Japanese will not agree to a course of action on the spot. They will not act until they have discussed the matter with their own people, because they do not feel empowered to act alone. Many Latin managers refuse to be held to a strict timetable, because they do not have the same time urgency that U.S. managers do. Here is another example, as described by a European manager:

> In attempting to plan a new project, a three-person team composed of managers from Britain, France, and Switzerland failed to reach agreement. To the others, the British representative appeared unable to accept any systematic approach; he wanted to discuss all potential problems before making a decision. The French and Swiss representatives agreed to examine everything before making a decision, but then disagreed on the sequence and scheduling of operations. The Swiss, being more pessimistic in their planning, allocated more time for each suboperation than did the French. As a result, although everybody agreed on its validity, we never started the project. If the project had been discussed by three Frenchmen, three Swiss, or three Britons, a decision, good or bad, would have been made. The project would not have been stalled for lack of agreement.[46]

多样性的优势
Advantages of Diversity

While there are some potential problems to overcome when using culturally diverse groups in today's MNCs, there are also very many benefits to be gained.[47] In particular, there is growing evidence that culturally diverse groups can enhance creativity, lead to better decisions, and result in more effective and productive performance.[48]

One main benefit of diversity is the generation of more and better ideas. Because group members come from a variety of cultures, they often are able to create a greater number of unique (and thus creative) solutions and recommendations. For example, a U.S. MNC recently was preparing to launch a new software package aimed at the mass consumer market. The company hoped to capitalize on the upcoming Christmas season with a strong advertising campaign in each of its international markets. A meeting of the sales managers from these markets in Spain, the Middle East, and Japan helped the company revise and better target its marketing effort. The Spanish manager suggested that the company focus its campaign around the coming of the Magi (January 6) and not Christmas (December 25), because in Latin cultures, gifts typically are exchanged on the date that the Magi brought their gifts. The Middle Eastern manager pointed out that most of his customers were not Christians, so a Christmas campaign would not have much meaning in his area. Instead, he suggested the company focus its sales campaign around the value of the software and how it could be useful to customers and not worry about getting the product shipped by early December at all. The Japanese manager concurred with his Middle Eastern colleague but further suggested that some of the colors being proposed for the sales brochure be changed to better fit with Japanese culture. Thanks to these diverse ideas, the sales campaign proved to be one of the most effective in the company's history.

A second major benefit is that culturally diverse groups can prevent **groupthink**, which is caused by social conformity and pressures on individual members of a group

groupthink
Consensus reached because of social conformity and pressures on individual members of a group to conform to group norms.

to conform and reach consensus. When groupthink occurs, group participants come to believe that their ideas and actions are correct and that those who disagree with them are either uninformed or deliberately trying to sabotage their efforts. Multicultural diverse groups often are able to avoid this problem, because the members do not think similarly or feel pressure to conform. As a result, they typically question each other, offer opinions and suggestions that are contrary to those held by others, and must be persuaded to change their minds. Therefore, unanimity is achieved only through a careful process of deliberation. Unlike homogeneous groups, where everyone can be "of one mind," diverse groups may be slower to reach a general consensus, but the decision may be more effective and free of "groupthink."

Diversity in the workplace enhances more than the internal operations but relationships to customers as well. It is commonly held that anyone will have insight into and connect better with others of the same nationality or cultural background, resulting in more quickly building trust and understanding of one another's preferences. Therefore, if the customer base is composed of many cultures, it may benefit the company to have representatives from corresponding nationalities. The U.S. multinational cosmetic firm Avon adopted this philosophy over a decade ago. When Avon observed an increase in the number of Korean shoppers at one of its U.S. locations, it quickly employed Korean sales staff.[49] The external environment, even in the MNC home country, can encompass many cultures that managers should bear in mind. Expanding diversity in the workplace to better serve the customer means that even local managers have an international exposure, further emphasizing the importance of learning about the multicultural surroundings.

建立多元文化团队的有效性
Building Multicultural Team Effectiveness

Multiculturally diverse teams have a great deal of potential, depending on how they are managed. As shown in Figure 3–5, Dr. Carol Kovach, who conducted research on the importance of leadership in managing cross-cultural groups, reports that if cross-cultural groups are led properly, they can indeed be highly effective; unfortunately, she also found that if they are not managed properly, they can be highly ineffective. In other words, diverse groups are more powerful than single-culture groups. They can hurt the organization, but if managed effectively, they can be the best.[50] The following sections provide the conditions and guidelines for managing diverse groups in today's organizations effectively.

Figure 3–5
Group Effectiveness and Culture

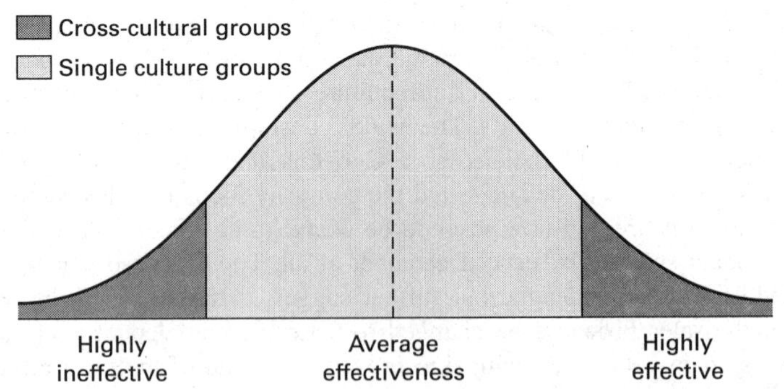

Source: From Adler. *International Dimensions of Organizational Behavior,* 5th ed. © 2008 South-Western, a part of Cengage Learning, Inc. Reproduced by permission. www.cengage.com/permissions.

理解有效性的条件

Understanding the Conditions for Effectiveness Multicultural teams are most effective when they face tasks requiring innovativeness. They are far less effective when they are assigned to routine tasks. As Adler explains:

> Cultural diversity provides the biggest asset for teams with difficult, discretionary tasks requiring innovation. Diversity becomes less helpful when employees are working on simple tasks involving repetitive or routine procedures. Therefore, diversity generally becomes more valuable during the planning and development of projects (the "work" stage) and less helpful during their implementation (the "action" stage). The more senior the team members, the more likely they are to be working on projects that can benefit from diversity. Diversity is therefore extremely valuable to senior executive teams, both within and across countries.[51]

To achieve the greatest effectiveness from diverse teams, the focus of attention must be determined by the stage of team development (e.g., entry, working, and action stages). In the entry stage, the focus should be on building trust and developing team cohesion, as we saw in The World of International Management at the opening of the chapter. This can be difficult for diverse teams, whose members are accustomed to working in different ways. For example, Americans, Germans, and Swiss typically spend little time getting to know each other; they find out the nature of the task and set about pursuing it on their own without first building trust and cohesion. This contrasts sharply with individuals from Latin America, Southern Europe, and the Middle East, where team members spend a great deal of initial time getting to know each other. This contrast between task-oriented and relationship-oriented members of a diverse team may slow progress due to communication and strategic barriers. To counteract this problem, it is common in the entry stage of development to find experienced multicultural managers focusing attention on the team members' equivalent professional qualifications and status. Once this professional similarity and respect are established, the group can begin forming a collective unit. In the work stage of development, attention may be directed more toward describing and analyzing the problem or task that has been assigned. This stage often is fairly easy for managers of multicultural teams, because they can draw on the diversity of the members in generating ideas. As noted earlier, diverse groups tend to be most effective when dealing with situations that require innovative approaches.

In the action stage, the focus shifts to decision making and implementation. This can be a difficult phase, because it often requires consensus building among the members. In achieving this objective, experienced managers work to help the diverse group recognize and facilitate the creation of ideas with which everyone can agree. In doing so, it is common to find strong emphasis on problem-solving techniques such as the nominal group technique (NGT), where the group members individually make contributions before group interaction takes place and consensus is reached.

应用恰当的指导方针

Using the Proper Guidelines Some specific guidelines have proved to be helpful as a quick reference for managers when setting out to manage a culturally diverse team. Here are some of the most useful ideas:

1. Team members must be selected for their task-related abilities and not solely based on ethnicity. If the task is routine, homogeneous membership often is preferable; if the task is innovative, multicultural membership typically is best.
2. Team members must recognize and be prepared to deal with their differences. The goal is to facilitate a better understanding of cross-cultural differences and generate a higher level of performance and rapport. In doing so, members need to become aware of their own stereotypes, as well as those of the others, and use this information to better understand the real differences that exist between them. This can then serve as a basis for determining how each individual member can contribute to the overall effectiveness of the team.
3. Because members of diverse teams tend to have more difficulty agreeing on their purpose and task than members of homogeneous groups, the team leader

must help the group to identify and define its overall goal. This goal is most useful when it requires members to cooperate and develop mutual respect in carrying out their tasks.

4. Members must have equal power so that everyone can participate in the process; cultural dominance always is counterproductive. As a result, managers of culturally diverse teams distribute power according to each person's ability to contribute to the task, not according to ethnicity.
5. It is important that all members have mutual respect for each other. This is often accomplished by managers' choosing members of equal ability, making prior accomplishments and task-related skills known to the group, and minimizing early judgments based on ethnic stereotypes.
6. Because teams often have difficulty determining what is a good or a bad idea or decision, managers must give teams positive feedback on their process and output. This feedback helps the members see themselves as a team, and it teaches them to value and celebrate their diversity, recognize contributions made by the individual members, and trust the collective judgment of the group.

再看国际化管理的世界
The World of International Management—Revisited

Our discussion in The World of International Management at the outset of the chapter introduced the challenges and the benefits of diverse, multicultural teams. These teams have become commonplace in organizations around the world as work becomes more flexible and less geographically bound. In addition, companies are looking to such teams to solve intractable problems and bring creativity and fresh thinking to their organizations. Using what you have learned from this chapter, answer the following: (1) What steps should organizations take to get the most out of their global virtual teams? (2) What types of organizational culture (family, Eiffel Tower, guided missile, incubator) would be best for leveraging global teams? (3) What advantages and problems associated with diversity have been experienced by global teams? How might they be overcome? (4) What features of multicultural teams are most critical for successful global team collaboration?

SUMMARY OF KEY POINTS

1. Organizational culture is a pattern of basic assumptions developed by a group as it learns to cope with its problems of external adaptation and internal integration and taught to new members as the correct way to perceive, think, and feel in relation to these problems. Some important characteristics of organizational culture include observed behavioral regularities, norms, dominant values, philosophy, rules, and organizational climate.
2. Organizational cultures are shaped by a number of factors. These include the general relationship between employees and their organization, the hierarchic system of authority that defines the roles of managers and subordinates, and the general views that employees hold about the organization's purpose, destiny, and goals and their place in the organization. When examining these differences, Trompenaars suggested the use of two continua: equity-hierarchy and person-task orientation, resulting in four basic types of organizational cultures: family, Eiffel Tower, guided missile, and incubator.
3. Family culture is characterized by strong emphasis on hierarchic authority and orientation to the person. Eiffel Tower culture is characterized by strong emphasis on hierarchy and orientation to the task. Guided missile culture is characterized by strong emphasis on equality in the workplace and orientation to the task. Incubator culture is characterized by strong emphasis on equality and orientation to the person.

4. Success in the international arena often is heavily determined by a company's ability to manage multiculturalism and diversity. Firms progress through four phases in their international evolution: (1) domestic corporation, (2) international corporation, (3) multinational corporation, and (4) global corporation.
5. There are a number of ways to examine multiculturalism and diversity. One is by looking at the domestic multicultural and diverse workforce that operates in the MNC's home country. Another is by examining the variety of diverse groups that exist in MNCs, including homogeneous groups, token groups, bicultural groups, and multicultural groups. Several potential problems as well as advantages are associated with multicultural, diverse teams. Diverse teams are not only helpful to internal operations but can enhance sales to customers as well, as shown at Avon.
6. A number of guidelines have proved to be particularly effective in managing culturally diverse groups. These include careful selection of the members, identification of the group's goals, establishment of equal power and mutual respect among the participants, and delivering positive feedback on performance.

KEY TERMS

bicultural group
Eiffel Tower culture
family culture
groupthink
guided missile culture
homogeneous group
incubator culture
multicultural group
organizational culture
token group

REVIEW AND DISCUSSION QUESTIONS

1. Some researchers have found that when Germans work for a U.S. MNC, they become even more German, and when Americans work for a German MNC, they become even more American. Why would this knowledge be important to these MNCs?
2. When comparing the negotiating styles and strategies of French versus Spanish negotiators, a number of sharp contrasts are evident. What are three of these, and what could MNCs do to improve their position when negotiating with either group?
3. In which of the four types of organizational cultures—family, Eiffel Tower, guided missile, incubator—would most people in the United States feel comfortable? In which would most Japanese feel comfortable? Based on your answers, what conclusions could you draw regarding the importance of understanding organizational culture for international management?
4. Most MNCs need not enter foreign markets to face the challenge of dealing with multiculturalism. Do you agree or disagree with this statement? Explain your answer.
5. What are some potential problems that must be overcome when using multicultural, diverse teams in today's organizations? What are some recognized advantages? Identify and discuss two of each.
6. A number of guidelines can be valuable in helping MNCs to make diverse teams more effective. What are five of these? How do these relate to the guidelines established by Matsushita, as discussed in the International Management in Action box?

INTERNET EXERCISE: LENOVO'S INTERNATIONAL FOCUS

Based in China, Lenovo is one of the largest computer brands in the world. Several years ago Lenovo purchased IBM's PC business and now sells more computers to retail customers and businesses than any company in the world. From its base in China, it is moving aggressively into global markets, especially emerging countries like India.

Visit Lenovo's website at lenovo.com, and review some of the latest developments. In particular, pay close attention to its product line and international expansion. Using the country/language tab in the upper center of the screen, choose three different countries where the firm is doing business: one from the Americas, one from Europe, and one from Southeast Asia or India. (The sites are all presented in the local language, so you might want to make India your choice because this site is in English.) Compare and contrast the product offerings and ways in which HP goes about marketing itself over the Web in these locations. What do you see as some of the major differences? Second, using Figure 3–2 and Table 3–3 as your guide, in what way are differences in organizational cultures internationally likely to present significant challenges to Lenovo efforts to create a smooth-running international enterprise? Look at the web page showing Lenovo's leadership team. What do you notice? What would you see as two of the critical issues with which management will have to deal? Third, what are two steps that you think Lenovo will have to take in order to build multicultural team effectiveness? What are two guidelines that can help it do this?

Japan

Japan is located in eastern Asia, and it comprises a curved chain of more than 3,000 islands. Four of these—Hokkaido, Honshu, Shikoku, and Kyushi—account for 89 percent of the country's land area. The population of Japan is approximately 128 million, with over 35 million people living in the metro of the nation's capital, Tokyo. According to the WorldBank, the country's gross domestic product in 2011 was approximately US$5.9 trillion, or US$45,900 per capita. Japan has faced a long period of stagnant economic growth. Japan's economy was especially hard hit by the global economic financial crisis, with GDP shrinking by 5.2 percent in 2009. The economy was still contracting in 2012 by about 1 percent.

Surprisingly, Japan has become a fashion mecca. Spanish clothing company Zara, Swedish brand H&M, French designer Louis Vuitton, and American jeweler Tiffany & Co. are very popular and prosperous throughout Japan. The new generation of fashion aficionados also makes Japan a country to watch. Japan is usually associated with a minimalist nature, not owning more than is necessary. In Tokyo, however, younger people are beginning to express themselves by quickly purchasing any item that appears to be part of a new trend, only to abandon it for the next craze in the blink of an eye. Investment in Japan has been supported by this phenomenon, since many fashion companies use Japan as their new testing ground before launching expensive lines in other markets. While New York City in the United States was once considered the primary region to try out new styles, experience has shown that what catches on in Japan often works across the globe as well and that the Japanese are much faster to respond to new products. This does not imply that everything that is tested in Japan will work worldwide. For example, bags with bubbly, cartoon printing containing the likes of Hello Kitty or indistinguishable characteristics that thrive in the kawaii, or "cute," market segment may not make a profit elsewhere. Essentially, there are times when Japan is distinctly ahead of the crowd, and it may take quite some time for the rest of the world to catch up.

Considering workplace ethics and customs in the home, most would not immediately think of Japan as such a vogue region. For instance, in business, employees often dress conservatively, are well groomed, and do not leave the work space until after the boss has left, which can be many hours after the office has officially closed. In fact, it is usually embarrassing for a worker to leave the moment the office closes, since that is seen as leaving "early," and it singles out the employee. Homes can be small, with little extra room for extravagant purchases, though with gift giving so prevalent in the country, it is unpredictable what someone else may procure for your household. These reasons and many more would imply that the Japanese would not want to call more attention to themselves. However, as Japan continues to move toward individualistic tendencies, citizens may be scrambling to find a way to express their own unique voice.

www.japanlink.com, www.businessweek.com, www.infoplease.com/ipa/A0107666.html, data.worldbank.org/country/japan

Questions

1. Based on their home country, how might the organizational cultures of the four fashion companies mentioned be distinct from one another, and in what ways could they be the same?
2. If the first two companies and the last two companies want to form joint ventures (Zara with H&M, and Louis Vuitton with Tiffany & Co.), what could be some potential ways the organizational cultures interact?
3. What types of problems might a culturally diverse top management team at headquarters create for the two joint ventures? Give some specific examples. How could these problems be overcome?
4. How could work structures and schedules of these companies at their respective headquarters affect operations in Japan? In what ways are they different or similar?

Chapter 4
跨文化沟通与谈判
CROSS-CULTURAL COMMUNICATION AND NEGOTIATION

OBJECTIVES OF THE CHAPTER

Communication takes on special importance in international management because of the difficulties in conveying meanings between parties from different cultures. The problems of misinterpretation and error are compounded in the international context. Chapter 4 examines how the communication process in general works, and it looks at the downward and upward communication flows that commonly are used in international communication. Then the chapter examines the major barriers to effective international communication and reviews ways of dealing with these communication problems. Finally, one important dimension of international communication, international negotiation, is examined, with particular attention to how negotiation approaches and strategies must be adapted to different cultural environments. The specific objectives of this chapter are:

1. **DEFINE** the term *communication,* examine some examples of verbal communication styles, and explain the importance of message interpretation.
2. **ANALYZE** the common downward and upward communication flows used in international communication.
3. **EXAMINE** the language, perception, and culture of communication and nonverbal barriers to effective international communications.
4. **PRESENT** the steps that can be taken to overcome international communication problems.
5. **DEVELOP** approaches to international negotiations that respond to differences in culture.
6. **REVIEW** different negotiating and bargaining behaviors that may improve negotiations and outcomes.

国际化管理的世界
The World of *International Management*
离岸文化和沟通
Offshoring Culture and Communication

Offshore call-center agents for a North American airline had difficulty relating to customers stranded at airports because of a snowstorm. The reason? These agents had never seen snow or been to an airport. The solution? The airline set up TVs broadcasting CNN in the break rooms so that agents could be exposed to snow, airports, and flight delays.

Offshoring, or the practice of a company moving certain services overseas, has highlighted cultural differences between employees around the world. Yet, if offshoring is managed correctly, companies can save money and increase productivity. By offshoring, Mamas and Papas, a U.K.-based baby stroller company, has benefited from the decreased labor and material costs and the ability to send work to places in the world best equipped to complete each piece of the manufacturing process. An employee of the company, Gill Kingston-Warren, told the Financial Times: "The U.K. is known for design and intellectual property and other countries have skills we are not known for any more. Some countries have strong traditions of craftsmanship, while others are focused on technology."[1] Offshoring enables companies to capitalize on other countries' cultural advantages. By the same token, however, these cultural differences can create challenges for firms that engage in offshoring.

文化挑战
Cultural Challenges

According to the global management consultants A.T. Kearney, when companies offshore certain operations, they face four main cultural challenges: communication, context, relationships, and working norms.

First, employees may encounter communication difficulties. In "The Offshore Cultural Clash," A.T. Kearney consultants wrote:

An American financial services manager e-mailed a counterpart in India laying out a project and asking for a work plan. Her counterpart's reply: "I will do the needful." The meaning, clear to people in India, is "I will do what's necessary to accomplish what we've been talking about." Most Westerners in Europe and North America have probably never heard the phrase and don't understand it. They prefer to convey their views directly and clarify the details of their contracts and intentions. In India, where e-mails are far less specific, such detail seems not only unnecessary, but also distrustful. The two cultures hold different expectations of what is said, what needs to be said, and what can remain unsaid but understood.[2]

Understanding the communication style of different cultures is key to managing employees in different regions of the world. In addition, it is essential to prevent communication lapses. For instance, an American bank had offshore service providers that it had worked with for the past five years, yet their relationships remained strained. The bank eventually discovered that U.S.-based IT teams received important updates for changing business requirements, but the offshore partners never received these updates. As a result, the bank had to re-do much of its work at significant cost. Companies can avoid this problem by having a dedicated liaison between the "home country" and offshore employees to verify that every team has clear information and work expectations.[3]

Second, managers must be aware of offshore workers' "context." Do these workers possess a cultural context necessary to understand the product or service? One credit card company executive told A.T. Kearney that his employees in India struggled to apply their accounting knowledge to credit card payment processing because "Consumer credit markets are not as pervasive in India as they are in the United States, where it's hard to find anyone who doesn't have an intuitive understanding of credit-card transactions. For our offshore agents, we had to develop that foundation."[4]

Third, companies need to understand how offshore agents perceive relationships. According to A.T. Kearney, one manager noticed that offshore agents are very deferential to their superiors. He said that if a manager is in the room, offshore agents "will not answer questions or make comments without specific invitations to do so."[5]

Fourth, managers must be aware of different cultural working norms. Indeed, by fostering collaboration between employees with cultural strengths, managers can increase productivity. One executive told A.T. Kearney that his company was very consensus-driven, but it lacked discipline. He found an offshore service provider that had a culture of discipline. Offshoring can be an opportunity for a company to find employees with different strengths to handle work that is best suited for them.[6]

离岸管理的技巧

Tips for Managing Offshoring

The following are a few tips for managing the cultural challenges of offshore operations.

Avoid an "us vs. them" mentality. Instead, insist on mutual respect. Companies that have a strong hierarchical and "clan" culture often resent their offshore colleagues. One manager compared this situation to a transplant patient rejecting a new organ. To prevent this problem, A.T. Kearney recommended: "All parties to the offshoring arrangement should understand that mutual respect for cultures, both national and corporate, is not negotiable. One way to demonstrate mutual respect is to send a healthy mix of rote and 'intelligent' activities to the offshore location. Delegating complex activities to the offshore team also requires a close working relationship, which can build trust."[7] Also, personal face-to-face interactions can help managers work through cultural differences so that offshore counterparts can be true partners.

Provide training to managers to meet new expectations. When companies move certain operations offshore, managers are often expected to be able to manage offshore employees without any additional training. Companies need to provide training opportunities to managers to fulfill their new roles, such as teaching them to use metrics to manage people rather than supervising by line of sight.[8]

Foster collaboration between "home country" and offshore employees. Based on their study of 130 offshore operations in India, Kannan Srikanth and

Phanish Puranam found that the operations that "paid close attention to managing coordination performed almost four times as well as their less-successful counterparts."[9] Furthermore, Srikanth and Puranam indicated that by focusing on teamwork between offshore and "home country" employees, companies could expand their offshore operations beyond merely call-centers and IT support. They noted that "if Western companies focused more on fostering collaboration between workers separated by geography and culture, and less on forcing offshore workers to perform tasks in very specific ways, the range of work they could source offshore would be significantly expanded."[10] How do managers achieve this collaboration? Srikanth and Puranam suggested that managers concentrate on "building common ground—essentially, shared knowledge—across locations, so that employees working offshore can anticipate the actions and decisions of their onshore counterparts without the need for extensive discussion."[11] Companies can develop common ground in two ways. Managers can train employees together so they become familiar with others' work habits and adopt the same business vocabulary. Also, firms can utilize technology that allows employees to see work across locations as it is being performed.[12]

As A.T. Kearney consultants point out, "Cultural issues are not insurmountable, but they must be purposely and diligently addressed."[13] In A.T. Kearney's 2007 study of offshoring performance, A.T. Kearney found that cross-border culture and communications issues were a significant problem for companies engaging in offshoring. By understanding cultural differences ahead of time, managers increase their chances that they can make offshoring operations a success for their companies.[14]

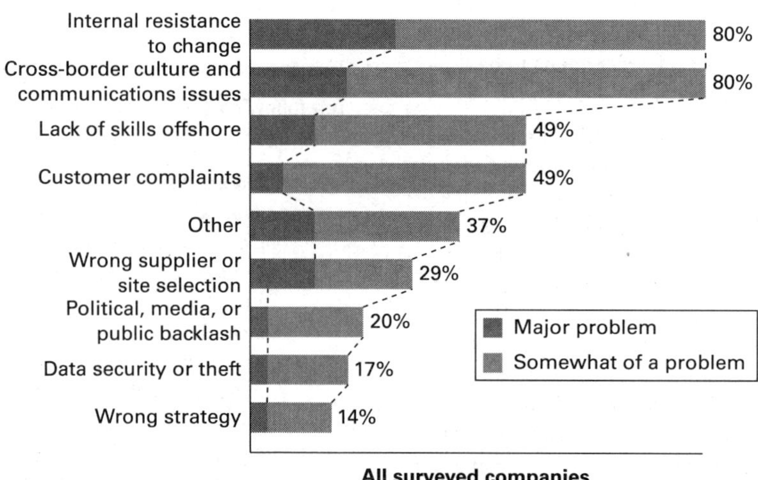

Source: Execution Is Everything: The Keys to Offshoring Success, copyright A. T. Kearney, 2007. All rights reserved. Reprinted with permission.

The opening World of International Management illustrates how cross-border communication is affected by cultural differences—both national and organizational—and how the increased offshoring of service tasks has exacerbated those challenges. Many firms offshore tasks in order to save costs without considering the implications for service and managerial oversight, issues that can quickly erode the cost benefits. The stark differences in culture, some emanating from basic variation in political, geographic, and even climatic realities (as in the example of the call-center staff who had never seen snow or been in an airport) can frustrate the coordination of global operations. Yet, there are some simple approaches that can alleviate some of these challenges and begin to bridge cultural divides. These center around anticipating, or at least responding quickly to, cultural gaps, and also creating an environment of continuous information exchange and communication. They also depend on deeper understanding of cultural differences and willingness to adapt and adjust to those differences when appropriate.

In this chapter, we explore communication and negotiation styles across cultures, emphasizing the importance of understanding different approaches to the development of effective international communication and negotiation strategies.

全面的沟通过程

The Overall Communication Process

Communication is the process of transferring meanings from sender to receiver. On the surface, this appears to be a fairly straightforward process. On analysis, however, there are a great many problems in the international arena that can result in the failure to transfer meanings correctly.

communication
The process of transferring meanings from sender to receiver.

In addition, as suggested in the opening World of International Management, the means and modes of communication have changed dramatically in recent decades. For example, the advent of the telephone, then Internet, and most recently personal communication devices ("smartphones") has influenced how, when, and why people communicate. These trends have both benefits and disadvantages. On the plus side, we have many more opportunities to communicate rapidly, without delays or filters, and often can incorporate rich content, such as photos, videos, and links to other information, in our exchanges. On the other hand, some are concerned that these devices are rendering our communication less meaningful and personal. In a recent book, Nicholas Carr argues that when we go online, "we enter an environment that promotes cursory reading, hurried and distracted thinking, and superficial learning." Mr. Carr calls the Web "a technology of forgetfulness." Web pages draw us into a myriad of embedded links while we are assaulted by other messages via e-mail, RSS, and Twitter and Facebook accounts. He suggests that greater access to knowledge is not the same as greater knowledge and that an ever-increasing plethora of facts and data is not the same as wisdom.[15]

Despite these concerns, communication—verbal and otherwise—remains an important dimension of international management. In this chapter, we survey different communication styles, how communication is processed and interpreted, and how culture and language influence communication (and miscommunication).

语言沟通方式

Verbal Communication Styles

One way of examining the ways in which individuals convey information is by looking at their communication styles. In particular, as has been noted by Hall, context plays a key role in explaining many communication differences.[16] **Context** is information that surrounds a communication and helps convey the message. In high-context societies, such as Japan and many Arab countries, messages are often highly coded and implicit. As a result, the receiver's job is to interpret what the message means by correctly filtering through what is being said and the way in which the message is being conveyed. This approach is in sharp contrast to low-context societies such as the United States and Canada, where the message is explicit and the speaker says precisely what he or she means. These contextual factors must be considered when marketing messages are being developed in disparate societies. For example, promotions in Japan should be subtle and convey a sense of community (high context). Similar segments in the United States, a low-context environment, should be responsive to expectations for more explicit messages. Figure 4–1 provides an international comparison of high-context/implicit and low-context/explicit societies. In addition, Table 4–1 presents some of the major characteristics of communication styles.

context
Information that surrounds a communication and helps convey the message.

间接方式和直接方式

Indirect and Direct Styles In high-context cultures, messages are implicit and indirect. One reason is that those who are communicating—family, friends, co-workers, clients—tend to have both close personal relationships and large information networks. As a result, each knows a lot about others in the communication network; they do not have to rely on language alone to communicate. Voice intonation, timing, and facial expressions can all play roles in conveying information.

Figure 4–1
Explicit-Implicit Communication: An International Comparison

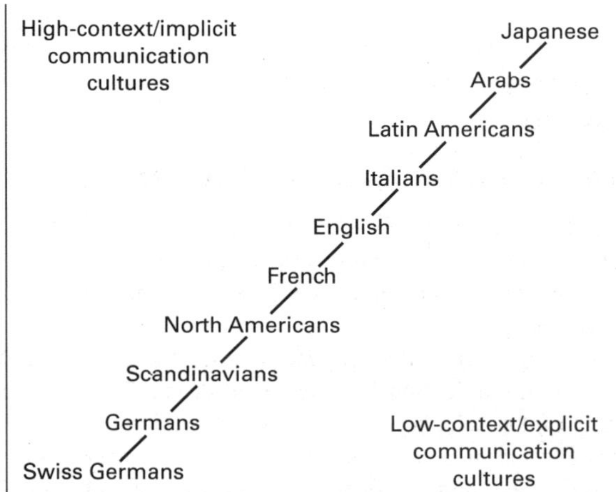

Source: Adapted from Martin Rosch, "Communications: Focal Point of Culture," *Management International Review* 27, no. 4 (1987), p. 60. Used with permission.

In low-context cultures, people often meet only to accomplish objectives. Since they do not know each other very well, they tend to be direct and focused in their communications.

One way of comparing these two kinds of culture—high context and low context—is by finding out what types of questions are typically asked when someone is contacted and told to attend a meeting. In a high-context culture it is common for the person to ask, "Who will be at this meeting?" so he or she knows how to prepare for appropriate personal interactions. In contrast, in a low-context culture the individual is likely to ask, "What is the meeting going to be about?" so he or she knows how to properly organize for the engagement. In the high-context society, the person focuses on the environment

Table 4–1
Major Characteristics of Verbal Styles

Verbal Style	Major Variation	Interaction Focus and Content	Cultures in Which Characteristic Is Found
Indirect vs. direct	Indirect	Implicit messages	Collective, high context
	Direct	Explicit messages	Individualistic, low context
Succinct vs. elaborate	Elaborate	High quantity of talk	Moderate uncertainty avoidance, high context
	Exacting	Moderate amount of talk	Low uncertainty avoidance, low context
	Succinct	Low amount of talk	High uncertainty avoidance, high context
Contextual vs. personal	Contextual	Focus on the speaker and role relationships	High power distance, collective, high context
	Personal	Focus on the speaker and personal relationships	Low power distance, individualistic, low context
Affective vs. instrumental	Affective	Process-oriented and receiver-focused language	Collective, high context
	Instrumental	Goal-oriented and sender-focused language	Individualistic, low context

in which the meeting will take place. In the low-context society, the individual is most interested in the objectives that are to be accomplished at the meeting.

从详尽的方式到简明的方式

Elaborate to Succinct Styles There are three degrees of communication quantity—elaborate, exacting, and succinct. In high-context societies, the elaborate style is often very common. There is a great deal of talking, description includes much detail, and people often repeat themselves. This elaborate style is widely used in Arabic countries.

The exacting style is more common in nations such as England, Germany, and Sweden. This style focuses on precision and the use of the right amount of words to convey the message. If a person uses too many words, this is considered exaggeration; if the individual relies on too few, the result is an ambiguous message.

The succinct style is most common in Asia, where people tend to say few words and allow understatements, pauses, and silence to convey meaning. In particular, in unfamiliar situations, communicators are succinct in order to avoid risking a loss of face.

Researchers have found that the elaborating style is more popular in high-context cultures that have a moderate degree of uncertainty avoidance. The exacting style is more common in low-context, low-uncertainty-avoidance cultures. The succinct style is more common in high-context cultures with considerable uncertainty avoidance.

背景方式和个人化的方式

Contextual and Personal Styles A contextual style is one that focuses on the speaker and relationship of the parties. For example, in Asian cultures people use words that reflect the role and hierarchical relationship of those in the conversation. As a result, in an organizational setting, speakers will choose words that indicate their status relative to the status of the others. Commenting on this idea, Yoshimura and Anderson have noted that white-collar, middle-management employees in Japan, commonly known as salarymen, quickly learn how to communicate with others in the organization by understanding the context and reference group of the other party:

> A salaryman can hardly say a word to another person without implicitly defining the reference groups to which he thinks both of them belong. . . . [This is because] failing to use proper language is socially embarrassing, and the correct form of Japanese to use with someone else depends not only on the relationship between the two people, but also on the relationship between their reference groups. Juniors defer to seniors in Japan, but even this relationship is complicated when the junior person works for a much more prestigious organization (for example, a government bureau) than the senior. [As a result, it is] likely that both will use the polite form to avoid social embarrassment.[17]

A personal style focuses on the speaker and the reduction of barriers between the parties. In the United States, for example, it is common to use first names and to address others informally and directly on an equal basis.

Researchers have found that the contextual style is often associated with high-power-distance, collective, high-context cultures. Examples include Japan, India, and Ghana. In contrast, the personal style is more popular in low-power-distance, individualistic, low-context cultures. Examples include the United States, Australia, and Canada.

情感方式和工具方式

Affective and Instrumental Styles The affective style is characterized by language that requires the listener to carefully note what is being said and to observe how the sender is presenting the message. Quite often the meaning that is being conveyed is nonverbal and requires the receiver to use his or her intuitive skills in deciphering what is being said. The part of the message that is being left out may be just as important as the part that is being included. In contrast, the instrumental style is goal-oriented and focuses on the sender. The individual clearly lets the other party know what he or she wants the other party to know.

The affective style is common in collective, high-context cultures such as the Middle East, Latin America, and Asia. The instrumental style is more commonly found in individualistic, low-context cultures such as Switzerland, Denmark, and the United States.

Table 4–2
Verbal Styles Used in 10 Select Countries

Country	Indirect vs. Direct	Elaborate vs. Succinct	Contextual vs. Personal	Affective vs. Instrumental
Australia	Direct	Exacting	Personal	Instrumental
Canada	Direct	Exacting	Personal	Instrumental
Denmark	Direct	Exacting	Personal	Instrumental
Egypt	Indirect	Elaborate	Contextual	Affective
England	Direct	Exacting	Personal	Instrumental
Japan	Indirect	Succinct	Contextual	Affective
Korea	Indirect	Succinct	Contextual	Affective
Saudi Arabia	Indirect	Elaborate	Contextual	Affective
Sweden	Direct	Exacting	Personal	Instrumental
United States	Direct	Exacting	Personal	Instrumental

Source: Anne Marie Francesco and Barry Allen Gold, *International Organizational Behavior: Text, Readings, Cases, and Skills,* 1st Edition © 1998. Reproduced by permission of Barry Allen Gold.

Table 4–2 provides a brief description of the four verbal styles that are used in select countries. A close look at the table helps explain why managers in Japan can have great difficulty communicating with their counterparts in the United States and vice versa: The verbal styles do not match in any context.

沟通解读
Interpretation of Communications

The effectiveness of communication in the international context often is determined by how closely the sender and receiver have the same meaning for the same message.[18] If this meaning is different, effective communication will not occur. A good example is the U.S. firm that wanted to increase worker output among its Japanese personnel. This firm put an individual incentive plan into effect, whereby workers would be given extra pay based on their work output. The plan, which had worked well in the United States, was a total flop. The Japanese were accustomed to working in groups and to being rewarded as a group. In another case, a U.S. firm offered a bonus to anyone who would provide suggestions that resulted in increased productivity. The Japanese workers rejected this idea, because they felt that no one working alone is responsible for increased productivity. It is always a group effort. When the company changed the system and began rewarding group productivity, it was successful in gaining support for the program.

A related case occurs when both parties agree on the content of the message but one party believes it is necessary to persuade the other to accept the message. Here is an example:

> Motorola University recently prepared carefully for a presentation in China. After considerable thought, the presenters entitled it "Relationships do not retire." The gist of the presentation was that Motorola had come to China in order to stay and help the economy to create wealth. Relationships with Chinese suppliers, subcontractors and employees would constitute a permanent commitment to building Chinese economic infrastructure and earning hard currency through exports. The Chinese audience listened politely to this presentation but was quiet when invited to ask questions. Finally one manager put up his hand and said: "Can you tell us about pay for performance?"[19]

Quite obviously, the Motorola presenter believed that it was necessary to convince the audience that the company was in China for the long run. Those in attendance, however, had already accepted this idea and wanted to move on to other issues.

Still another example has been provided by Adler, who has pointed out that people doing business in a foreign culture often misinterpret the meaning of messages. As a result, they arrive at erroneous conclusions, as in the following story of a Canadian doing business in the Middle East. The Canadian was surprised when his meeting with a high-ranking official was not held in a closed office and was constantly interrupted:

> Using the Canadian-based cultural assumptions that (a) important people have large private offices with secretaries to monitor the flow of people into the office, and (b) important business takes precedence over less important business and is therefore not interrupted, the Canadian interprets the . . . open office and constant interruptions to mean that the official is neither as high ranking nor as interested in conducting the business at hand as he had previously thought.[20]

沟通方向

Communication Flows

Communication flows in international organizations move both down and up. However, as Figure 4–2 humorously, but in many ways accurately, portrays, there are some unique differences in organizations around the world.

向下沟通

Downward Communication

downward communication The transmission of information from manager to subordinate.

Downward communication is the transmission of information from manager to subordinate. The primary purpose of the manager-initiated communication flow is to convey orders and information. Managers use this channel to let their people know what is to be done and how well they are doing. The channel facilitates the flow of information to those who need it for operational purposes.

Communicating with subordinates can be both challenging and difficult, especially if the manager delivering the news does not believe in the decision. Some suggest that managers should consider pushing back with superiors to gauge whether there is some flexibility. If you haven't fully bought into it, "your employees will be able to tell in the tone of your voice or your body language that you do not believe in what you are doing," says Ray Skiba, director of human resources at Streck, a manufacturer of clinical laboratory products in Omaha, Nebraska. Whether or not this is successful, sending a mixed signal is never helpful.

> "Once you've done your internal work, prepare yourself to deliver the message. If there was team involvement in the decision, ask one of the team members to listen to how you plan to address your employees. The more prepared you are, the better the outcome," says Mr. Skiba. Next, consider your communication strategy. "Explain why the decision is important to the business, how the decision was made, and why it is important that the plan be executed," says Kimberly Bishop, founder of a career management and leadership services consulting firm in New York. Give your employees ample time to digest the message. Since it took you some time to accept the information, realize that your employees will need time as well. "When the message has been delivered, be available to answer questions, be visible and approachable to help individuals get to the point of acceptance," says Mr. Skiba.[21]

In the international context, downward communication poses special challenges. For example, in Asian countries, as noted earlier, downward communication is less direct than in the United States. Orders tend to be implicit in nature. Conversely, in some European countries, downward communication is not only direct but extends beyond business matters. For example, one early study surveyed 299 U.S. and French managers regarding the nature of downward communication and the managerial authority they perceived themselves as having. This study found that U.S. managers basically used downward communication for work-related matters. A follow-up study investigated matters that U.S. and French managers felt were within the purview of their authority.[22] The major differences involved work-related and nonwork-related activities: U.S. managers felt that it was within their authority to communicate or attempt to influence their people's

Figure 4–2
Communication Epigrams

There are a number of different "organization charts" that have been constructed to depict international organizations. An epigram is a poem or line of verse that is witty or satirical in nature. The following organization designs are epigrams that show how communication occurs in different countries. In examining them, remember that each contains considerable exaggeration and humor, but also some degree of truth.

In America, everyone thinks he or she has a communication pipeline directly to the top.

America

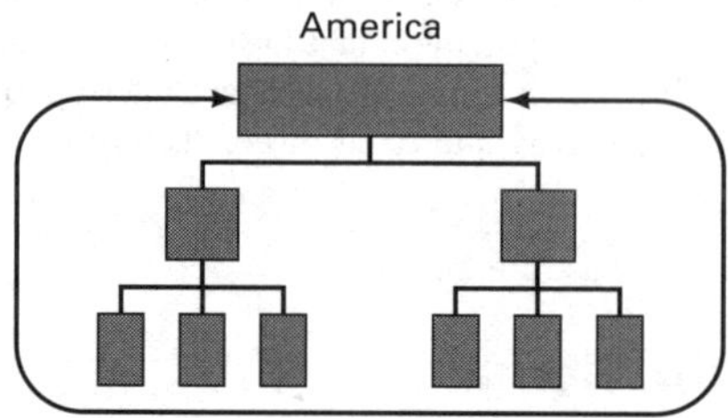

There are so many people in China that organizations are monolithic structures characterized by copious levels of bureaucracy. All information flows through channels.

China

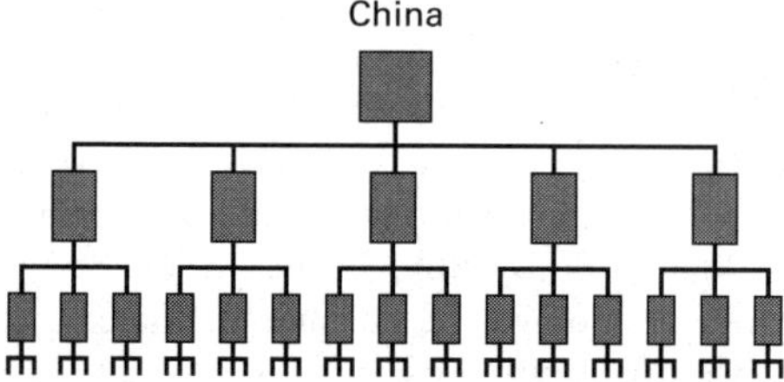

At the United Nations everyone is arranged in a circle so that no one is more powerful than anyone else. Those directly in front or behind are philosophically aligned, and those nearby form part of an international bloc.

United Nations

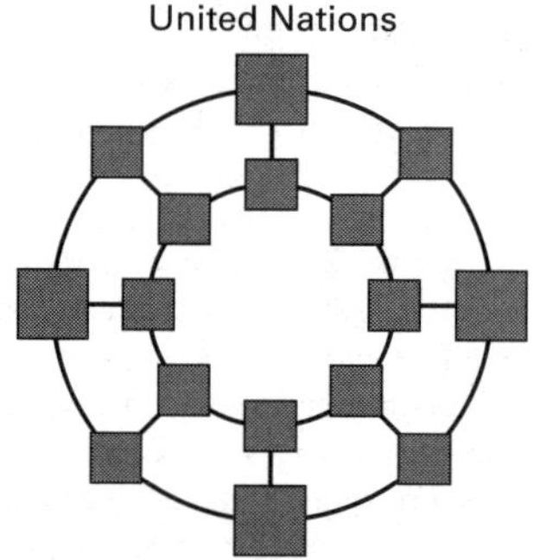

In France some people in the hierarchy are not linked to anyone, indicating how haphazard the structure can be.

France

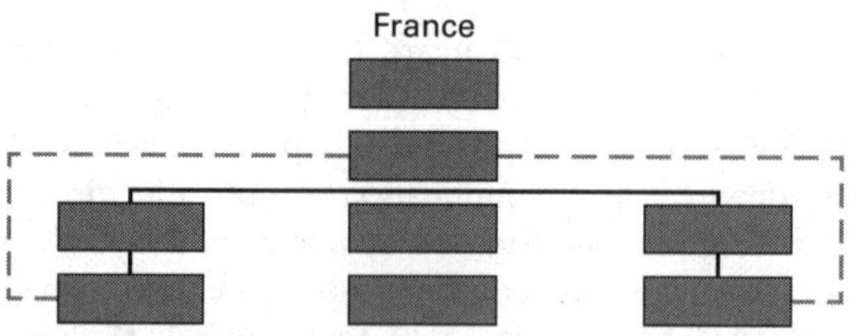

Source: Adapted from Simcha Ronen, *Comparative and Multinational Management* (New York: Wiley, 1986), pp. 318–319. The epigrams in turn were derived from a variety of sources, including Robert M. Worchester of the U.K.-based Market and Opinion Research International (MORI), Ole Jacob Raad of Norway's PM Systems, and anonymous managers.

social behavior only if it occurred on the job or it directly affected their work. For example, U.S. managers felt that it was proper to look into matters such as how much an individual drinks at lunch, whether the person uses profanity in the workplace, and how active the individual is in recruiting others to join the company. The French managers were not as supportive of these activities. The researcher concluded that "the Americans find it as difficult [as] or more difficult than the French to accept the legitimacy of managerial authority in areas unrelated to work."[23]

Harris and Moran have noted that, when communicating downward with nonnative speakers, it is extremely important to use language that is easy to understand and allows the other person to ask questions. Here are 10 suggestions that apply not only for downward but for all types of communication with nonnative speakers:

1. Use the most common words with their most common meanings.
2. Select words that have few alternative meanings.
3. Strictly follow the basic rules of grammar—more so than would be the case with native speakers.
4. Speak with clear breaks between the words so that it is easier for the person to follow.
5. Avoid using words that are esoteric or culturally biased such as "he struck out" or "the whole idea is Mickey Mouse" because these clichés often have no meaning for the listener.
6. Avoid the use of slang.
7. Do not use words or expressions that require the other person to create a mental image such as "we were knee deep in the Big Muddy."
8. Mimic the cultural flavor of the nonnative speaker's language, for example, by using more flowery communication with Spanish-speaking listeners than with Germans.
9. Continually paraphrase and repeat the basic ideas.
10. At the end, test how well the other person understands by asking the individual to paraphrase what has been said.[24]

向上沟通
Upward Communication

Upward communication is the transfer of information from subordinate to superior. The primary purpose of this subordinate-initiated upward communication is to provide feedback, ask questions, or obtain assistance from higher-level management. In recent years, there has been a call for and a concerted effort to promote more upward communication in the United States. In other countries and regions, such as in Japan, Chinese Hong Kong, and Singapore, upward communication has long been a fact of life. Managers in these countries have extensively used suggestion systems and quality circles to get employee input and always are available to listen to their people's concerns.

upward communication
The transfer of meaning from subordinate to superior.

Here are some observations from the approach the Japanese firm Matsushita uses in dealing with employee suggestions:

> Matsushita views employee recommendations as instrumental to making improvements on the shop floor and in the marketplace. [It believes] that a great many little people, paying attention each day to how to improve their jobs, can accomplish more than a whole headquarters full of production engineers and planners. Praise and positive reinforcement are an important part of the Matsushita philosophy. . . . Approximately 90 percent of . . . suggestions receive rewards; most only a few dollars per month, but the message is reinforced constantly: "Think about your job; develop yourself and help us improve the company." The best suggestions receive company-wide recognition and can earn substantial monetary rewards. Each year, many special awards are also given, including presidential prizes and various divisional honors.[25]

Matsushita has used the same approach wherever it has established plants worldwide, and the strategy has proved very successful. The company has all its employees

Table 4–3
Matsushita's Philosophy

Basic Business Principles

To recognize our responsibilities as industrialists, to foster progress, to promote the general welfare of society, and to devote ourselves to the further development of world culture.

Employees Creed

Progress and development can be realized only through the combined efforts and cooperation of each member of the company. Each of us, therefore, shall keep this idea constantly in mind as we devote ourselves to the continuous improvement of our company.

The Seven Spiritual Values

1. National service through industry
2. Fairness
3. Harmony and cooperation
4. Struggle for betterment
5. Courtesy and humility
6. Adjustment and assimilation
7. Gratitude

begin the day by reciting its basic principles, beliefs, and values, which are summarized in Table 4–3, to reinforce in all employees the reason for the company's existence and to provide a form of spiritual fabric to energize and sustain them. All employees see themselves as important members of a successful team, and they are willing to do whatever is necessary to ensure the success of the group.

Outside these Asian countries, upward communication is not as popular. For example, in South America, many managers believe that employees should follow orders and not ask a lot of questions. German managers also make much less use of this form of communication. In most cases, however, evidence shows that employees prefer to have downward communication at least supplemented by upward channels. Unfortunately, such upward communication does not always occur because of a number of communication barriers.

沟通障碍

Communication Barriers

A number of common communication barriers are relevant to international management. The more important barriers involve language, perception, culture, and nonverbal communication.

语言障碍

Language Barriers

Knowledge of the home country's language (the language used at the headquarters of the MNC) is important for personnel placed in a foreign assignment. If managers do not understand the language that is used at headquarters, they likely will make a wide assortment of errors. Additionally, many MNCs now prescribe English as the common language for internal communication, so that managers can more easily convey information to their counterparts in other geographically dispersed locales.[26] Despite such progress, however, language training continues to lag in many areas, although in an increasing number of European countries, more and more young people are becoming multilingual.[27] Table 4–4 shows the percentage of European students who are studying English, French, or German.

Language education is a good beginning, but it is also important to realize that the ability to speak the language used at MNC headquarters is often not enough to ensure that the personnel are capable of doing the work. Stout recently noted that many MNCs worldwide place a great deal of attention on the applicant's ability to speak English without considering if the person has other necessary skills, such as the ability to interact well with others and the technical knowledge demanded by the job.[28] Additionally, in interviewing people for jobs, he has noted that many interviewers fail to take into

Table 4–4
Multilingualism in the EU Classroom

	Percentage of Pupils in General Secondary Education Learning English, French, or German as a Foreign Language, 2009/2010		
	English	**French**	**German**
European Union	92.7	23.2	23.9
Finland	99.1	17.4	25.7
Germany	91.1	27.3	–
Denmark	91.7	10.6	34.7
Spain	94.7	22.3	1.0
France	99.5	–	21.6
Greece	91.4	6.9	2.9
Italy	97.7	19.5	6.9
Romania	98.7	86.3	11.8
Britain	–	27.4	10.3
Ireland	–	58.2	16.4
Poland	92.4	8.6	52.4

Source: Eurostat (2011). http://eacea.ec.europa.eu/education/eurydice/documents/key_data_series/143EN.pdf

account the applicant's culture. As a result, interviewers misinterpret behaviors such as quietness or shyness and use them to conclude that the applicant is not sufficiently confident or self-assured. Still another problem is that nonnative speakers may know the language but not be fully fluent, so they end up asking questions or making statements that convey the wrong message. After studying Japanese for only one year, Stout began interviewing candidates in their local language and made a number of mistakes. In one case, he reports, "a young woman admitted to having an adulterous affair—even though this was not even close to the topic I was inquiring about—because of my unskilled use of the language."[29]

Written communication has been getting increased attention, because poor writing is proving to be a greater barrier than poor talking. For example, Hildebrandt has found that among U.S. subsidiaries studied in Germany, language was a major problem when subsidiaries were sending written communications to the home office. The process often involved elaborate procedures associated with translating and reworking the report. Typical steps included (1) holding a staff conference to determine what was to be included in the written message; (2) writing the initial draft in German; (3) rewriting the draft in German; (4) translating the material into English; (5) consulting with bilingual staff members regarding the translation; and (6) rewriting the English draft a series of additional times until the paper was judged to be acceptable for transmission. The German managers admitted that they felt uncomfortable with writing, because their command of written English was poor. As Hildebrandt noted:

> All German managers commanding oral English stated that their grammatical competence was not sufficiently honed to produce a written English report of top quality. Even when professional translators from outside the company rewrote the German into English, German middle managers were unable to verify whether the report captured the substantive intent or included editorial alterations.[30]

Problems associated with the translation of information from one language to another have been made even clearer by Schermerhorn, who conducted research among 153 Hong Kong Chinese bilinguals who were enrolled in an undergraduate management course at a major Hong Kong university. The students were given two scenarios, written in either

English or Chinese. One scenario involved a manager who was providing some form of personal support or praise for a subordinate. The research used the following procedures:

> [A] careful translation and back-translation method was followed to create the Chinese language versions of the research instruments. Two bilingual Hong Kong Chinese, both highly fluent in English and having expertise in the field of management, shared roles in the process. Each first translated one scenario and the evaluation questions into Chinese. Next they translated each other's Chinese versions back into English, and discussed and resolved translation differences in group consultation with the author. Finally, a Hong Kong professor read and interpreted the translations correctly as a final check of equivalency.[31]

The participants were asked to answer eight evaluation questions about these scenarios. A significant difference between the two sets of responses was found. Those who were queried in Chinese gave different answers from those who were queried in English. This led Schermerhorn to conclude that language plays a key role in conveying information between cultures and that in cross-cultural management research, bilingual individuals should not be queried in their second language.

语言中的文化障碍

Cultural Barriers in Language Geographic distance poses challenges for international managers, but so do cultural and institutional distance. Previous research has conceptualized and measured cross-national differences primarily in terms of dyadic cultural distance; that is, comparing the "distance" of one culture to another. Some, however, have suggested that distance is a multidimensional construct which includes economic, financial, political, administrative, cultural, demographic, knowledge, and global connectedness as well as geographic distance and cannot be summarized in one "score."[32] Nowhere does such cultural distance show up more vividly than in challenges to accurate communications.

As one dimension of such distance, cultural barriers have significant ramifications for international communications. For example, research by Sims and Guice compared 214 letters of inquiry written by native and nonnative speakers of English to test the assumption that cultural factors affect business communication. Among other things, the researchers found that nonnative speakers used exaggerated politeness, provided unnecessary professional and personal information, and made inappropriate requests of the other party. Commenting on the results and implications of their study, the researchers noted that their investigation indicated that the deviations from standard U.S. business communication practices were not specific to one or more nationalities. The deviations did not occur among specific nationalities but were spread throughout the sample of nonnative letters used for the study. Therefore, we can speculate that U.S. native speakers of English might have similar difficulties in international settings. In other words, a significant number of native speakers in the U.S. might deviate from the standard business communication practices of other cultures. Therefore, these native speakers need specific training in the business communication practices of the major cultures of the world so they can communicate successfully and acceptably with readers in those cultures.[33]

Research by Scott and Green has extended these findings, showing that even in English-speaking countries, there are different approaches to writing letters. In the United States, for example, it is common practice when constructing a bad-news letter to start out "with a pleasant, relevant, neutral, and transitional buffer statement; give the reasons for the unfavorable news before presenting the bad news; present the refusal in a positive manner; imply the bad news whenever possible; explain how the refusal is in the reader's best interest; and suggest positive alternatives that build goodwill."[34] In Great Britain, however, it is common to start out by referring to the situation, discussing the reasons for the bad news, conveying the bad news (often quite bluntly), and concluding with an apology or statement of regret (something that is frowned on by business-letter experts in the United States) designed to keep the reader's goodwill. Here is an example:

> Lord Hanson has asked me to reply to your letter and questionnaire of February 12 which we received today.

> As you may imagine, we receive numerous requests to complete questionnaires or to participate in a survey, and this poses problems for us. You will appreciate that the time it would take to complete these requests would represent a full-time job, so we decided some while ago to decline such requests unless there was some obvious benefit to Hanson PLC and our stockholders. As I am sure you will understand, our prime responsibility is to look after our stockholders' interests.
>
> I apologize that this will not have been the response that you were hoping for, but I wish you success with your research study.[35]

U.S. MNC managers would seldom, if ever, send that type of letter; it would be viewed as blunt and tactless. However, the indirect approach that Americans use would be viewed by their British counterparts as overly indirect and obviously insincere.

On the other hand, when compared to Asians, many American writers are far more blunt and direct. For example, Park, Dillon, and Mitchell reported that there are pronounced differences between the ways in which Americans and Asians write business letters of complaint. They compared the approach used by American managers for whom English is a first language, who wrote international business letters of complaint, with the approach of Korean managers for whom English is a second language, who wrote the same types of letters. They found that American writers used a direct organizational pattern and tended to state the main idea or problem first before sharing explanatory details that clearly related to the stated problem. In contrast, the standard Korean pattern was indirect and tended to delay the reader's discovery of the main point. This led the researchers to conclude that the U.S.-generated letter might be regarded as rude by Asian readers, while American readers might regard the letter from the Korean writer as vague, emotional, and accusatory.[36]

感知障碍
Perceptual Barriers

perception
A person's view of reality.

Perception is a person's view of reality. How people see reality can vary and will influence their judgment and decision making.[37] Examples abound, of course, of how perceptions play an important role in international management. Japanese stockbrokers who perceived that the chances of improving their career would be better with U.S. firms have changed jobs. Hong Kong hoteliers bought U.S. properties because they had the perception that if they could offer the same top-quality hotel service as back home, they could dominate the U.S. markets. Unfortunately, misperceptions can become a barrier to effective communication and thus decision making. In international incidents such as this, perception is critical, and misperceptions may get out of hand. The following sections provide examples of perceptual barriers and their results in the international business arena.

广告信息

Advertising Messages One way that perception can prove to be a problem in international management communication is the very basic misunderstandings caused when one side uses words or symbols that simply are misinterpreted by others. Many firms have found to their dismay that a failure to understand home-country perceptions can result in disastrous advertising programs, for instance. Here are two examples:

> Ford . . . introduced a low cost truck, the "Fiera," into some Spanish-speaking countries. Unfortunately, the name meant "ugly old woman" in Spanish. Needless to say, this name did not encourage sales. Ford also experienced slow sales when it introduced a top-of-the-line automobile, the "Comet," in Mexico under the name "Caliente." The puzzling low sales were finally understood when Ford discovered that "caliente" is slang for a street walker.[38]

> One laundry detergent company certainly wishes now that it had contacted a few locals before it initiated its promotional campaign in the Middle East. All of the company's advertisements pictured soiled clothes on the left, its box of soap in the middle, and clean clothes on the right. But, because in that area of the world people tend to read from the right to the left, many potential customers interpreted the message to indicate the soap actually soiled the clothes.[39]

There have been countless other such advertising blunders. Some speak to the political context, such as when Mercedes-Benz introduced its Grand Sports Tourer, or Mercedes GST, in Canada. Canadians were not very impressed, since they used the letters GST to refer to Canadian socialism. Other times, the advertising is simply offensive. Bacardi, for example, advertised the fruity drink "Pavian" in Germany, believing that it was tres chic. "Pavian" to the German population, however, meant "baboon." Needless to say, sales did not exceed expectations. The food and beverage industry may have experienced the worst string of bloopers. The Coors slogan "Turn It Loose" dismayed the Spanish who thought it would cause intestinal problems. In China's Taiwan, Pepsi's "Come live with Pepsi" frightened consumers, since it literally meant "Pepsi will bring your ancestors back from the grave." Finally, even though Kentucky Fried Chicken is performing better in the Chinese market than in America, its catchphrase "Finger-licking good" was originally translated as "Eat your fingers off."[40]

Managers must be very careful when they translate messages. As mentioned, some common phrases in one country will not mean the same thing in others. Evidently from the many examples, errors in translation occur frequently, but MNCs can still come out on top with care and persistence, always remembering that perception may create new reality.

View of Others Perception influences how individuals "see" others. A good example is provided by the perception of foreigners who reside in the United States by Americans and the perception of Americans by the rest of the world. Most Americans see themselves as extremely friendly, outgoing, and kind, and they believe that others also see them in this way. At the same time, many are not aware of the negative impressions they give to others. This has become especially salient in light of Americans' reaction to September 11, 2001, and their conduct of the Iraq War, which have at times shaken the world view of the United States. It becomes a trying exercise to sort through truth and error in such circumstances.

An example in the business world where perception is all important and misperception may abound is the way in which people act, or should act, when initially meeting others. The International Management in Action feature, "Doing It Right the First Time," provides some insight regarding how to conduct oneself when doing business in Japan.

Perceptions of others obviously may play a major role in the context of international management in the effects of the ways that international managers perceive their subordinates and their peers. For example, a study examined the perceptions that German and U.S. managers had of the qualifications of their peers (those on the same level and status), managers, and subordinates in Europe and Latin America.[41] The findings showed that both the German and the U.S. respondents perceived their subordinates to be less qualified than their peers. However, although the Germans perceived their managers to have more managerial ability than their peers, the Americans felt that their South American peers in many instances had qualifications equal to or better than the qualifications of their own managers. Quite obviously, these perceptions will affect how German and U.S. expatriates communicate with their South American and other peers and subordinates, as well as how the expatriates communicate with their bosses.

Another study found that Western managers have more favorable attitudes toward women as managers than do Asian or Saudi managers.[42] Japanese managers, according to one survey, also still regard women as superfluous to the effective running of their organizations and generally continue to not treat women as equals.[43] Such perceptions obviously affect the way these managers interact and communicate with their female counterparts.

International Management in Action

Doing It Right the First Time

Like other countries of the world, Japan has its own business customs and culture. And when someone fails to adhere to tradition, the individual runs the risk of being perceived as ineffective or uncaring. The following addresses three areas that are important in being correctly perceived by one's Japanese counterparts.

Business Cards

The exchange of business cards is an integral part of Japanese business etiquette, and Japanese businesspeople exchange these cards when meeting someone for the first time. Additionally, those who are most likely to interface with non-Japanese are supplied with business cards printed in Japanese on one side and a foreign language, usually English, on the reverse side. This is aimed at enhancing recognition and pronunciation of Japanese names, which are often unfamiliar to foreign businesspeople. Conversely, it is advisable for foreign businesspeople to carry and exchange with their Japanese counterparts a similar type of card printed in Japanese and in their native language. These cards can often be obtained through business centers in major hotels.

When receiving a card, it is considered common courtesy to offer one in return. In fact, not returning a card might convey the impression that the manager is not committed to a meaningful business relationship in the future.

Business cards should be presented and received with both hands. When presenting one's card, the presenter's name should be facing the person who is receiving the card so the receiver can easily read it. When receiving a business card, it should be handled with care, and if the receiver is sitting at a conference or other type of table, the card should be placed in front of the individual for the duration of the meeting. It is considered rude to put a prospective business partner's card in one's pocket before sitting down to discuss business matters.

Bowing

Although the handshake is increasingly common in Japan, bowing remains the most prevalent formal method of greeting, saying goodbye, expressing gratitude, or apologizing to another person. When meeting foreign businesspeople, however, Japanese will often use the handshake or a combination of both a handshake and a bow, even though there are different forms and styles of bowing, depending on the relationship of the parties involved. Foreign businesspeople are not expected to be familiar with these intricacies, and therefore a deep nod of the head or a slight bow will suffice in most cases. Many foreign businesspeople are unsure whether to use a handshake or to bow. In these situations, it is best to wait and see if one's Japanese counterpart offers a hand or prefers to bow and then to follow suit.

Attire

Most Japanese businessmen dress in conservative dark or navy blue suits, although slight variations in style and color have come to be accepted in recent years. As a general rule, what is acceptable business attire in virtually any industrialized country is usually regarded as good business attire in Japan as well. Although there is no need to conform precisely to the style of dress of the Japanese, good judgment should be exercised when selecting attire for a business meeting. If unsure about what constitutes appropriate attire for a particular situation, it is best to err on the conservative side.

文化的影响
The Impact of Culture

Besides language and perception, another major barrier to communication is culture, a topic that was given detailed attention in Chapter 1. Culture can affect communication in a number of ways, and one way is through the impact of cultural values.

文化价值观

Cultural Values One expert on Middle Eastern countries notes that people there do not relate to and communicate with each other in a loose, general way as do those in the United States. Relationships are more intense and binding in the Middle East, and a wide variety of work-related values influence what people in the Middle East will and will not do.

In North American society, the generally professed prevalent pattern is one of nonclass-consciousness, as far as work is concerned. Students, for example, make extra pocket money by taking all sorts of part-time jobs—manual and otherwise—regardless of the socioeconomic stratum to which the individual belongs. The attitude is uninhibited. In the Middle East, the overruling obsession is how the money is made and via what kind of job.[44]

Table 4–5
U.S. Proverbs Representing Cultural Values

Proverb	Cultural Value
A penny saved is a penny earned.	Thriftiness
Time is money.	Time thriftiness
Don't cry over spilt milk.	Practicality
Waste not, want not.	Frugality
Early to bed, early to rise, makes one healthy, wealthy, and wise.	Diligence; work ethic
A stitch in time saves nine.	Timeliness of action
If at first you don't succeed, try, try again.	Persistence; work ethic
Take care of today, and tomorrow will take care of itself.	Preparation for future

Source: Adapted from Nancy J. Adler (with Allison Gunderson), *International Dimensions of Organizational Behavior,* 5th ed. (Mason, OH: South-Western, 2008), p. 84.

These types of values indirectly, and in many cases directly, affect communication between people from different cultures. For example, one would communicate differently with a "rich college student" from the United States than with one from Saudi Arabia. Similarly, when negotiating with managers from other cultures, knowing the way to handle the deal requires an understanding of cultural values.[45]

Another cultural value is the way that people use time. In the United States, people believe that time is an asset and is not to be wasted. This is an idea that has limited meaning in some other cultures. Various values are reinforced and reflected in proverbs that Americans are taught from an early age. These proverbs help to guide people's behavior. Table 4–5 lists some examples.

Misinterpretation Cultural differences can cause misinterpretations both in how others see expatriate managers and in how the latter see themselves. For example, U.S. managers doing business in Austria often misinterpret the fact that local businesspeople always address them in formal terms. They may view this as meaning that they are not friends or are not liked, but in fact, this formal behavior is the way that Austrians always conduct business. The informal, first-name approach used in the United States is not the style of the Austrians.

Culture even affects day-to-day activities of corporate communications.[46] For example, when sending messages to international clients, American managers have to keep in mind that there are many things that are uniquely American and overseas managers may not be aware of them. As an example, daylight savings time is known to all Americans, but many Asian managers have no idea what the term means. Similarly, it is common for American managers to address memos to their "international office" without realizing that the managers who work in this office regard the American location as the "international" one! Other suggestions that can be of value to American managers who are engaged in international communications include:

- Be careful not to use generalized statements about benefits, compensation, pay cycles, holidays, or policies in your worldwide communications. Work hours, vacation accrual, general business practices, and human resource issues vary widely from country to country.
- Since most of the world uses the metric system, be sure to include converted weights and measures in all internal and external communications.
- Keep in mind that even in English-speaking countries, words may have different meanings. Not everyone knows what is meant by "counterclockwise," or "quite good."

- Remember that letterhead and paper sizes differ worldwide. The 8½ × 11 inch page is a U.S. standard, but most countries use an A4 (8¼ × 11½ inch) size for their letterhead, with envelopes to match.
- Dollars are not unique to the United States. There are Australian, Bermudian, Canadian, Hong Kong and New Zealand dollars, among others.
  So when referring to American dollars, it is important to use "US$."

Many Americans also have difficulty interpreting the effect of national values on work behavior. For example, why do French and German workers drink alcoholic beverages at lunchtime? Why are many European workers unwilling to work the night shift? Why do overseas affiliates contribute to the support of the employees' work council or donate money to the support of kindergarten teachers in local schools? These types of actions are viewed by some people as wasteful, but those who know the culture of these countries realize that such actions promote the long-run good of the company. It is the outsider who is misinterpreting why these culturally specific actions are happening, and such misperceptions can become a barrier to effective communication.

非语言沟通
Nonverbal Communication

Another major source of communication and perception problems is **nonverbal communication**, which is the transfer of meaning through means such as body language and use of physical space. Table 4–6 summarizes a number of dimensions of nonverbal communication. The general categories that are especially important to communication in international management are kinesics, proxemics, chronemics, and chromatics.

身体语言学

Kinesics **Kinesics** is the study of communication through body movement and facial expression. Primary areas of concern include eye contact, posture, and gestures. For example, when one communicates verbally with someone in the United States, it is good manners to look the other person in the eye. This area of communicating through the use of eye contact and gaze is known as **oculesics**. In some areas of the world oculesics is an important

nonverbal communication
The transfer of meaning through means such as body language and the use of physical space.

kinesics
The study of communication through body movement and facial expression.

oculesics
The area of communication that deals with conveying messages through the use of eye contact and gaze.

Table 4–6
Common Forms of Nonverbal Communication

1. Hand gestures, both intended and self-directed (autistic), such as the nervous rubbing of hands.
2. Facial expressions, such as smiles, frowns, and yawns.
3. Posture and stance.
4. Clothing and hair styles (hair being more like clothes than like skin, both subject to the fashion of the day).
5. Interpersonal distance (proxemics).
6. Eye contact and direction of gaze, particularly in "listening behavior."
7. "Artifacts" and nonverbal symbols, such as lapel pins, walking sticks, and jewelry.
8. Paralanguage (though often in language, just as often treated as part of nonverbal behavior—speech rate, pitch, inflections, volume).
9. Taste, including symbolism of food and the communication function of chatting over coffee or tea, and oral gratification such as smoking or gum chewing.
10. Cosmetics: temporary—powder; permanent—tattoos.
11. Time symbolism: when is too late or too early to telephone or visit a friend, or what is too long or too short to make a speech or stay for dinner.
12. Timing and pauses within verbal behavior.

Source: From John C. Condon and Fathi S. Yousef, *An Introduction to Intercultural Communication,* 1st Edition. Published by Allyn and Bacon, Boston, MA. Copyright © 1975 by Pearson Education. Reprinted by permission of the publisher.

consideration because of what people should not do, such as stare at others or maintain continuous eye contact, because it is considered impolite to do these things.

Another area of kinesics is posture, which can also cause problems. For example, when Americans are engaged in prolonged negotiations or meetings, it is not uncommon for them to relax and put their feet up on a chair or desk, but this is insulting behavior in the Middle East. Here is an example from a classroom situation:

> In the midst of a discussion of a poem in the sophomore class of the English Department, the professor, who was British, took up the argument, started to explain the subtleties of the poem, and was carried away by the situation. He leaned back in his chair, put his feet up on the desk, and went on with the explanation. The class was furious. Before the end of the day, a demonstration by the University's full student body had taken place. Petitions were submitted to the deans of the various facilities. The next day, the situation even made the newspaper headlines. The consequences of the act, that was innocently done, might seem ridiculous, funny, baffling, incomprehensible, or even incredible to a stranger. Yet, to the native, the students' behavior was logical and in context. The students and their supporters were outraged because of the implications of the breach of the native behavioral pattern. In the Middle East, it is extremely insulting to have to sit facing two soles of the shoes of somebody.[47]

haptics
Communicating through the use of bodily contact.

Gestures are also widely used and take many different forms. For example, Canadians shake hands, Japanese bow, and Middle Easterners of the same sex kiss on the cheek. Communicating through the use of bodily contact is known as **haptics**, and it is a widely used form of nonverbal communication.

Sometimes gestures present problems for expatriate managers because these behaviors have different meanings depending on the country. For example, in the United States, putting the thumb and index finger together to form an "O" is the sign for "okay." In Japan, this is the sign for money; in southern France, the gesture means "zero" or "worthless"; and in Brazil, it is regarded as a vulgar or obscene sign. In France and Belgium, snapping the fingers of both hands is considered vulgar; in Brazil, this gesture is used to indicate that something has been done for a long time. In Britain, the "V for victory" sign is given with the palm facing out; if the palm is facing in, this roughly means "shove it"; in non-British countries, the gesture means two of something and often is used when placing an order at a restaurant.[48] Gibson, Hodgetts, and Blackwell found that many foreign students attending school in the United States have trouble communicating because they are unable to interpret some of the most common nonverbal gestures.[49] A survey group of 44 Jamaican, Venezuelan, Colombian, Peruvian, Thai, Indian, and Japanese students at two major universities were given pictures of 20 universal cultural gestures, and each was asked to describe the nonverbal gestures illustrated. In 56 percent of the choices the respondents either gave an interpretation that was markedly different from that of Americans or reported that the nonverbal gesture had no meaning in their culture. These findings help to reinforce the need to teach expatriates about local nonverbal communication.

proxemics
The study of the way people use physical space to convey messages.

intimate distance
Distance between people that is used for very confidential communications.

personal distance
In communicating, the physical distance used for talking with family and close friends.

social distance
In communicating, the distance used to handle most business transactions.

public distance
In communicating, the distance used when calling across the room or giving a talk to a group.

人际距离学

Proxemics **Proxemics** is the study of the way that people use physical space to convey messages. For example, in the United States, there are four "distances" people use in communicating on a face-to-face basis (see Figure 4–3). **Intimate distance** is used for very confidential communications. **Personal distance** is used for talking with family and close friends. **Social distance** is used to handle most business transactions. **Public distance** is used when calling across the room or giving a talk to a group.

One major problem for Americans communicating with people from the Middle East or South America is that the intimate or personal distance zones are violated. Americans often tend to be moving away in interpersonal communication with their Middle Eastern or Latin counterparts, while the latter are trying to physically close the gap. The American cannot understand why the other is standing so close; the latter cannot understand why the American is being so reserved and standing so far away. The result is a breakdown in communication.

Office layout is another good example of proxemics. In the United States, the more important the manager, the larger the office, and often a secretary screens visitors and

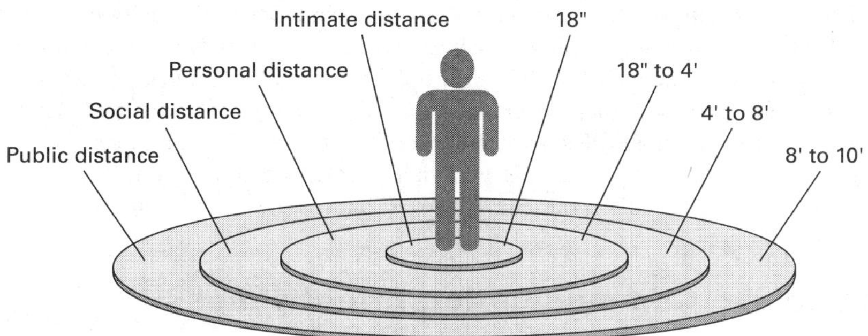

Figure 4–3
Personal Space Categories for Those in the United States

Source: Adapted from Richard M. Hodgetts and Donald F. Kuratko, *Management,* 2nd ed. (San Diego, CA: Harcourt Brace Jovanovich, 1991), p. 384.

keeps away those whom the manager does not wish to see. In Japan, most managers do not have large offices, and even if they do, they spend a great deal of time out of the office and with the employees. Thus, the Japanese have no trouble communicating directly with their superiors. A Japanese manager staying in his office would be viewed as a sign of distrust or anger toward the group.

Another way that office proxemics can affect communication is that in many European companies, no wall separates the space allocated to the senior-level manager from that of the subordinates. Everyone works in the same large room. These working conditions often are disconcerting to Americans, who tend to prefer more privacy.

语言时位学

Chronemics **Chronemics** refers to the way in which time is used in a culture. When examined in terms of extremes, there are two types of time schedules: *monochronic* and *polychronic*. A **monochronic time schedule** is one in which things are done in a linear fashion. A manager will address Issue A first and then move on to Issue B. In individualistic cultures such as the United States, Great Britain, Canada, and Australia, as well as many of the cultures in Northern Europe, managers adhere to monochronic time schedules. In these societies, time schedules are very important, and time is viewed as something that can be controlled and should be used wisely.

chronemics
The way in which time is used in a culture.

monochronic time schedule
A time schedule in which things are done in a linear fashion.

polychronic time schedule
A time schedule in which people tend to do several things at the same time and place higher value on personal involvement than on getting things done on time.

This is in sharp contrast to **polychronic time schedules**, which are characterized by people tending to do several things at the same time and placing higher value on personal involvement than on getting things done on time. In these cultures, schedules are subordinated to personal relationships. Regions of the world where polychronic time schedules are common include Latin America and the Middle East.

When doing business in countries that adhere to monochronic time schedules, it is important to be on time for meetings. Additionally, these meetings typically end at the appointed time so that participants can be on time for their next meeting. When doing business in countries that adhere to polychronic time schedules, it is common to find business meetings starting late and finishing late.

色彩学

Chromatics **Chromatics** is the use of color to communicate messages. Every society uses chromatics, but in different ways. Colors that mean one thing in the United States may mean something entirely different in Asia. For example, in the United States it is common to wear black when one is in mourning, while in some locations in India people wear white when they are in mourning. In Chinese Hong Kong red is used to signify happiness or luck and traditional bridal dresses are red; in the United States it is common for the bride to wear white. In many Asian countries shampoos are dark in color because users want the soap to be the same color as their hair and believe that if it were a light color, it would remove color from their hair. In the United States shampoos tend to be light in color because people see this as a sign of cleanliness and hygiene. In Chile a gift of yellow roses conveys the message "I don't like you," but in the United States it says quite the opposite.

chromatics
The use of color to communicate messages.

Knowing the importance and the specifics of chromatics in a culture can be very helpful because, among other things, such knowledge can help you avoid embarrassing situations. A good example is the American manager in Peru who, upon finishing a one-week visit to the Lima subsidiary, decided to thank the assistant who was assigned to him. He sent her a dozen red roses. The lady understood the faux pas, but the American manager was somewhat embarrassed when his Peruvian counterpart smilingly told him, "It was really nice of you to buy her a present. However, red roses indicate a romantic interest!"

达到有效沟通
Achieving Communication Effectiveness

A number of steps can be taken to improve communication effectiveness in the international arena. These include improving feedback systems, providing language and cultural training, and increasing flexibility and cooperation.

改善反馈系统
Improve Feedback Systems

One of the most important ways of improving communication effectiveness in the international context is to open up feedback systems. Feedback is particularly important between parent companies and their affiliates. There are two basic types of feedback systems: personal (e.g., face-to-face meetings, telephone conversations, and personalized e-mail) and impersonal (e.g., reports, budgets, and plans). Both systems help affiliates keep their home office aware of progress and, in turn, help the home office monitor and control affiliate performance as well as set goals and standards.

At present, there seem to be varying degrees of feedback between the home offices of MNCs and their affiliates. For example, one study evaluated the communication feedback between subsidiaries and home offices of 63 MNCs headquartered in Europe, Japan, and North America.[50] A marked difference was found between the way that U.S. companies communicated with their subsidiaries and the way that European and Japanese firms did. Over one-half of the U.S. subsidiaries responded that they received monthly feedback from their parent companies, in contrast to less than 10 percent for the subsidiaries of European and Japanese firms. In addition, the Americans were much more inclined to hold regular management meetings on a regional or worldwide basis. Seventy-five percent of the U.S. companies had annual meetings for their affiliate top managers, compared with less than 50 percent for the Europeans and Japanese. These findings may help explain why many international subsidiaries and affiliates are not operating as efficiently as they should. The units may not have sufficient contact with the home office. They do not seem to be getting continuous assistance and feedback that are critical to effective communication.

提供语言培训
Provide Language Training

Besides improving feedback systems, another way to make communication more effective in the international arena is through language training. Many host-country managers cannot communicate well with their counterparts at headquarters. Because English has become the international language of business, those who are not native speakers of English should learn the language well enough so that face-to-face and telephone conversations and e-mail are possible. If the language of the home office is not English, this other language also should be learned. As a U.S. manager working for a Japanese MNC recently told one of the authors, "The official international language of this company is English. However, whenever the home-office people show up, they tend to cluster together with their countrymen and speak Japanese. That's why I'm trying to learn Japanese. Let's face it. They say all you need to know is English, but if you want to really know what's going on, you have to talk their language."

Written communication also is extremely important in achieving effectiveness. As noted earlier, when reports, letters, and e-mail messages are translated from one language to another, preventing a loss of meaning is virtually impossible. Moreover, if the communications are not written properly, they may not be given the attention they deserve. The reader will allow poor grammar and syntax to influence his or her interpretation and subsequent actions. Moreover, if readers cannot communicate in the language of those who will be receiving their comments or questions about the report, their messages also must be translated and likely will further lose meaning. Therefore, the process can continue on and on, each party failing to achieve full communication with the other. Hildebrandt has described the problems in this two-way process when an employee in a foreign subsidiary writes a report and then sends it to his or her boss for forwarding to the home office:

> The general manager or vice president cannot be asked to be an editor. Yet they often send statements along, knowingly, which are poorly written, grammatically imperfect, or generally unclear. The time pressures do not permit otherwise. Predictably, questions are issued from the States to the subsidiary and the complicated bilingual process now goes in reverse, ultimately reaching the original . . . staff member, who receives the English questions retranslated.[51]

Language training would help to alleviate such complicated communication problems.

提供文化培训
Provide Cultural Training

It is very difficult to communicate effectively with someone from another culture unless at least one party has some understanding of the other's culture.[52] Otherwise, communication likely will break down. This is particularly important for multinational companies that have operations throughout the world.[53] Although there always are important differences between countries, and even between subcultures of the same country, firms that operate in South America find that the cultures of these countries have certain commonalities. These common factors also apply to Spain and Portugal. Therefore, a basic understanding of Latin cultures can prove to be useful throughout a large region of the world. The same is true of Anglo cultures, where norms and values tend to be somewhat similar from one country to another. When a multinational has operations in South America, Europe, and Asia, however, multicultural training becomes necessary. The International Management in Action on the following page, "Communicating in Europe," provides some specific examples of cultural differences.

As Chapter 4 pointed out, it is erroneous to generalize about an "international" culture, because the various nations and regions of the globe are so different. Training must be conducted on a regional or country-specific basis. Failure to do so can result in continuous communication breakdown.[54] Many corporations are investing in programs to help train their executives in international communication. Such training has become more common since it began in the 1970s as many Americans returned from the Peace Corps with increased awareness of cultural differences. And this training is not limited to those who travel themselves but is increasingly important for employees who frequently interact with individuals from other cultures in their workplace or in their communication.

"Whether a multinational or a start-up business out of a garage, everybody is global these days," said Dean Foster, president of Dean Foster Associates, an intercultural consultancy in New York. "In today's economy, there is no room for failure. Companies have to understand the culture they are working in from Day 1." Mr. Foster recounted how an American businessman recently gave four antique clocks wrapped in white paper to a prospective client in China. What the man did not realize, he said, was that the words in Mandarin for clock and the number four are similar to the word for death, and white is a funeral color in many Asian countries. "The symbolism was so powerful," Mr. Foster said that the man lost the deal.[55]

加强灵活性和合作
Increase Flexibility and Cooperation

Effective international communications require increased flexibility and cooperation by all parties.[56] To improve understanding and cooperation, each party must be prepared to give a little.[57] Take the case of International Computers Ltd., a mainframe computer firm

Communicating in Europe

In Europe, many countries are within easy commuting distance of their neighbors, so an expatriate who does business in France on Monday may be in Germany on Tuesday, Great Britain on Wednesday, Italy on Thursday, and Spain on Friday. Each country has its own etiquette regarding how to greet others and conduct oneself during social and business meetings. The following sections examine some of the things that expatriate managers need to know to communicate effectively.

France

When one is meeting with businesspeople in France, promptness is expected, although tardiness of 5 to 10 minutes is not considered a major gaffe. The French prefer to shake hands when introduced, and it is correct to address them by title plus last name. When the meeting is over, a handshake again is proper manners.

French executives try to keep their personal and professional lives separate. As a result, most business entertaining is done at restaurants or clubs. When gifts are given to business associates, they should appeal to intellectual or aesthetic pursuits as opposed to being something that one's company produces for sale on the world market. In conversational discussions, topics such as politics and money should be avoided. Also, humor should be used carefully during business meetings.

Germany

German executives like to be greeted by their title, and one should never refer to someone on a first-name basis unless invited to do so. When introducing yourself, do not use a title, just state your last name. Business appointments should be made well in advance, and punctuality is important. Like the French, the Germans usually do not entertain clients at home, so an invitation to a German manager's home is a special privilege and always should be followed with a thank-you note. Additionally, as is the case in France, one should avoid using humor during business meetings. They are very serious when it comes to business, so be as prepared as possible and keep light-hearted banter to the German hosts' discretion.

Great Britain

In Britain, it is common to shake hands on the first meeting, and to be polite one should use last names and appropriate titles when addressing the host, until invited to use their first name. Punctuality again is important to the British, so be prepared to be on time and get down to business fairly quickly. The British are quite warm, though, and an invitation to a British home is more likely than in most areas of Europe. You should always bring a gift if invited to the host's house; flowers, chocolates, or books are acceptable.

During business meetings, suits and ties are common dress; however, striped ties should be avoided if they appear to be a copy of those worn by alumni of British universities and schools or by members of military or social clubs. Additionally, during social gatherings it is a good idea not to discuss politics, religion, or gossip about the monarchy unless the British person brings the topic up first.

Italy

In traditional companies, executives are referred to by title plus last name. It is common to shake hands when being introduced, and if the individual is a university graduate, the professional title *dottore* should be used.

Business appointments should be made well in advance, and if you expect to be late, call the host and explain the situation. In most cases, business is done at the office, and when someone is invited to a restaurant, this invitation is usually done to socialize and not to continue business discussions. If an expatriate is invited to an Italian home, it is common to bring a gift for the host, such as a bottle of wine or a box of chocolates. Flowers are also acceptable, but be sure to send an uneven number and avoid chrysanthemums, a symbol of death, and red roses, a sign of deep passion. Be sure to offer high-quality gifts with the wrapping done well, as the Italians are very generous when it comes to gifts. It is not a common practice to exchange them during business, but it is recommended that you are prepared. During the dinner conversation, there is a wide variety of acceptable topics, including business, family matters, and soccer.

Spain

It is common to use first names when introducing or talking to people in Spain, and close friends typically greet each other with an embrace. Appointments should be made in advance, but punctuality is not essential.

If one is invited to the home of a Spanish executive, flowers or chocolates for the host are acceptable gifts. If the invitation includes dinner, any business discussions should be delayed until after coffee is served. During the social gathering, some topics that should be avoided include religion, family, and work. Additionally, humor rarely is used during formal occasions.

that does a great deal of business in Japan. This firm urges its people to strive for successful collaboration in their international partnerships and ventures. At the heart of this process is effective communication. As Kenichi Ohmae put it:

> We must recognize and accept the inescapable subtleties and difficulties of intercompany relationships. This is the essential starting point. Then we must focus not on contractual or equity-related issues but on the quality of the people at the interface between organizations. Finally, we must understand that success requires frequent, rapport-building meetings by at least three organizational levels: top management, staff, and line management at the working level.[58]

管理跨文化谈判
Managing Cross-Cultural Negotiations

Closely related to communications but deserving special attention is managing negotiations.[59] **Negotiation** is the process of bargaining with one or more parties to arrive at a solution that is acceptable to all. It has been estimated that managers can spend 50 percent or more of their time on negotiation processes.[60] Therefore, it is a learnable skill that is imperative not only for the international manager but for the domestic manager as well, since more and more domestic businesses are operating in multicultural environments (see Chapter 3). Negotiation often follows assessing political environments and is a natural approach to conflict management. Often, the MNC must negotiate with the host country to secure the best possible arrangements. The MNC and the host country will discuss the investment the MNC is prepared to make in return for certain guarantees or concessions. The initial range of topics typically includes critical areas such as hiring practices, direct financial investment, taxes, and ownership control. Negotiation also is used in creating joint ventures with local firms and in getting the operation off the ground. After the firm is operating, additional areas of negotiation include expansion of facilities, use of more local managers, additional imports or exports of materials and finished goods, and recapture of profits.

> **negotiation**
> Bargaining with one or more parties for the purpose of arriving at a solution acceptable to all.

On a more macro level of international trade are the negotiations conducted between countries. The current balance-of-trade problem between the United States and China is one example. The massive debt problems of less developed countries and the opening of trade with Eastern European and newly emerging economies are other current examples.

谈判的类型
Types of Negotiation

People enter into negotiations for a multitude of reasons, but the nature of the goal determines what kind of negotiation will take place. There are two types of negotiations that we will discuss here: distributive and integrative negotiation. **Distributive negotiations** occur when two parties with opposing goals compete over a set value.[61] Consider a person who passes a street vendor and sees an item he likes but considers the price, or set value, a bit steep. The goal of the buyer is to procure the item at the lowest price, getting more value for his money, while the goal of the seller is to collect as much as possible to maximize profits. Both are trying to get the best deal, but what translates into a gain by one side is usually experienced as a loss by the other, otherwise known as a win-lose situation. The relationship is focused on the individual and based on a short-term interaction. More often than not, the people involved are not friends, or at least their personal relationship is put aside in the matter. Information also plays an important role, since you do not want to expose too much and be vulnerable to counterattack.

> **distributive negotiations**
> Bargaining that occurs when two parties with opposing goals compete over a set value.

Research has shown that first offers in a negotiation can be good predictors of outcomes, which is why it is important to have a strong initial offer.[62] This does not imply that overly greedy or aggressive behavior is acceptable; this could be off-putting to the other negotiator, causing her or him to walk away. In addition to limiting the amount of information you disclose, it can be advantageous to know a little about the other side.

Table 4–7
Negotiation Types and Characteristics

Characteristic	Distributive Negotiations	Integrative Negotiations
Objective	Claim maximum value	Create and claim value
Motivation	Individual-selfish benefit	Group-cooperative benefit
Interests	Divergent	Overlapping
Relationship	Short term	Long term
Outcome	Win-lose	Win-win

Source: Adapted from *Harvard Business Essentials: Negotiation* (Boston: Harvard Business School Press, 2003), pp. 2–6.

integrative negotiation
Bargaining that involves cooperation between two groups to integrate interests, create value, and invest in the agreement.

Integrative negotiation involves cooperation between the two groups to integrate interests, create value, and invest in the agreement. Both groups work toward maximizing benefits for both sides and distributing those benefits. This method is sometimes called the win-win scenario, which does not mean that everyone receives exactly what they wish for, but instead that the compromise allows both sides to keep what is most important and still gain on the deal. The relationship in this instance tends to be more long term, since both sides take time to really get to know the other side and what motivates them. The focus is on the group, reaching for a best-case outcome where everyone benefits. This is the most useful tactic when dealing with business negotiation, so from this point on, we assume the integrative approach. Table 4–7 provides a summary of the two types of negotiation.

谈判过程
The Negotiation Process

Several basic steps can be used to manage the negotiation process. Regardless of the issues or personalities of the parties involved, this process typically begins with planning.

计划

Planning Planning starts with the negotiators identifying the objectives they would like to attain. Then they explore the possible options for reaching these objectives. Research shows that the greater the number of options, the greater the chances for successful negotiations. While this appears to be an obvious statement, research also reveals that many negotiators do not alter their strategy when negotiating across cultures.[63] Next, consideration is given to areas of common ground between the parties. Other major areas include (1) the setting of limits on single-point objectives, such as deciding to pay no more than $10 million for the factory and $3 million for the land; (2) dividing issues into short- and long-term considerations and deciding how to handle each; and (3) determining the sequence in which to discuss the various issues.

建立人际关系

Interpersonal Relationship Building The second phase of the negotiation process involves getting to know the people on the other side. This "feeling out" period is characterized by the desire to identify those who are reasonable and those who are not. In contrast to negotiators in many other countries, those in the United States often give little attention to this phase; they want to get down to business immediately, which often is an ineffective approach. Adler notes:

> Effective negotiators view luncheon, dinner, reception, ceremony, and tour invitations as times for interpersonal relationship building and therefore as key to the negotiating process. When American negotiators, often frustrated by the seemingly endless formalities, ceremonies, and "small talk," ask how long they must wait before beginning to "do business," the answer is simple: wait until your counterparts bring up business (and they will). Realize that the work of conducting a successful negotiation has already begun, even if business has yet to be mentioned.[64]

交流与任务相关的信息

Exchanging Task-Related Information In this part of the negotiation process, each group sets forth its position on the critical issues. These positions often will change later in the negotiations. At this point, the participants are trying to find out what the other party wants to attain and what it is willing to give up.

说服

Persuasion This step of negotiations is considered by many to be the most important. No side wants to give away more than it has to, but each knows that without giving some concessions, it is unlikely to reach a final agreement. The success of the persuasion step often depends on (1) how well the parties understand each other's position; (2) the ability of each to identify areas of similarity and difference; (3) the ability to create new options; and (4) the willingness to work toward a solution that allows all parties to walk away feeling they have achieved their objectives.

同意

Agreement The final phase of negotiations is the granting of concessions and hammering out a final agreement. Sometimes, this phase is carried out piecemeal, and concessions and agreements are made on issues one at a time. This is the way negotiators from the United States like to operate. As each issue is resolved, it is removed from the bargaining table, and interest is focused on the next. Asians and Russians, on the other hand, tend to negotiate a final agreement on everything, and few concessions are given until the end.

Once again, as in all areas of communication, to negotiate effectively in the international arena, it is necessary to understand how cultural differences between the parties affect the process.

文化差异影响谈判
Cultural Differences Affecting Negotiations

In international negotiations, participants tend to orient their approach and interests around their home culture and their group's needs and aspirations. This is natural. Yet, to negotiate effectively, it is important to have a sound understanding of the other side's culture and position to better empathize and understand what they are about.[65] The cultural aspects managers should consider include communication patterns, time orientation, and social behaviors.[66] A number of useful steps can help in this process of understanding. One negotiation expert recommends the following:

1. Do not identify the counterpart's home culture too quickly. Common cues (e.g., name, physical appearance, language, accent, location) may be unreliable. The counterpart probably belongs to more than one culture.
2. Beware of the Western bias toward "doing." In Arab, Asian, and Latin groups, ways of being (e.g., comportment, smell), feeling, thinking, and talking can shape relationships more powerfully than doing.
3. Try to counteract the tendency to formulate simple, consistent, stable images.
4. Do not assume that all aspects of the culture are equally significant. In Japan, consulting all relevant parties to a decision is more important than presenting a gift.
5. Recognize that norms for interactions involving outsiders may differ from those for interactions between compatriots.
6. Do not overestimate your familiarity with your counterpart's culture. An American studying Japanese wrote New Year's wishes to Japanese contacts in basic Japanese characters but omitted one character. As a result, the message became "Dead man, congratulations."[67]

Other useful examples have been offered by Trompenaars and Hampden-Turner, who note that a society's culture often plays a major role in determining the effectiveness of a negotiating approach. This is particularly true when the negotiating groups come from decidedly different cultures such as an ascription society and an achievement society.

As noted in Chapter 1, in an ascription society status is attributed based on birth, kinship, gender, age, and personal connections. In an achievement society, status is determined by accomplishments. As a result, each side's cultural perceptions can affect the outcome of the negotiation. Here is an example:

> Sending whiz-kids to deal with people 10–20 years their senior often insults the ascriptive culture. The reaction may be: "Do these people think that they have reached our own level of experience in half the time? That a 30-year-old American is good enough to negotiate with a 50-year-old Greek or Italian?" Achievement cultures must understand that some ascriptive cultures, the Japanese especially, spend much on training and in-house education to ensure that older people actually are wiser for the years they have spent in the corporation and for the sheer number of subordinates briefing them. It insults an ascriptive culture to do anything which prevents the self-fulfilling nature of its beliefs. Older people are held to be important so that they will be nourished and sustained by others' respect. A stranger is expected to facilitate this scheme, not challenge it.[68]

U.S. negotiators have a style that often differs from that of negotiators in many other countries. Americans believe it is important to be factual and objective. In addition, they often make early concessions to show the other party that they are flexible and reasonable. Moreover, U.S. negotiators typically have authority to bind their party to an agreement, so if the right deal is struck, the matter can be resolved quickly. This is why deadlines are so important to Americans. They have come to do business, and they want to get things resolved immediately.

A comparative example would be the Arabs, who in contrast to Americans, with their logical approach, tend to use an emotional appeal in their negotiation style. They analyze things subjectively and treat deadlines as only general guidelines for wrapping up negotiations. They tend to open negotiations with an extreme initial position. However, the Arabs believe strongly in making concessions, do so throughout the bargaining process, and almost always reciprocate an opponent's concessions. They also seek to build a long-term relationship with their bargaining partners. For these reasons, Americans typically find it easier to negotiate with Arabs than with representatives from many other regions of the world.

Another interesting comparative example is provided by the Chinese. In initial negotiation meetings, it is common for Chinese negotiators to seek agreement on the general focus of the meetings. The hammering out of specific details is postponed for later get-togethers. By achieving agreement on the general framework within which the negotiations will be conducted, the Chinese seek to limit and focus the discussions. Many Westerners misunderstand what is happening during these initial meetings and believe the dialogue consists mostly of rhetoric and general conversation. They are wrong and quite often are surprised later on when the Chinese negotiators use the agreement on the framework and principles as a basis for getting agreement on goals—and then insist that all discussions on concrete arrangements be in accord with these agreed-upon goals. Simply put, what is viewed as general conversation by many Western negotiators is regarded by the Chinese as a formulation of the rules of the game that must be adhered to throughout the negotiations. So in negotiating with the Chinese, it is important to come prepared to ensure that one's own agenda, framework, and principles are accepted by both parties.

Before beginning any negotiations, negotiators should review the negotiating style of the other parties. (Table 4–8 provides some insights regarding negotiation styles of the Americans, Japanese, Arabs, and Mexicans.) This review should help to answer certain questions: What can we expect the other side to say and do? How are they likely to respond to certain offers? When should the most important matters be introduced? How quickly should concessions be made, and what type of reciprocity should be expected? These types of questions help effectively prepare the negotiators. In addition, the team will work on formulating negotiation tactics. The International Management in Action on page 228, "Negotiating with the Japanese," demonstrates such tactics, and the following discussion gets into some of the specifics.

Table 4–8
Negotiation Styles from a Cross-Cultural Perspective

Element	United States	Japanese	Arabians	Mexicans
Group composition	Marketing oriented	Function oriented	Committee of specialists	Friendship oriented
Number involved	2–3	4–7	4–6	2–3
Space orientation	Confrontational; competitive	Display harmonious relationship	Status	Close, friendly
Establishing rapport	Short period; direct to task	Longer period; until harmony	Long period; until trusted	Longer period; discuss family
Exchange of information	Documented; step by step; multimedia	Extensive; concentrate on receiving side	Less emphasis on technology, more on relationship	Less emphasis on technology, more on relationship
Persuasion tools	Time pressure; loss of saving/making money	Maintain relationship references; intergroup connections	Go-between; hospitality	Emphasis on family and on social concerns; goodwill measured in generations
Use of language	Open, direct, sense of urgency	Indirect, appreciative, cooperative	Flattery, emotional, religious	Respectful, gracious
First offer	Fair ±5 to 10%	±10 to 20%	±20 to 50%	Fair
Second offer	Add to package; sweeten the deal	−5%	−10%	Add an incentive
Final offer package	Total package	Makes no further concessions	−25%	Total
Decision-making process	Top management team	Collective	Team makes recommendation	Senior manager and secretary
Decision maker	Top management team	Middle line with team consensus	Senior manager	Senior manager
Risk taking	Calculated personal responsibility	Low group responsibility	Religion based	Personally responsible

Source: Lillian H. Chaney and Jeanette S. Martin, *International Business Communication*, 3rd Edition © 2004. Electronically reproduced by permission of Pearson Education, Inc., Upper Saddle River, New Jersey.

Sometimes, simply being familiar with the culture is still falling short of being aptly informed. We knew how the political and legal environment of a country can have an influence over an MNC's decision to open operations, and those external factors are good to bear in mind when coming to an agreement. Both parties may believe that the goals have been made clear, and on the surface a settlement may deliver positive results. However, the subsequent actions taken by either company could prove to exhibit even more barriers. Take Pirelli, an Italian tire maker that acquired Continental Gummiwerke, its German competitor. Pirelli purchased the majority holdings of Continental's stock, a transaction which would translate into Pirelli having control of the company if it occurred in the United States. When Pirelli attempted to make key managerial decisions for its Continental unit, it discovered that in Germany, the corporate governance in place allows German companies to block such actions, regardless of the shareholder position. Furthermore, the labor force has quite a bit of leverage with its ability to elect members of the supervisory board, which in turn chooses the management board.[69] Pirelli essentially lost on an investment; that is, unless Continental can be profitable under its current management. If Pirelli had known that this was going to happen, it probably would have reconsidered. One solution could be for Pirelli's management to begin some positive rapport with the labor force to try to sway viewpoints internally. The better option, though, would be for international managers to be as informed as possible and avoid trouble before it occurs.

International Management in Action

Negotiating with the Japanese

Some people believe that the most effective way of getting the Japanese to open up their markets to the United States is to use a form of strong-arm tactics, such as putting the country on a list of those to be targeted for retaliatory action. Others believe that this approach will not be effective, because the interests of the United States and Japan are intertwined and we would be hurting ourselves as much as them. Regardless of which group is right, one thing is certain: U.S. MNCs must learn how to negotiate more effectively with the Japanese. What can they do? Researchers have found that besides patience and a little table pounding, a number of important steps warrant consideration.

First, business firms need to prepare for their negotiations by learning more about Japanese culture and the "right" ways to conduct discussions. Those companies with experience in these matters report that the two best ways of doing this are to read books on Japanese business practices and social customs and to hire experts to train the negotiators. Other steps that are helpful include putting the team through simulated negotiations and hiring Japanese to assist in the negotiations.

Second, U.S. MNCs must learn patience and sincerity. Negotiations are a two-way street that require the mutual cooperation and efforts of both parties. The U.S. negotiators must understand that many times, Japanese negotiators do not have full authority to make on-the-spot decisions. Authority must be given by someone at the home office, and this failure to act quickly should not be interpreted as a lack of sincerity on the part of the Japanese negotiators.

Third, the MNC must have a unique good or service. So many things are offered for sale in Japan that unless the company has something that is truly different, persuading the other party to buy it is difficult.

Fourth, technical expertise often is viewed as a very important contribution, and this often helps to win concessions with the Japanese. The Japanese know that the Americans, for example, still dominate the world when it comes to certain types of technology and that Japan is unable to compete effectively in these areas. When such technical expertise is evident, it is very influential in persuading the Japanese to do business with the company.

These four criteria are critical to effective negotiations with the Japanese. MNCs that use them report more successful experiences than those that do not.

谈判策略
Negotiation Tactics

A number of specific tactics are used in international negotiation. The following discussion examines some of the most common.

地点

Location Where should negotiations take place? If the matter is very important, most businesses will choose a neutral site. For example, U.S. firms negotiating with companies from the Far East will meet in Hawaii, and South American companies negotiating with European firms will meet halfway, in New York City. A number of benefits derive from using a neutral site. One is that each party has limited access to its home office for receiving a great deal of negotiating information and advice and thus gaining an advantage on the other. A second is that the cost of staying at the site often is quite high, so both sides have an incentive to conclude their negotiations as quickly as possible. (Of course, if one side enjoys the facilities and would like to stay as long as possible, the negotiations could drag on.) A third is that most negotiators do not like to return home with nothing to show for their efforts, so they are motivated to reach some type of agreement.

时间限制

Time Limits Time limits are an important negotiation tactic when one party is under a time constraint. This is particularly true when this party has agreed to meet at the home site of the other party. For example, U.S. negotiators who go to London to discuss a joint venture with a British firm often will have a scheduled return flight. Once their hosts find out how long these individuals intend to stay, the British can plan their strategy accordingly. The "real" negotiations are unlikely to begin until close to the time that the Americans must leave. The British know that their guests will be anxious to strike some type of deal before returning home, so the Americans are at a disadvantage.

Time limits can be used tactically even if the negotiators meet at a neutral site. For example, most Americans like to be home with their families for Thanksgiving, Christmas, and the New Year holiday. Negotiations held right before these dates put

Americans at a disadvantage, because the other party knows when the Americans would like to leave.

买卖者的关系

Buyer-Seller Relations How should buyers and sellers act? As noted earlier, Americans believe in being objective and trading favors. When the negotiations are over, Americans walk away with what they have received from the other party, and they expect the other party to do the same. This is not the way negotiators in many other countries think, however.

The Japanese, for example, believe that the buyers should get most of what they want. On the other hand, they also believe that the seller should be taken care of through reciprocal favors. The buyer must ensure that the seller has not been "picked clean." For example, when many Japanese firms first started doing business with large U.S. firms, they were unaware of U.S. negotiating tactics. As a result, the Japanese thought the Americans were taking advantage of them, whereas the Americans believed they were driving a good, hard bargain.

The Brazilians are quite different from both the Americans and Japanese. Researchers have found that Brazilians do better when they are more deceptive and self-interested and their opponents more open and honest than they are.[70] Brazilians also tend to make fewer promises and commitments than their opponents, and they are much more prone to say no. However, Brazilians are more likely to make initial concessions. Overall, Brazilians are more like Americans than Japanese in that they try to maximize their advantage, but they are unlike Americans in that they do not feel obligated to be open and forthright in their approach. Whether they are buyer or seller, they want to come out on top.

互利共赢的谈判
Negotiating for Mutual Benefit

When managers enter a negotiation with the intent to win and are not open to flexible compromises, it can result in a stalemate. Ongoing discussion with little progress can increase tensions between the two groups and create an impasse where groups become more frustrated and aggressive, and no agreement can be reached.[71] Ultimately, too much focus on the plan with little concern for the viewpoint of the other group can lead to missed opportunities. It is important to keep objectives in mind and at the forefront, but it should not be a substitute for constructive discussions. Fisher and Ury, authors of the book *Getting to Yes*, present five general principles to help avoid such disasters: (1) separate the people from the problem, (2) focus on interests rather than positions, (3) generate a variety of options before settling on an agreement (as mentioned earlier in this section), (4) insist that the agreement be based on objective criteria, and (5) stand your ground.[72]

将人与问题分开看

Separating the People from the Problem Often, when managers spend so much time getting to know the issue, many become personally involved. Therefore, responses to a particular position can be interpreted as a personal affront. In order to preserve the personal relationship and gain a clear perspective on the issue, it is important to distinguish the problem from the individual.

When dealing with people, one barrier to complete understanding is the negotiating parties' perspectives. Negotiators should try to put themselves in the other's shoes. Avoid blame, and keep the atmosphere positive by attempting to alter proposals to better translate the objectives. The more inclusive the process, the more willing everyone will be to find a solution that is mutually beneficial.

Emotional factors arise as well. Negotiators often experience some level of an emotional reaction during the process, but it is not seen by the other side. Recognize your own emotions, and be open to hearing and accepting emotional concerns of the other party. Do not respond in a defensive manner or give in to intense impulses. Ignoring the intangible tension is not recommended; try to alleviate the situation through sympathetic gestures such as apologies.

As mentioned earlier, good communication is imperative to reaching an agreement. Talk to each other, instead of just rehashing grandiose aspects of the proposal. Listen to responses, and avoid passively sitting there while formulating a response. When appropriate, summarize the key points by vocalizing your interpretation to the other side to ensure correct evaluation of intentions.

Overall, don't wait for issues to arise and react to them. Instead, go into discussion with these guidelines already in play.

站在双方的立场关注利益

Focusing on Interests over Positions The position one side takes can be expressed through a simple outline, but still does not provide the most useful information. Focusing on interests gives one insight into the motivation behind why a particular position was chosen. Digging deeper into the situation by both recognizing your own interests and becoming more familiar with others' interests will put all active partners in a better position to defend their proposal. Simply stating, "This model works, and it is the best option," may not have much leverage. Discussing your motivation, such as, "I believe our collaboration will enhance customer satisfaction, which is why I took on this project," will help others see the why, not just the what.

Hearing the incentive behind the project will make both sides more sympathetic, and may keep things consistent. Be sure to consider the other side, but maintain focus on your own concerns.

提供多种选择

Generating Options Managers may feel pressured to come to an agreement quickly for many reasons, especially if they hail from a country that puts a value on time. If negotiations are with a group that does not consider time constraints, there may be temptation to have only a few choices to narrow the focus and expedite decisions. It turns out, though, that it is better for everyone to have a large number of options in case some proposals prove to be unsatisfactory.

How do groups go about forming these proposals? First, they can meet to brainstorm and formulate creative solutions through a sort of invention process. This includes shifting thought focus among stating the problem, analyzing the issue, pondering general approaches, and strategizing the actions. After creating the proposals, the groups can begin evaluating the options and discuss improvements where necessary. Try to avoid the win-lose approach by accentuating the points of parity. When groups do not see eye to eye, find options that can work with both viewpoints by "look[ing] for items that are of low cost to you and high benefit to them, and vice versa."[73] By offering proposals that the other side will agree to, you can pinpoint the decision makers and tailor future suggestions toward them. Be sure to support the validity of your proposal, but not to the point of being overbearing.

应用客观标准

Using Objective Criteria In cases where there are no common interests, avoid tension by looking for objective options. Legitimate, practical criteria could be formed by using reliable third-party data, such as legal precedent. If both parties would accept being bound to certain terms, then chances are the suggestions were derived from objective criteria. The key is to emphasize the communal nature of the process. Inquire about why the other group chose its particular ideas. It will help you both see the other side and give you a springboard from which you can argue your views, which can be very persuasive. Overall, effective negotiations will result from international managers being flexible but not folding to external pressures.

These are just general guidelines to abide by to try and reach a mutual agreement. The approaches will be more effective if the group adhering to the outline was the one with more power. Fisher and Ury also looked at what managers should do if the other party has the power.

基本原则

Standing Ground Every discussion will have some imbalance of power, but there is something negotiators can do to defend themselves. It may be tempting to create a "bottom line," or lowest possible set of options that one will accept, but it does not necessarily accomplish the objective. When negotiators make a definitive decision before engaging in discussion, they may soon find out that the terms never even surface. That is not to say that their bottom line is below even the lowest offer, but instead that without working with the other negotiators, they cannot accurately predict the proposals that will be devised. So what should the "weaker" opponent do?

The reason two parties are involved in a negotiation is because they both want a situation that will leave them better off than before. Therefore, no matter how long negotiations drag on, neither side should agree to terms that will leave it worse off than its best alternative to a negotiated agreement, or BATNA. Clearly defining and understanding the BATNA will make it easier to know when it is time to leave a negotiation and empower that side. An even better scenario would be if the negotiator learns of the other side's BATNA. As Fisher and Ury say: "Developing your BATNA thus not only enables you to determine what is a minimally acceptable agreement, it will probably raise that minimum."[74]

Even the most prepared manager can walk into a battle zone. At times, negotiators will encounter rigid, irritable, caustic, and selfish opponents. A positional approach to bargaining can cause tension, but the other side can opt for a principled angle. This entails a calm demeanor and a focus on the issues. Instead of counterattacking, redirect the conversation to the problem, and do not take any outbursts as personal attacks. Inquire about their reasoning and try to take any negative statements as constructive. If no common ground is reached, a neutral third party can come in to assess the desires of each side and compose an initial proposal. Each group has the right to suggest alternative approaches, but the third-party person has the last word in what the true "final draft" is. If the parties decide it is still unacceptable, then it is time to walk away from negotiations.

Fisher and Ury compiled a comprehensive guide as to how to approach negotiations. While no guideline has a 100 percent effective rate, their method helps gain a position where both sides win.

讨价还价行为
Bargaining Behaviors

Closely related to the discussion of negotiation tactics are the different types of bargaining behaviors, including both verbal and nonverbal behaviors. Verbal behaviors are an important part of the negotiating process, because they can improve the final outcome. Research shows that the profits of the negotiators increase when they make high initial offers, ask a lot of questions, and do not make many verbal commitments until the end of the negotiating process. In short, verbal behaviors are critical to the success of negotiations.

使用极端行为

Use of Extreme Behaviors Some negotiators begin by making extreme offers or requests. The Chinese and Arabs are examples. Some negotiators, however, begin with an initial position that is close to the one they are seeking. The Americans and Swedes are examples here.

Is one approach any more effective than the other? Research shows that extreme positions tend to produce better results. Some of the reasons relate to the fact that an extreme bargaining position (1) shows the other party that the bargainer will not be exploited; (2) extends the negotiation and gives the bargainer a better opportunity to gain information on the opponent; (3) allows more room for concessions; (4) modifies the opponent's beliefs about the bargainer's preferences; (5) shows the opponent that the bargainer is willing to play the game according to the usual norms; and (6) lets the bargainer gain more than would probably be possible if a less extreme initial position had been taken.

Although the use of extreme position bargaining is considered to be "un-American," many U.S. firms have used it successfully against foreign competitors. When Peter Ueberroth managed the Olympic Games in the United States in 1984, he turned a profit of well over $100 million—and that was without the participation of Soviet-bloc countries, which would have further increased the market potential of the games. In past Olympiads, sponsoring countries had lost hundreds of millions of dollars. How did Ueberroth do it? One way was by using extreme position bargaining. For example, the Olympic Committee felt that the Japanese should pay $10 million for the right to televise the games in the country, so when the Japanese offered $6 million for the rights, the Olympic Committee countered with $90 million. Eventually, the two sides agreed on $18.5 million. Through the effective use of extreme position bargaining, Ueberroth got the Japanese to pay over three times their original offer, an amount well in excess of the committee's budget.

承诺、威胁和其他行为

Promises, Threats, and Other Behaviors Another approach to bargaining is the use of promises, threats, rewards, self-disclosures, and other behaviors that are designed to influence the other party. These behaviors often are greatly influenced by the culture. Graham conducted research using Japanese, U.S., and Brazilian businesspeople and found that they employed a variety of different behaviors during a buyer-seller negotiation simulation.[75] Table 4–9 presents the results.

Table 4–9
Cross-Cultural Differences in Verbal Behavior of Japanese, U.S., and Brazilian Negotiators

	Number of Times Tactic Was Used in a Half-Hour Bargaining Session		
Behavior and Definition	**Japanese**	**United States**	**Brazilian**
Promise. A statement in which the source indicated an intention to provide the target with a reinforcing consequence which source anticipates target will evaluate as pleasant, positive, or rewarding.	7	8	3
Threat. Same as promise, except that the reinforcing consequences are thought to be noxious, unpleasant, or punishing.	4	4	2
Recommendation. A statement in which the source predicts that a pleasant environmental consequence will occur to the target. Its occurrence is not under the source's control.	7	4	5
Warning. Same as recommendation except that the consequences are thought to be unpleasant.	2	1	1
Reward. A statement by the source that is thought to create pleasant consequences for the target.	1	2	2
Punishment. Same as reward, except that the consequences are thought to be unpleasant.	1	3	3
Positive normative appeal. A statement in which the source indicates that the target's past, present, or future behavior was or will be in conformity with social norms.	1	1	0
Negative normative appeal. Same as positive normative appeal, except that the target's behavior is in violation of social norms.	3	1	1
Commitment. A statement by the source to the effect that its future bids will not go below or above a certain level.	15	13	8
Self-disclosure. A statement in which the source reveals information about itself.	34	36	39
Question. A statement in which the source asks the target to reveal information about itself.	20	20	22
Command. A statement in which the source suggests that the target perform a certain behavior.	8	6	14
First offer. The profit level associated with each participant's first offer.	61.5	57.3	75.2
Initial concession. The differences in profit between the first and second offer.	6.5	7.1	9.4
Number of no's. Number of times the word "no" was used by bargainers per half-hour.	5.7	9.0	83.4

Source: Adapted from John L. Graham, "The Influence of Culture on the Process of Business Negotiations in an Exploratory Study," *Journal of International Business Studies,* Spring 1983, p. 88. Reprinted by permission from Macmillan Publishers Ltd., *Journal of International Business Studies,* March 1, 1985. Published by Palgrave Macmillan. Palgrave Macmillan.

The table shows that Americans and Japanese make greater use of promises than do Brazilians. The Japanese also rely heavily on recommendations and commitment. The Brazilians use a discussion of rewards, commands, and self-disclosure more than Americans and Japanese. The Brazilians also say no a great deal more and make first offers that have higher-level profits than those of the others. Americans tend to operate between these two groups, although they do make less use of commands than either of their opponents and make first offers that have lower profit levels than their opponents'.

Nonverbal Behaviors Nonverbal behaviors also are very common during negotiations. These behaviors refer to what people do rather than what they say. Nonverbal behaviors sometimes are called the "silent language." Typical examples include silent periods, facial gazing, touching, and conversational overlaps. As seen in Table 4–10, the Japanese tend to use silent periods much more often than either Americans or Brazilians during negotiations. In fact, in this study, the Brazilians did not use them at all. The Brazilians did, however, make frequent use of other nonverbal behaviors. They employed facial gazing almost four times more often than the Japanese and almost twice as often as the Americans. In addition, although the Americans and Japanese did not touch their opponents, the Brazilians made wide use of this nonverbal tactic. They also relied heavily on conversational overlaps, employing them more than twice as often as the Japanese and almost three times as often as Americans. Quite obviously, the Brazilians rely very heavily on nonverbal behaviors in their negotiating.

The important thing to remember is that in international negotiations, people use a wide variety of tactics, and the other side must be prepared to counter or find a way of dealing with them. The response will depend on the situation. Managers from different cultures will employ different tactics. Table 4–11 suggests some characteristics needed in effective negotiators, as exemplified by various cultures. To the extent that international managers have these characteristics, their success as negotiators should increase.

Table 4–10
Cross-Cultural Differences in Nonverbal Behavior of Japanese, U.S., and Brazilian Negotiators

	Number of Times Tactic Was Used in a Half-Hour Bargaining Session		
Behavior and Definition	**Japanese**	**United States**	**Brazilian**
Silent period. The number of conversational gaps of 10 seconds or more per 30 minutes.	5.5	3.5	0
Facial gazing. The number of minutes negotiators spend looking at their opponent's face per randomly selected 10-minute period.	1.3 minutes	3.3 minutes	5.2 minutes
Touching. Incidents of bargainers' touching one another per half-hour (not including handshakes).	0	0	4.7
Conversational overlaps. The number of times (per 10 minutes) that both parties to the negotiation would talk at the same time.	12.6	10.3	28.6

Source: Adapted from John L. Graham, "The Influence of Culture on the Process of Business Negotiations in an Exploratory Study," *Journal of International Business Studies,* Spring 1983, p. 88. Reprinted by permission from Macmillan Publishers Ltd., *Journal of International Business Studies,* March 1, 1985. Published by Palgrave Macmillan. Palgrave Macmillan.

Table 4–11
Culture-Specific Characteristics Needed by International Managers for Effective Negotiations

U.S. managers	Preparation and planning skill
	Ability to think under pressure
	Judgment and intelligence
	Verbal expressiveness
	Product knowledge
	Ability to perceive and exploit power
	Integrity
Japanese managers	Dedication to job
	Ability to perceive and exploit power
	Ability to win respect and confidence
	Integrity
	Listening skill
	Broad perspective
	Verbal expressiveness
China's Taiwan managers	Persistence and determination
	Ability to win respect and confidence
	Preparation and planning skill
	Product knowledge
	Interesting
	Judgment and intelligence
Brazilian managers	Preparation and planning skill
	Ability to think under pressure
	Judgment and intelligence
	Verbal expressiveness
	Product knowledge
	Ability to perceive and exploit power
	Competitiveness

Source: Adapted from Nancy J. Adler, *International Dimensions of Organizational Behavior,* 2nd ed. (Boston: PWS-Kent Publishing, 1991), p. 187; and from material provided by Professor John Graham, School of Business Administration, University of Southern California, 1983.

再看国际化管理的世界

■ The World of International Management—Revisited

The chapter's opening World of International Management surveyed some of the international communication and negotiation challenges that have emerged as a result of the increasing prevalence of offshoring. Offshoring has increased telephone and e-mail communication, which may exacerbate already substantial cultural differences in communication. In the opening World of International Management, recall how an e-mailed reply from an Indian colleague stating "I will do the needful" resulted in confusion on the part of an American manager. Even cultures that are speaking the same language (English, in this instance) may experience such difficulties. Understanding the communication styles of different cultures is a critical variable in managing relationships among employees and customers, managers and subordinates, and in all business relationships.

A key to success in today's global economy is being able to communicate effectively within and across national boundaries and to engage in effective negotiations across cultures. Considering the communication challenges faced by offshoring firms, along with what you have read in this chapter, answer the following questions: (1) How is communication in India similar to that of Europe and North America? How is it different? (2) What kind of managerial relationships could you assume exist between the American financial services firm (mentioned in The World of International Management) and its employees in India? (3) What kind of negotiations could help engage Indian employees and overcome some of the cultural problems encountered? How might culture play a role in the approach the Indian employees take in their negotiation with the financial firm?

SUMMARY OF KEY POINTS

1. Communication is the transfer of meaning from sender to receiver. The key to the effectiveness of communication is how accurately the receiver interprets the intended meaning.
2. Communicating in the international business context involves both downward and upward flows. Downward flows convey information from superior to subordinate; these flows vary considerably from country to country. For example, the downward system of organizational communication is much more prevalent in France than in Japan. Upward communication conveys information from subordinate to superior. In the United States and Japan, the upward system is more common than in South America or some European countries.
3. The international arena is characterized by a number of communication barriers. Some of the most important are intrinsic to language, perception, culture, and nonverbal communication. Language, particularly in written communications, often loses considerable meaning during interpretation. Perception and culture can result in people's seeing and interpreting things differently, and as a result, communication can break down. Nonverbal communication such as body language, facial expressions, and use of physical space, time, and even color often varies from country to country and, if improper, often results in communication problems.
4. A number of steps can be taken to improve communication effectiveness. Some of the most important include improving feedback, providing language and cultural training, and encouraging flexibility and cooperation. These steps can be particularly helpful in overcoming communication barriers in the international context and can lead to more effective international management.
5. Negotiation is the process of bargaining with one or more parties to arrive at a solution that is acceptable to all. There are two basic types of negotiation: distributive negotiation involves bargaining over opposing goals while integrative negotiation involves cooperation aimed at integrating interests. The negotiation process involves five basic steps: planning, interpersonal relationship building, exchanging task-related information, persuasion, and agreement. The way in which the process is carried out often will vary because of cultural differences, and it is important to understand them.
6. There are a wide variety of tactics used in international negotiating. These include location, time limits, buyer-seller relations, verbal behaviors, and nonverbal behaviors.
7. Negotiating for mutual benefit is enhanced by separating the people from the problem, focusing on interests rather than positions, generating a variety of options, insisting that the agreement be based on objective criteria, and standing one's ground.

KEY TERMS

chromatics
chronemics
communication
context
distributive negotiations
downward communication
haptics
integrative negotiation
intimate distance
kinesics
monochronic time schedule
negotiation
nonverbal communication
oculesics
perception
personal distance
polychronic time schedule
proxemics
public distance
social distance
upward communication

REVIEW AND DISCUSSION QUESTIONS

1. How does explicit communication differ from implicit communication? Which is one culture that makes wide use of explicit communication? Implicit communication? Describe how one would go about conveying the following message in each of the two cultures you identified: "You are trying very hard, but you are still making too many mistakes."
2. One of the major reasons that foreign expatriates have difficulty doing business in the United States is that they do not understand American slang. A business executive recently gave the authors the following three examples of statements that had no direct meaning for her because she was unfamiliar with slang: "He was laughing like hell." "Don't worry; it's a piece of cake." "Let's throw these ideas up against the wall and see if any of them stick." Why did the foreign expat have trouble understanding these statements, and what could be said instead?
3. Yamamoto Iron & Steel is considering setting up a minimill outside Atlanta, Georgia. At present, the company is planning to send a group of executives to the area to talk with local and state officials regarding this plant. In what way might misperception be a barrier to effective communication between the representatives for both sides? Identify and discuss two examples.
4. Diaz Brothers is a winery in Barcelona. The company would like to expand operations to the United States and begin distributing its products in the Chicago area. If things work out well, the company then will expand to both coasts. In its business dealings in the Midwest, how might culture prove to be a communication barrier for the company's representatives from Barcelona? Identify and discuss two examples.
5. Why is nonverbal communication a barrier to effective communication? Would this barrier be greater for Yamamoto Iron & Steel (question 3) or Diaz Brothers (question 4)? Defend your answer.
6. For U.S. companies going abroad for the first time, which form of nonverbal communication barrier would be the greatest, kinesics or proxemics? Why? Defend your answer.
7. If a company new to the international arena was negotiating an agreement with a potential partner in an overseas country, what basic steps should it be prepared to implement? Identify and describe them.
8. Which elements of the negotiation process should be done with only your group? Which events should take place with all sides present? Why?
9. An American manager is trying to close a deal with a Brazilian manager, but has not heard back from him for quite some time. The American is getting very nervous that if he waits too long, he is going to miss out on any backup options lost while waiting for the Brazilian. What should the American do? How can the American tell it is time to drop the deal? Give some signs that suggest negotiations will go no further.
10. Wilsten Inc. has been approached by a Japanese firm that wants exclusive production and selling rights for one of Wilsten's new high-tech products. What does Wilsten need to know about Japanese bargaining behaviors to strike the best possible deal with this company? Identify and describe five.

INTERNET EXERCISE: WORKING EFFECTIVELY AT TOYOTA

For 11 straight years, the Toyota Camry has been the best-selling car in the United States, and the firm's share of the American automobile market was solid. However, the company is not resting on its laurels. Toyota has expanded worldwide and is now doing business in scores of countries. Visit the firm's website and find out what it has been up to lately. The address is www.toyota.com. Then take a tour of the company's products and services including cars, air services, and sports vehicles. Next, go to the jobs section site, and see what types of career opportunities there are at Toyota. Finally, find out what Toyota is doing in your particular locale. Then, drawing upon this information and the material you read in the chapter, answer these three questions: (1) What type of communication and negotiation challenges do you think you would face if you worked for Toyota and were in constant communication with home-office personnel in Japan? (2) What type of communication training do you think the firm would need to provide to you to ensure that you were effective in dealing with senior-level Japanese managers in the hierarchy? (3) Using Table 4–1 as your guide, what conclusions can you draw regarding communicating with the Japanese managers, and what guidelines would you offer to a non-Japanese employee who just entered the firm and is looking for advice and guidance regarding how to communicate and negotiate more effectively?

China

China, with more than 1.3 billion people, is the world's most populous country and has a rapidly growing economy. Economic development has proceeded unevenly. Urban coastal areas, particularly in the southeast, are experiencing more rapid economic development than other areas of the country. By 2011, just 10.1 percent of the GDP consisted of agriculture, while industry constituted 46.8 percent. China has a mixed economy, with a combination of state-owned and private firms. A number of state-owned enterprises (SOEs) have undergone partial or full privatization in recent years. The Chinese government has encouraged foreign investment—in some sectors of the economy and subject to constraints—since the 1980s, defining several "special economic zones" in which foreign investors receive preferable tax, tariff, and investment treatment. Since 2003 Hu Jintao has been the country's president, and since 2004 he also has the chairman of the Central Military Commission.

With China's entry into the World Trade Organization in November 2001, the Chinese government made a number of specific commitments to trade and investment liberalization that have substantially opened the Chinese economy to foreign firms. In telecommunications, this means the lifting or sharp reduction of tariffs and foreign ownership limitations, although China retains the right to limit foreign majority ownership of telecom firms. There has been increasing concern on the part of foreign MNCs that China has not moved fast enough in opening up previously protected sectors and generally favors Chinese firms for large government tenders such as those issued as part of the government's US$586 billion stimulus package, designed to counteract the effects of the global economic crisis. China's successful hosting of the 2008 Summer Olympics in Beijing reinforced the country's pride and position as a global leader in economics, culture, foreign relations, and sports.

China's real GDP grew by 9.2 percent in 2011, an impressive performance given the global economic crisis. This growth brought China's GDP to US$7.3 trillion and boosted per capita GDP to US$8,500.

Despite this impressive growth, employees are increasingly demanding higher wages and better working conditions. Widespread strikes at firms such as Foxconn (a large contract manufacturer that assembles Apple's iPhone, along with many other products), Honda, and Toyota underscore the desire by workers to receive a greater share of company profits and to have a stronger voice in decisions that affect them. In June 2010 a plant of Toyoda Gosei, a car parts manufacturer affiliated with Toyota, was forced to halt production in Tianjin due to a strike. The cause of the strike was the workers' demand for higher wages.

Some analysts believe that the era of China's reliance on low-cost labor to fuel its economic growth may be coming to an end. Increasingly, the Chinese government and Chinese industry are investing in higher value-added products such as clean energy technology, aviation and avionics, and health care equipment. China's growth has been unparalleled and China will no doubt play an increasingly important role in global economic affairs in the future.

www.cnbc.com/id/37768476,
www.1stheadlines.com/china.htm,
www.infoplease.com

Questions

1. Do you think China will continue to achieve record growth? What factors could hurt its prospects?
2. Because of an abundance of cheap labor, China has been called "the workshop of the world." Do you think this will still be the case a decade from now? Why or why not?
3. What communication and negotiation approaches are likely to work best when foreign MNCs experience demands from Chinese workers for higher wages?

Brief Integrative Case 1.1

Coca-Cola in India

Coca-Cola is a brand name known throughout the entire world. It covers 60 percent of the $1.6 billion soft drink market. In 2006–2007, Coca-Cola faced some difficult challenges in the region of Kerala, India. The company was accused of using water that contained pesticides in its bottling plants in Kerala. An environmental group, the Center for Science and Environment (CSE), found 57 bottles of Coke and Pepsi products from 12 Indian states that contained unsafe levels of pesticides.[1]

The Kerala minister of health, Karnataka R. Ashok, imposed a ban on the manufacture and sale of Coca-Cola products in the region. Coca-Cola then arranged to have its drinks tested in a British lab, and the report found that the amount of pesticides found in Pepsi and Coca-Cola drinks was harmless to the body.[2] Coca-Cola then ran numerous ads to regain consumers' confidence in its products and brand. However, these efforts did not satisfy the environmental groups or the minister of health.

India's Changing Marketplace

During the 1960s and 1970s, India's economy faced many challenges, growing only an average of 3–3.5 percent per year. Numerous obstacles hindered foreign companies from investing in India, and many restrictions on economic activity caused huge difficulties for Indian firms and a lack of interest among foreign investors. For many years the government had problems implementing reform and overcoming bureaucratic and political divisions. Business activity has traditionally been undervalued in India; leisure is typically given more value than work. Stemming from India's colonial legacy, Indians are highly suspicious of foreign investors. Indeed, there have been a few well-publicized disputes between the Indian government and foreign investors.[3]

More recently, however, many Western companies are finding an easier time doing business in India.[4] In 1991, political conditions had changed, many restrictions were eased, and economic reforms came into force. With more than 1 billion consumers, India has become an increasingly attractive market.[5] From 2003–2006, foreign investment doubled to $6 billion. Imported goods have become a status symbol for the burgeoning middle class.[6]

Coca-Cola has been targeting India for potential growth, as Indians consume an average of 12 eight-ounce beverages per year. In comparison, Brazil consumers drink roughly 240 beverages per year on average. Despite the relatively low amount of beverages consumed by India on average, India has been one of Coke's best emerging market plays. During the January to March period of 2012, sales in India increased 20 percent. This compares very favorably with Coca-Cola's other emerging market operations in China (9 percent growth over the same period) and Brazil (4 percent growth over the same period). As part of the investment plan, Coca-Cola plans to expand capacity at all 13 of its bottling plants, which should help expand the company's distribution throughout the country. Coca-Cola is aiming to double both revenue and volume in India by the year 2020.[7]

In 2008–2009 FDI in India stood at $27.31 billion.[8] In 2009, India was the third highest recipient of FDI and was likely to continue to remain among the top five attractive destinations for international investors during the following two years, according to a United Nations Conference on Trade and Development (UNCTAD) report.[9] The 2009 survey of the Japan Bank for International Cooperation conducted among Japanese investors continued to rank India as the second most promising country for overseas business operations, after China. According to the Minister of Commerce and Industry, Mr. Anand Sharma, FDI equity inflows as a percentage of GDP have grown from 0.75 percent in 2005–2006 to nearly 2.49 percent in 2008–2009.[10]

India's GDP has grown at the impressive average annual rate of 8.5 percent during the six years spanning 2003/04–2008/09. Even the global financial crisis, which began in September 2008, has cut the rate of growth by only 2–3 percentage points, and the economy continued to grow at the annual rate of 6 percent during the three quarters following the crisis.[11] But the country needs more investment in manufacturing if it hopes to improve the lives of the 350 million people living in poverty.[12]

Coca-Cola and Other Soft Drink Investment in India

Coca-Cola had experienced previous confrontations with the Indian government. In 1977, Coke had pulled out of India when the government demanded its secret formula.[13]

Circumstances have dramatically improved over the years for soft drink providers of India. Coke and Pepsi have invested nearly $2 billion in India over the years. They employ about 12,500 people directly and support 200,000 indirectly through their purchases of sugar, packaging material, and shipping services. Coke is India's number-one consumer of mango pulp for its local soft drink offerings.[14] Coca-Cola in India is also the largest domestic buyer of sugar and green coffee beans.[15] From 1994 to 2003, Coca-Cola sales in India more than doubled.

In 2008–2009 Coca-Cola announced its plans to invest more than $250 million in India over the next three years. The money would be used for everything from expanding bottling capacity to buying delivery trucks and refrigerators for small retailers. The new money will mean around a 20 percent increase in the total Coca-Cola has invested in India.[16] Coca-Cola's sales in India climbed 31 percent in the three months ended March 31, 2009, compared to a year earlier. That's the highest volume growth of any of Coke's markets.[17]

Furthermore, Coca-Cola announced plans in 2012 to invest upwards of US$5 billion in India by 2020. This investment marks a 150 percent increase over the announced plans from 2011 to invest up to US$2 billion in India over the next five years. Putting this investment in perspective, Coca-Cola has invested a total of just over US$2 billion in its India operations over the past 20 years. Despite the large investment in India, Coca-Cola will see serious competition from Pepsi in this market. Together Coke and Pepsi make up 97 percent of the market for carbonated soft drinks in India, where soda sales overall are estimated to be US$1.05 billion. Coke accounted for 60 percent of all sales in 2011 while Pepsi received 37 percent of the market share.[18]

Royal Crown Cola (RC Cola) is the world's third largest brand of soft drinks. The brand was purchased in 2000 by Cadbury Schweppes and entered the Indian market in 2003. For production in India, the company hired three licensing and franchising bottlers. In order to ensure that it was not associated with the pesticide accusations against Pepsi and Coke, RC Cola immediately had its groundwater tested by the testing institute SGS India Pvt Ltd.[19]

The Charges against Coke

The pesticide issue began in 2002, in Plachimada, India. Villagers thought that water levels had sunk and the drinking water was contaminated by Coke's plant. They launched a vigil at the plant, and two years later, Coke's license was canceled. Coca-Cola's most recent pesticide issue began at a bottling plant in Mehdiganj. The plant was accused of exploiting the groundwater and polluting it with toxic metals.[20] Karnataka R. Ashok, the health minister of Kerala, India, banned the sale of all Coca-Cola and PepsiCo products, claiming that the drinks contained unsafe levels of pesticides.

The alleged contamination of the water launched a debate on everything from pesticide-polluted water to the Indian middle-class's addiction to unhealthy, processed foods. "It's wonderful," said Sunita Narin, director of CSE. "Pepsi and Coke are doing our work for us. Now the whole nation knows that there is a pesticide problem."[21]

Coca-Cola fought back against the accusations. "No Indian soft drink makers have been tested for similar violations even though pesticides could be in their products such as milk and bottled teas. If pesticides are in the groundwater, why isn't anyone else being tested? We are continuously being challenged because of who we are," said Atul Singh, CEO of Coca-Cola India.[22]

Some believe that Coca-Cola was targeted to bring the subject of pesticides in consumer products to light. "If you target multinational corporations, you get more publicity," adds Arvind Kumar, a researcher at the watchdog group Toxic Links. "Pesticides are in everything in India."[23]

India's Response to the Allegations

After CSE's discovery of the unsafe levels of pesticides,[24] some suggested the high levels of pesticides came from sugar, which is 10 percent of the soft drink content. However laboratories found the sugar samples to be pesticide free.[25]

Kerala is run by a communist government and a chief minister who still claims to have a revolutionary objection to the evils of capitalism.[26] Defenders of Coca-Cola claim that this is a large reason for the pesticide findings in Coca-Cola products. After the ban was placed on all Coca-Cola and PepsiCo products in the region of Kerala, Coca-Cola took its case to the state court to defend its products and name. The court said that the state government had no jurisdiction to impose a ban on the manufacture and sale of products.[27] Kerala then lifted the statewide ban on Coke products.[28]

In March 2010, after several years of tense battles, the Indian unit of Coca-Cola Company was asked to pay $47 million in compensation for causing environmental damage at its bottling plant in the southern Indian state of Kerala. A state government panel said Coca-Cola's subsidiary, Hindustan Coca-Cola Beverages Pvt Ltd (HCBPL), was responsible for depleting groundwater and dumping toxic waste around its Palakkad plant between 1999 and 2004. Protests by farmers, complaining about the alleged pollution, forced Coca-Cola to close down the plant in 2005. Coca-Cola responded that HCBPL was not responsible for pollution in Palakkad, but the final decision on the compensation will be taken by the state government.[29]

Pepsi's Experience in India

PepsiCo has had an equally noticeable presence in India; and it is not surprising that the company has weathered the same storms as its rival Coca-Cola. In addition to claims of excessive water use, a CSE pesticide study, performed in August 2006, accused Pepsi of having 30 times the "unofficial" pesticide limit in its beverages (Coke was claimed to be 27 times the limit in this study).[30] These findings, coupled with the original 2003 CSE study that first tarnished the cola companies' image, have prompted numerous consumers to stop their cola consumption. Some have even taken to the streets, burning pictures of Pepsi bottles in protest.

Indra Nooyi, CEO of PepsiCo Inc. and a native of India, is all too familiar with the issues of water contamination and water shortages. Yet, in light of the recent claims made against Pepsi, she has expressed frustration with the exaggerated CSE findings (local tea and coffee have thousands of times the alleged pesticide level found in Pepsi products) and the disproportionate reaction to Pepsi's water-use practices (pointing out that soft drinks and bottled water account for less than 0.04 percent of industrial water usage in India).[31]

In order to reaffirm the safety and popularity of its products, Pepsi has taken on a celebrity-studded ad campaign across India, as well as continued its legacy of corporate social responsibility (CSR). Some of Pepsi's CSR efforts have involved digging village wells, "harvesting" rainwater, and teaching better techniques for growing rice and tomatoes.[32] Pepsi has also initiated efforts to reduce water waste at its Indian facilities.

Although Pepsi sales are back on the rise, Nooyi realizes that she should have acted sooner to counteract CSE's claims about Pepsi products. From here on out, the company must be more attentive to its water-use practices; but Nooyi also notes, "We have to invest, too, in educating communities in how to farm better, collect water, and then work with industry to retrofit plants and recycle."[33]

Coke's Social Responsibility Commitments

Coca-Cola has recently employed The Energy and Resources Institute (TERI) to assess its operations in India. The investigations have been conducted because of claims that Coca-Cola has engaged in unethical production practices in India. These alleged practices include causing severe water shortages, locating water-extracting plants in "drought prone" areas, further limiting water access by contaminating the surrounding land and groundwater, and irresponsibly disposing of toxic waste. Colleges and universities throughout the United States, U.K., and Canada have joined in holding the company accountable for its overseas business practices by banning Coca-Cola products on their campuses until more positive results are reported. However, critics have argued that TERI's assessment would undoubtedly be biased since the organization has been largely funded by the Coca-Cola Company.[34]

Coca-Cola stands behind the safety of its products. "Multinational corporations provide an easy target," says Amulya Ganguli, a political analyst in New Delhi. "These corporations are believed to be greedy, devoted solely to profit, and uncaring about the health of the consumers." There is also a deeply rooted distrust of big business, and particularly foreign big business, in India.[35] This is a reminder that there will continue to be obstacles, as there were in the past, to foreign investments in India.

In order to reaffirm their presence in India, Coke and Pepsi have run separate ads insisting that their drinks are safe. Coke's ad said, "Is there anything safer for you to drink?" and invited Indians to visit its plants to see how the beverage is made.[36] Nevertheless, in July 2006, Coke reported a 12 percent decline in sales.[37]

Coca-Cola has undertaken various initiatives to improve the drinking water conditions around the world. It has formally pledged support for the United Nations Global Compact and co-founded the Global Water Challenge, which improves water access and sanitation in countries in critical need. It is improving energy efficiency through the use of hydrofluorocarbon-free insulation for 98 percent of new refrigerater sales and marketing equipment. Specifically, in India, Coke has stated, "More than one-third of the total water that is used in operations is renewed and returned to groundwater systems."[38] Among its first water renewal projects was installation of 270 rainwater catching devices.[39]

Table 1 A Timeline of Coca-Cola in Kerala, India

1977:	Coca-Cola pulls out of India when the government demands its secret formula.
1991:	Restrictions are eased in India for easier international business development.
1999:	A report is published by the All-Indian Coordinated Research Program stating that 20% of all Indian food commodities exceed the maximum pesticide residue level and 43% of milk exceeds the maximum residue levels of DDT.
2002:	Villagers in Plachimada, India, make the accusation that Coke's bottling plant is contaminating their drinking water.
2003:	The Center for Science and Environment produces a study that finds unsafe levels of pesticides in Coca-Cola products in India.
January 2004:	Parliament in India forms a Joint Parliamentary Committee to investigate the charges by the CSE.
March 2004:	A Coca-Cola bottling facility is shut down in Plachimada, India.
2004:	Indian government announces new regulations for carbonated soft drinks based on European Union standards.
2005:	Coca-Cola co-founds the Global Water Challenge, develops the Global Community-Watershed Partnership, and establishes the Ethics and Compliance Committee.
August 2006:	The CSE produces another report finding 57 Coke and Pepsi products from 12 Indian states that contain unsafe pesticide levels.
September 2006:	India's high court overturns the ban on the sale of Coke products in Kerala.
March 2010:	Indian unit of Coca-Cola Co asked by state government to pay $47 million compensation for causing environmental damage at its bottling plant in Kerala.

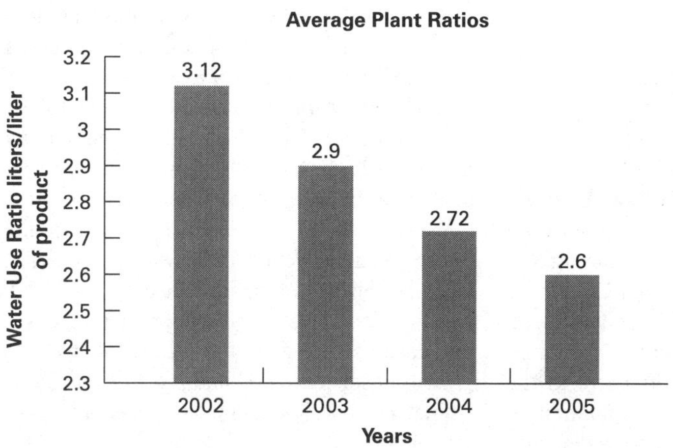

Figure 1

Coca-Cola's Water Use: Average Plant Ratios

Source: The Coca-Cola Company, *2005 Environmental Report,* www.thecocacolacompany.com/citizenship/environmental_report2005.pdf.

Later, Coca-Cola expanded the number of rainwater harvesting projects by partnering with the Central Ground Water Authority (CGWA), State Ground Water Boards, schools, colleges, NGOs, and local communities to combat water scarcity. According to Coca-Cola India's 2007–2008 Environment Report, the company was actively engaged in 400 rainwater harvesting projects running across 17 states. These efforts were contributing to the company's eventual target of being a "net zero" user of groundwater by the end of 2009.[40]

Having inspected its own water-use habits, Coca-Cola has vowed to reduce the amount of water it uses in its bottling operations. As of June 2007, Coca-Cola had reduced the amount of water needed to make one liter of Coke to 2.54 liters (compared with 3.14 liters five years earlier).[41]

At the June 2007 annual meeting of the World Wildlife Fund (WWF) in Beijing, Coca-Cola announced its multi-year partnership with the organization "to conserve and protect freshwater resources." E. Neville Isdell, chairman and CEO of the Coca-Cola Company, said, "Our goal is to replace every drop of water we use in our beverages and their production. For us that means reducing the amount of water used to produce our beverages, recycling water used for manufacturing processes so it can be returned safely to the environment, and replenishing water in communities and nature through locally relevant projects." Coca-Cola hopes to spread these practices to other members of its supply chain, particularly the sugar cane industry. The Coca-Cola–WWF partnership is also focused on climate protection and protection of seven of the world's "most critical freshwater basins," including the Yangtze in China. Although Coca-Cola's corporate social responsibility efforts have included other projects with the WWF in the past, it hopes that this official partnership will help achieve larger-scale results.[42] Figures 1 and 2 show Coca-Cola's declining water use on a per-plant and systemwide basis.

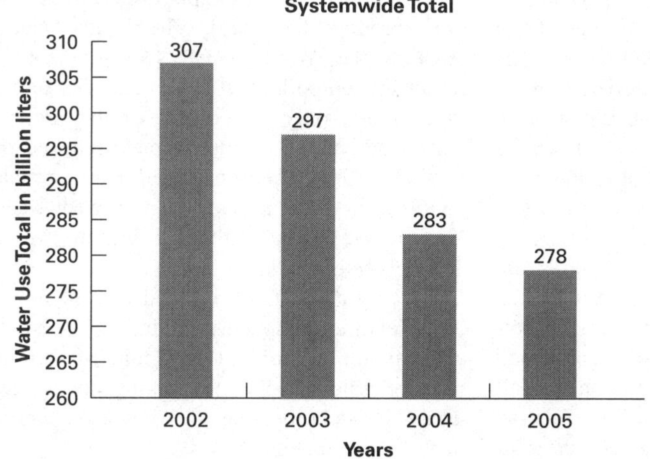

Figure 2

Coca-Cola's Water Use: Systemwide Total

Source: The Coca-Cola Company, *2005 Environmental Report,* www.thecocacolacompany.com/citizenship/environmental_report2005.pdf.

Coca-Cola has also established EthicsLine, which is a global Web and telephone information and reporting service that allows anyone to report confidential information to a third party. Service is toll free—24 hours a day—and translators are available. Coca-Cola is currently focusing on improving standards through the global water challenge and enhancing global packaging to make it more environmentally friendly. It is also working on promoting nutrition and physical education by launching programs throughout the world. For example, in January 2009, Coca-Cola India announced a partnership with the Bharat Integrated Social Welfare Agency (BISWA) to build awareness regarding micro-nutrient malnutrition (or "Hidden Hunger") in the "bottom of the socio-economic pyramid" population in India. The two partners will work together to establish a successful income-generation model for communities through Self-Help Groups in Sambalpur in Orissa and also provide them with affordable alternatives to alleviate "Hidden Hunger." The first product developed by Coca-Cola India to address the issue of "hidden hunger" is Vitingo, a tasty, affordable and refreshing orange-flavored beverage fortified with micro-nutrients.

During the past decade, the Coca-Cola Company has invested more than US$1 billion in India, making it one of India's top international investors. Almost all the goods and services required to produce and market Coca-Cola are made in India. The Coca-Cola Company directly employs approximately 5,500 local people in India; and indirectly, its business in India creates employment for more than 150,000 people.[43] Hindustan Coca-Cola Beverages Pvt Ltd operates 22 bottling plants, some of which are located in economically underdeveloped areas of the country. The Coca-Cola system also includes 23 franchise operated plants, and has one facility that manufactures concentrates or beverage bases.[44]

Lessons Learned

Yet Coca-Cola was caught off guard by its experience in India. Coke did not fully appreciate how quickly local politicians would attack Coke in light of the test results, nor did it respond quickly enough to the anxieties of its consumers. The company failed to realize how fast news travels in modern India. India represents only about 1 percent of Coca-Cola's global volume, but it is central to the company's long-term growth strategy. The company needed to take action fast.[45]

In what Coke thought to be a respectful and immediate time frame, it formed committees in India and the United States. The committees worked on rebuttals and had their own labs commission the tests, and then they commented in detail. Coke also directed reporters to Internet blogs full of entries that were pro-Coke. Critics say that Coke focused too much on the charges instead of winning back the support of its customers. "Here people interpret silence as guilt," said Mr. Seth, Coke's Indian public relations expert.

Ms. Bjorhus, the Coke communications director, said she could now see how the environmental group had picked Coca-Cola as a way of attracting attention to the broader problem of pesticide contamination in Indian food products. Coca-Cola stands behind its products as being pesticide free. It is now up to the Indian consumer to decide the success of Coca-Cola in future years.

Nevertheless, Coca-Cola has been optimistic about its future in India. While India was still among the countries with the lowest per capita consumption of Coke, in 2009 it was the second fastest growing region in terms of Coca-Cola unit case volume growth.[46] Coca-Cola recorded a 3 percent growth in sales in 2009 and most of it came from India and China, even as the company faced hard economic times elsewhere in the world.[47]

The Global Water Challenge

In 2007, one out of every five people globally lacked access to clean drinking water.[48] In August 2006, an international conference was held in Stockholm, Sweden, to discuss global water issues. A UN study reported that many large water corporations have decreased their investments in developing countries because of high political and financial risks. Even nations that have had abundant water supplies are experiencing significant reductions. These reductions are believed to be caused by two factors: the decline in rainfall and increased evaporation of water due to global warming and the loss of wetlands. Water is something that affects every person each and every day. The executive director of the Stockholm Water Institute, Anders Berntell, noted that water affects the areas of agriculture, energy, transportation, forestry, trade, financing, and social and political security. The Food and Agriculture Organization points out, "Agriculture is the world's largest water consumer. Any water crisis will therefore also create a food crisis."

There have been attempts to improve the water conditions around the world. The United Nations recently released the World Water Development Report. This report was compiled by 24 UN agencies and claimed that, in actuality, only 12 percent of the funds targeted for water and sanitation improvement reached those most in need. The United Nations stated that more than 1.1 billion people still lack access to improved water resources. Nearly two-thirds of the 1.1 billion live in Asia.[49]
The Institute of Public and
Environmental Affairs reported that 34 foreign-owned or joint-venture companies, including Pepsi, have caused water pollution problems in China. Ma Jun, the institute's founder, said, "We're not talking about very high standards. These companies are known for their commitment to the environment."[50]

According to the 2009 UN World Water Development Report, the world's population is growing by about 80 million people a year, implying increased freshwater demand of about 64 billion cubic meters a year. An estimated 90 percent of the 3 billion people who are expected to be added to the population by 2050 will be in developing countries, many in regions where the current population does not have sustainable access to safe drinking water or adequate sanitation. The world will have substantially more people in vulnerable urban and coastal areas in the next 20 years.[51]

With businesses expanding globally every day, water is a crucial resource, and water issues will increasingly affect all industries. With water conditions improving at a slower rate than business development, businesses will have to take on the responsibility of not only finding an adequate supply of the diminishing resource but also making sure the water is safe for all to consume. This responsibility is going to be an additional cost to companies, but a necessary one that will prevent loss of sales in the future. Coca-Cola's specific situation in India is a reminder for all global corporations.

Questions for Review

1. What aspects of U.S. culture and of Indian culture may have been causes of Coke's difficulties in India?
2. How might Coca-Cola have responded differently when this situation first occurred, especially in terms of responding to negative perceptions among Indians of Coke and other MNCs?
3. If Coca-Cola wants to obtain more of India's soft drink market, what changes does it need to make?
4. How might companies like Coca-Cola and PepsiCo demonstrate their commitment to working with different countries and respecting the cultural and natural environments of those societies?

Source: This case was prepared by Jaclyn Johns of Villanova University under the supervision of Professor Jonathan Doh as the basis for class discussion. It is not intended to illustrate either effective or ineffective managerial capability or administrative responsibility. Research assistance was provided by Courtney Asher, Tetyana Azarova, and Benjamin Littell.

Brief Integrative Case 1.2

Danone's Wrangle with Wahaha

In 1996, Danone Group and Wahaha Group combined forces in a joint venture (JV) to form the largest beverage company in China. A longstanding trademark dispute between the JV members, embedded within a broader clash of national and organizational cultures, came to a head. Valuable lessons can be learned from this dispute for investors considering joint ventures in China.[1]

The Wahaha Joint Venture was established in 1996 by Hangzhou Wahaha Food Group Co. Ltd., Danone Group, and Bai Fu Qin Ltd. In 1997, Danone bought the interests of Bai Fu Qin and gained legal control of the JV with 51 percent of shares. While members of the JV are entitled to use the JV's Wahaha trademark, in 2000, the Wahaha Group developed companies outside of the JV that sold products similar to those of the JV and used the JV's trademark. The Danone Group objected and sought to purchase those non-JV companies.[2]

In April 2007, Danone offered RMB4 billion to acquire 51 percent of the shares of Wahaha's five non-JV companies. Wahaha Group rejected the offer. Subsequently, Danone filed more than 30 lawsuits against Wahaha for violating the contract and illegally using the JV's Wahaha trademark in countries such as France, Italy, the U.S., and China.[3]

Danone's Background

Danone traces its routes to Europe in the early 20th century. In 1919, Isaac Carasso opened a small yogurt stand in Spain. He named it "Danone," meaning "Little Daniel," after his son. Carasso was aware of new methods of milk fermentation conducted at the Pasteur Institute in Paris. He decided to merge these new techniques with traditional practices for making yogurt. The first industrial manufacturer of yogurt was started.[4]

Following his success in Europe, Carasso immigrated to the U.S. to expand his market. He changed the Danone name to Dannon Milk products, Inc., and founded the first American yogurt company in 1942 in New York. Distribution began on a small scale. When Dannon introduced the "fruit on the bottom" line in 1947, sales soared. The following year, he sold his company's interest and returned to Spain to manage his family's original business.[5]

By 1950, Dannon had expanded to other U.S. states in the Northeast. It also broadened the line by introducing low-fat yogurt that targeted the health-conscious consumer. Sales continued to rise. Dannon expanded across the country throughout the 1960s and 1970s. In 1979, Dannon became the first company to sell perishable dairy products coast to coast in the U.S.[6]

In 1967, Danone merged with leading French fresh cheese producer Gervais to become Gervais Danone. In 1973, Gervais Danone merged with Boussois-Souchon-Neuvesel (BSN), a company which had also acquired the Alsacian brewer Kronenbourg and Evian mineral water.[7] In 1987, Gervais Danone acquired European biscuit manufacturer Général Biscuit, owners of the LU brand, and in 1989, it bought out the European biscuit operations of Nabisco.

In 1994, BSN changed its name to Groupe Danone, adopting the name of the Group's best known international brand. Under its current CEO, Franck Riboud, the company has pursued its focus on the three product groups: dairy, beverages, and cereals.[8]

Today, Danone is a Fortune 500 company with a mission to produce healthy, nutritious, and affordable food and beverage products for as many people as possible.

Danone's Global Growth

Danone, with 160 plants and around 80,000 employees, has a presence in all five continents and over 120 countries. In 2008, Danone recorded €15.2 billion in sales. Danone enjoys leading positions in healthy food:[9]

- No. 1 worldwide in fresh dairy products
- No. 2 worldwide in bottled water
- No. 2 worldwide in baby nutrition
- No. 1 in Europe in medical nutrition

Its portfolio of brands and products includes Activia, a probiotic dairy product line; Danette, a brand of cream desserts; Nutricia, an infant product line; Danonino, a brand of yogurts; and Evian, a brand of bottled water.[10]

Listed on Euronext Paris, Danone is also ranked among the main indexes of social responsibility: Dow Jones Sustainability Index Stoxx and World, ASPI Eurozone (Advanced Sustainable Performance Indices), and Ethibel Sustainability index.[11] Danone has ranked number 60 in top 100 international brands according to Interbrand 2009 Best Global Brand valuation, with the brand value of $5.96 billion.[12]

In 2008, Danone recorded an organic growth rate of 8.4 percent. With its operating margin increasing for the 14th year running, the group further strengthened its global standing. The group's performance is the result of a balanced strategy that builds on international expansion, a growing commitment to innovation, and strengthening health-oriented brands. Danone invests heavily in research and development—€208 million in 2008. One hundred percent of projects currently in the pipeline focus on health and nutrition.[13]

With a total of roughly 18 billion liters of bottled water marketed in 2008, Danone is the world's second largest producer (its global market share is approximately 11 percent). Danone owns the world's top-selling brand of packaged water, Aqua, which recorded sales of 6 billion liters. With Evian and Volvic, Danone also owns two of the five worldwide brands of bottled water.[14] Its revenue from water products amounted to €2.9 billion in 2008: Europe accounted for 47 percent of this total, Asia 31 percent, and the rest of the world 22 percent. At constant structure and exchange rates, the proportion of sales in emerging countries rose in 2008 to 52 percent.[15]

In the mid-1990s, Danone did 80 percent of its business in Western Europe. Until 1996, the company was present in about a dozen markets including pasta, confectionery, biscuits, ready-to-serve meals, and beer. The company realized that it is difficult to achieve simultaneous growth in all these markets. Therefore, they decided to concentrate on the few markets that showed the most growth potential and were consistent with Danone's focus on health. Starting in 1997, the Group decided to focus on three business lines worldwide (Fresh Dairy Products, Beverages, as well as Biscuits and Cereal Products), and the rest of the business lines were divested. This freed the company's financial and human resources and allowed for quick expansion into new markets in Asia, Africa, Eastern Europe, and Latin America. In less than 10 years, the contribution of emerging markets to sales rose from zero to 40 percent while that of Western Europe went below 50 percent.[16]

The 2007 year marked the end of a 10-year refocusing strategy period during which the Group's activities were refocused in the area of health. That year, the Group sold nearly all of its Biscuits and Cereal Products business to the Kraft Foods group, while adding Baby Nutrition and Medical Nutrition to its portfolio by acquiring Numico.

Danone is now centered on 4 business lines:

1. Fresh Dairy Products, representing approximately 57 percent of consolidated sales for 2008
2. Waters, representing approximately 19 percent of consolidated sales for 2008
3. Baby Nutrition, representing approximately 18 percent of consolidated sales for 2008
4. Medical Nutrition, representing approximately 6 percent of consolidated sales for 2008

Danone Strategy in China

Danone entered the Chinese market in the late 1980s. Since then, it has invested heavily in China, building factories and expanding production. Today, Danone has 70 factories in China, including Danone Biscuits, Robust, Wahaha, and Health. Danone sells primarily yogurt, biscuits, and beverages in China.[17]

Danone's Asia-Pacific division employs 23,000 people in the Asia-Pacific area, which is almost 30 percent of Danone's total employees. Of Danone's Asian sales, 57 percent were in China. Danone's Wahaha was China's largest beverage company. Two billion liters of Wahaha were sold in 2004, making it the market leader in China with a 30 percent market share.[18] In Asia, in 2007, Danone Group was the market leader with a 20 percent share of a 34-billion liter market. In comparison, rivals Coca-Cola and Nestlé had a 7 percent and 2 percent share, respectively. Evian, its global brand, was sold alongside of local brands such as China's Wahaha.

In the past 20 years, Danone has purchased shares of many of the top beverage companies in China: 51 percent of shares of the companies owned by Wahaha Group, 98 percent of Robust Group, 50 percent of Shanghai Maling Aquarius Co., Ltd., 54.2 percent of Shenzhen Yili Mineral Water Company, 22.18 percent of China Huiyuan Group, 50 percent of Mengniu, and 20.01 percent of Bright dairy. These companies, leaders in their industry, all own trademarks that are well-known in China.[19]

However, while expanding into the Chinese market, Danone faced challenges due to lack of market knowledge. In 2000, Danone purchased Robust, the then-second-largest company in the Chinese beverage industry. Sales of Robust had reached RMB2 billion in 1999. After the purchase, Danone dismissed the original management and managed Robust directly. Because its new management was not familiar with the Chinese beverage market, Robust struggled. Its tea and milk products almost disappeared from the market. During 2005–2006, the company lost RMB 150 million.[20]

Wahaha Company

The Wahaha company was established in 1987 by a retired teacher, Mr. Zong Qinghou. In 1989, the enterprise opened its first plant, Wahaha Nutritional Food Factory, to produce "Wahaha Oral Liquid for Children," a nutritional drink for kids. The name Wahaha was meant to evoke a laughing child, combining the character for baby (wa) with the sound of laughter.[21] After its launch, Wahaha won a rapid public acceptance. By 1991, the company's sales revenue grew beyond 100 million renminbi (¥).[22]

In 1991, with the support of the Hangzhou local district government, Wahaha Nutritional Food Factory merged with Hangzhou Canning Food Factory, a state-owned enterprise, to form the Hangzhou Wahaha Group Corporation. After mergers with three more companies, Wahaha became the biggest corporation of its district.[23]

Since 1997, Wahaha has set up new many subsidiaries. It was aided by state and local government since its continuous expansion helped create new jobs and its increased profits led to more tax revenues.

In 1996, the Hangzhou Wahaha Group Corporation began a joint venture with Danone Group and formed five new subsidiaries, which attracted a $45 million foreign investment and then added another $26.2 million investment. With the investment funds, Wahaha brought world-class advanced production lines from Germany, America, Italy, Japan, and Canada into its sites. The terms of the Danone–Wahaha joint venture allowed Wahaha to retain all managerial and operating rights as well as the brand name Wahaha. In the next eight years, the company established 40 subsidiaries in China, and in 1998 launched its own brand, "Future Cola," to compete against Coke and Pepsi.[24]

In 2000, the company produced 2.24 million tons of beverages with sales revenue of $5.4 billion. The production accounted for 15 percent of the Chinese output of beverages. The group became the biggest company in the beverage industry of China with total assets of $4.4 billion.[25]

In 2007, it produced 6.89 million tons of beverage with a sales revenue of $25.8 billion. Today, Hangzhou Wahaha Group Co., Ltd., is still the leading beverage producer in China and has more than 100 subsidiary companies with total assets of $17.8 billion. The company product category contains more than 100 varieties, such as milk drinks, drinking water, carbonated drinks, tea drinks, canned food, and health care products.[26]

According to a report on the "Top 10 Beverage Companies" released by the China Beverage Industry Association, Wahaha contributed 55.57 percent to the Association Top 10's overall production, 65.84 percent to its revenue, and 73.16 percent to its profit tax. According to Zong Qinghou, the president of Wahaha: "As China becomes the world's largest food and beverage market, we'll be a major player in the global market." Wahaha implements a strategy of "local production and local distribution" and has built an excellent production-distribution network. Its Wahaha R&D center and Analysis Center provide guarantees for high product quality.[27]

Danone–Wahaha Joint Venture Conflict

The Wahaha joint venture (JV) was formed in 1996 with three participants: Hangzhou Wahaha Food Group (Wahaha Group); Danone Group, a French corporation (Danone); and Bai Fu Qin, a Hong Kong corporation (Baifu). Danone and Baifu did not invest directly in the JV. Instead, Danone and Baifu formed Jin Jia Investment, a Singapore corporation (Jinjia). Upon the formation of the JV, Wahaha Group owned 49 percent of the shares of the JV and Jinjia owned 51 percent of the shares of the JV. This structure led to immediate misunderstandings between the participants. From Wahaha Group's point of view—with the division of ownership at 49 percent Wahaha Group, 25.5 percent Danone, and 25.5 percent Baifu—it was the majority shareholder in the JV. Since Wahaha Group felt it controlled the JV, it was relatively unconcerned when it transferred its trademark to the JV.[29]

In 1998, Danone bought out the interest of Baifu in Jinjia, becoming 100 percent owner of Jinjia and effectively the 51 percent owner of the JV. This gave it legal control over the JV because of its right to elect the board of directors. For the first time, the Wahaha Group and Zong realized two things: (1) They had given complete control over their trademark to the JV; (2) A foreign company was now in control of the JV. From a legal standpoint, this result was implied by the structure of the JV from the very beginning. However, it is clear from public statements that the Wahaha Group did not understand the implications when they entered into the venture. The Danone "takeover" in 1998 therefore produced significant resentment on the part of Wahaha Group. Rightly or not, Wahaha felt that Danone misled them from the very beginning.[30]

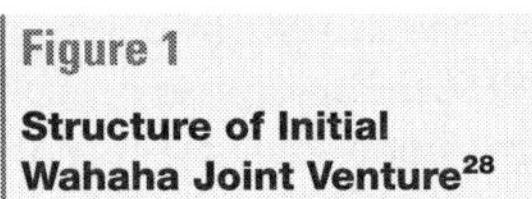

Figure 1

Structure of Initial Wahaha Joint Venture[28]

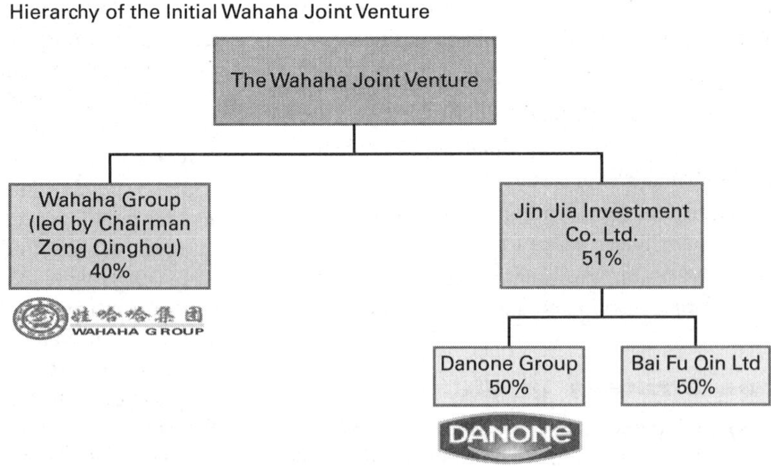

Source: Danone website.

When the JV was formed, Wahaha Group was a state-owned enterprise owned by the Hangzhou city government. After formation of the JV, it was converted into a private corporation, effectively controlled by Zong. This set the stage for Wahaha Group's decision to take back control of the trademark it felt had been unfairly transferred to Danone. Zong and his employees now viewed the transferred trademark as their personal property.[31]

When the JV was formed, Wahaha Group obtained an appraisal of its trademark valuing it at RMB100 million (US$13.2 million). The trademark was its sole contribution to the JV, while Jinjia contributed RMB500 million (US$66.1 million) in cash. Wahaha Group also agreed not to use the trademark for any independent business activity or allow it to be used by any other entity. However, the trademark transfer was rejected by China's Trademark Office. It took the position that, as the well-known mark of a state-owned enterprise, the trademark belonged to the state and Wahaha Group did not have the right to transfer it to a private company.[32]

Rather than terminate the JV, the shareholders (now Danone and Wahaha Group) decided to work around the approval issue by entering into an exclusive license agreement for the trademark in 1999. Since the license agreement was intended to be the functional equivalent of a sale of the trademark, they were concerned the Trademark Office would refuse to register the license. Therefore, they only registered an abbreviated license. This was accepted by the Trademark Office, which never saw the full license. As a result, Wahaha Group never transferred ownership of the Wahaha trademark to the JV, just the exclusive license. Thus, Wahaha Group never complied with its basic obligation for capitalization of the JV. It does not appear that any of the JV documents were revised to deal with this changed situation.[33]

Although Danone was the majority shareholder and maintained a majority interest on the board of directors, day-to-day management of the JV was delegated entirely to Zong. He filled management positions with his family members and employees of the Wahaha Group. Under Zong's management, the JV became the largest Chinese bottled water and beverage company.[34]

Beginning in 2000, the Wahaha Group created a series of companies that sold the same products as the JV and used the Wahaha trademark. The non-JV companies appear to have been owned in part by Wahaha Group and in part by an offshore British Virgin Islands company controlled by Zong's daughter and wife. Neither Danone nor Wahaha group receives any benefits from the profits of these non-JV companies. According to press reports in China, products from the non-JV companies and the JV were sold by the same sales staff working for the same sales company, all ultimately managed by Zong.[35]

In 2005, Danone realized the situation and insisted it be given a 51 percent ownership interest in the non-JV companies. Wahaha Group and Zong, who by this time was one of the richest men in China, refused.[36]

Details of the Dispute

In April 2006, Wahaha was informed by its 10-year JV partner Danone that it had breached the contract by establishing nonjoint ventures, which had infringed upon the interests of Danone. Danone proposed to purchase 51 percent of shares of Wahaha's nonjoint ventures.[37] The move was opposed by Wahaha. In May 2007, Danone formally initiated a proceeding, claiming that Wahaha's establishment of nonjoint ventures as well as the illegal use of "Wahaha" trademark had seriously violated the noncompete clause. The two parties carried on 10 lawsuits in and out of China, and all the ruled cases between Wahaha and Danone have ended in Wahaha's favor.[38]

On February 3, 2009, a California court in the United States dismissed Danone's accusation against the wife and daughter of Zong Qinghou and ruled that the dispute between Danone and Wahaha should be settled in China. In addition, Danone's lawsuits against Wahaha were rejected by courts in Italy and France; and a series of lawsuits brought by Danone in China against Zong Qinghou and Wahaha's nonjoint ventures all ended in failure.[39]

The rationality of the existence of the nonjoint ventures, the ownership of the "Wahaha" trademark, and the noncompete clause issue were the key points of the Danone-Wahaha dispute.[40] In 1996, Wahaha offered a list of 10 subsidiaries to Danone, which after evaluation selected four. Jinja Investments Pte Ltd. (a Singapore-based joint venture between Danone Asia Pte Ltd. and Hong Kong Peregrine Investment, of which Danone is the controlling shareholder), Hangzhou Wahaha Group Co., Ltd., and Zhejiang Wahaha Industrial Holdings Ltd. jointly invested to form five joint venture enterprises, with shareholdings of 51 percent, 39 percent, and 10 percent, respectively. In 1998, Hong Kong Peregrine sold its stake in Jinja Investments to Danone, which makes Danone the sole shareholder of Jinja Investments, giving it the control of over 51 percent of the joint ventures. Wahaha and Danone cooperated on the basis of joint venture enterprises, rather than the complete acquisition of Wahaha by Danone. As a result, Wahaha was always independent, and its nonjoint ventures have existed and developed since 1996. Relevant transactions of Wahaha's nonjoint ventures and joint ventures were disclosed fully and frankly by the auditing reports of PricewaterhouseCoopers, an accounting firm appointed by Danone. Meanwhile, during the 11-year cooperation, Danone assigned a Finance Director to locate in the headquarters of Wahaha Group to audit the latter's financial information.[41]

Danone and Wahaha had signed in succession three relevant agreements concerning the ownership of the "Wahaha" brand name. In 1997, the two parties signed a trademark transfer agreement, with an intention to transfer the "Wahaha" trademark to the joint ventures. The move, however, was not approved by the State Trademark Office.[42] For this reason, the two parties signed in 1999 the trademark licensing contract. According to law, the same subject cannot be synchronously transferred and licensed the use to others by the same host. Therefore, the signing and fulfillment of the trademark licensing contract showed that the two parties had agreed to the invalidation of the transfer agreement. The "Wahaha" brand should belong to the Wahaha Group, while the joint ventures only have right of use.[43]

In October 2005, the two parties signed the No. 1 amendment agreement to the trademark licensing contract, in which it confirmed Party A (Hangzhou Wahaha Group Co., Ltd.) as owner of the trademark. In addition, the second provision of the amendment agreement clearly stated that the several Wahaha subsidiaries listed in the fifth annex of the licensing contract as well as other Wahaha subsidiaries (referred to as "licensed Wahaha enterprises") established by Party A or its affiliates following the signing of the licensing contract also have right granted by one party to use the trademark. The "licensed Wahaha enterprises" involved in the amendment agreement refer to the nonjoint ventures.[44] According to related files, Wahaha owns the ownership of the "Wahaha" trademark, while its nonjoint ventures have the right to use the trademark.[45] The Wahaha brand is among the most famous in China. It ranked No. 16 among domestic brands and is worth $2.2 billion, according to a recent report by Shanghai research firm Hurun Report. Wahaha doesn't publicly disclose financial figures.[46]

Ventures and Acquisitions

Several years ago, as Wahaha sought to expand its market, Wahaha suggested adding online new production lines by increasing investment, while Danone requested Wahaha outsource to product processing suppliers for its joint ventures. Wahaha saw the shortcomings in using product processing suppliers, so it set up nonjoint ventures to meet production needs. Wahaha believed that the existence and operation of the nonjoint ventures did not adversely affect the interest of Danone.[47]

During the 11 years that followed 1996, Danone invested less than RMB1.4 billion in Wahaha's joint ventures, but received a profit of RMB3.554 billion as of 2007. On the other hand, Danone acquired several strong competitors of Wahaha including Robust, Huiyuan, and Shanghai Maling Aquariust. Wahaha saw Robust as its biggest rival. Wahaha was disappointed that Danone failed to hold up its end of the bargain of "jointly exploring markets in and out of China" listed in the JV contract.[48]

Through influence of the Chinese and French governments, Danone and Wahaha reached a peaceful settlement in late 2007. However, Danone's proposal to sell its shares in the joint ventures to Wahaha for RMB50 billion (finally reduced to approximately RMB20 billion) was rejected by Wahaha.[49]

After the negotiations were suspended, the two parties again turned to legal action. As of April 2009, all the ruled cases both in China and abroad have ruled against Danone.[50]

Conflict Resolution

In late September 2009, France's Groupe Danone SA agreed to accept a cash settlement to relinquish claims to the name Wahaha. In a joint statement issued September 30, 2009, Danone announced a settlement with China's Hangzhou Wahaha Group Co. by saying its 51 percent share in joint ventures that make soft drinks and related products will be sold to the businesses' Chinese partners. "The completion of this settlement will put an end to all legal proceedings related to the disputes between the two parties," the statement said.[51]

The feud over control of the Wahaha empire offered a glimpse into the breakup of a major Asian-foreign joint venture. Danone's strategy to publicly confront its partner and Wahaha's strategy to respond with its own accusations marked a break with prevailing business practice in China, where problems have usually been settled with face-saving, private negotiations.[52]

Analysts said the case served to reinforce how difficult it is to operate a partnership in China. "That's a key lesson: To build a [brand] business in China you need to build from the ground up," said Jonathan Chajet, China managing director for consultancy Interbrand.[53] Foreign firms such as Procter & Gamble, Starbucks, and General Motors have operated wholly or in part through joint ventures in China. But executives involved say the expectations of foreign and local parties can conflict in a JV.

Danone, which reported the Wahaha business generated about 10 percent of its global revenue in 2006 but has since adjusted how it accounted for Wahaha, said it expects no impact on its income statement from the settlement. In China, it will be left with a much smaller footprint and is essentially starting over.[54] Danone's CEO Franck Riboud stated: "Danone has a long-standing commitment to China, where it has been present since 1987, and we are keen to accelerate the success of our Chinese activities." China is Danone's fourth-largest market after France, Spain, and the U.S., contributing about €1bn, or 8 percent, of Danone's revenues.[55]

Questions for Review

1. When and how did Danone expand into the Chinese market? What problems did Danone Group encounter while operating in China?
2. How was the Danone and Wahaha JV formed? What was its structure? Why did Danone decide to form a joint venture rather than establish a 100 percent–owned subsidiary?
3. What was the problem of Danone Wahaha joint venture that triggered the conflict between the companies? What were the differences in Danone's and Wahaha's understanding of their own respective roles and responsibilities in this venture? What aspects of national and organizational culture affected this perspective?
4. Was Danone successful in proving its claims in court? How was the conflict between the two companies resolved? What were the key lessons for Danone about doing business in China?
5. Did Danone follow the advice regarding JVs in China mentioned in the list just above? Which aspects did it follow and which did it not?

Source: This case was prepared by Tetyana Azarova of Villanova University under the supervision of Professor Jonathan Doh as the basis for class discussion. Research assistance was provided by Kelley Bergsma and Benjamin Littell. It is not intended to illustrate either effective or ineffective managerial capability or administrative responsibility.

In-Depth Integrative Case 1.1a

Euro Disneyland

On January 18, 1993, Euro Disneyland chairperson Robert Fitzpatrick announced he would leave that post on April 12 to begin his own consulting company. Quitting his position exactly one year after the grand opening of Euro Disneyland, Fitzpatrick with his resignation removed U.S. management from the helm of the French theme park and resort.

Fitzpatrick's position was taken by a Frenchman, Philippe Bourguignon, who had been Euro Disneyland's senior vice president for real estate. Bourguignon, 45 years old, faced a net loss of FFr 188 million for Euro Disneyland's fiscal year, which ended September 1992. Also, between April and September 1992, only 29 percent of the park's total visitors were French. Expectations were that closer to half of all visitors would be French.

It was hoped that the promotion of Philippe Bourguignon would have a public relations benefit for Euro Disneyland—a project that had been a publicist's nightmare from the beginning. One of the low points was at a news conference prior to the park's opening when protesters pelted Michael Eisner, CEO of the Walt Disney Company, with rotten eggs. Within the first year of operation, Disney had to compromise its "squeaky clean" image and lift the alcohol ban at the park. Wine is now served at all major restaurants.

Euro Disneyland, 49 percent owned by Walt Disney Company, Burbank, California, originally forecasted 11 million visitors in the first year of operation. In January 1993 it appeared attendance would be closer to 10 million. In response, management temporarily slashed prices at the park for local residents to FFr 150 ($27.27) from FFr 225 ($40.91) for adults and to FFr 100 from FFr 150 for children in order to lure more French during the slow, wet winter months. The company also reduced prices at its restaurants and hotels, which registered occupancy rates of just 37 percent.

Bourguignon also faced other problems, such as the second phase of development at Euro Disneyland, which was expected to start in September 1993. It was unclear how the company planned to finance its FFr 8–10 billion cost. The company had steadily drained its cash reserves (FFr 1.9 billion in May 1993) while piling up debt (FFr 21 billion in May 1993). Euro Disneyland admitted that it and the Walt Disney Company were "exploring potential sources of financing for Euro Disneyland." The company was also talking to banks about restructuring its debts.

Despite the frustrations, Eisner was tirelessly upbeat about the project. "Instant hits are things that go away quickly, and things that grow slowly and are part of the culture are what we look for," he said. "What we created in France is the biggest private investment in a foreign country by an American company ever. And it's gonna pay off."

In the Beginning

Disney's story is the classic American rags-to-riches story, which started in a small Kansas City advertising office where Mickey was a real mouse prowling the unknown Walt Disney floor. Originally, Mickey was named Mortimer, until a dissenting Mrs. Disney stepped in. How close Mickey was to Walt Disney is evidenced by the fact that when filming, Disney himself dubbed the mouse's voice. Only in later films did Mickey get a different voice. Disney made many sacrifices to promote his hero-mascot, including selling his first car, a beloved Moon Cabriolet, and humiliating himself in front of Louis B. Mayer. "Get that mouse off the screen!" was the movie mogul's reported response to the cartoon character. Then, in 1955, Disney had the brainstorm of sending his movie characters out into the "real" world to mix with their fans, and he battled skeptics to build the very first Disneyland in Anaheim, California.

When Disney died in 1966, the company went into virtual suspended animation. Its last big hit of that era was 1969's *The Love Bug,* about a Volkswagen named Herbie. Today, Disney executives trace the problem to a tyrannical CEO named E. Cardon Walker, who ruled the company from 1976 to 1983, and to his successor, Ronald W. Miller. Walker was quick to ridicule underlings in public and impervious to any point of view but his own. He made decisions according to what he thought Walt would have done. Executives clinched arguments by quoting Walt like the Scriptures or Marx, and the company eventually supplied a little book of the founder's sayings. Making the wholesome family movies Walt would have wanted formed a key article of Walker's creed. For example, a poster advertising the unremarkable Condorman featured actress Barbara Carrera in a slit skirt. Walker had the slit painted over. With this as the context, studio producers ground out a thin stream of tired, formulaic movies that fewer and fewer customers would pay to see. In mid-1983, a similar low-horsepower approach to television production led to CBS's cancellation of the hour-long program *The Wonderful World of Disney,* leaving the company without a regular network show for the first time in 29 years. Like a reclusive hermit, the company lost touch with the contemporary world.

Ron Miller's brief reign was by contrast a model of decentralization and delegation. Many attributed Miller's ascent to his marrying the boss's daughter rather than to any special gift. To shore Miller up, the board installed Raymond L. Watson, former head of the Irvine Co., as part-time chairperson. He quickly became full time.

Miller sensed the studio needed rejuvenation, and he managed to produce the hit film *Splash,* featuring an apparently (but not actually) bare-breasted mermaid, under the newly devised Touchstone label. However, the reluctance of freelance Hollywood talent to accommodate Disney's narrow range and stingy compensation often kept his sound instincts from bearing fruit. "Card [Cardon Walker] would listen but not hear," said a former executive. "Ron [Ron Miller] would listen but not act."

Too many box office bombs contributed to a steady erosion of profit. Profits of $135 million on revenues of $915 million in 1980 dwindled to $93 million on revenues of $1.3 billion in 1983. More alarmingly, revenues from the company's theme parks, about three-quarters of the company's total revenues, were showing signs of leveling off. Disney's stock slid from $84.375 a share to $48.75 between April 1983 and February 1984.

Through these years, Roy Disney Jr. simmered while he watched the downfall of the national institution that his uncle, Walt, and his father, Roy Disney Sr., had built. He had long argued that the company's constituent parts all worked together to enhance each other. If movie and television production weren't revitalized, not only would that source of revenue disappear but the company and its activities would also grow dim in the public eye. At the same time the stream of new ideas and characters that kept people pouring into the parks and buying toys, books, and records would dry up. Now his dire predictions were coming true. His own personal shareholding had already dropped from $96 million to $54 million. Walker's treatment of Ron Miller as the shining heir apparent and Roy Disney as the idiot nephew helped drive Roy to quit as Disney vice president in 1977 and to set up Shamrock Holdings, a broadcasting and investment company.

In 1984, Roy teamed up with Stanley Gold, a tough-talking lawyer and a brilliant strategist. Gold saw that the falling stock price was bound to flush out a raider and afford Roy Disney a chance to restore the company's fortunes. They asked Frank Wells, vice chairperson of Warner Bros., if he would take a top job in the company in the event they offered it. Wells, a lawyer and a Rhodes scholar, said yes. With that, Roy knew that what he would hear in Disney's boardroom would limit his freedom to trade in its stock, so he quit the board on March 9, 1984. "I knew that would hang a 'For Sale' sign over the company," said Gold.

By resigning, Roy pushed over the first of a train of dominoes that ultimately led to the result he most desired. The company was raided, almost dismantled, greenmailed, raided again, and sued left and right. But it miraculously emerged with a skilled new top management with big plans for a bright future. Roy Disney proposed Michael Eisner as the CEO, but the board came close to rejecting Eisner in favor of an older, more buttoned-down candidate. Gold stepped in and made an impassioned speech to the directors. "You see guys like Eisner as a little crazy . . . but every studio in this country has been run by crazies. What do you think Walt Disney was? The guy was off the goddamned wall. This is a creative institution. It needs to be run by crazies again."[1]

Meanwhile Eisner and Wells staged an all-out lobbying campaign, calling on every board member except two, who were abroad, to explain their views about the company's future. "What was most important," said Eisner, "was that they saw I did not come in a tutu, and that I was a serious person, and I understood a P&L, and I knew the investment analysts, and I read Fortune."

In September 1984, Michael Eisner was appointed CEO and Frank Wells became president. Jeffrey Katzenberg, the 33-year-old, maniacal production chief, followed Fisher from Paramount Pictures. He took over Disney's movie and television studios. "The key," said Eisner, "is to start off with a great idea."

Disneyland in Anaheim, California

For a long time, Walt Disney had been concerned about the lack of family-type entertainment available for his two daughters. The amusement parks he saw around him were mostly filthy traveling carnivals. They were often unsafe and allowed unruly conduct on the premises. Disney envisioned a place where people from all over the world would be able to go for clean and safe fun. His dream came true on July 17, 1955, when the gates first opened at Disneyland in Anaheim, California.

Disneyland strives to generate the perfect fantasy. But magic does not simply happen. The place is a marvel of modern technology. Literally dozens of computers, huge banks of tape machines, film projectors, and electronic controls lie behind the walls, beneath the floors, and above the ceilings of dozens of rides and attractions. The philosophy is that "Disneyland is the world's biggest stage, and the audience is right here on the stage," said Dick Hollinger, chief industrial engineer at Disneyland. "It takes a tremendous amount of work to keep the stage clean and working properly."

Cleanliness is a primary concern. Before the park opens at 8 a.m., the cleaning crew will have mopped, hosed, and dried every sidewalk, street, floor, and counter. More than 350 of the park's 7,400 employees come on duty at 1 a.m., to begin the daily cleanup routine. The thousands of feet that walk through the park each day and chewing gum do not mix; gum has always presented major cleanup problems. The park's janitors found long ago that fire hoses with 90 pounds of water pressure would not do the job. Now they use steam machines, razor scrapers, and mops towed by Cushman scooters to literally scour the streets and sidewalks daily.

It takes one person working a full eight-hour shift to polish the brass on the Fantasyland merry-go-round. The scrupulously manicured plantings throughout the park are treated with growth-retarding hormones to keep the trees and bushes from spreading beyond their assigned spaces and destroying the carefully maintained five-eighths scale modeling that is utilized in the park. The maintenance supervisor of the Matterhorn bobsled ride personally walks every foot of track and inspects every link of tow chain every night, thus trusting his or her own eyes more than the $2 million in safety equipment that is built into the ride.

Eisner himself pays obsessive attention to detail. Walking through Disneyland one Sunday afternoon, he peered at the plastic leaves on the Swiss Family Robinson tree house noting that they periodically wear out and need to be replaced leaf by leaf at a cost of $500,000. As his family strolled through the park, he and his eldest son Breck stooped to pick up the rare piece of litter that the cleanup crew had somehow missed. This old-fashioned dedication has paid off. Since opening day in 1955, Disneyland has been a consistent moneymaker.

Disney World in Orlando, Florida

By the time Eisner arrived, Disney World in Orlando was already on its way to becoming what it is today—the most popular vacation destination in the United States. But the company had neglected a rich niche in its business: hotels. Disney's three existing hotels, probably the most profitable in the United States, registered unheard-of occupancy rates of 92 percent to 96 percent versus 66 percent for the industry. Eisner promptly embarked on an ambitious $1 billion hotel expansion plan. Two major hotels, Disney's Grand Floridian Beach Resort and Disney's Caribbean Beach Resort, were opened during 1987–89. Disney's Yacht Club and Beach Resort along with the Dolphin and Swan Hotels, owned and operated by Tishman Realty & Construction, Metropolitan Life Insurance, and Aoki Corporation opened during 1989–90. Adding 3,400 hotel rooms and 250,000 square feet of convention space made it the largest convention center east of the Mississippi.

In October 1982, Disney made a new addition to the theme park—the Experimental Prototype Community of Tomorrow, or EPCOT Center. E. Cardon Walker, then president of the company, announced that EPCOT would be a "permanent showcase, industrial park, and experimental housing center." This new park consists of two large complexes: Future World, a series of pavilions designed to show the technological advances of the next 25 years, and World Showcase, a collection of foreign "villages."

Tokyo Disneyland

It was Tokyo's nastiest winter day in four years. Arctic winds and 8 inches of snow lashed the city. Roads were clogged and trains slowed down. But the bad weather didn't keep 13,200 hardy souls from Tokyo Disneyland. Mikki Mausu, better known outside Japan as Mickey Mouse, had taken the country by storm.

Located on a fringe of reclaimed shoreline in Urayasu City on the outskirts of Tokyo, the park opened to the public on April 15, 1983. In less than one year, over 10 million people had passed through its gates, an attendance figure that has been bettered every single year. On August 13, 1983, 93,000 people helped set a one-day attendance record that easily eclipsed the old records established at the two parent U.S. parks. Four years later, records again toppled as the turnstiles clicked. The total this time: 111,500. By 1988, approximately 50 million people, or nearly half of Japan's population, had visited Tokyo Disneyland since its opening. The steady cash flow pushed revenues for fiscal year 1989 to $768 million, up 17 percent from 1988.

The 204-acre Tokyo Disneyland is owned and operated by Oriental Land under license from the Walt Disney Co. The 45-year contract gives Disney 10 percent of admissions and 5 percent of food and merchandise sales, plus licensing fees. Disney opted to take no equity in the project and put no money down for construction. "I never had the slightest doubt about the success of Disneyland in Japan," said Masatomo Takahashi, president of Oriental Land Company. Oriental Land was so confident of the success of Disney in Japan that it financed the park entirely with debt, borrowing ¥180 billion ($1.5 billion at February 1988 exchange rates). Takahashi added, "The debt means nothing to me," and with good reason. According to Fusahao Awata, who co-authored a book on Tokyo Disneyland: "The Japanese yearn for [American culture]."

Soon after Tokyo Disneyland opened in April 1983, five Shinto priests held a solemn dedication ceremony near Cinderella's castle. It is the only overtly Japanese ritual seen so far in this sprawling theme park. What visitors see is pure Americana. All signs are in English, with only small katakana (a phonetic Japanese alphabet)

Exhibit 1 How the Theme Parks Grew

1955	Disneyland
1966	Walt Disney's death
1971	Walt Disney World in Orlando
1982	Epcot Center
1983	Tokyo Disneyland
1992	Euro Disneyland

Stephen Koepp, "Do You Believe in Magic?" *Time,* April 25, 1988, pp. 66–73.

translations. Most of the food is American style, and the attractions are cloned from Disney's U.S. parks. Disney also held firm on two fundamentals that strike the Japanese as strange—no alcohol is allowed and no food may be brought in from outside the park.

However, in Disney's enthusiasm to make Tokyo a brick-by-brick copy of Anaheim's Magic Kingdom, there were a few glitches. On opening day, the Tokyo park discovered that almost 100 public telephones were placed too high for Japanese guests to reach them comfortably. And many hungry customers found countertops above their reach at the park's snack stands.

"Everything we imported that worked in the United States works here," said Ronald D. Pogue, managing director of Walt Disney Attractions Japan Ltd. "American things like McDonald's hamburgers and Kentucky Fried Chicken are popular here with young people. We also wanted visitors from Japan and Southeast Asia to feel they were getting the real thing," said Toshiharu Akiba, a staff member of the Oriental Land publicity department.

Still, local sensibilities dictated a few changes. A Japanese restaurant was added to please older patrons. The Nautilus submarine is missing. More areas are covered to protect against rain and snow. Lines for attractions had to be redesigned so that people walking through the park did not cross in front of patrons waiting to ride an attraction. "It's very discourteous in Japan to have people cross in front of somebody else," explained James B. Cora, managing director of operations for the Tokyo project. The biggest differences between Japan and America have come in slogans and ad copy. Although English is often used, it's "Japanized" English—the sort that would have native speakers shaking their heads while the Japanese nod happily in recognition. "Let's Spring" was the motto for one of their highly successful ad campaigns.

Pogue, visiting frequently from his base in California, supervised seven resident American Disney managers who work side by side with Japanese counterparts from Oriental Land Co. to keep the park in tune with the Disney doctrine. American it may be, but Tokyo Disneyland appeals to such deep-seated Japanese passions as cleanliness, order, outstanding service, and technological wizardry. Japanese executives are impressed by Disney's detailed training manuals, which teach employees how to make visitors feel like VIPs. Most worth emulating, say the Japanese, is Disney's ability to make even the lowliest job seem glamorous. "They have changed the image of dirty work," said Hakuhodo Institute's Sekizawa.

Disney Company did encounter a few unique cultural problems when developing Tokyo Disneyland:

> *The problem:* how to dispose of some 250 tons of trash that would be generated weekly by Tokyo Disneyland visitors?
> *The standard Disney solution:* trash compactors.
> *The Japanese proposal:* pigs to eat the trash and be slaughtered and sold at a profit.

Exhibit 2 Investor's Snapshot: The Walt Disney Company (December 1989)

Sales (latest four quarters)	$4.6 billion
Change from year earlier	Up 33.6%
Net profit	$703.3 million
Change	Up 34.7%
Return on common stockholders' equity	23.4%
Five year average	20.3%
Stock price average (last 12 months)	$60.50–$136.25
Recent share price	$122.75
Price/Earnings Multiple	27
Total return to investor (12 months to 11/3/89)	90.6%

Source: Fortune, December 4, 1989.

James B. Cora and his team of some 150 operations experts did a little calculating and pointed out that it would take 100,000 pigs to do the job. And then there would be the smell . . .

The Japanese relented.

The Japanese were also uneasy about a rustic-looking Westernland, Tokyo's version of Frontierland. "The Japanese like everything fresh and new when they put it in," said Cora. "They kept painting the wood and we kept saying, 'No, it's got to look old.'" Finally the Disney crew took the Japanese to Anaheim to give them a firsthand look at the Old West.

Tokyo Disneyland opened just as the yen escalated in value against the dollar, and the income level of the Japanese registered a phenomenal improvement. During this era of affluence, Tokyo Disneyland triggered an interest in leisure. Its great success spurred the construction of "leisurelands" throughout the country. This created an increase in the Japanese people's orientation toward leisure. But demographics are the real key to Tokyo Disneyland's success. Thirty million Japanese live within 30 miles of the park. There are three times more than the number of people in the same proximity to Anaheim's Disneyland. With the park proven such an unqualified hit, and nearing capacity, Oriental Land and Disney mapped out plans for a version of the Disney-MGM studio tour next door. This time, Disney talked about taking a 50 percent stake in the project.

Building Euro Disneyland

On March 24, 1987, Michael Eisner and Jacques Chirac, the French prime minister, signed a contract for the building of a Disney theme park at Marne-la-Vallee. Talks between Disney and the French government had dragged on for more than a year. At the signing, Robert Fitzpatrick, fluent in French, married to the former Sylvie Blondet, and the recipient of two awards from the French government, was introduced as the president of Euro Disneyland. He was expected to be a key player in wooing support from the French establishment for the theme park. As one analyst put it, Disney selected him to set up the park because he is "more French than the French."

Disney had been courted extensively by Spain and France. The prime ministers of both countries ordered their governments to lend Disney a hand in its quest for a site. France set up a five-person team headed by Special Advisor to Foreign Trade and Tourism Minister Edith Cresson, and Spain's negotiators included Ignacio Vasallo, Director-General for the Promotion of Tourism. Disney pummeled both governments with requests for detailed information. "The only thing they haven't asked us for is the color of the tourists' eyes," moaned Vasallo.

The governments tried other enticements too. Spain offered tax and labor incentives and possibly as much as 20,000 acres of land. The French package, although less generous, included spending of $53 million to improve highway access to the proposed site and perhaps speeding up a $75 million subway project. For a long time, all that smiling Disney officials would say was that Spain had better weather while France had a better population base.

Officials explained that they picked France over Spain because Marne-la-Vallee is advantageously close to one of the world's tourism capitals, while also being situated within a day's drive or train ride of some 30 million people in France, Belgium, England, and Germany. Another advantage mentioned was the availability of good transportation. A train line that serves as part of the Paris Metro subway system ran to Torcy, in the center of Marne-la-Vallee, and the French government promised to extend the line to the actual site of the park. The park would also be served by A-4, a modern highway that runs from Paris to the German border, as well as a freeway that runs to Charles de Gaulle airport.

Once a letter of intent had been signed, sensing that the French government was keen to not let the plan fail, Disney held out for one concession after another. For example, Disney negotiated for VAT (value-added tax) on ticket sales to be cut from a normal 18.6 percent to 7 percent. A quarter of the investment in building the park would come from subsidized loans. Additionally, any disputes arising from the contract would be settled not in French courts but by a special international panel of arbitrators. But Disney did have to agree to a clause in the contract which would require it to respect and utilize French culture in its themes.

The park was built on 4,460 acres of farmland in Marne-la-Vallee, a rural corner of France 20 miles east of Paris known mostly for sugar beets and Brie cheese. Opening was planned for early 1992, and planners hoped to attract some 10 million visitors a year. Approximately $2.5 billion was needed to build the park, making it the largest single foreign investment ever in France. A French "pivot" company was formed to build the park with starting capital of FFr 3 billion, split 60 percent French and 40 percent foreign, with Disney taking 16.67 percent. Euro Disneyland was expected to bring $600 million in foreign investment into France each year.

As soon as the contract had been signed, individuals and businesses began scurrying to somehow plug into the Mickey Mouse money machine—all were hoping to benefit from the American dream without leaving France. In fact, one Paris daily, *Liberation,* actually sprouted mouse ears over its front-page flag.

The $1.5 to $2 billion first phase investment would involve an amusement complex including hotels and restaurants, golf courses, and an aquatic park in addition to a European version of the Magic Kingdom. The second phase, scheduled to start after the gates opened in 1992, called for the construction of a community around the park, including a sports complex, technology park, conference center, theater, shopping mall, university campus, villas, and condominiums. No price tag had been put on the second phase, although it was expected to rival, if not surpass, the first phase investment. In November 1989, Fitzpatrick announced that the Disney–MGM Studios, Europe, would also open at Euro Disneyland in 1996, resembling the enormously successful Disney–MGM Studios theme park at Disney World in Orlando. The new studios would greatly enhance the Walt Disney Company's strategy of increasing its production of live action and animated filmed entertainment in Europe for both the European and world markets.

"The phone's been ringing here ever since the announcement," said Marc Berthod of EpaMarne, the government body that oversees the Marne-la-Vallee region. "We've gotten calls from big companies as well as small—everything from hotel chains to language interpreters all asking for details on Euro Disneyland. And the individual mayors of the villages around here have been swamped with calls from people looking for jobs," he added.

Euro Disneyland was expected to generate up to 28,000 jobs, providing a measure of relief for an area that had suffered a 10 percent–plus unemployment rate for the previous year. It was also expected to light a fire under France's construction industry, which had been particularly hard hit by France's economic problems over the previous year. Moreover, Euro Disneyland was expected to attract many other investors to the depressed outskirts of Paris. International Business Machines (IBM) and Banque National de Paris were among those already building in the area. In addition one of the new buildings going up was a factory that would employ 400 outside workers to wash the 50 tons of laundry expected to be generated per day by Euro Disneyland's 14,000 employees.

The impact of Euro Disneyland was also felt in the real estate market. "Everyone who owns land around here is holding on to it for the time being, at least until they know what's going to happen," said Danny Theveno, a spokesman for the town of Villiers on the western edge of Marne-la-Vallee. Disney expected 11 million visitors in the first year. The break-even point was estimated to be between 7 and 8 million. One worry was that Euro Disneyland would cannibalize the flow of European visitors to Walt Disney World in Florida, but European travel agents said that their customers were still eagerly signing up for Florida, lured by the cheap dollar and the promise of sunshine.

Protests of Cultural Imperialism

Disney faced French communists and intellectuals who protested the building of Euro Disneyland. Ariane Mnouchkine, a theater director, described it as a "cultural Chernobyl." "I wish with all my heart that the rebels would set fire to Disneyland," thundered a French intellectual in the newspaper *La Figaro*. "Mickey Mouse," sniffed another, "is stifling individualism and transforming children into consumers." The theme park was damned as an example of American "neoprovincialism."

Farmers in the Marne-la-Vallee region posted protest signs along the roadside featuring a mean looking Mickey Mouse and touting sentiments such as "Disney go home," "Stop the massacre," and "Don't gnaw away our national wealth." Farmers were upset partly because under the terms of the contract, the French government would expropriate the necessary land and sell it without profit to the Euro Disneyland development company.

While local officials were sympathetic to the farmers' position, they were unwilling to let their predicament interfere with what some called "the deal of the century." "For many years these farmers have had the fortune to cultivate what is considered some of the richest land in France," said Berthod. "Now they'll have to find another occupation."

Also less than enchanted about the prospect of a magic kingdom rising among its midst was the communist-dominated labor federation, the Confédération Générale du Travail (CGT). Despite the job-creating potential of Euro Disney, the CGT doubted its members would benefit. The union had been fighting hard to stop the passage of a bill which would give managers the right to establish flexible hours for their workers. Flexible hours were believed to be a prerequisite to the profitable operation of Euro Disneyland, especially considering seasonal variations.

However, Disney proved to be relatively immune to the anti-U.S. virus. In early 1985, one of the three state-owned television networks signed a contract to broadcast two hours of dubbed Disney programming every Saturday evening. Soon after, *Disney Channel* became one of the top-rated programs in France.

In 1987, the company launched an aggressive community relations program to calm the fears of politicians, farmers, villagers, and even bankers that the project would bring traffic congestion, noise, pollution, and other problems to their countryside. Such a public relations program was a rarity in France, where businesses make little effort to establish good relations with local residents. Disney invited 400 local children to a birthday party for Mickey Mouse, sent Mickey to area hospitals, and hosted free trips to Disney World in Florida for dozens of local officials and children.

"They're experts at seduction, and they don't hide the fact that they're trying to seduce you," said Vincent Guardiola, an official with Banque Indosuez, one of the 17 banks wined and dined at Orlando and subsequently one of the venture's financial participants. "The French aren't used to this kind of public relations—it was unbelievable." Observers said that the goodwill efforts helped dissipate initial objections to the project.

Financial Structuring at Euro Disneyland

Eisner was so keen on Euro Disneyland that Disney kept a 49 percent stake in the project, while the remaining 51 percent of stock was distributed through the London, Paris, and Brussels stock exchanges. Half the stock under the offer was going to the French, 25 percent to the English, and the remainder distributed in the rest of the European community. The initial offer price of FFr 72 was considerably higher than the pathfinder prospectus estimate because the capacity of the park had been slightly extended. Scarcity of stock was likely to push up the price, which was expected to reach FFr 166 by opening day in 1992. This would give a compound return of 21 percent.

Exhibit 3 Chronology of the Euro Disneyland Deal

1984–85	Disney negotiates with Spain and France to create a European theme park. Chooses France as the site.
1987	Disney signs letter of intent with the French government.
1988	Selects lead commercial bank lenders for the senior portion of the project. Forms the Société en Nom Collectif (SNC). Begins planning for the equity offering of 51% of Euro Disneyland as required in the letter of intent.
1989	European press and stock analysts visit Walt Disney World in Orlando. Begin extensive news and television campaign. Stock starts trading at 20–25 percent premium from the issue price.

Source: Geraldine E. Willigan, "The Value-Adding CFO: An Interview with Disney's Gary Wilson," *Harvard Business Review,* January–February 1990, pp. 85–93.

Walt Disney Company maintained management control of the company. The U.S. company put up $160 million of its own capital to fund the project, an investment which soared in value to $2.4 billion after the popular stock offering in Europe. French national and local authorities, by comparison, were providing about $800 million in low-interest loans and poured at least that much again into infrastructure.

Other sources of funding were the park's 12 corporate sponsors, and Disney would pay them back in kind. The "autopolis" ride, where kids ride cars, features coupes emblazoned with the "Hot Wheels" logo. Mattel Inc., sponsor of the ride, was grateful for the boost to one of its biggest toy lines.

The real payoff would begin once the park opened. The Walt Disney Company would receive 10 percent of admission fees and 5 percent of food and merchandise revenue, the same arrangement as in Japan. But in France, it would also receive management fees, incentive fees, and 49 percent of the profits.

A Saloman Brothers analyst estimated that the park would pull in 3 to 4 million more visitors than the 11 million the company expected in the first year. Other Wall Street analysts cautioned that stock prices of both Walt Disney Company and Euro Disney already contained all the Euro optimism they could absorb. "Europeans visit Disney World in Florida as part of an 'American experience,'" said Patrick P. Roper, marketing director of Alton Towers, a successful British theme park near Manchester. He doubted they would seek the suburbs of Paris as eagerly as America and predicted attendance would trail Disney projections.

The Layout of Euro Disneyland

Euro Disneyland is determinedly American in its theme. There was an alcohol ban in the park despite the attitude among the French that wine with a meal is a God-given right. Designers presented a plan for a Main Street USA based on scenes of America in the 1920s, because research indicated that Europeans loved the Prohibition era. Eisner decreed that images of gangsters and speakeasies were too negative. Though made more ornate and Victorian than Walt Disney's idealized Midwestern small town, Main Street remained Main Street. Steamships leave from Main Street through the Grand Canyon Diorama en route to Frontierland.

The familiar Disney Tomorrowland, with its dated images of the space age, was jettisoned entirely. It was replaced by a gleaming brass and wood complex called Discoverland, which was based on themes of Jules Verne and Leonardo da Vinci. Eisner ordered $8 or $10 million in extras to the "Visionarium" exhibit, a 360-degree movie about French culture which was required by the French in their original contract. French and English are the official languages at the park, and multilingual guides are available to help Dutch, German, Spanish, and Italian visitors.

With the American Wild West being so frequently captured on film, Europeans have their own idea of what life was like back then. Frontierland reinforces those images. A runaway mine train takes guests through the canyons and mines of Gold Rush country. There is a paddle wheel steamboat reminiscent of Mark Twain, Indian explorer canoes, and a phantom manor from the Gold Rush days.

In Fantasyland, designers strived to avoid competing with the nearby European reality of actual medieval towns, cathedrals, and chateaux. While Disneyland's castle is based on Germany's Neuschwanstein and Disney World's is based on a Loire Valley chateau, Euro Disney's *Le Château de la Belle au Bois Dormant,* as the French insisted Sleeping Beauty be called, is more cartoonlike with stained glass windows built by English craftspeople and depicting Disney characters. Fanciful trees grow inside as well as a beanstalk.

The park is criss-crossed with covered walkways. Eisner personally ordered the installation of 35 fireplaces in hotels and restaurants. "People walk around Disney World in Florida with humidity and temperatures in the 90s and they walk into an air-conditioned ride and say, 'This is the greatest,'" said Eisner. "When it's raining and miserable, I hope they will walk into one of these lobbies with the fireplace going and say the same thing."

Children all over Europe were primed to consume. Even one of the intellectuals who contributed to *Le Figaro's* Disney-bashing broadsheet was forced to admit with resignation that his 10-year-old son "swears by Michael Jackson." At Euro Disneyland, under the name "Captain EO," Disney just so happened to have a Michael Jackson attraction awaiting him.

Food Service and Accommodations at Euro Disneyland

Disney expected to serve 15,000 to 17,000 meals per hour, excluding snacks. Menus and service systems were developed so that they varied both in style and price. There is a 400-seat buffeteria, 6 table service restaurants, 12 counter service units, 10 snack bars, 1 Discovery food court seating 850, 9 popcorn wagons, 15 ice-cream carts, 14 specialty food carts, and 2 employee cafeterias. Restaurants were, in fact, to be a showcase for American foods. The only exception to this is Fantasyland which re-creates European fables. Here, food service will reflect the fable's country of origin: Pinocchio's facility having German food; Cinderella's, French; Bella Notte's, Italian; and so on.

Of course recipes were adapted for European tastes. Since many Europeans don't care much for very spicy food, Tex-Mex recipes were toned down. A special coffee blend had to be developed which would have universal appeal. Hot dog carts would reflect the regionalism of

Exhibit 4 The Euro Disneyland Resort

5,000 acres in size
30 attractions
12,000 employees
6 hotels (with 5,184 rooms)
10 theme restaurants
414 cabins
181 camping sites

Source: Roger Cohen, "Threat of Strikes in Euro Disney Debut," *New York Times,* April 10, 1992, p. 20.

American tastes. There would be a ball park hot dog (mild, steamed, a mixture of beef and pork), a New York hot dog (all beef, and spicy), and a Chicago hot dog (Vienna-style, similar to bratwurst).

Euro Disneyland has six theme hotels which would offer nearly 5,200 rooms on opening day, a campground (444 rental trailers and 181 camping sites), and single family homes on the periphery of the 27-hole golf course.

Disney's Strict Appearance Code

Antoine Guervil stood at his post in front of the 1,000-room Cheyenne Hotel at Euro Disneyland, practicing his "Howdy!" When Guervil, a political refugee from Haiti, said the word, it sounded more like "Audi." Native French speakers have trouble with the aspirated "h" sound in words like "hay" and "Hank" and "howdy." Guervil had been given the job of wearing a cowboy costume and booming a happy, welcoming howdy to guests as they entered the Cheyenne, styled after a Western movie set.

"Audi," said Guervil, the strain of linguistic effort showing on his face. This was clearly a struggle. Unless things got better, it was not hard to imagine objections from Renault, the French car company that was one of the corporate sponsors of the park. Picture the rage of a French auto executive arriving with his or her family at the Renault-sponsored Euro Disneyland, only to hear the doorman of a Disney hotel advertising a German car.

Such were the problems Disney faced while hiring some 12,000 people to maintain and populate its Euro Disneyland theme park. A handbook of detailed rules on acceptable clothing, hairstyles, and jewelry, among other things, embroiled the company in a legal and cultural dispute. Critics asked how the brash Americans could be so insensitive to French culture, individualism, and privacy. Disney officials insisted that a ruling that barred them from imposing a squeaky-clean employment standard could threaten the image and long-term success of the park.

"For us, the appearance code has a real effect from a product identification standpoint," said Thor Degelmann, vice president for human resources for Euro Disneyland. "Without it we wouldn't be presenting the Disney product that people would be expecting."

The rules, spelled out in a video presentation and detailed in a guide handbook, went beyond height and weight standards. They required men's hair to be cut above the collar and ears with no beards or mustaches. Any tattoos must be covered. Women must keep their hair in one "natural color" with no frosting or streaking, and they may make only limited use of makeup like mascara. False eyelashes, eyeliners, and eye pencil were completely off limits. Fingernails can't pass the end of the fingers. As for jewelry, women can wear only one earring in each ear, with the earring's diameter no more than three-quarters of an inch. Neither men nor women can wear more than one ring on each hand. Further, women were required to wear appropriate undergarments and only transparent panty hose, not black or anything with fancy designs. Though a daily bath was not specified in the rules, the applicant's video depicted a shower scene and informed applicants that they were expected to show up for work "fresh and clean each day." Similar rules are in force at Disney's three other theme parks in the United States and Japan.

In the United States, some labor unions representing Disney employees have occasionally protested the company's strict appearance code, but with little success. French labor unions began protesting when Disneyland opened its "casting center" and invited applicants to "play the role of [their lives]" and to take a "unique opportunity to marry work and magic." The CGT handed out leaflets in front of the center to warn applicants of the appearance code, which they believed represented "an attack on individual liberty." A more mainstream union, the Confédération Française Démocratique du Travail (CFDT), appealed to the Labor Ministry to halt Disney's violation of "human dignity." French law prohibits employers from restricting individual and collective liberties unless the restrictions can be justified by the nature of the task to be accomplished and are proportional to that end.

Degelmann, however, said that the company was "well aware of the cultural differences" between the United States and France and as a result had "toned down" the wording in the original American version of the guidebook. He pointed out that many companies, particularly airlines, maintained appearance codes just as strict. "We happened to put ours in writing," he added. In any case, he said that he knew of no one who had refused to take the job because of the rules and that no more than 5 percent of the people showing up for interviews had decided not to proceed after watching the video, which also detailed transportation and salary.

Fitzpatrick also defended the dress code, although he conceded that Disney might have been a little naive in presenting things so directly.

Another big challenge lay in getting the mostly French "cast members," as Disney calls its employees, to break their ancient cultural aversions to smiling and being consistently polite to park guests. The individualistic French had to be molded into the squeaky-clean Disney image. Rival theme parks in the area, loosely modeled on the Disney system, had already encountered trouble keeping smiles on the faces of the staff, who sometimes took on the demeanor of subway ticket clerks.

The delicate matter of hiring French citizens as opposed to other nationals was examined in the more than two-year-long preagreement negotiations between the French government and Disney. The final agreement called for Disney to make a maximum effort to tap into the local labor market. At the same time, it was understood that for Euro Disneyland to work, its staff must mirror the multicountry makeup of its guests. "Casting centers" were set up in Paris, London, Amsterdam, and Frankfurt. "We are concentrating on the local labor market, but we are also looking for workers who are German, English, Italian, Spanish, or other nationalities and who have good communication skills, are outgoing, speak two European languages—French plus one other—and like being around people," said Degelmann.

Stephane Baudet, a 28-year-old trumpet player from Paris, refused to audition for a job in a Disney brass band when he learned he would have to cut his ponytail. "Some people will turn themselves into a pumpkin to work at Euro Disneyland," he said. "But not me."

Opening Day at Euro Disneyland

A few days before the grand opening of Euro Disneyland, hundreds of French visitors were invited to a preopening party. They gazed perplexed at what was placed before them. It was a heaping plate of spare ribs. The visitors were at the Buffalo Bill Wild West Show, a cavernous theater featuring a panoply of "Le Far West," including 20 imported buffaloes. And Disney deliberately didn't provide silverware. "There was a moment of consternation," recalls Fitzpatrick. "Then they just kind of said, 'The hell with it,' and dug in." There was one problem. The guests couldn't master the art of gnawing ribs and applauding at the same time. So Disney planned to provide more napkins and teach visitors to stamp with their feet.

On April 12, 1992, the opening day of Euro Disneyland, France-Soir enthusiastically predicted Disney dementia. "Mickey! It's Madness" read its front-page headline, warning of chaos on the roads and suggesting that people might have to be turned away. A French government survey indicated that half a million might turn up with 90,000 cars trying to get in. French radio warned traffic to avoid the area.

By lunchtime on opening day, the Euro Disneyland car park was less than half full, suggesting an attendance of below 25,000, less than half the park's capacity and way below expectations. Many people may have heeded the advice to stay home or, more likely, were deterred by a one-day strike that cut the direct rail link to Euro Disneyland from the center of Paris. Queues for the main rides, such as Pirates of the Caribbean and Big Thunder Mountain railroad, were averaging around 15 minutes less than on an ordinary day at Disney World, Florida.

Disney executives put on a brave face, claiming that attendance was better than at first days for other Disney theme parks in Florida, California, and Japan. However, there was no disguising the fact that after spending thousands of dollars on the preopening celebrations, Euro Disney would have appreciated some impressively long traffic jams on the auto route.

Other Operating Problems

When the French government changed hands in 1986, work ground to a halt, as the negotiator appointed by the Conservative government threw out much of the groundwork prepared by his Socialist predecessor. The legalistic approach taken by the Americans also bogged down talks, as it meant planning ahead for every conceivable contingency. At the same time, right-wing groups who saw the park as an invasion of "chewing-gum jobs" and U.S. pop culture also fought hard for a greater "local cultural context."

On opening day, English visitors found the French reluctant to play the game of queuing. "The French seem to think that if God had meant them to queue, He wouldn't have given them elbows," they commented. Different cultures have different definitions of personal space, and Disney guests faced problems of people getting too close or pressing around those who left too much space between themselves and the person in front.

Exhibit 5 What Price Mickey?

	Euro Disneyland	Disney World, Orlando
	Peak Season Hotel Rates	
4-person room	$97–$345	$104–$455
	Campground Space	
	$48	$30–$49
	One-Day Pass	
Children	$26	$26
Adults	$40	$33

Source: BusinessWeek, March 30, 1992.

A Further Look at Euro Disneyland in Recent Years:

As discussed in In-Depth Integrative Case 2.1a, Euro Disneyland faced major hurdles in its early years. In May 1992, roughly 25 percent of Euro Disney's workforce (approximately 3,000 people) resigned from their jobs citing unacceptable working conditions. As a result, the Euro Disney Company stock price declined and Euro Disney announced an expected net loss in its first year of operation of approximately 300 million French francs in July of 1992.[1] Since then, Euro Disneyland has enacted some major changes—many with great success.

In an effort to improve attendance, Disney began serving alcoholic beverages with meals inside the Euro Disneyland Park in June of 1993.[2] In March of 1994, Disney offered the banks a deal: Disney would provide additional capital to ensure that it continues to operate if the banks agreed to restructure the US$1 billion of debt. If the banks did not agree, Disney was prepared to close the park and default on the loans. Disney put additional pressure on the banks by publically announcing the possible closure of the park unless the debt was restructured. The banks agreed to Disney's demands and wrote off the next two years of interest payments along with a three year period where loan repayments would be postponed. In return, The Walt Disney Company agreed to restructure its own loan arrangements at the new park valued at US$210 million.[3]

A turnaround began to blossom shortly after restructuring. In 1995, Disney reported that attendance had increased 21 percent from 8.8 million to 10.7 million year over year with hotel occupancy also increasing from 60 percent to 68.5 percent.[4] The Euro Disney Resort was renamed to Disneyland Paris in 1994 and, in July of 1995, the company reported its first quarterly profit of US$35.3 million. Disneyland Paris ended 1995 with a profit of US$22.8 million. Disney opened a second theme park in France, Walt Disney Studios Park in March of 2002.[5] The two combined parks had a total attendance in 2012 of over 15 million, making it Europe's most visited themed attraction.[6]

In September 2012, the Walt Disney Co. assumed Euro Disney S.C.A.'s debt under a new refinancing deal. The new 1.23 billion euro loan aims to free Euro Disney of debt covenants that have restricted capital expenditures and future investments.[7]

Disney placed its first ads for work bids in English, leaving small- and medium-sized French firms feeling like foreigners in their own land. Eventually, Disney set up a data bank with information on over 20,000 French and European firms looking for work, and the local Chamber of Commerce developed a video text information bank with Disney that small- and medium-sized companies through France and Europe would be able to tap into. "The work will come, but many local companies have got to learn that they don't simply have the right to a chunk of work without competing," said a chamber official.

Efforts were made to ensure that sooner, rather than later, European nationals take over the day-to-day running of the park. Although there were only 23 U.S. expatriates among the employees, they controlled the show and held most of the top jobs. Each senior manager had the task of choosing his or her European successor.

Disney was also forced to bail out 40 subcontractors who were working for the Gabot-Eremco construction contracting group, which had been unable to honor all of its commitments. Some of the subcontractors said they faced bankruptcy if they were not paid for their work on Euro Disneyland. A Disney spokesperson said that the payments would be less than $20.3 million and the company had already paid Gabot-Eremco for work on the park. Gabot-Eremco and 15 other main contractors demanded $157 million in additional fees from Disney for work that they said was added to the project after the initial contracts were signed. Disney rejected the claim and sought government intervention. Disney said that under no circumstances would it pay Gabot-Eremco and accused its officers of incompetence. As Bourguignon thought about these and other problems, the previous year's losses and the prospect of losses again in the current year, with their negative impact on the company's stock price, weighed heavily on his mind.

Questions for Review

1. Using Hofstede's four cultural dimensions as a point of reference, what are some of the main cultural differences between the United States and France?
2. In what way has Trompenaars's research helped explain cultural differences between the United States and France?
3. In managing its Euro Disneyland operations, what are three mistakes that the company made? Explain.
4. Based on its experience, what are three lessons the company should have learned about how to deal with diversity? Describe each.

Source: This case was prepared by Research Assistant Sonali Krishna under the direction of Professors J. Stewart Black and Hal B. Gregersen as the basis for class discussion. It is not intended to illustrate either effective or ineffective managerial capability or administrative responsibility. Reprinted by permission of the authors.

In-Depth Integrative Case 1.1b

Beyond Tokyo: Disney's Expansion in Asia

After its success with Tokyo Disneyland in the 1980s, Disney began to realize the vast potential of the Asian market. The theme park industry throughout Asia has been very successful in recent years, with a range of regional and international companies all trying to enter the market. Disney has been one of the major participants, opening Hong Kong Disneyland in 2005 and discussing future operations in at least three other Asian cities.

Disney in China

After Disney's success in Tokyo, China, in particular, became a serious option for its next theme park venture in light of the country's impressive population and economic growth throughout the 1990s. Successful sales associated with the Disney movie *The Lion King*, in 1996, also convinced Disney officials that China was a promising location. However, consumer enthusiasm for theme parks in China was at a low in the late 1990s. "Between 1993 and 1998, more than 2,000 theme parks had been opened in China," and "many projects were swamped by excessive competition, poor market projections, high costs, and interference from local officials," forcing several hundred to be closed.[8] Nevertheless, Disney continued to pursue plans in both Shanghai and Hong Kong.

Shanghai, known as the "Paris of the Orient," was an attractive site for Disney officials because of its growing commercialization and industrialization and its already extant transportation access. The projected $1 billion project was scheduled to be built across the Huangpu River from Shanghai's world-famous waterfront promenade, the Bund, on a 200-square-mile expanse called The Pudong New Area. The first phase of construction included a Magic Kingdom park, while an EPCOT-style theme park was to be added after at least five years of operations.[9]

A Disney theme park in Shanghai would be mutually beneficial for the company and the nation of China. From Disney's perspective, it would gain access to one of the world's largest potential markets (and also compete with Universal Studios' new theme park). From the perspective of Chinese government officials, Disney's park would be a long-awaited mark of international success.[10]

Initially planners hoped to have a Disneyland operating in Shanghai prior to the World Expo in 2010. However the project stalled, and as of late 2006, "the chances of Beijing approving the project have shrunk since Shanghai's official was implicated in a big corruption investigation in September [2005]." This led Disney to consider other options for the construction of a new park.[11]

Hong Kong Disneyland

Plans in Hong Kong, which culminated in the opening of Hong Kong Disneyland in September 2005, began after the 1997–1998 Asian financial crisis. Despite the poor economic condition of Hong Kong in the late 1990s, Disney was still optimistic about prospects for a theme park in the "city of life." Hong Kong, already an international tourist destination, would draw Disneyland patrons primarily from Southeast Asia, Chinese mainland and Taiwan.

The official park plans were announced in November 1999 as a joint venture between the Walt Disney Company and the Hong Kong SAR Government. Unlike its experience in Tokyo, where Disney handed the reins over completely to a foreign company (the Oriental Land Company), Disney decided to take more direct control over this new park. The park was built on Lantau Island at Penny's Bay, within the 6-mile stretch separating the international airport and downtown. Hong Kong Disneyland was estimated to create 18,000 jobs upon opening and ultimately 36,000 jobs. The first phase of the park was to include a 10 million annual visitor Disneyland-based theme park, 2,100 hotel rooms, and a 300,000-square-foot retail, dining and entertainment complex.[12]

In order to make the park "culturally sensitive," Jay Rasulo, president of Walt Disney Parks & Resorts, announced that Hong Kong Disneyland would be trilingual with English, Cantonese, and Mandarin. The park would also include a fantasy garden for taking pictures with the Disney characters (popular among Asian tourists), as well as more covered and rainproof spaces to accommodate the "drizzly" climate.[13]

Unfortunately, Disney soon realized that its attempts at cultural sensitivity had not gone far enough. For instance, the decision to serve shark fin soup, a local favorite, greatly angered environmentalists. The park ultimately had to remove the dish from its menus. Park executives also failed to plan for the large influx of visitors around the Chinese New Year in early 2006, forcing them to turn away numerous patrons who had valid tickets. Unsurprisingly, this led to customer outrage and negative media coverage of the relatively new theme park.

Other criticisms of the park have included its small scale and slow pace of expansion. Hong Kong Disneyland has only 16 attractions and "one classic Disney thrill ride, Space Mountain, compared to 52 at Disneyland Resort Paris [formerly Euro Disneyland]."[14] However the government has made plans to increase the size of the park by acquiring land adjacent to the existing facilities. Likely due to its small size and fewer attractions, Hong Kong Disneyland pulled in only 5.2 million guests during its first 12 months, less than the estimated 5.6 million.[15] Failure to meet its projected levels of attendance and guest spending could cause the park to look toward other sources of funding for these expansions.

Battle over Hong Kong Park Expansion

Disney had plans to expand the size of the theme park in Hong Kong by about a third and it had been trying to obtain the local government's financial support for these plans since 2007. However, Disney's Park in Hong Kong had been performing well below the projected sales number in 2007–2008, and the government, which is 57 percent stockholder in this business, has expressed serious doubts in the need to fund the further expansion. As noted by *Financial Times* analysts, in one of the March 2009 reports, Hong Kong Disneyland has attracted about 15m visitors since its opening in September 2005, or about 4.3m a year. That figure fell short of the original projection of more than 5m a year.[16] Although Disney did not release financial figures to the public, Euromonitor estimated the park had an operating loss of $46 million in the year ended June 2006, and lost $162 million the following year.[17]

Disney's officials have been trying to stress the importance of park expansion for the overall viability of the project. So far, the park occupied 126 hectares and had only four "lands"—Fantasyland, Tomorrowland, Adventureland, and Main Street USA—and two hotels. Hong Kong Disneyland Managing Director Andrew Kam said expansion is vital to the park's success. In one of the September 2008 releases, Kam said the park had plenty of room to grow, since it was only using half of the land available. "Expansion is part of the strategy to make this park work for Hong Kong," he said.[18] An expansion could cost as much as 3 billion Hong Kong dollars, or $387 million, local media have reported. In December 2008, the Sing Tao Daily newspaper in Hong Kong reported that Disney, in what was deemed an unusual concession, might give the government a greater share in the project in repayment of a cash loan of nearly $800 million that the city had extended previously to the theme park.[19]

Unable to come to agreement with the Hong Kong government, Disney has indicated that it is putting on hold long-awaited plans to expand the park. In a statement from Disney's Burbank (Calif.) office released in March 2009, the company said it was laying off employees in Hong Kong after failing to reach an agreement with the Hong Kong government to fund a much-needed expansion. According to Disney, "The uncertainty of the outcome requires us to immediately suspend all creative and design work on the project." Thirty Hong Kong–based Disney "Imagineers," who helped to plan and design new parks, will be losing their jobs.[20] Business news sources had noted that one reason Disney might be willing to end negotiations with the Hong Kong government is the company's progress in negotiations with Shanghai officials to open a theme park there that would be much larger and arguably a more exciting China project. This park is expected to be easier for many Chinese families to visit. However, the possible shift of mainland Chinese away from Hong Kong to Shanghai could mean a drop of as much as 60 percent in visitor numbers to the Hong Kong park, according to Euromonitor's estimates.[21]

In June of 2009 Disney and Hong Kong's government finally reached a deal to expand the territories of the Disneyland theme park at a cost of about $465 million. Under terms of the deal, the entertainment giant will contribute all the necessary new capital for construction as well as sustaining the park's operation during the building phases. It will also convert into equity about $350 million in loans to the venture to help with funding and will keep open a credit facility of about $40 million. Hong Kong, which shouldered much of the $3.5 billion original construction cost, will not add any new capital. "Disney is making a substantial investment in this important project," Leslie Goodman, a Disney vice president, said in a statement.[22]

Disney Gets Green Light for Shanghai Park

In spite of the global economic downturn, Walt Disney Co. has revisited its plans to build a park in Shanghai, China. In January 2009 Disney presented to the Chinese central government a $3.59 billion proposal that outlined the plans for a jointly owned park, hotel, and shopping development. Shanghai Disneyland, if the project succeeds, would be one of the largest-ever foreign investments in China.[23] Though Disney had been unsuccessful in its negotiations with the Chinese government a few years earlier, and almost abandoned its plans of expansion to Shanghai, the global economic crisis played a role making the prospective creation of 50,000 new jobs amid a cooling Chinese economy especially attractive, and gave Disney the grounds to revisit its plans.[24]

The preliminary agreement signed in January represented a framework to be considered by China's State Council, the central government's highest administrative body. According to the proposal Disney would take a 43 percent equity stake in Shanghai Disneyland with 57 percent owned by the Shanghai government forming a joint-venture company.[25] The park's first phase would include building a theme park, a hotel, and shopping outlets on about 1.5 square kilometers (371 acres) site near

Shanghai's Pudong International Airport.[26] The preliminary agreement outlined a six-year construction period for the first phase with the projected opening of the park in 2014. Disney will likely pay $300 million to $600 million in capital expenses for the park in exchange for 5 percent of the ticket sales and 10 percent of the concessions.[27] Shanghai Disneyland will incorporate Chinese cultural features as well as attractions built around traditional Disney characters and themes. The ownership structure will contain some aspects of Disney's Hong Kong joint venture agreement. But the details of the Shanghai project will need to be further negotiated and the actual contract will have to be approved by the central government. According to *The Wall Street Journal,* a newly formed Shanghai company named Shendi will hold the local government's interest in the park. Shendi is owned by two business entities under district governments in Shanghai, as well as a third company owned by the municipal government's propaganda bureau.[28]

After almost a year of negotiation, in November 2009, Disney finally received an approval from the Chinese government to proceed with its Shanghai park plan.[29] The new park planned for the Pudong new district of China's financial capital will take years to contribute to a company that takes in more than $30 billion in annual revenue. But analysts see the move as an important step forward for Disney and other Western media firms to make inroads into the vast and untapped Chinese media and entertainment market.

"They've been laying the groundwork for a park for many years by exposing the population to Disney properties, film, TV and merchandising," said Christopher Marangi, senior analyst with Gabelli and Co in New York.[30]

There are certain public concerns that the new Shanghai park, which would be Disney's sixth, will inevitably affect the Hong Kong park. The main concern is that Hong Kong park's revenue may be cannibalized which will make the financial perspectives of this underperforming park even sadder looking. However, Disney thinks that both parks will complement each other rather than be competitors. Disney's main points are that Shanghai is close to a number of other major cities within easy driving distance, including Nanjing, Suzhou, and Hangzhou, and that Shanghai's own population of around 19 million, combined with tens of millions more within a three-hour driving radius, would provide a more-than-ample base of local users for the park. There are analysts, like Paul Tang, chief economist at Bank of East Asia, who share this optimism, projecting that "visitors from Guangdong and southern China will still find Hong Kong more convenient, while Shanghai will attract visitors from northern and eastern China."[31] Indeed, when Disney reported its 2012 results, it noted that the Hong Kong park turned a modest profit, its first since opening, with overall attendance up 13 percent to 6.7 million, and revenue up 18 percent.[32]

The critics of the Shanghai park on the other hand are convinced that this project is a bigger threat to the Hong Kong park than anybody can imagine. According to Parita Chitakasem, research manager at Euromonitor International in Singapore, who specializes in theme parks, "Disneyland Shanghai will have two big features which will make it more attractive than its Hong Kong counterpart: Although it is still early days, Disneyland in Shanghai will probably offer a much better experience for your money than Disneyland in Hong Kong—initial plans show that Shanghai's Disneyland will be six times bigger compared to the current size of Hong Kong Disneyland, which is very small (only 16 attractions). Also, for visitors from mainland China, it will be much easier to travel to Disneyland in Shanghai, as there are no visa/cross border concerns to take care of."[33]

While the public is debating the project, Disney is not wasting time and moves on with getting all other necessary approvals and documents that are needed for the park construction, which still may take long to obtain. In April 2010 the company received approval for the land. Authorities have also confirmed that 97 percent of residents have been already relocated, and the land would be transferred over to Disney in July. Over 2,000 households and 297 companies have to be relocated to make way for the first phase of construction. The head of Pudong New District where Shanghai Disney will be sited informed the public that the first phase of the project, including a theme park and supporting facilities, will span four square km with the theme park covering one square km. The project would take five to six years to finish.[34]

Other Asian Ventures

The Walt Disney Company has also looked into building other theme parks and resorts in Asia. Based on its successful operation of two theme parks in the United States (at Anaheim and Orlando), Disney believes that it can have more than one park per region. Another strategically located park in Asia, officials agreed, would not compete with Tokyo Disneyland or Hong Kong Disneyland, but rather bring in a new set of customers.

One such strategic location is the state of Johor in Malaysia. Malaysian officials wanted to develop Johor in order to rival its neighbor, Singapore, as a tourist attraction. (Two large casinos were built in Singapore in 2006.) However, Disney claimed to have no existing plans or discussions for building a park in Malaysia. Alannah Goss, a spokeswoman for Disney's Asian operations based in Hong Kong, said, "We are constantly evaluating strategic markets in the world to grow our park and resort business and the Disney brand. We continue to evaluate markets but at this time, we have no plans to announce regarding a park in Malaysia."[35]

Singapore, in its effort to expand its tourism industry, had also expressed interest in being host to the next Disneyland theme park. Although rumors of a Singapore Disneyland were quickly dismissed, some reports suggested there were exploratory discussions of locations at either Marina East or Seletar. Residents of Singapore expressed concern that the park would not be competitive, even against the smaller-scale Hong Kong Disneyland. Their primary fears included limited attractions (based on size and local regulations), hot weather, and high ticket prices.

Disney's Future in Asia

Although Disney is wise to enter the Asian market with its new theme parks, it still faces many obstacles. One is finding the right location. Lee Hoon, professor of tourism management at Yanyang University in Seoul, noted, "Often, more important than content is whether a venue is located in a metropolis, whether it's easily accessible by public transportation." Often tied to issues of location is the additional threat of competition, both from local attractions and those of other international corporations. It seems that Asian travelers are loyal to their local attractions, evidenced by the success of South Korea's Everland theme park and Hong Kong's own Ocean Park (which brought in more visitors than Hong Kong Disneyland in 2006).[36] The stiff competition of the theme park industry in Asia will center on not only which park can create a surge of interest in its first year but also which can build a loyal base of repeat customers.

Despite its already large size, the Asian theme park industry is still developing. Disney officials will need to be innovative and strategic in order to maintain sales. After Universal Studios in Japan witnessed a 20 percent drop in attendance between 2001 and 2006 and Hong Kong Disneyland failed to meet its estimated attendance level in 2006, Disney officials might want to think twice about building additional parks in Asia.[37]

In spite of underperformance of some theme parks, and a recent world economic crisis, Asia is still viewed by many as the most attractive region for the entertainment industry. Attendance may be stagnating in some parts of the world, but a growing middle class with disposable incomes to match is making the Asia-Pacific region a prime target for investors and theme park owners. "China will lead the way," said Kelven Tan, Southeast Asia's representative for the International Association of Amusement Parks and Attractions, an industry group. "The critical mass really came about with the resurgence of China. You need a good source of people; you also need labor and you need cheap land."[38]

That's what the people behind the just-completed Universal Studios in Singapore are betting. Developers aim to tap the wallets of Singapore's 4.6 million residents and 9.7 million tourists a year and its proximity to populous areas of Indonesia and southern Malaysia. After opening in spring of 2010, it will be the island nation's first bona fide amusement park. Outside this and other foreign brands like Legoland, which plan to open a park in Johor, Malaysia, for 2013, home-grown companies like Genting in Malaysia and OTC Enterprise Corp. in China are aggressively looking to take advantage of the burgeoning market in their backyards.[39]

Overall spending on entertainment and media in Asia Pacific is set to increase 4.5 percent each year, jumping to $413 billion in 2013 from $331 billion in 2008, according to PricewaterhouseCoopers, with places like South Korea, Australia, and China posting the biggest increases. "It's an up-and-coming market, and growing quite fast," said Christian Aaen, Hong Kong–based regional director for AECOM Economics, a consulting firm that specializes in the entertainment and leisure industries. MGM Studios and Paramount, too, are scouting around Asia for future projects. PricewaterhouseCoopers predicted the region's market will be worth nearly $8.5 billion by 2012, up from $6.4 billion in 2007.[40]

In light of these optimistic projections, it is reasonable to assume that Disney may consider expansion to other Asian countries such as Malaysia, South Korea, or Singapore, where Disney appeared to have seriously considered a park. Given that the Hong Kong park expansion and Shanghai park construction are on track, Disney now has the experience and motivation to further penetrate the Asian region. In this regard, Disney announced in mid-2010 a comprehensive plan to develop and operate English language schools throughout China.[41] Such a move could constitute a broader push by Disney to establish a strong Asian presence across its businesses and brands, a move that would undoubtedly involve the theme park operations as a central component.

Questions for Review

1. What cultural challenges are posed by Disney's expansion into Asia? How are these different from those in Europe?
2. How do cultural variables influence the location choice of theme parks around the world?
3. Why was Disney's Shanghai theme park so controversial? What are the risks and benefits of this project?
4. What location would you recommend for Disney's next theme park in Asia? Why?

Source: This case was prepared by Courtney Asher under the supervision of Professor Jonathan Doh of Villanova University as the basis for class discussion. Additional research assistance was provided by Benjamin Littell.

In-Depth Integrative Case 1.2

Walmart's Global Strategies

Introduction

In 1991, Walmart became an international company when it opened a Sam's Club near Mexico City. Just two years later, Walmart International was created. Since venturing into Mexico in 1991, Walmart International has grown somewhat erratically. During the 1990s the retailer exported its big-box, low-price model, an approach the company expected to be as successful in foreign markets as it was in the United States. Although Walmart has had success in several overseas markets, this success has been far from universal. For example, in Mexico, China, and the U.K., the company's efforts to offer the lowest price to customers backfired because of resistance from established retailers. And in Germany, Walmart could not seem to fit its model to local tastes and preferences. In Japan, its joint venture had a series of setbacks, many related to buying habits for which the Walmart model did not respond well. In Mexico, three of the largest domestic retailers constructed a joint buying and operational alliance solely to compete with Walmart.[1] Its presence in Chinese Hong Kong ended after only two years during the 1990s, and it shuttered operations in Indonesia in the mid-1990s after rioting incidents in Jakarta. Walmart also owned approximately 16 stores in South Korea and 85 in Germany; however, it sold off these operations in 2006 after merchandise failed to match consumer tastes, distribution and re-bagging problems arose, and strong loyalties to other brands made attracting customers difficult and expensive.[2]

In addition, labor advocates and environmentalists have created headaches for the U.S. behemoth, making continued expansion both cumbersome and expensive. For instance, in 2006, Walmart faced a strong public relations campaign from the All-China Federation of Trade Unions (ACFTU) over Walmart's refusal to let its workers in China unionize. Walmart was eventually forced to concede, perhaps because the Chinese government also lent its weight to the ACFTU's campaign in its effort to establish unions in all foreign-funded enterprises throughout the country. As of October 2006, almost 6,000 of Walmart China's 30,000 employees were union members.[3] Despite its public battle with the ACFTU, Fortune China and Watson Wyatt still voted Walmart China as one of the "Top 10 Best Companies to Work for" in 2005.[4] As Walmart continues to expand its global operations, analysts are curious to see how the company is received and whether consumers' opinions in fragmented market settings are a match with Walmart's low price model.

Notwithstanding these challenges, today, Walmart International is a fast-growing part of Walmart's overall operations, with 6,155 stores and more than 800,000 associates in 26 countries outside the continental U.S.[5] (See Exhibit 1.) According to international chief C. Douglas McMillon, Walmart is "progressing from being a domestic company with an international division to being a global company." In two decades Walmart International had become a $100 billion business. Had it been a standalone company, it would have ranked among the top five global retailers.[6] (See Exhibit 2.) Walmart International's business represents a solid chunk of Walmart's overall $405 billion revenues for the fiscal year 2010.[7]

Exhibit 1 Walmart International Operations, April 2010[8]

Market	Retail Units (04/2010)	Date of Entry
Mexico	1,479	November 1991
Canada	317	November 1994
Brazil	438	May 1995
Argentina	44	August 1995
China	284	August 1996
United Kingdom	374	July 1999
Japan	371	March 2002
Costa Rica	170	September 2005
El Salvador	77	September 2005
Guatemala	164	September 2005
Honduras	53	September 2005
Nicaragua	55	September 2005
Chile	254	January 2009
India	1	May 2009

With a market capitalization of more than $200 billion in 2010, Walmart is worth as much as the gross domestic product of Nigeria. Four of America's 10 richest individuals are from Walmart's low-profile Walton family, which still owns a 40 percent controlling stake. The company's portfolio ranges from superstores in the U.S. to neighborhood markets in Brazil, bodegas in Mexico, the ASDA supermarket chain in Britain, and Japan's nationwide network of Seiyu shops. Walmart sources many of its products from low-cost Chinese suppliers. The pressure group China Labour Watch estimates that if it were a country, Walmart would rank as China's seventh largest trading partner, just ahead of the U.K., spending more than $18bn annually on Chinese goods.[9]

Walmart Early Internationalization

In venturing beyond its large domestic market, Walmart had a number of regional options, including entering

Exhibit 2 The Largest Global Companies and Retailers, 2008

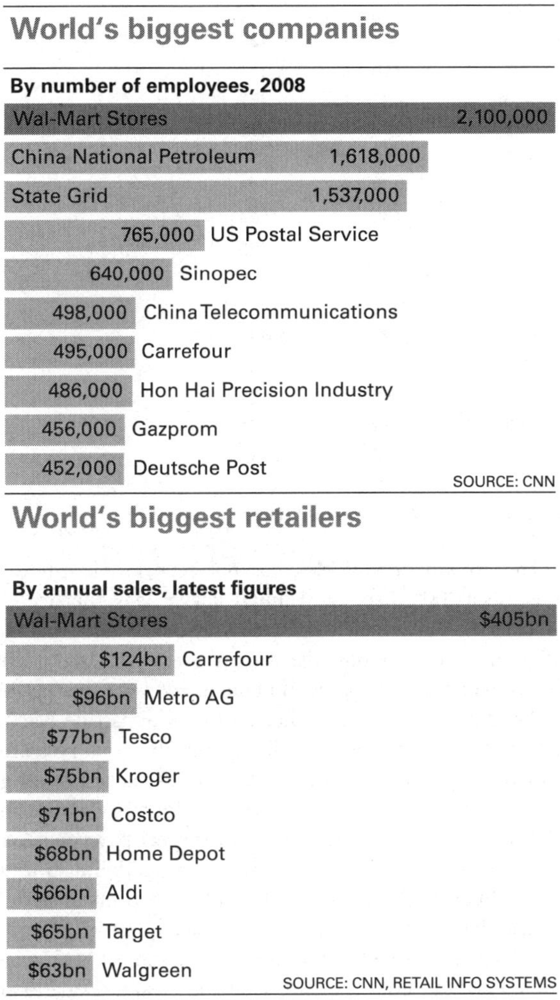

World's biggest companies

By number of employees, 2008

Company	Employees
Wal-Mart Stores	2,100,000
China National Petroleum	1,618,000
State Grid	1,537,000
US Postal Service	765,000
Sinopec	640,000
China Telecommunications	498,000
Carrefour	495,000
Hon Hai Precision Industry	486,000
Gazprom	456,000
Deutsche Post	452,000

SOURCE: CNN

World's biggest retailers

By annual sales, latest figures

Retailer	Sales
Wal-Mart Stores	$405bn
Carrefour	$124bn
Metro AG	$96bn
Tesco	$77bn
Kroger	$75bn
Costco	$71bn
Home Depot	$68bn
Aldi	$66bn
Target	$65bn
Walgreen	$63bn

SOURCE: CNN, RETAIL INFO SYSTEMS

Source: Guardian (http://www.guardian.co.uk/business/2010/jan/12/walmart-companies-to-shape-the-decade).

Europe, Asia, or other countries in the Western hemisphere. (See Exhibits 3 and 4.) At the time, however, Walmart lacked the requisite financial, organizational, and managerial resources to pursue multiple countries simultaneously. Instead, it opted for a logically sequenced approach to market entry that would allow it to apply the learning gained from its initial entries to subsequent ones. In the end, during the first five years of its globalization (1991 to 1995), Walmart decided to concentrate heavily on establishing a presence in the Americas: Mexico, Brazil, Argentina, and Canada. Obviously, Canada had the business environment closest to the U.S. and appeared the easiest entry destination. The other countries that Walmart chose as its first global points of entry—Mexico (1991), Brazil (1994), and Argentina (1995)—were those with the three largest populations in Latin America.[10]

The European market had certain characteristics that made it less attractive to Walmart as a first point of entry. The European retail industry was mature, implying that a new entrant would have to take market share away from an existing player—a very difficult task. Additionally, there were well-entrenched competitors on the scene (e.g., Carrefour in France and Metro A.G. in Germany) that would likely retaliate vigorously against any new player. Further, as with most newcomers, Walmart's relatively small size and lack of strong local customer relationships would be severe handicaps in the European arena. In addition, the higher growth rates of Latin American and Asian markets would have made a delayed entry into those markets extremely costly in terms of lost opportunities. In contrast, the opportunity costs of delaying acquisition-based entries into European markets appeared to be relatively small.[11]

While the Asian markets had huge potential when Walmart launched its globalization effort in 1991, they were the most distant geographically and different culturally and logistically from the United States market. It would have taken considerable financial and managerial resources to establish a presence in Asia.[12] However, by 1996, Walmart

Exhibit 3 Walmart International Retail Unit Count (2001–2006)

Country	2001	2002	2003	2004	2005	2006
Argentina	11	11	11	11	11	11
Brazil	20	22	22	25	149	295
Canada	174	196	213	235	262	278
China	11	19	26	34	43	56
Germany	94	95	94	92	91	88
Japan	0	0	0	0	0	398
Mexico	499	551	597	623	679	774
Puerto Rico	15	17	52	53	54	54
UK	241	250	258	267	282	315
South Korea	6	9	15	15	16	16
Total	1,071	1,170	1,288	1,355	1,587	2,285

Source: Walmart Annual Reports for fiscal years 2001, 2002, 2003, 2004, 2005, 2006.

Exhibit 4 Walmart International Retail Unit Count (2006–2010)

Country	2007	2008	2009	2010
Argentina	13	21	28	43
Brazil	299	313	345	434
Canada	289	305	318	317
Chile	0	0	197	252
China	73	202	243	279
Costa Rica	137	149	164	170
El Salvador	63	70	77	77
Guatemala	132	145	160	164
Honduras	41	47	50	53
India	0	0	0	1
Japan	392	394	371	371
Mexico	889	1,023	1,197	1,469
Nicaragua	40	46	51	55
Puerto Rico	54	54	56	56
UK	335	352	358	371
Total	2,757	3,121	3,615	4,112

Source: Walmart Annual Reports for fiscal years 2007, 2008, 2009, 2010.

felt ready to take on the Asian challenge and it targeted China. This choice made sense in that the lower purchasing power of the Chinese consumer offered huge potential to a low-price retailer like Walmart. Still, China's cultural, linguistic, and geographical distance from the United States presented relatively high entry barriers, so Walmart decided to use two beachheads as learning vehicles for establishing an Asian presence.[13]

During 1992–93, Walmart agreed to sell low-priced products to two Japanese retailers, Ito-Yokado and Yaohan, that would market these products in Japan, Singapore, Chinese Hong Kong, Malaysia, Thailand, Indonesia, and the Philippines. Then, in 1994, Walmart entered Hong Kong through a joint venture with the C.P. Pokphand Company, a Thailand-based conglomerate, to open three Value Club membership discount stores in Hong Kong.[14]

Success in Mexico and China

Overall, Walmart has had a very successful experience in Mexico. In 1991 Walmart entered into a joint venture with retail conglomerate Cifra and opened a Sam's Club in Mexico City. In 1997 it gained a majority position in the company and in 2001 changed the store name to Walmart de Mexico, or more commonly, "Wal-Mex." In addition to its 195 Walmart Supercenters and Sam's Club warehouses, Wal-Mex also operates Bodega food and general merchandise discount stores, Superama supermarkets, Suburbia apparel stores, and Vips and El Portón restaurants. The majority of its stores are located in and around Mexico City; however, it does business in over 145 cities throughout Mexico. Wal-Mex has shown no signs of slowing down. In 2005 Walmart opened 93 new stores and saw a 13.7 percent increase in net sales overall. As of February 2007, it operated 889 stores in Mexico and had plans to open another 125 that year.[15]

The growth of Wal-Mex has not been problem-free. In September 2005 a senior Walmart lawyer was contacted by a former executive at Walmart de Mexico. In the e-mail and follow-up conversations, the former executive (later identified as the lawyer in charge of obtaining construction permits for Walmart de Mexico) indicated that Walmart de Mexico had paid bribes for permits throughout the country to fuel growth prospects. In response, Walmart dispatched investigators to Mexico City. Those investigators found overwhelming evidence of bribery and hundreds of suspect payments totaling more than US$24 million. The investigation also found that Walmart de Mexico's top executives had taken steps to conceal the evidence from Walmart's headquarters.[16] Regulatory filings confirmed that Walmart is the subject of an investigation by the both the SEC and the Justice Department. Walmart warned shareholders that its reputation could be affected by the bribery scandal. In a statement Walmart said that inquiries from media and law enforcement could affect the "perception among certain audiences of its role as a corporate citizen."[17] In response to the investigation and bribery charges, Walmart has created a new executive position to ensure that all Walmart employees are complying with the U.S. Foreign Corrupt Practices Act.[18]

In late 2006 the company was also approved by Mexico's Finance Ministry to open its own bank. In a country where 75 percent of citizens have never had a bank account due to high fees, "Banco Walmart de Mexico Adelante" added much-needed competition to the financial services industry and it was hoped would begin to offer consumers lower fees than traditional banks.[19] In November 2007, Wal-Mex opened its first consumer bank, Banco Walmart, in Toluca; by August 2010, the company had opened nearly 250 branches. Banco Walmart is especially targeting the low-income market in a country where just 24 percent of households have savings accounts, compared with 55 percent in Chile. Wal-Mex plans to boost sales via debit cards, later ease users into more profitable services like insurance, and make money on interest-rate spreads. Wal-Mex's mission is to lure newcomers with easy instructions and entry points, like minimum balances of less than $5 and no commissions, compared with $100 minimums at competing banks. Wal-Mex is also eyeing the $23 billion remittances market—the amount sent home every year by Mexican immigrants in the U.S.[20]

Wal-Mex's plans for future growth involve more heavily targeting the 16–24-year-old age group, which constitutes 55 percent of Mexico's population. In April 2010, Mexico ranked as Walmart's number one international destination with 1,479 retail outlets, far ahead of its second major international destination Brazil, which had only 438 stores.[21] In 2011, Walmart de Mexico was a top performer globally with an operating margin of 7.9 percent, compared to 4.9 percent in total for all global operations during this same time.[22]

Though not as easy as its experience in Mexico, Walmart has also found decent success in China. Walmart entered the Chinese market in 1996 when it opened a Supercenter and Sam's Club in Shenzen. As of late 2006 the company had expanded to 73 stores in 36 cities. In order to cater to its Chinese shoppers, Walmart has introduced "retail-tainment" and attempted to create a more hands-on shopping experience.[23] China's Tourism Bureau even named one underground Walmart store a tourist destination.[24]

In addition to its own stores, Walmart has had a stake in the Bounteous Company Ltd., which owned the popular chain of Trust-Mart stores.[25] In late 2006, *The Wall Street Journal* publicized a $1 billion deal between Walmart and Bounteous, in which Walmart would acquire Trust-Mart's 100 stores over the course of three years. In light of Walmart's slowing U.S. sales and the termination of its operations in Germany and South Korea, the company's expansion in China is quite timely. Like its operations in Mexico, Walmart has also entered the Chinese financial service industry, by introducing a credit card with Bank of Communications Ltd. in late 2006.[26]

Walmart's expansion has not gone unnoticed. Domestic Chinese rivals have also built up their businesses in order to compete. In 2005 Shanghai Bailan Group purchased four rival supermarkets and department stores and now operates over 5,000 stores. China Resources Enterprise has hired away managers from foreign chains and cut staff in order to increase its profitability.[27] While these efforts signal greater competition for Walmart in particular, they are necessary for domestic companies to survive in China's $841 billion retail market,[28] which has been increasingly competitive ever since the country joined the WTO and dropped restrictions on foreign retailers.

Mixed Results in Europe and Japan

In 1998 Walmart entered the European market through Germany by acquiring 21 Wertkauf hypermarkets, one-stop shopping centers that offered a broad assortment of high quality general merchandise and food. Germany was seen as the largest single base for retailing in Europe. Wertkauf's annual sales were about $1.4 billion, and its stores operated similar to the popular Walmart Supercenter format in the U.S. Walmart's executives considered Wertkauf as an "excellent fit" for Walmart and hoped that it would provide the company with an ideal entry into a new market.[29]

However, Walmart's operations in Germany quickly turned into a costly struggle. There were a number of critical factors that the company underestimated when it entered the new market. First of all, the stores of the acquired German retail chain were geographically dispersed and often in poor locations. Also, Walmart had faced some serious cultural differences, which it tried to resolve by making one error after another. For example, the company initially installed American managers, who made some well-intentioned cultural gaffes, like offering to bag groceries for customers (Germans prefer to bag their own groceries) or instructing clerks to smile at customers (Germans, used to brusque service, were put off).[30]

Other problems, however, were largely outside Walmart's control. Two German discounters, Aldi and Lidl, dominated the grocery business, with smaller shops that featured cut-rate, though still good-quality, food. Aldi also heavily promoted one-week sales, featuring deeply discounted merchandise, ranging from wine to garden hoses, which draw customers back. While Walmart's vast size gave it enormous leverage in purchasing clothing and other goods, it had to buy much of the food for its German stores locally. And there, it lacked the muscle of Aldi, which had 4,100 shops and a presence in nearly every town in the country.[31]

"Germany is the home of the discounter," said Mark Josefson, a retail analyst at Kepler Securities in Frankfurt. "Walmart is not competing on price, and that is one of its main attributes in its home market." Beyond these competitive pressures there was another serious factor to consider, namely that the German consumer was one of the most parsimonious and price-conscious in Europe. Profit margins in German retailing were the lowest in Europe.[32]

Walmart had struggled in Germany for almost 8 years. Analysts said that Walmart Germany was losing about €200 million (£137 million) a year on a turnover of about €2 billion, despite several attempts to turn around the business. In 2006 it finally made the decision to withdraw from the German market, by selling its 85 German stores to the rival supermarket chain Metro and taking a pre-tax loss of about $1 billion (£536 million) on the failed venture.[33] The decision to sell out to the Metro Group came two months after Walmart sold its 16 stores in South Korea and it appeared a rare retreat by the world's largest retailer from its breakneck global expansion.[34]

In contrast, Walmart's second retail destination in Europe, the United Kingdom, has brought the company much needed success. Walmart entered the U.K. market in June 1999 by acquiring ASDA Group PLC, Britain's third-largest food retailer. Walmart offered £6.7 billion ($10.8 billion). The cash deal, which topped a rival bid from the British retail group Kingfisher PLC, was predicted to double Walmart's international business at a stroke and put it in a position to expand its retailing expertise throughout Europe.[35]

Walmart executives said they hoped to draw upon ASDA's management talent and experience. ASDA's 229 stores are a little less than half the size of Walmart's supercenters of more than 200,000 square feet (18,000 square meters) in the United States, but the lack of space in much of Europe for new out-of-town shopping developments could make ASDA's formula more relevant as a platform for expansion.[36]

However, while the chain has been only a moderate success, delivering consistent results, Walmart has been frustrated in its efforts to expand, though competing in Britain's feverishly competitive supermarket industry has taught Walmart a good deal. Nevertheless, ASDA is now something of a center for excellence for its global grocery sales. The head of global marketing for Walmart is based at ASDA's head office in Leeds. And, in an example of Walmart's global distribution muscle, *The Wall Street Journal* recently reported that the best-selling wine in the whole of Japan is an own-label ASDA Bordeaux.[37]

The third major strategic step in Walmart's early 2000s global expansion was entering the Japanese market. In 2002 Walmart set foot in Japan with the purchase of a 6 percent stake in the 371-store Seiyu chain. Despite continued losses, Walmart gradually raised its stake, making Seiyu a wholly owned subsidiary in June 2008. Walmart has had to confront numerous issues in Japan, from longtime Seiyu managers resisting its initiatives to a tendency among Japanese shoppers to equate low prices with inferior products. Also, bulk deals did not play well in a country where many lived in small urban apartments, and the country's grocery distribution system was populated with wholesalers who brokered deals between suppliers and retailers, skimming profits. Even rival Carrefour abandoned this market.[38]

Edward J. Kolodzieski was the man in charge of turning Seiyu around. As CEO of Walmart Japan, Kolodzieski has slashed expenses, closed 20 stores, and cut 29 percent of corporate staff. In-store butchers were removed, with most meat now processed in a central facility. With the freed-up floor space, Seiyu bulked up meals-to-go offerings. To bypass the middlemen, Seiyu has also boosted the number of products it imports directly from manufacturers by 25 percent in 2009, and was also focusing on increasing sales of its own private-label brands.[39]

The biggest change, however, was a shift away from weekly specials to "everyday low prices" in areas like baby care and pet products, and, eventually, throughout the store. Taking a page from Britain's ASDA, Seiyu instead used its marketing dollars to compare prices against competitors. With the pressure of prolonged recession Japanese consumers have finally accepted that they can buy quality merchandise for a lower price.[40] After spending 100 billion yen (roughly $1.2 billion), by 2010, Walmart's situation in Japan had stabilized, with two years of profits and reports that it was looking for further expansion through acquisition.[41]

After 2005: Refocusing on Latin America

2005 became another turning point in Walmart's strategy. Somewhat frustrated by strategic failure in Germany, and very slow expansion in the developed countries like Canada and the U.K., the company has turned its focus toward Latin America. Walmart has decided to leverage its positive experience in Mexico toward other South American countries. In 2005 Walmart successfully entered this market with the purchase of a 33-ss 1/3 percent interest in Central American Retail Holding Company (CARHCO) from the Dutch retailer Royal Ahold NV. CARHCO is Central America's largest retailer, with 363 supermarkets and other stores in the following five countries: Guatemala (120), El Salvador (57), Honduras (32), Nicaragua (30), and Costa Rica (124). CARHCO has approximately 23,000 associates. Its sales during 2004 were approximately $2.0 billion.[42]

Prior to that, in March 2004, Walmart bought a 118-store supermarket chain, Bompreco, in northeastern Brazil for $300 million, also from Royal Ahold of the Netherlands. This acquisition has significantly increased Walmart's competitive position in the country. In 2006 the company made another successful deal with Portugal-based Sonae by purchasing its 140 Brazilian stores for $757 million. The Sonae purchase was expected to boost Walmart's presence in Brazil's wealthier southern states. With the Sonae acquisition, Walmart store count increased to 295 units in 17 of Brazil's 26 states. However, this move made Walmart only the third-largest retailer in Brazil, following Carrefour of France and Companhia Brasileira de Distribuio Po de Acar.[43]

The last step in the sequence of its strategic moves in Latin America was Walmart's expansion into Chile. In 2009 Walmart acquired a majority stake of D&S (short for Distribución y Servicio) 224-store chain for $1.6 billion. In acquiring D&S, the nation's leading grocer and third-largest retailer, Walmart hopes to cement its dominance in Latin America, where it is by far the biggest retailer with $38 billion in sales, estimates research firm Planet Retail, double that of its closest rival, Carrefour. In Chile, Walmart enters a market that has long been inhospitable to foreign retailers. Home Depot, Carrefour, and JC Penney are among the companies that have tried, and failed, to make it in Chile, a nation of 17 million with the sixth-largest retail market in Latin America.[44]

Walmart has increased D&S's expansion budget from $150 million to $250 million, which would go toward opening nearly 70 stores in fiscal year 2010, many of them small stores that cater to lower-income shoppers, according to Vicente Trius, Walmart Latin America's president and CEO.

The appeal of D&S goes well beyond its stores. About 1.7 million Chileans carry a Presto card issued by its financial services unit, up from 1.2 million in 2004. "There is a saying here that large retailers generate sales with [stores] and earnings with their credit cards," says Rodrigo Rivera, a partner with the Boston Consulting Group in Santiago.[45]

Indeed, analysts estimate some South American retail chains generate upwards of 70 percent of their profits from financial services. (At D&S that figure is just 17 percent.) Walmart already offers financial services in Mexico and Brazil, though its attempts to launch a bank in the U.S. have failed. The retailer is keen to grow the Presto business by adding more low-risk services such as selling life insurance for outside vendors.[46]

Walmart's Plans for 2010–2011

In October 2009 Walmart Stores, Inc., presented its global plans for store and club growth in the next year at its annual conference for the investment community and updated its projections for capital expenditures through the fiscal year ending on January 31, 2011. According to this plan, total capital spending for the fiscal year ending January 31, 2010, is projected to be in a range of $12.5 to $13.1 billion, up from approximately $11.5 billion in fiscal year 2009. Total capital spending for the fiscal year ending January 31, 2011, is projected to be in a range of $13.0 to $15.0 billion.[47]

"Our plan for growth is clearly intended to increase shareholder value," said Tom Schoewe, executive vice president and chief financial officer. "In the U.S., we're building new stores and accelerating the pace of our remodels because they have been so successful at winning and retaining customers. We're stepping up growth in our International operations to take advantage of growing economies and opportunities in emerging markets, such as China and Brazil."[48] Capital expenditures for all purposes are projected as shown in Exhibit 5 and exclude the impact of any future acquisitions.

If fiscal year 2009 were placed on a constant currency basis with fiscal year 2010, international capital expenditures in fiscal year 2009 would have been approximately $3.8 billion. In the fiscal year ending January 31, 2010, the company expected to add approximately 38 million square feet globally, compared to approximately 44 million square feet added in the prior year (excluding square footage added by acquisition). Walmart expects to increase global square footage by approximately 37 million square feet in fiscal year 2011.[49] Square footage growth (excluding any acquisitions) is projected as shown in Exhibit 6.

Exhibit 5 Walmart Actual and Projected Capital Expenditure 2009–2011 (US$ billions)

	Actual	Projected	
Segment	FY09	FY10	FY11
Walmart U.S.	$5.8	$6.6–6.8	$7.0–8.0
Sam's Club U.S.	$0.8	$0.8–0.9	$0.7–1.0
Walmart International	$4.1	$4.2–4.4	$4.5–5.0
Corporate	$0.8	$0.9–1.0	$0.8–1.0
Total	$11.5	$12.5–13.1	$13.0–15.0

Source: walmartstores.com.

Exhibit 6 Walmart Actual and Projected Square Footage Growth by Segment (in millions)

	Actual	Projected	
Additional Square Footage for:	FY09	FY10	FY11
Walmart U.S.	23	14	11
Sam's Club U.S.	2	1	1
Walmart International	19	23	25
Total Company	44	38	37

Source: walmartstores.com.

Walmart International plans aggressive investment, particularly in growth markets such as China and Brazil. The International portfolio includes a variety of formats, from supercenters to small grocery stores. New stores are expected to add approximately 23 million square feet in fiscal year 2010, and approximately 25 million more square feet in fiscal year 2011. These projections are based on the existing store base and do not include possible acquisitions.[50]

"We will continue our organic growth strategy, with strong capital discipline and optimization of our portfolio of formats and brands worldwide," said Doug McMillon, president and CEO of Walmart International in a company press release in October 2009. "We will allocate capital, by country and by format, to improve returns from these investments."[51]

Walmart, whose international business is its fastest growing segment and already makes up roughly one-quarter of its total business, is positioning itself for 20 years of worldwide growth according to the CEO.[52] Walmart is projected to spend up to US$750 million to build, renovate, or relocate roughly 73 stores in Canada in 2012.[53] If Walmart International (with over 9,000 stores under 60 different names in 15 foreign countries) was viewed as a stand-alone company, it would be the third largest retailer in the world as of 2010 with sales of US$109 billion and a growth rate of 12.1 percent. Seventy-five percent of Walmart's stores outside of the U.S. operate under a different name as Walmart has shifted towards smaller formats and smaller acquisitive growth for global strategy. In comparison, Walmart's domestic unit did not experience any significant growth and virtually remained flat for 2010.[54]

China

In March 2010, the official website of China's Ministry of Commerce reported that Walmart had set up a new wholly owned subsidiary in Hebei. This move is reportedly designed to help Walmart's smooth expansion and localization of Walmart in China. An insider from Walmart revealed to the local media that the company will continue to speed up its expansion in China in 2010 and in the future the Chinese market is expected to have the most Walmart stores worldwide, exceeding even its domestic American market.[55]

Since 2009, Walmart has set up more than 10 wholly owned subsidiaries in Chinese cities and provinces, including Hunan, Chongqing, Hubei, and Dongguan. Before setting up these regional subsidiaries, Walmart cooperated with Chinese companies, including Shenzhen International Trust & Investment, for expansion in China. However, the complicated operating processes slowed down the retailer's expansion. With the help of these new subsidiaries, Walmart opened nearly 40 new outlets in 2009 and the total number of Walmart stores in China exceeded that of its competitor Carrefour for the first time.[56]

Brazil

In this most open of the large emerging economies, the world's two biggest supermarket chains and a homegrown competitor are battling for dominance. Leading the field is Companhia Brasileira de Distribuicão Grupo Pão de Açúcar, with revenues of $13 billion in 2009. Close behind is France's Carrefour, with sales last year of $12.6 billion. In third place, but making a big push, is the world's No. 1 retailer, Walmart Stores, which operates under several names in Brazil. It racked up $9.5 billion in sales in Brazil in 2009.[57]

All three plan to invest big in Brazil in coming years. As its middle class expands, annual spending on food is expected to rise 50 percent over the next five years, to $406 billion, says Carlos Hernandez, a Madrid-based analyst at consultant Planet Retail. Among the emerging nations known as the BRICs, Brazil offers fewer barriers to business than Russia, India, and China. India bans foreign stores that sell multiple brands, and Russia limits expansion by retailers. China is attractive because of its rapid economic growth, expected to be 8 percent in 2010, versus 5.8 percent in Brazil. However, "Brazil is more developed in terms of infrastructure and wealth creation," says Justin Scarborough, a retail analyst at Royal Bank of Scotland in London. "Consumers are used to shopping in hypermarkets, whereas retail in China is more traditional."[58]

Already No. 1 in Mexico, Walmart aims to overtake Carrefour to become No. 2 or No. 1 in Latin America's largest market. The Bentonville (Arkansas) retailer plans to spend $1.2 billion this year to open 110 new stores in Brazil, on top of the 436 it now operates. It may also scout out an acquisition, says Héctor Núñez, president of Walmart Brazil. "We have a very, very clear plan to win here in Brazil," he says. "We are investing heavily to start having a much more solid and persuasive presence."[59]

Walmart is opening the cash spigot at a time when Carrefour is contending with the recession in Europe, which accounts for 80 percent of its revenues. Annual sales growth for the Paris-based chain at home has averaged less than 1 percent over the last 10 years. To defend its No. 2 position in Brazil, Carrefour is planning to spend $1.4 billion over the next two years. The goal: to add 70 stores and double Brazil's share of Carrefour's overall sales to 20 percent by 2015. Pão de Açúcar, which is 34 percent owned by French supermarket chain Casino, says it will invest $2.8 billion to add 300 stores to its 1,080-store chain by 2012.[60]

India and Russia

The other two attractive growing markets from the BRIC group that also draw Walmart's attention are India and Russia. India and Russia are widely regarded as two of the world's fastest-growing retail markets—and two of the most frustrating for foreign retailers. Walmart boasts one wholesale outlet so far in India, and it has only a 30-person development administrative office in Moscow to show after more than five years of scouting in Russia. But through a combination of joint ventures, acquisitions, and expansion, the retailer is hoping to become a major player in both countries.[61]

India's $350 billion retail sector is composed of small family-run ventures, with organized chains accounting for less than 5 percent of sales. To get around government restrictions on foreign retailers selling to consumers, Walmart recently teamed up with Bharti Enterprises to open a cash-and-carry operation in the northern city of Amritsar. Best Price Modern Wholesale, as it's called, technically caters to merchants and small businesses. But with few restrictions, more than 30,000 members have signed up for the first store.[62]

As in the U.S., the emphasis is on a wide selection of goods in one location at a low cost—everything from Castrol motor oil and sneakers to milk in large canisters that can be tied to the side of bicycles. Best Price employs 25 people to go around the region each week and check prices at mom-and-pop shops, to ensure that they're consistently offering the best value. Raj Jain, a former Whirlpool executive who now heads Walmart's Indian operations, also opened a training institute in Amritsar last December in partnership with Bharti and the Punjab government.[63]

Walmart plans to open 10 to 15 outlets through the partnership over the next three years, eventually employing about 5,000 people. But McMillon wants to see Walmart running its own retail stores there, too. He pressed his case with commerce and agriculture ministers in New Delhi in July. "What I tried to convey is that we would invest more, and faster, if we had the opportunity to do so," he says. A representative from the Indian government declined to comment.[64] As of 2013, Walmart only had 20 wholesale stores in India.[65]

In April of 2010 Scott Price, president and CEO of Walmart Asia, reinforced the major points of Walmart's Asian strategy: "We will capture 10 to 15 markets in Asia in ten years. At present, expansion plans for India alone is the full time job for us." He also noted that India has a lot of potential as it has availability of a highly educated workforce. "The retail giant would also like to increase sourcing from India for their stores all over the world," he said.[66]

In Russia, the impediments to retail development are less visible but no less worrisome. Corruption is rampant with various administrative authorities capable of gumming up operations if payments are not made. Anticorruption group Transparency International ranked Russia 147th out of 180 countries on its most recent corruption perception index. While Walmart is looking at opening its own stores in Russia, it's far more likely it will start by acquiring a local retailer. Analysts say the prime candidate is Lenta, a fast-growing, privately held chain of 34 hypermarkets and the nation's fifth-largest retailer. Lenta founder Oleg Zherebtsov is saddled with debts and sold his 35 percent stake to the investment group of private equity firm TPG and the private equity arm of Russian state bank VTB in early September 2010.[67]

According to another source Walmart made a preliminary offer to the Kopeika store chain in June 2009.[68] Walmart is not the first retailer Kopeika has dealt with. X5 Retail Group tried to negotiate a deal at the end of 2008 and it was in discussions with Magnit in January 2009. Kopeika operates a network of around 500 supermarkets in Moscow and the Moscow region, where it competes with around 400 X5 Retail Group Pyaterochka stores and Dixy Group's outlets. Walmart is actively seeking a partner in Russia. It was in negotiations with St. Petersburg–based hypermarket operator Lenta in 2008, but no deal was reached.[69] With rivals such as Metro expanding their presence through new stores, and Carrefour opening its second outlet in September, "they cannot wait," says Planet Retail analyst Milos Ryba.[70]

Canada

Established in 1994 and headquartered in Mississauga, Ontario, Walmart Canada currently operates 317 stores and serves more than 1 million customers each day across Canada. Walmart is Canada's third-largest employer with more than 85,000 associates, and was recently named one of Canada's top 10 corporate cultures by Waterstone Human Capital.[71]

In February 2010 Walmart Canada announced that the company will open 35 to 40 supercentres in 2010. According to Walmart, the projects will include new stores, relocations of existing stores, store expansions, and store remodels, representing a combined investment of almost half a billion dollars in Canadian communities. The supercentres are expected to generate approximately 6,500 store and construction jobs, with specific store locations to be announced over the coming weeks and months. "The combination of one-stop shopping and low prices that our supercentres provide has been embraced by our customers," said David Cheesewright, president and CEO of Walmart Canada. "We look forward to bringing this popular format to a new range of shoppers."[72]

In addition to store expansions, Walmart Canada is investing in its first sustainable refrigerated distribution center, which is anticipated to open in Balzac, Alberta, in the fall of this year. The company is investing $115 million in its construction. The center will create 1,400 jobs, including trade and construction jobs.[73]

Expected to be one of the most energy-efficient distribution facilities of its kind in North America, the cutting-edge distribution center will be an estimated 60 percent more energy-efficient than Walmart's traditional refrigerated distribution centers. The center will include a pilot of fuel cell technology and many other sustainable features. Walmart Canada is committed to reducing costs while implementing energy-saving strategies across its operations. The company's new stores are now 30 percent more energy-efficient than previous prototypes.[74]

Despite its growth in Canada, Walmart is not without competition. Target opened 150 locations in Canada in 2011 alone.[75]

South Africa

In October of 2010, it was announced that Walmart was conducting due diligence on Massmart, a leading retailer in South Africa which operates 288 large stores located in 14 African countries, most of them in South Africa where it has a strong presence catering to a range of customers. Initially, reports suggested that Walmart would offer 32 billion rand ($4.63 billion) to own Massmart outright.[76] Subsequently, it was reported that Walmart would bid only for a majority controlling share (more than 50 percent but less than 100 percent) in order to preserve Massmart's listing on the Johannesburg stock exchange.[77] If either deal goes through, it would place Walmart ahead of its European competitors Tesco PLC and Carrefour SA, which don't have any stores in Africa.

Walmart's Global.com Challenge to Amazon.com

In January 2010 Vice Chairman Eduardo Castro-Wright announced that Walmart is creating a new unit that will be responsible for driving online growth around the world, both in developed markets where the company has stores and an online presence and in markets it doesn't. This new organization will be called Global.com.[78]

Wan Ling Martello, formerly the Ccief financial officer of Walmart International, will be the executive vice president and chief operating officer of Global.com. In her new role, Wan Ling's primary responsibilities will include (1) development and execution of a global strategy for e-commerce; (2) establishing cross-functional and cross-border Walmart relationships designed to accelerate and broaden growth in the global online channel; and (3) the creation of technology platforms and applications that can be used effectively in every Walmart market.[79]

In early 2008, the retailer said it would invest "millions of dollars" in its global e-commerce initiative, which it labeled "a multi-billion dollar opportunity over the next three to five years." Walmart, with stores in 15 countries, currently operates separate e-commerce sites in the U.S., U.K., Mexico, and Brazil. It has been working on developing a single global e-commerce platform that would be replicable in all of its markets, similar to the model developed by its rival Amazon.[80]

In the U.S., where the retailer competes directly with Amazon, Walmart has named Steve Nave, currently chief operating officer, as general manager of its website, taking over from Raul Vazquez, who has taken a new position as head of the retailer's new Walmart West division.

But Mr. Nave will now report directly to John Fleming, the chief merchandising officer who himself previously served as CEO of Walmart.com. Mr. Castro-Wright said Walmart hopes to "integrate merchandising and operations capabilities of the dot-com organization with those of our traditional retail business." Walmart's online marketing will now be overseen directly by Stephen Quinn, its chief marketing officer.

The changes reflect Walmart's strategy of tying its website closely to its stores, which some argue could give it a long-term strategic advantage over Amazon. Currently around 40 percent of its U.S. business is delivered to stores for pickup under its "site to store" service, which it sees as also augmenting the development of smaller format stores in the future.[81]

Continued Challenges with Corporate Responsibility

Like other retailers, Walmart continues to face challenges from its exposure to the realities of production and sales in emerging and developing regions. On the sales side, as noted above, Walmart has been embroiled in corruption scandals in Mexico and India. On the production side, a fire at a Bangalore textile factory in late 2012, and two horrific accidents at garment factories in Bangladesh in 2013, have placed renewed pressure on U.S. and European clothing brands to take greater responsibility for the working conditions of the factories from which they source products. What happened in Bangladesh has underscored the difficulties and vulnerabilities of outsourcing production to sometimes unreliable and unethical suppliers.

In early 2013, more than 1,000 workers were killed when an eight-story garment factory in Dhaka caught firewhile thousands worked inside. Not two weeks later, a fire killed eight workers in another site in Bangladesh. After initially denying it had production at these locations, Walmart eventurlly confirmed that it had ordered garments from a supplier who utilized the plant.[82] Then on June 11 another fire erupted at a Dickies garment factory on the outskirts of Dhaka, causing employees to run from the building, raising further questions about safety in Bangladeshi factories.[83]

As a result Walmart and the Gap Inc. subsequently announced their signing of the Bangladesh Worker Safety Initiative to ensure factory safety in Bangladesh. This agreement, backed by a $50 million commitment, will be overseen by the Bipartisan Policy Center, a nonprofit group based in Washington. As part of this effort, various U.S. retail trade groups who had been concerned about the legal liability associated with the competing, European-dominated agreement will join with Walmart and the Gap.[84] On June 25, the Obama Administration announced it was suspending trade privileges with Bangladesh, removing the country from the list of countries with most favored trade status. The move came after pressure from unions and continuing concerns about the Bangladeshi government's ability to maintain safe working conditions in its factories.[85] Walmart and other retailers continue to struggle with how to manage extended global supply chains with multiple layers of suppliers.

Questions for Review

1. What was Walmart's early global expansion strategy? Why did it choose to first enter Mexico and Canada rather than expand into Europe and Asia?
2. What cultural problems did Walmart face in some of the international markets it entered? Which early strategies succeeded and which failed? Why? What lessons did Walmart learn from its experience in Germany and in Japan?
3. How would you characterize Walmart's Latin America strategy? What countries were targeted as part of this strategy? What potential does this region brings to Walmart's future global expansion? What cultural challenges and opportunities have Walmart faced in Latin America?
4. What group of countries will be targeted for Walmart's future growth? What are the attractiveness and risk profiles of these countries? What regions of the world do you think will be vital for Walmart's future global expansion?
5. How would you characterize Walmart's response to pressure for greater ethics and social responsibilities in its expansion strategy and supply chain? Are its responses appropriate and adequate?

Exercise

You are part of Walmart's global strategic planning group and have been asked to explore the benefits and challenges of expansion into the following regions. Divide your group into six teams, each representing a country or region of the world other than North America.

Team	Country/Region
1	Latin America
2	Western Europe
3	Central/Eastern Europe
4	Japan
5	China
6	Russia

Describe the opportunities and challenges of expansion in your assigned country or region. Be sure to summarize the cultural environment, how it differs from the U.S., and what challenges that might pose for the company.

Source: This case was prepared by Tetyana Azarova of Villanova University under the supervision of Professor Jonathan Doh as the basis for class discussion. Additional research assistance was provided by Benjamin Littell.

Endnotes
注释

Chapter 1

1. Associated Press, "Dealers and Car Owners Await Answers as Toyota's Massive Recalls go Global," *New York Daily News Online,* January 28, 2010, http://www.nydailynews.com/news/money/dealers-car-owners-await-answers-toyota-massive-recalls-global-article-1.193302.
2. Jeff Kingston, "A Crisis Made in Japan," *The Wall Street Journal,* February 5, 2010, http://online.wsj.com/article/SB10001424052748704533204575047370633234414.html..
3. Joseph B. White, "U.S. Fines Toyota for Defect Report Delays," *The Wall Street Journal Online*, December 18, 2012, http://online.wsj.com/article/SB10001424127887324407504578186993119562224.html?mg=id-wsj.
4. Jeff Kingston, "A Crisis Made in Japan," *The Wall Street Journal,* February 5, 2010, http://online.wsj.com/article/SB10001424052748704533204575047370633234414.html.
5. Ibid.
6. "Independent Commission Releases Report on Fukushima Meltdown: Blames Japanese Culture," *Time,* July 5, 2012, http://science.time.com/2012/07/05/independent-commission-releases-report-on-fukushima-meltdown-blames-japanese-culture/.
7. "Fukushima Disaster Due to Japan's Culture? Ruth Benedict Would Have Said So," *East Asia Gazette,* July 13, 2012, http://asia-gazette.com/news/japan/157.
8. Jeff Kingston, "A Crisis Made in Japan," *The Wall Street Journal,* February 5, 2010, http://online.wsj.com/article/SB10001424052748704533204575047370633234414.html.
9. Akio Toyoda, "Back to Basics for Toyota," *The Wall Street Journal,* February 23, 2010, http://online.wsj.com/article/SB10001424052748704454304575081644051321722.html.
10. Jeffrey Johnson, Seongbae Lim, and Prasad Padmanabhan, "Important Lessons Need to Be Learned from the Toyota Recall," *San Antonio Business Journal,* March 19, 2010, http://www.bizjournals.com/birmingham/othercities/sanantonio/stories/2010/03/22/editorial1.html?b=1269230400%5E3064371&s=industry&i=manufacturing.
11. Ibid.
12. Bill Fischer, "Lessons from the Toyota Recall," *Management Issues.com,* February 9, 2010, http://www.management-issues.com/2010/2/9/opinion/lessons-from-the-toyota-recall.asp.
13. Jeffrey Johnson, Seongbae Lim, and Prasad Padmanabhan, "Important Lessons Need to Be Learned from the Toyota Recall," *San Antonio Business Journal,* March 19, 2010, http://www.bizjournals.com/birmingham/othercities/sanantonio/stories/2010/03/22/editorial1.html?b=1269230400%5E3064371&s=industry&i=manufacturing.
14. Pat Joynt and Malcolm Warner, "Introduction: Cross-Cultural Perspectives," in *Managing Across Cultures: Issues and Perspectives,* ed. Pat Joynt and Malcolm Warner (London: International Thomson Business Press, 1996), p. 3.
15. For additional insights see Gerry Darlington, "Culture—A Theoretical Review," in Pat Joynt and Malcolm Warner, *Managing Across Cultures: Issues and Perspectives* (London: International Thomson Business Press, 1996), pp. 33–55.
16. Fred Luthans, *Organizational Behavior,* 7th ed. (New York: McGraw-Hill, 1995), pp. 534–535.
17. Gary Bonvillian and William A. Nowlin, "Cultural Awareness: An Essential Element of Doing Business Abroad," *Business Horizons,* November–December 1994, pp. 44–54.
18. Roger E. Axtell, ed., *Do's and Taboos Around the World*, 2nd ed. (New York: Wiley, 1990), p. 3.
19. Lillian H. Chaney and Jeanette S. Martin, *Intercultural Business Communication* (Englewood Cliffs, NJ: Prentice Hall, 1995), p. 115.
20. Fons Trompenaars and Charles Hampden-Turner, *Riding the Waves of Culture: Understanding Diversity in Global Business,* 2nd ed. (New York: McGraw-Hill, 1998), p. 23.
21. Christopher Orpen, "The Work Values of Western and Tribal Black Employees," *Journal of Cross-Cultural Psychology,* March 1978, pp. 99–111.
22. William Whitely and George W. England, "Variability in Common Dimensions of Managerial Values Due to Value Orientation and Country Differences," *Personnel Psychology,* Spring 1980, pp. 77–89.
23. Ibid., p. 87.
24. George W. England and Raymond Lee, "The Relationship Between Managerial Values and Managerial Success in the United States, Japan, India, and Australia," *Journal of Applied Psychology,* August 1974, pp. 418–419.
25. George W. England, "Managers and Their Value Systems: A Five-Country Comparative Study," *Columbia Journal of World Business,* Summer 1978, p. 39.
26. A. Reichel and D. M. Flynn, "Values in Transition: An Empirical Study of Japanese Managers in the U.S.," *Management International Review* 23, no. 4 (1984), pp. 69–70.
27. Yumiko Ono and Bill Spindle, "Japan's Long Decline Makes One Thing Rise: Individualism," *The Wall Street Journal,* December 29, 2000, pp. A1, A4.
28. Sang M. Lee and Suzanne J. Peterson, "Culture, Entrepreneurial Orientation, and Global Competitiveness," *Journal of World Business* 35, no. 4 (2000), pp. 411–412.
29. "Confucius Makes a Comeback," *The Economist*, May 17, 2007, www.economist.com/world/asia/displaystory.cfm?story_id=9202957.
30. Geert Hofstede, *Culture's Consequences: International Differences in Work-Related Values* (Beverly Hills, CA: Sage, 1980).

31. Geert Hofstede, *Cultures and Organizations: Software of the Mind* (London: McGraw-Hill U.K., 1991), pp. 251–252.
32. Ibid.
33. Geert Hofstede and Michael Bond, "The Need for Synergy Among Cross-Cultural Studies," *Journal of Cross-Cultural Psychology,* December 1984, p. 419.
34. A. R. Negandhi and S. B. Prasad, *Comparative Management* (New York: Appleton-Century-Crofts, 1971), p. 128.
35. For additional insights, see Mark F. Peterson et al., "Role Conflict, Ambiguity, and Overload: A 21–Nation Study," *Academy of Management Journal,* June 1995, pp. 429–452.
36. Hofstede, *Culture's Consequences.*
37. Ibid.
38. Ibid.
39. Also see Chao C. Chen, Xiao-Ping Chen, and James R. Meindl, "How Can Cooperation Be Fostered? The Cultural Effects of Individualism-Collectivism," *Academy of Management Review* 23, no. 2 (1998), pp. 285–304.
40. Hofstede, *Culture's Consequences*, pp. 419–420.
41. Ibid., p. 420.
42. Geert Hofstede, "National Culture: Dimensions," http://geert-hofstede.com/dimensions.html.
43. Ibid.
44. Geert Hofstede. "Dimensionalizing Cultures: The Hofstede Model in Context," *Online Readings in Psychology and Culture:* Unit 2, 2011, http://scholarworks.gvsu.edu/orpc/vol2/iss1/8.
45. Geert Hofstede, "National Culture: Dimensions," http://geert-hofstede.com/dimensions.html.
46. Geert Hofstede. "Dimensionalizing Cultures: The Hofstede Model in Context," *Online Readings in Psychology and Culture:* Unit 2, 2011, http://scholarworks.gvsu.edu/orpc/vol2/iss1/8.
47. Fons Trompenaars, *Riding the Waves of Culture: Understanding Diversity in Global Business* (New York: Irwin, 1994), p. 10.
48. Talcott Parsons, *The Social System* (New York: Free Press, 1951).
49. Also see Lisa Hoecklin, *Managing Cultural Differences* (Workingham, England: Addison-Wesley, 1995).
50. Charles M. Hampden-Turner and Fons Trompenaars, "A World Turned Upside Down: Doing Business in Asia," in *Managing Across Cultures,* ed. Joynt and Warner (London: International Thomson Business Press, 1996), p. 279.
51. Ibid., p. 288.
52. Trompenaars, *Riding the Waves of Culture,* p. 131.
53. Ibid., p. 140.
54. Peter Dorfman, Mansour Javidan, Paul Hanges, Ali Dastmalchian, and Robert House, "GLOBE: A Twenty Year Journey into the Intriguing World of Culture and Leadership," *Journal of World Business* 47, (2012), pp. 504–518.
55. Ibid.
56. Mansour Javidan and Robert House, "Leadership and Cultures around the World: Findings from GLOBE: An Introduction to the Special Issue," *Journal of World Business* 37, no. 1 (2002), pp. 1–2.
57. Robert House, Paul J. Hanges, Mansour Javidan, Peter W. Dorfman, and Vipin Gupta, *Culture, Leadership, and Organizations: The GLOBE Study of 62 Societies* (London: Sage, 2004).
58. Kwong Leung, "Editor's Introduction to the Exchange between Hofstede and GLOBE," *Journal of International Business Studies* 37 (2006), p. 881.
59. Peter Dorfman, Mansour Javidan, Paul Hanges, Ali Dastmalchian, and Robert House, "GLOBE: A Twenty Year Journey into the Intriguing World of Culture and Leadership," *Journal of World Business* 47, (2012), pp. 504–518.
60. House et al., *Culture, Leadership, and Organizations: The GLOBE Study.*
61. Mansour Javidan and Robert House, "Cultural Acumen for the Global Manager: Lessons from Project GLOBE," *Organizational Dynamics* 29, no. 4 (2001), pp. 289–305.
62. Robert House, Mansour Javidan, Paul Hanges, and Peter Dorfman, "Understanding Cultures and Implicit Leadership Theories Across the Globe: An Introduction to Project GLOBE," *Journal of World Business* 37, no. 1 (2002), pp. 3–10.
63. Ibid.
64. David A. Waldman, Mary Sully de Luque et al., "Cultural and Leadership Predictors of Corporate Social Responsibility Values of Top Management: A GLOBE Study of 15 Countries," *Journal of International Business Studies* 37 (2006), pp. 823–837.
65. Geert Hofstede, "What Did GLOBE Really Measure? Researchers' Minds versus Respondents' Minds," *Journal of International Business Studies* 37 (2006), pp. 882–896.
66. P. Christopher Earley, "Leading Cultural Research in the Future: A Matter of Paradigms and Taste," *Journal of International Business Studies* 37 (2006), pp. 922–931; Peter B. Smith, "When Elephants Fight, the Grass Gets Trampled: The GLOBE and Hofstede Projects," *Journal of International Business Studies* 37 (2006), pp. 915–921.
67. Mansour Javidan, Peter W. Dorfman, et al., "In the Eye of the Beholder: Cross Cultural Lessons in Leadership from Project GLOBE," *Academy of Management Perspectives* 20, no. 1 (2006), pp. 67–90.
68. Ibid.

Chapter 2

1. Nancy J. Adler, *International Dimensions of Organizational Behavior,* 5th ed. (Cincinnati, OH: Southwestern, 2007).
2. Dylan Love, "At Apple, They Really Are After You," *Business Insider,* January 9, 2013. http://www.businessinsider.com/apple-corporate-culture-2013-1.
3. Adam Lashinsky, "The Secrets Apple Keeps," *Fortune,* January 28, 2012. http://tech.fortune.cnn.com/2012/01/18/inside-apple-adam-lashinsky/.
4. Sam Grobart, "How Samsung became the World's No. 1 Smartphone Maker," *Bloomberg Businessweek.* March 28, 2013. http://www.businessweek.com/articles/2013-03-28/how-samsung-became-the-worlds-no-dot-1-smartphone-maker#p1.
5. Miyoung Kim, "Samsung's Crisis Culture: a Driver and a Drawback," *Reuters,* September 2, 2012. http://www.reuters.com/article/2012/09/02/us-samsung-culture-idUSBRE8810B320120902.
6. Sam Grobart, "How Samsung Became the World's No. 1 Smartphone Maker," *Bloomberg Businessweek.* March 28, 2013. http://www.businessweek.com/articles/2013-03-28/how-samsung-became-the-worlds-no-dot-1-smartphone-maker#p1.
7. David M. Barreda, "Who Supplies Apple?" *China File,* http://www.chinafile.com/who-supplies-apple-it-s-not-just-china-interactive-map.
8. Peter Cohan, "Apple Can't Innovate or Manage Supply Chain," *Forbes,* October 26, 2012. http://www.forbes.com/sites/petercohan/2012/10/26/apple-cant-innovate-or-manage-supply-chain/.
9. Miyoung Kim, "Samsung Says to Fix Outsourcing Issues, but Keep Most Production Inhouse," *Reuters,* November 11, 2012. http://www.reuters.com/article/2012/11/30/us-samsung-labour-idUSBRE8AT09220121130.

10. Sam Grobart, "How Samsung Became the World's No. 1 Smartphone Maker," *Bloomberg Businessweek,* March 28, 2013. http://www.businessweek.com/articles/2013-03-28/how-samsung-became-the-worlds-no-dot-1-smartphone-maker#p1.
11. Ibid.
12. Leo Kelion, "Apple v Samsung Patent Verdict Reconsidered in Court," *BBC,* December 6, 2012. http://www.bbc.co.uk/news/technology-20615376.
13. Jung-ah Lee and Evan Ramstad, "Samsung's Smartphone Sales Surpass Apple's," *Wall Street Journal,* October 28, 2011. http://online.wsj.com/article/SB10001424052970203687504577002571419254242.html.
14. Brian S. Hall, "Samsung vs. Apple: Samsung is Winning Every Way But One," *Readwrite Mobile.* March 5, 2013. http://readwrite.com/2013/03/05/samsung-vs-apple-samsung-is-winning-every-way-but-one-infographic.
15. Ibid.
16. Market Data, Income Statement, *The Wall Street Journal.*
17. World Motor Vehicle Production (OICA, November 2012).
18. Luca Ciferri, "How Renault's Low-cost Dacia has Become a 'Cash Cow'," *Automotive News Europe,* January 2, 2013, http://europe.autonews.com/apps/pbcs.dll/article?AID=/20130102/ANE/312259994/how-renaults-low-cost-dacia-has-become-a-cash-cow.
19. Laurence Frost and Gilles Guillaume, "Renault Taps Logan Creator for Low-Cost Car for India," *Livemint,* December 16, 2012, http://www.livemint.com/Industry/lHHQsNgTS3bJKWMa1jvicK/Renault-taps-Logan-creator-for-5500-India-car.html.
20. "Renault-Nissan Alliance Recognises Its 10–Year Anniversary," *The Auto Channel,* March 27, 2009, http://www.theautochannel.com/news/2009/03/26/454752.html.
21. Lisa Hoecklin, *Managing Cultural Differences: Strategies for Competitive Advantage* (Workingham, England: Addison-Wesley, 1995), pp. 98–99.
22. Marcy Beitle, Arjun Sethi, Jessica Milesko, and Alyson Potenza, "The Offshore Culture Clash," *AT Kearney Executive Agenda* XI, no. 2 (2008), pp. 32–39.
23. Matt Ackerman, "State St.: New Markets Key to Growth," *American Banker,* May 3, 2004, p. 1.
24. Linda M. Randall and Lori A. Coakley, "Building a Successful Partnership in Russia and Belarus: The Impact of Culture on Strategy," *Business Horizons,* March–April 1998, pp. 15–22.
25. Fons Trompenaars and Charles Hampden-Turner, *Riding the Waves of Culture: Understanding Diversity in Global Business,* 2nd ed. (New York: McGraw-Hill, 1998), p. 202.
26. See, for example, Anisya S. Thomas and Stephen L. Mueller, "A Case for Comparative Entrepreneurship: Assessing the Relevance of Culture," *Journal of International Business Studies,* Second Quarter 2000, pp. 287–301.
27. Adapted from Richard Mead, *International Management* (Cambridge, MA: Blackwell, 1994), pp. 57–59.
28. Derived from www.communicaid.com/Malaysia-business-culture.asp.
29. Fred Luthans, Dianne H. B. Welsh, and Stuart A. Rosenkrantz, "What Do Russian Managers Really Do? An Observational Study with Comparisons to U.S. Managers," *Journal of International Business Studies,* Fourth Quarter 1993, pp. 741–761.
30. Diane H. B. Welsh, Fred Luthans, and Steven M. Sommer, "Organizational Behavior Modification Goes to Russia: Replicating an Experimental Analysis Across Cultures and Tasks," *Journal of Organizational Behavior Management* 13, no. 2 (1993), pp. 15–35; Diane H. B. Welsh, Fred Luthans, and Steven M. Sommer, "Managing Russian Factory Workers: The Impact of U.S.-Based Behavioral and Participative Techniques," *Academy of Management Journal,* February 1993, pp. 58–79.
31. Welsh, Luthans, and Sommer, "Organizational Behavior Modification," p. 31. The summary of positive (17 percent average) performance from O.B.Mod. for U.S. samples can be found in Fred Luthans and Alexander Stajkovic, "Reinforce for Performance," *Academy of Management Executive* 13, no. 2 (1999), pp. 49–57.
32. Steven M. Sommer, Seung-Hyun Bae, and Fred Luthans, "The Structure-Climate Relationship in Korean Organizations," *Asia Pacific Journal of Management* 12, no. 2 (1995), pp. 23–36. Also see Steven Sommer, Seung-Hyun Bae, and Fred Luthans, "Organizational Commitment Across Cultures: The Impact of Antecedents on Korean Employees," *Human Relations* 49, no. 7 (1996), pp. 977–993.
33. Sommer, Bae, and Luthans, "The Structure-Climate Relationship."
34. Trompenaars and Hampden-Turner, *Riding the Waves of Culture,* p. 196.
35. Shari Caudron, "Lessons for HR Overseas," *Personnel Journal,* February 1995, p. 92.
36. Richard M. Hodgetts and Fred Luthans, "U.S. Multinationals' Compensation Strategies for Local Management: Cross-Cultural Implications," *Compensation and Benefits Review,* March–April 1993, pp. 42–48.
37. Philip M. Rosenzweig and Nitin Nohria, "Influences on Human Resource Management Practices in Multinational Corporations," *Journal of International Business Studies,* Second Quarter 1994, pp. 229–251.
38. "Disillusioned Workers Cost Japanese Economy up to $180.18 Billion," *The Wall Street Journal,* September 5, 2001, p. B18.
39. Also see Richard W. Wright, "Trends in International Business Research: Twenty-Five Years Later," *Journal of International Business Studies,* Fourth Quarter 1994, pp. 687–701; Schon Beechler and John Zhuang Yang, "The Transfer of Japanese-Style Management to American Subsidiaries: Contingencies, Constraints, and Competencies," *Journal of International Business Studies,* Third Quarter 1994, pp. 467–491.
40. Jacob M. Schlesinger, "Another Foreign CEO Leaves Japan's Executive Ranks," *The Wall Street Journal online,* April 18, 2012.
41. Jean Lee, "Emerging Need: How Companies in Developing Markets Can Cultivate the Leaders They Lack," *The Wall Street Journal online,* May 24, 2010.
42. John Boudreau and Brandon Bailey, "Doing Business in China Getting Tougher for U.S. Companies," *Mercury News,* March 27, 2010; Emily Rauhala, "Q. and A.: Doing Business in China," *New York Times online,* June 16, 2010.
43. Eric W. K. Tsang, "Can Guanxi Be a Source of Sustained Competitive Advantage for Doing Business in China?" *Academy of Management Executive* 12, no. 2 (1998), p. 64.
44. Stephen S. Standifird and R. Scott Marshall, "The Transaction Cost Advantage of Guanxi-Based Business Practices," *Journal of World Business* 35, no. 1 (2000), pp. 21–42.
45. Lee Mei Yi and Paul Ellis, "Insider-Outsider Perspective of Guanxi," *Business Horizons,* January–February 2000, p. 28.
46. Rosalie L. Tung, "Managing in Asia: Cross-Cultural Dimensions," in *Managing Across Cultures: Issues and Perspectives,* ed. Pat Joynt and Malcolm Warner (London: International Thomson Business Press, 1996), p. 239.
47. Michelle Conlin, "Go-Go-Going to Pieces in China," *BusinessWeek,* April 23, 2007, p. 88.
48. For more on this topic, see Philip R. Harris and Robert T. Moran, *Managing Cultural Differences,* 3rd ed. (Houston: Gulf Publishing, 1991), pp. 410–411.

49. Ming-Jer Chen, *Inside Chinese Business* (Boston: Harvard Business School Press, 2001), p. 153.
50. Conlin, "Go-Go-Going to Pieces in China."
51. William B. Snavely, Serguel Miassaoedov, and Kevin McNeilly, "Cross-Cultural Peculiarities of the Russian Entrepreneur: Adapting to the New Russians," *Business Horizons*, March–April 1998, pp. 10–13.
52. For additional insights into how to interact and negotiate effectively with the Russians, see Richard D. Lewis, *When Cultures Collide* (London: Nicholas Brealey, 1999), pp. 314–318.
53. Snavely, Miassaoedov, and McNeilly, "Cross-Cultural Peculiarities," p. 13.
54. "The Challenges for India," *Chicago Tribune*, May 27, 2004, p. 28; Amy Waldman, "In India, Economic Growth and Democracy Do Mix," *New York Times*, May 26, 2004, p. A13.
55. Adapted from Harris and Moran, *Managing Cultural Differences*, p. 447.
56. Also see Lewis, *When Cultures Collide*, pp. 341–346.
57. Jean-Louis Barsoux and Peter Lawrence, "The Making of a French Manager," *Harvard Business Review*, July–August 1991, pp. 58–67.
58. Adapted from Harris and Moran, *Managing Cultural Differences*, p. 471.
59. Lewis, *When Cultures Collide*, pp. 231–232.
60. T. Lenartowicz and James Patrick Johnson, "A Cross-National Assessment of Values of Latin America Managers: Contrasting Hues or Shades of Gray?" *Journal of International Business Studies* 34, no. 3 (May 2003), p. 270.
61. Reed E. Nelson and Suresh Gopalan, "Do Organizational Cultures Replicate National Cultures? Isomorphism, Rejection and Reciprocal Opposition in the Corporate Values of Three Countries," *Organization Studies* 24, no. 7 (September 2003), pp. 1115–1154.
62. Derived from Raul Gouvea, "Brazil: A Strategic Approach," *Thunderbird International Business Review* 46, no. 2 (March–April 2004), pp. 183–184; David Hannon, "Brazil Offers the Best of Both Worlds," *Purchasing,* October 5, 2006, pp. 51–52, www.careerjournaleurope.com/myc/workabroad/countries/brazil.html.
63. Sean Van Zyl, "Global Political Risks: Post 9/11," *Canadian Underwriter* 71, no. 3 (March 2004), p. 16; Marvin Zonis, "Mideast Hopes: Endless Surprises," *Chicago Tribune*, January 18, 2004, p. 1.
64. Changiz Pezeshkpur, "Challenges to Management in the Arab World," *Business Horizons*, August 1978, p. 50.
65. Adapted from Harris and Moran, *Managing Cultural Differences*, p. 503.

Chapter 3

1. "Innovation through Diversity," *Applied Materials,* http://www.appliedmaterials.com/careers/diversity.html.
2. Bradley L. Kirkman, Benson Rosen, Cristina Gibson, and Paul E. Tesluk, "Five Challenges to Virtual Team Success: Lessons from Sabre, Inc.," *Academy of Management Executive* 16, no. 3 (August 2002), pp. 67–79, retrieved from EBSCOhost: http://turbo.kean.edu/~jmcgill/sabre.htm.
3. Ibid.
4. Surinder Kahai, "Culture Matters in Virtual Teams," *Leading Virtually: Leadership in the Digital Age*, December 31, 2007, http://www.leadingvirtually.com/?p=22.
5. Ibid.
6. Ibid.
7. Ibid.
8. Melanie Doulton, "Tips for Working in Global Teams," *Career Guidance*, *The Institute*, January 5, 2007, http://www.ieee.org/portal/site/tionline/menuitem.130a3558587d56e8fb2275875bac26c8/index.jsp?&pName=institute_level1_article&TheCat=1002&article=tionline/legacy/inst2007/jan07/career.xml.
9. Steven R. Rayner, "The Virtual Team Challenge," Rayner & Associates, Inc., 1997, http://raynerassoc.com/Resources/Virtual.pdf.
10. Bradley L. Kirkman, Benson Rosen, Cristina Gibson, and Paul E. Tesluk, "Five Challenges to Virtual Team Success: Lessons from Sabre, Inc.," *Academy of Management Executive* 16, no. 3 (August 2002), pp. 67–79, retrieved from EBSCOhost: http://turbo.kean.edu/~jmcgill/sabre.htm.
11. Steven R. Rayner, "The Virtual Team Challenge," Rayner & Associates, Inc., 1997, http://raynerassoc.com/Resources/Virtual.pdf.
12. Bradley L. Kirkman, Benson Rosen, Cristina Gibson, and Paul E. Tesluk, "Five Challenges to Virtual Team Success: Lessons from Sabre, Inc.," *Academy of Management Executive* 16, no. 3 (August 2002), pp. 67–79, retrieved from EBSCOhost: http://turbo.kean.edu/~jmcgill/sabre.htm.
13. Melanie Doulton, "Tips for Working in Global Teams," *Career Guidance, The Institute*, January 5, 2007, http://www.ieee.org/portal/site/tionline/menuitem.130a3558587d56e8fb2275875bac26c8/index.jsp?&pName=institute_level1_article&TheCat=1002&article=tionline/legacy/inst2007/jan07/career.xml.
14. Bradley L. Kirkman, Benson Rosen, Cristina Gibson, and Paul E. Tesluk, "Five Challenges to Virtual Team Success: Lessons from Sabre, Inc.," *Academy of Management Executive* 16, no. 3 (August 2002), pp. 67–79, retrieved from EBSCOhost: http://turbo.kean.edu/~jmcgill/sabre.htm.
15. Ibid.
16. Bradley L. Kirkman, Benson Rosen, Cristina Gibson, and Paul E. Tesluk, "Five Challenges to Virtual Team Success: Lessons from Sabre, Inc.," *Academy of Management Executive* 16, no. 3 (August 2002), pp. 67–79, retrieved from EBSCOhost: http://turbo.kean.edu/~jmcgill/sabre.htm.
17. Steven R. Rayner, "The Virtual Team Challenge," Rayner & Associates, Inc., 1997, http://raynerassoc.com/Resources/Virtual.pdf.
18. Ibid.
19. Lisa Hoecklin, *Managing Cultural Differences: Strategies for Competitive Advantage* (Workingham, England: Addison-Wesley, 1995), p. 146.
20. Edgar H. Schein, *Organizational Culture and Leadership,* 2nd ed. (San Francisco: Jossey-Bass, 1997), p. 12.
21. Fred Luthans, *Organizational Behavior,* 10th ed. (New York: McGraw-Hill/Irwin, 2005), pp. 110–111.
22. In addition see W. Mathew Jeuchter, Caroline Fisher, and Randall J. Alford, "Five Conditions for High-Performance Cultures," *Training and Development Journal,* May 1998, pp. 63–67.
23. AstraZeneca, *Diversity and Inclusion*, http://www.astrazeneca.com/Responsibility/Our-people/.
24. Ibid.
25. Ibid.
26. Hoecklin, *Managing Cultural Differences,* p. 145.
27. Andre Laurent, "The Cultural Diversity of Western Conceptions of Management," *International Studies of Management and Organization,* Spring–Summer 1983, pp. 75–96.
28. Nancy J. Adler, *International Dimensions of Organizational Behavior,* 2nd ed. (Boston: PWS-Kent Publishing, 1991), pp. 58–59.

29. Robert Frank and Thomas M. Burton, "Cross-Border Merger Results in Headaches for a Drug Company," *The Wall Street Journal,* February 4, 1997, p. A1.
30. Hoecklin, *Managing Cultural Differences,* p. 151.
31. Robert Hughes, "Weekend Journal: Futures and Options: Global Culture," *The Wall Street Journal,* October 10, 2003, p. W2.
32. Rita A. Numeroff and Michael N. Abrams, "Integrating Corporate Culture from International M&As," *HR Focus,* June 1998, p. 12.
33. See Maddy Janssens, Jeanne M. Brett, and Frank J. Smith, "Confirmatory Cross-Cultural Research: Testing the Viability of a Corporation-Wide Safety Policy," *Academy of Management Journal,* June 1995, pp. 364–382.
34. Fons Trompenaars, *Riding the Waves of Culture: Understanding Diversity in Global Business* (Burr Ridge, IL: Irwin, 1994), p. 154.
35. Ibid.
36. Ibid., p. 156.
37. Ibid., p. 164.
38. Ibid., p. 167.
39. Ibid., p. 172.
40. For more see Rose Mary Wentling and Nilda Palma-Rivas, "Current Status of Diversity Initiatives in Selected Multinational Corporations," *Human Resource Development Quarterly,* Spring 2000, pp. 35–60.
41. Adler, *International Dimensions of Organizational Behavior,* p. 121.
42. Jean Lee, "Culture and Management: A Study of Small Chinese Family Business in Singapore," *Journal of Small Business Management,* July 1996, p. 65.
43. Noboru Yoshimura and Philip Anderson, *Inside the Kaisha: Demystifying Japanese Business Behavior* (Boston: Harvard Business School Press, 1997).
44. Edmund L. Andrews, "Meet the Maverick of Japan, Inc." *New York Times,* October 12, 1995, pp. C1, C4.
45. Sheryl WuDunn, "Incubators of Creativity," *New York Times,* October 9, 1997, pp. C1, C21.
46. Adler, *International Dimensions of Organizational Behavior,* p. 132.
47. Adele Thomas and Mike Bendixen, "The Management Implications of Ethnicity in South Africa," *Journal of International Business Studies,* Third Quarter 2000, pp. 507–519.
48. John M. Ivencevich and Jacqueline A. Gilbert, "Diversity Management: Time for a New Approach," *Public Personnel Management,* Spring 2000, pp. 75–92.
49. "Over the Rainbow," *Economist online,* November 20, 1997, www.economist.com/business/displaystory.cfm?story_id=E1_TDGQRP.
50. See, for example, Betty Jane Punnett and Jason Clemens, "Cross-National Diversity: Implications for International Expansion Decisions," *Journal of World Business* 34, no. 2 (1999), pp. 128–138.
51. Adler, *International Dimensions of Organizational Behavior,* p. 137.

Chapter 4

1. Ed Hammond, "Offshoring: Still in Control although at Arm's Length," *Financial Times,* June 24, 2010, http://www.ft.com/cms/s/0/6769a858-7d8e-11df-a0f5-00144feabdc0.html.
2. Marcy Beitle, Arjun Sethi, Jessica Milesko, and Alyson Potenza, "The Offshore Culture Clash," A.T. Kearney Global Management Consultants, http://www.atkearney.com/index.php/Publications/the-offshore-culture-clash.html.
3. Ibid.
4. Ibid.
5. Ibid.
6. Ibid.
7. Ibid.
8. Ibid.
9. Kannan Srikanth and Phanish Puranam, "Business Insight (A Special Report): Global Business—Advice for Outsourcers: Think Bigger: Too Many Companies Mistakenly Limit Offshore Work to Routine Tasks," *The Wall Street Journal (Europe),* January 25, 2010, http://online.wsj.com/article/SB10001424052748704007804574574161967309526.html.
10. Ibid.
11. Ibid.
12. Ibid.
13. Marcy Beitle, Arjun Sethi, Jessica Milesko, and Alyson Potenza, "The Offshore Culture Clash," A.T. Kearney Global Management Consultants, http://www.atkearney.com/index.php/Publications/the-offshore-culture-clash.html.
14. Ibid.
15. Nicholas Carr, *The Shallows* (New York: Norton, 2010).
16. E. T. Hall and E. Hall, "How Cultures Collide," in *Culture, Communication, and Conflict: Readings in Intercultural Relations,* ed. G. R. Weaver (Needham Heights, MA: Ginn Press, 1994).
17. Noboru Yoshimura and Philip Anderson, *Inside the Kaisha: Demystifying Japanese Business Behavior* (Boston: Harvard Business School Press, 1997), p. 59.
18. William C. Byham and George Dixon, "Through Japanese Eyes," *Training and Development Journal*, March 1993, pp. 33–36; Linda S. Dillon, "West Meets East," *Training and Development Journal*, March 1993, pp. 39–43.
19. Fons Trompenaars and Charles Hampden-Turner, *Riding the Waves of Culture: Understanding Diversity in Global Business*, 2nd ed. (New York: McGraw-Hill, 1998), p. 204.
20. Nancy J. Adler (with Allison Gunderson), *International Dimensions of Organizational Behavior*, 5th ed. (Mason, OH: South-Western, 2008), p. 80.
21. Toddi Gunter, "Delivering Unpopular News When You Haven't Bought In," *New York Times online*, June 14, 2010.
22. Giorgio Inzerilli, "The Legitimacy of Managerial Authority: A Comparative Study," *National Academy of Management Proceedings* (Detroit, 1980), pp. 58–62.
23. Ibid., p. 62.
24. Philip R. Harris and Robert T. Moran, *Managing Cultural Differences*, 3rd ed. (Houston: Gulf Publishing, 1996), pp. 36–37.
25. Richard Tanner Pascale and Anthony G. Athos, *The Art of Japanese Management* (New York: Warner Books, 1981), pp. 82–83.
26. Justin Fox, "The Triumph of English," *Fortune,* September 18, 2000, pp. 209–212.
27. See "Double or Quits," *Economist*, February 25, 1995, pp. 84–85.
28. Brock Stout, "Interviewing in Japan," *HR Magazine*, June 1998, p. 73.
29. Ibid., p. 75.
30. H. W. Hildebrandt, "Communication Barriers Between German Subsidiaries and Parent American Companies," *Michigan Business Review*, July 1973, p. 9.
31. John R. Schermerhorn Jr., "Language Effects in Cross-Cultural Management Research: An Empirical Study and a Word of Caution," *National Academy of Management Proceedings* (New Orleans, 1987), p. 103.

32. Heather Berry, Mauro F. Guillén, and Nan Zhou, "An Institutional Approach to Cross-national Distance," *Journal of International Business Studies* (advance online publication), July 1, 2010, doi: 10.1057/jibs.2010.28.

33. Brenda R. Sims and Stephen Guice, "Differences Between Business Letters from Native and Non-Native Speakers of English," *Journal of Business Communication*, Winter 1991, p. 37.

34. James Calvert Scott and Diana J. Green, "British Perspectives on Organizing Bad-News Letters: Organizational Patterns Used by Major U.K. Companies," *The Bulletin*, March 1992, p. 17.

35. Ibid., pp. 18–19.

36. Mi Young Park, W. Tracy Dillon, and Kenneth L. Mitchell, "Korean Business Letters: Strategies for Effective Complaints in Cross-Cultural Communication," *Journal of Business Communication*, July 1998, pp. 328–345.

37. As an example see Jeremiah Sullivan, "What Are the Functions of Corporate Home Pages?" *Journal of World Business* 34, no. 2 (1999), pp. 193–211.

38. David A. Ricks, *Big Business Blunders: Mistakes in Multinational Marketing* (Homewood, IL: Dow Jones/Irwin, 1983), p. 39.

39. Ibid., p. 55.

40. John Kass, "Some Bright Ideas Get Lost in Translation," *Chicago Tribune online edition*, April 20, 2007, www.chicagotribune.com/news/columnists/chi-0704190692apr20,1,6809930.column.

41. Edwin Miller, Bhal Bhatt, Raymond Hill, and Julian Cattaneo, "Leadership Attitudes of American and German Expatriate Managers in Europe and Latin America," *National Academy of Management Proceedings* (Detroit, 1980), pp. 53–57.

42. Abdul Rahim A. Al-Meer, "Attitudes Towards Women as Managers: A Comparison of Asians, Saudis and Westerners," *Arab Journal of the Social Sciences*, April 1988, pp. 139–149.

43. Sheryl WuDunn, "In Japan, Still Getting Tea and No Sympathy," *New York Times*, August 27, 1995, p. E3.

44. Fathi S. Yousef, "Cross-Cultural Communication: Aspects of the Contrastive Social Values Between North Americans and Middle Easterners," *Human Organization*, Winter 1974, p. 385.

45. Peter McKiernan and Chris Carter, "The Millennium Nexus: Strategic Management at the Crossroads," *European Management Review* 1, no. 1 (Spring 2004), p. 3.

46. R. Bruce Money, "Word-of-Mouth Referral Sources for Buyers of International Corporate Financial Services," *Journal of World Business* 35, no. 3 (2000), pp. 314–329.

47. Yousef, "Cross-Cultural Communication," p. 383.

48. See Roger E. Axtell, ed., *Do's and Taboos Around the World* (New York: Wiley, 1990), chapter 2.

49. Jane Whitney Gibson, Richard M. Hodgetts, and Charles W. Blackwell, "Cultural Variations in Nonverbal Communication," *55th Annual Business Communication Proceedings*, San Antonio, November 8–10, 1990, pp. 211–229.

50. William K. Brandt and James M. Hulbert, "Patterns of Communications in the Multinational Corporation: An Empirical Study," *Journal of International Business Studies*, Spring 1976, pp. 57–64.

51. Hildebrandt, "Communication Barriers," p. 9.

52. See for example George Ming-Hong Lai, "Knowing Who You Are Doing Business with in Japan: A Managerial View of Keiretsu and Keiretsu Business Groups," *Journal of World Business* 34, no. 4 (1999), pp. 423–449.

53. Nicholas Athanassiou and Douglas Nigh, "Internationalization, Tacit Knowledge and the Top Management Teams of MNCs," *Journal of International Business Studies*, Third Quarter 2000, pp. 471–487.

54. Also see Linda Beamer, "Bridging Business Cultures," *China Business Review*, May–June 1998, pp. 54–58.

55. Tanya Mohn, "Going Global, Stateside," *New York Times*, March 9, 2010, p. B9.

56. Michael D. Lord and Annette L. Ranft, "Organizational Learning about New International Markets: Exploring the Internal Transfer of Local Market Knowledge," *Journal of International Business Studies*, Fourth Quarter 2000, pp. 573–589.

57. Jennifer W. Spencer, "Knowledge Flows in the Global Innovation System: Do U.S. Firms Share More Scientific Knowledge than Their Japanese Rivals?" *Journal of International Business Studies*, Third Quarter 2000, pp. 521–530.

58. Kenichi Ohmae, "The Global Logic of Strategic Alliances," *Harvard Business Review*, March–April 1989, p. 154.

59. See Hildy Teegen and Jonathan P. Doh, "U.S./Mexican Alliance Negotiations: Cultural Impacts on Trust, Authority and Performance," *Thunderbird International Business Review* 44, no. 6 (2002), pp. 749–775; Elise Campbell and Jeffrey J. Reuer, "International Alliance Negotiations: Legal Issues for General Managers," *Business Horizons*, January–February 2001, pp. 19–26.

60. Nina Reynolds, Antonis Simintiras, and Efi Vlachou, "International Business Negotiations: Present Knowledge and Direction for Future Research," *International Marketing Review* 20, no. 3 (2003), p. 236.

61. Harvard Business Essentials: Negotiation (Boston: Harvard Business School Press, 2003), p. 2.

62. Ibid., p. 4.

63. David K. Tse, June Francis, and Ian Walls, "Cultural Differences in Conducting Intra- and Inter-Cultural Negotiations: A Sino-Canadian Comparison," *Journal of International Business Studies,* Third Quarter 1994, pp. 537–555; Teegen and Doh, "U.S./Mexican Alliance Negotiations," pp. 749–775.

64. Adler and Gundersen, *International Dimensions of Organizational Behavior*, p. 241.

65. Daniel Druckman, "Group Attachments in Negotiation and Collective Action," *International Negotiation* 11 (2006), pp. 229–252.

66. Jeanne M. Brett, Debra L. Shapiro, and Anne L. Lytle, "Breaking the Bonds of Reciprocity in Negotiations," *Academy of Management Journal*, August 1998, pp. 410–424.

67. Stephen E. Weiss, "Negotiating with 'Romans'—Part 2," *Sloan Management Review,* Spring 1994, p. 89.

68. Trompenaars and Hampden-Turner, *Riding the Waves of Culture*, p. 112.

69. James K. Sebenius, "The Hidden Challenge of Cross-Border Negotiations," *Harvard Business Review*, March 2002, pp. 4–12.

70. John L. Graham, "Brazilian, Japanese, and American Business Negotiations," *Journal of International Business Studies*, Spring–Summer 1983, pp. 47–61; John L. Graham, "The Influence of Culture on the Process of Business Negotiations in an Exploratory Study," *Journal of International Business Studies,* Spring 1983, pp. 81–96.

71. William Zartman, "Negotiating Internal, Ethnic and Identity Conflicts in a Globalized World," *International Negotiation* 11 (2006), pp. 253–272.

72. Roger Fisher and William Ury, *Getting to Yes: Negotiating Agreement Without Giving In* (New York: Penguin Books, 1983), p. 11.

73. Ibid., p. 79.

74. Ibid., p. 111.
75. Graham, "The Influence of Culture on the Process of Business Negotiations in an Exploratory Study," pp. 84, 88.

Brief Integrative Case 1.1

1. Peter Wonacott and Chad Terhune, "Politics & Economics: Path to India's Market Dotted with Potholes; Savvy Cola Giants Stumble over Local Agendas; KFC Climbs Back from Abyss," *Wall Street Journal,* September 12, 2006, p. A6.
2. "CSE Report on Pesticide Residue Inconclusive," *Businessline,* August 27, 2006, p. 1.
3. Rajesh Kumar and Verner Worm, "Institutional Dynamics and the Negotiation Process: Comparing India and China," *International Journal of Conflict Management* 15, no. 3 (2004), p. 304.
4. Wonacott and Terhune, "Politics & Economics."
5. Archna Shukla, "Message Will Always Be More Important than Medium," *Business Today,* August 27, 2006, p. 102.
6. Mark Sappenfield, "India's Cola Revolt Taps into Old Distrust: Behind Contradictory Reports of Pesticides in Coke and Pepsi Is an Underlying Wariness of Foreign Companies," *The Christian Science Monitor,* September 1, 2006, p. 6.
7. Nikhil Gulati and Runman Ahmed, "India has 1.2 Billion People But Not Enough Drink Coke," *The Wall Street Journal Online,* July 13, 2012, http://online.wsj.com/article/SB1000142405270230 4870304577490092413939410.
8. "India 2009/10 FDI Flows Seen at $18 bn—Trade Min," *Reuters,* December 4, 2009, http://www.reuters.com/article/ idUSDEL00240820091204.
9. UNCTAD, *World Investment Prospects Survey,* 2010.
10. "Foreign Direct Investment," *India Brand Equity Foundation,* February 2010, http://www.ibef.org/economy/fdi.aspx.
11. Arvind Panagariya, "Building a Modern India," *Business Standard India 2010.*
12. Brian Bremner, Nandini Lakshman, and Diane Brady, "India: Behind the Scare over Pesticides in Pepsi and Coke," *BusinessWeek,* September 4, 2006, p. 43.
13. Sappenfield, "India's Cola Revolt Taps into Old Distrust."
14. Bremner, Lakshman, and Brady, "India: Behind the Scare over Pesticides in Pepsi and Coke."
15. Coca-Cola India, "Environment Report 2007–2008."
16. Eric Bellman, "Coke Sees Strong Demand across India, Plans Investment," *The Wall Street Journal,* June 30, 2009, http:// online.wsj.com/article/SB124055692273452331.html?mod= googlenews_wsj.
17. Ibid.
18. Nikhil Gulati and Runman Ahmed, "India Has 1.2 Billion People But Not Enough Drink Coke," *The Wall Street Journal Online,* July 13, 2012, http://online.wsj.com/article/SB1000142405270230 4870304577490092413939410.
19. Ratna Bhushan, "RC Cola Comes to India," *Businessline,* October 7, 2003, p. 1.
20. "India: Reports of Contaminated Soda Dry up Coke, Pepsi Sales," *Global Information Network,* September 7, 2006, p. 1.
21. Aryn Baker, "India's Storm in a Cola Cup," *Time International,* August 21, 2006, p. 8.
22. Bremner, Lakshman, and Brady, "India: Behind the Scare over Pesticides in Pepsi and Coke."
23. Sappenfield, "India's Cola Revolt Taps into Old Distrust."
24. Wonacott and Terhune, "Politics & Economics."
25. "India: Reports of Contaminated Soda Dry up Coke, Pepsi Sales."
26. Sappenfield, "India's Cola Revolt Taps into Old Distrust."
27. "Coca-Cola Co.: India's Kerala State Cancels Ban on Coke, Pepsi Drinks," *The Wall Street Journal,* September 25, 2006, p. A11.
28. Ibid.
29. "Coca-Cola India Unit Asked to Pay $47 Million Damages," *Reuters,* March 23, 2010, http://www.reuters.com/article/ idUSSGE62M0AV20100323.
30. Diane Brady, "Pepsi: Repairing a Poisoned Reputation in India," *BusinessWeek,* June 11, 2007.
31. Ibid.
32. Ibid.
33. Ibid.
34. Amit Srivastava, "Coca-Cola Funded Group Investigates Coca-Cola in India," India Resource Center, April 16, 2007, www.indiaresource.org/campaigns/coke/2007/coketeri.html.
35. Sappenfield, "India's Cola Revolt Taps into Old Distrust."
36. Amelia Gentleman, "For 2 Giants of Soft Drinks, a Crisis in Crucial Market," *New York Times,* August 23, 2006, p. C3.
37. Wonacott and Terhune, "Politics & Economics."
38. "Coca-Cola-India: Key Facts," www.cokefacts.org.
39. Ibid.
40. Coca-Cola India, "Environment Report 2007–2008."
41. Ben Blanchard, "Coke Vows to Reduce Water Used in Drink Production," June 5, 2007, www.reuters.com.
42. "The Coca-Cola Company Pledges to Replace the Water It Uses in Its Beverages and Their Production," press release, June 5, 2007, www.thecoca-colacompany.com/presscenter/nr_20070605_ tccc_and_wwf_partnership.html.
43. Coca-Cola India, "Environment Report 2007–2008."
44. Ibid.
45. Gentleman, "For 2 Giants of Soft Drinks, a Crisis in Crucial Market."
46. Coca-Cola, "2009 Annual Review."
47. Brad Dorfman and Martinne Geller, "Coca-Cola Sales Rise, Led by Emerging Markets," *Reuters,* February 9, 2010, http://www. reuters.com/article/idUSTRE61829W20100209.
48. Kenneth E. Behring, "Water Research; Researchers Are Raising Awareness of the Global Drinking Water Crisis," *Health & Medicine Week,* October 16, 2006, p. 1339.
49. Thalif Deen, "Development: Water, Water Everywhere Is Thing of the Past," *Global Information Network,* August 22, 2006, p. 1.
50. Loretta Chao and Shai Oster, "China Study Says Foreigners Violate Clean-Water Rules," *The Wall Street Journal,* October 30, 2006, p. B7.
51. *The 3rd United Nations World Water Development Report: Water in a Changing World* (WWDR-3), 2009.

Brief Integrative Case 1.2

1. Steve Dickinson, JP Morgan's Hand-On China Series: "Views You Can Use," July 2007, http://query.jpmorgan.com/inetSearch/ index_redesign.jsp?q=wahaha&image=Go+%BB&pageType=_ JPMC&sort=2&num=10&lr=&site=jpmorgan.
2. J. Zhou, "Trademark Disputes between Danone and Wahaha Group," *China Business Law,* August 2009, http://www.china-business-law. com/trademark-disputes-between-danone-and-wahaha-group/.

3. "Danone Encounters Continuous Frustration in China and a Murky Future Due to Unsuccessful Litigations," Wahaha Group, October 9, 2008, *PR Newswire,* http://www.highbeam.com/doc/1G1–184638322.html.
4. http://www.brandchannel.com/features_profile.asp?pr_id=120.
5. Ibid.
6. Ibid.
7. B. Bruce, "Danone Celebrates Its 90th Birthday," March 14, 2009, http://www.foodbev.com/article/danone-celebrates-its-90th-birthday.
8. Ibid.
9. Danone, corporate press release, September 30, 2009, http://phx.corporate-ir.net/phoenix.zhtml?c=95168&p=irol-newsArticle&ID=1336626.
10. Danone S.A. Profile, *Reuters,* http://www.reuters.com/finance/stocks/companyProfile?symbol=DANO.PA.
11. http://www.finance.danone.com/phoenix.zhtml?c=95168&p=irol-newsArticle&ID=1336626&highlight=.
12. http://www.interbrand.com/best_global_brands.aspx?year=2009&langid=1000.
13. http://www.danone.com/en/company/introduction.html.
14. http://www.danone.com/en/brands/business/beverages.html.
15. Ibid.
16. Danone 2008 Annual Report: *Economic and Social Report.*
17. Shangguan Zhoudong, "Danone's Quick Expansion in China," *China Daily,* June 15, 2007, http://www.chinadaily.com.cn/bizchina/2007–06/15/content_895462.htm.
18. T. C. Melewar, E. Badal, and J. Small, "Danone Branding Strategy in China," *Brand Management* 13, no. 6 (July 2006), pp. 407–417.
19. "Danone Encounters Continuous Frustration in China and a Murky Future Due to Unsuccessful Litigations," *Thomson Reuters,* September 9, 2008, http://www.reuters.com/article/pressRelease/idUS113471+09–Sep-2008+PRN20080909.
20. Ibid.
21. Vivian Wai-yin Kwok, "A Pyrrhic Victory for Danone in China," *Forbes,* August 6, 2007, http://www.forbes.com/2007/06/08/wahaha-danone-zong-markets-equity-cx_vk_0608markets2.html.
22. http://en.wahaha.com.cn/aboutus/history/.
23. Ibid.
24. Ibid.
25. Ibid.
26. Ibid.
27. Ibid.
28. S. M. Dickinson, "Danone v. Wahaha," *China Economic Review,* September 2007, http://www.chinaeconomicreview.com/cer/2007_09/Danone_v_Wahaha.html.
29. Ibid.
30. Steve Dickinson, JP Morgan's Hand-On China Series: "Views You Can Use," July 2007, http://query.jpmorgan.com/inetSearch/index_redesign.jsp.
31. Dickinson, "Danone v. Wahaha."
32. Ibid.
33. Ibid.
34. Ibid.
35. Ibid.
36. Ibid.
37. Baoxiu Ye, "Wahaha Reviews 21:0 Whitewash Against Danone," *Thomson Reuters,* April 13, 2009, http://www.reuters.com/article/pressRelease/idUS69637+13–Apr-2009+PRN20090413.
38. Ibid.
39. Ibid.
40. Ibid.
41. Ibid.
42. Ibid.
43. Ibid.
44. Ibid.
45. Ibid.
46. Ibid.
47. Ibid.
48. Ibid.
49. Ibid.
50. Ibid.
51. J. T. Areddy, "Danone Pulls Out of Disputed China Venture," *The Wall Street Journal,* October 1, 2009, http://online.wsj.com/article/SB125428911997751859.html.
52. Ibid.
53. Ibid.
54. Ibid.
55. P. Waldmeir and S. Tucker, "Danone to Quit Joint Venture with Wahaha," *Financial Times,* September 30, 2009, http://www.ft.com/cms/s/0/849e7eda-ad87–11de-bb8a-00144feabdc0,dwp_uuid=eced8d08–6d64–11da-a4df-0000779e2340.html.

In-Depth Integrative Cases 1.1a and 1.1b

1. Anna Willard, James Mackenzie, James Grubel, Wayne Cole, Tova Cohen, Alan Raybould and Jonathan Thatcher. "FACTBOX:Who's next? Countries at risk of recession." March 3, 2009. http://www.reuters.com.
2. "Euro Disney Adding Alcohol," *The New York Times,* June 12, 1993. http://www.nytimes.com/1993/06/12/business/euro-disney-adding-alcohol.html.
3. "The History of DisneyLand Paris," Solarius, July 4, 2006. http://www.solarius.com/dvp/dlp/dlp-history.htm.
4. Christian Sylt, "Magic Results: Euro Disney Plans New Hotels." August 17, 2008. http://www.independent.co.uk/news/business/news/magic-results-euro-disney-plans-new-hotels-899529.html.
5. Euro Disney S.C.A. "EURO DISNEY S.C.A. Reports Fiscal Year 2011 Results." November 9, 2011. http://corporate.disneylandparis.com/CORP/EN/Neutral/Images/uk-2011-11-09-euro-disney-sca-reports-annual-results-for-fiscal-year-2011.pdf.
6. Peter Gumbel, "Disney's $1.7 Billion French Birthday Gift." *Time,* September 19, 2012. http://business.time.com/2012/09/19/disneys-1-7-billion-french-birthday-gift/.
7. Ibid.
8. Raymond H. Lopez, "Disney in China Again?" March 2002, appserv.pace.edu/emplibrary/FINAL.Asiacasestudy.doc.
9. Ibid.
10. Ibid.
11. "Disney's Shanghai Park Plan in Doubt: Company Mulls Move to Another Location in China," *Msnbc.com,* December 11, 2006.
12. Lopez, "Disney in China Again?"
13. Thomas Crampton, "Disney's New Hong Kong Park to be 'Culturally Sensitive': Mickey Mouse Learns Chinese," *International Herald Tribune,* January 13, 2003, www.iht.com/articles/2003/01/13/disney_ed3__0.php.

14. Michael Schuman, "Disney's Hong Kong Headache," *Time Magazine,* May 8, 2006, www.time.com/time/magazine/article/0,9171,501060515–1191881,00.html.
15. Kim Soyoung and George Chen, "Hollywood Chases Asia Theme Park Rainbow," *Turkish Daily News*, May 29, 2007, www.turkishdailynews.com.tr/article.php?enewsid=74352.
16. "Cuts Cloud Hong Kong Disneyland Expansion," *Financial Times,* March 17, 2009, http://www.ft.com/cms/s/0/c59c5a72–12bb-11de-9848–0000779fd2ac.html.
17. "Hong Kong Disneyland's Future Is in Danger," *BusinessWeek,* March 17, 2009, http://www.businessweek.com/globalbiz/content/mar2009/gb20090317_923737.htm.
18. Ibid.
19. "Disney Puts Hong Kong Expansion on Hold," *Reuters,* March 16, 2009, http://www.reuters.com/article/industryNews/idUSTRE52G0I120090317.
20. "Hong Kong Disneyland's Future Is in Danger."
21. Ibid.
22. "Disney, Hong Kong Reach $465m Expansion Deal," *China Daily,* June 30, 2009, http://www.chinadaily.com.cn/china/2009–06/30/content_8338445.htm.
23. J. T. Areddy and P. Sanders, "Disney's Shanghai Park Plan Advances," *The Wall Street Journal,* January 12, 2009, p. A1.
24. Ibid.
25. "Disney Announces Shanghai Theme Park," Disney news release, January 11, 2009, http://www.magicalmountain.net/WDWNewsDetail.asp?page=4&NewsID=2103&type=1&tag=.
26. "Walt Disney, Shanghai Propose New Theme Park in China (Update 1)," *Bloomberg,* January 9, 2009, http://www.bloomberg.com/apps/news?pid=20601080&sid=atGa2ymXAMM8&refer=asia.
27. Ibid.
28. Areddy and Sanders, "Disney's Shanghai Park Plan Advances."
29. Samuel Shen and Sue Zeidler, "Disney Takes China Stride as Shanghai Park Gets Nod," *Reuters,* November 4, 2009, http://www.reuters.com/article/idUSTRE5A31TC20091104.
30. Ibid.
31. Ibid.
32. Brooks Barnes, "Hong Kong Disneyland turns a Profit." *New York Times*, February 18, 2013. NTY.com.
33. Frederik Balfour, "Disney Shanghai: Good for China, Bad for Hong Kong," *BusinessWeek,* November 5, 2009.
34. "Shanghai Disney to Get Approved Land in July," *China Daily,* April 4, 2010, http://www.chinadaily.com.cn/china/2010–04/14/content_9730662.htm.
35. "Malaysia Discussing Building Disney Park: Would Be First Such Attraction in Southeast Asia," *Associated Press,* May 30, 2006, www.msnbc.msn.com/id/13045465/.
36. Soyoung and Chen, "Hollywood Chases Asia Theme Park Rainbow."
37. Ibid.
38. Hana R. Alberts, "Tokyo Disneyland? Asia's Top 12 Amusement Parks," February 13, 2010, http://www.ctv.ca/servlet/ArticleNews/story/CTVNews/20100212/forbes_amusement_100213/20100213?hub=World.
39. Ibid.
40. Ibid.
41. James T. Areddy and Peter Sanders, "Chinese Learn English the Disney Way," *The Wall Street Journal,* April 20, 2009, p. B1.

In-Depth Integrative Case 1.2

1. Jennifer McTaggart, "Walmart versus the World," *Progressive Grocer,* October 15, 2003, p. 20.
2. "'Walmart' in Japan Sees Losses," *Associated Press*, August 23, 2006, www.sptimes.com/2006/08/23/Business/_Wal_Mart__in_Japan_s.shtml.
3. David Lague, "Unions Triumphant at Walmart in China," *International Herald Tribune,* October 12, 2006, www.iht.com/-articles/2006/10/12/business/unions.php.
4. Walmart Inc., "China Fact Sheet," www.walmartstores.com.
5. Walmart corporate website, "Where in the World Is Walmart?" retrieved April 1, 2013, http://corporate.walmart.com/our-story/locations.
6. Matthew Boyle, "Walmart's Painful Lessons," *BusinessWeek,* October 13, 2009, http://www.businessweek.com/managing/content/oct2009/ca20091013_227022.htm.
7. walmartstores.com.
8. International Data Sheet, April 2010, http://walmartstores.com/pressroom/news/9865.aspx.
9. Andrew Clark, "Walmart, the U.S. Retailer Taking Over the World by Stealth," *Guardian,* January 12, 2010, http://www.guardian.co.uk/business/2010/jan/12/walmart-companies-to-shape-the-decade.
10. Vijay Govindarajan and Anil K. Gupta, "Taking Walmart Global: Lessons From Retailing's Giant," *Strategy + Business,* June 19, 2002, http://www.strategy-business.com/article/13866?pg=all.
11. Ibid.
12. Ibid.
13. Ibid.
14. Ibid.
15. "Walmart to Add 125 Stores in Mexico," *Arkansas Business Staff,* February 14, 2007, www.arkansasbusiness.com/article.aspx?aID=97026.13096.109168.
16. David Barstow, "Vast Mexico Bribery Case Hushed Up by Wal-Mart After Top-Level Struggle," *New York Times.* April 21, 2012. http://www.nytimes.com/2012/04/22/business/at-wal-mart-in-mexico-a-bribe-inquiry-silenced.html?_r=1.
17. Stephanie Clifford, "Bribery Case at Wal-Mart May Widen," *New York Times*. May 17, 2012. http://www.nytimes.com/2012/05/18/business/wal-mart-concedes-bribery-case-may-widen.html?pagewanted=all.
18. David Welch, (4/25/12). http://www.businessweek.com. In Wal-Mart Mexico Probe Threatening Global Growth Success: Retail, retrieved 7/24/12, from http://www.businessweek.com/news/2012-04-25/wal-mart-mexico-probe-threatening-global-growth-success-retail#p2.
19. Geri Smith, "In Mexico, Banco Walmart," *BusinessWeek,* November 20, 2006.
20. Carolyn Whelan, "Walmart Gets Its Bank—In Mexico," *Fortune,* January 29, 2008, www.fortune.com.
21. Walmart corporate website, "April 2010 Data Sheet," walmartstores.com.
22. David Welch, "Wal-Mart Mexico Probe Threatening Global Growth Success: Retail," *BusinessWeek*. April 25, 2012. http://www.businessweek.com/news/2012-04-25/wal-mart-mexico-probe-threatening-global-growth-success-retail#p1
23. Clay Chandler, "The Great Walmart of China," *Fortune,* July 25, 2005, money.cnn.com/magazines/fortune/fortune_archive/2005/07/25/8266651/index.htm.
24. Pallavi Gogoi, "Walmart's China Card," *BusinessWeek,* July 26, 2005.

25. "Walmart's Cheap Doubling in China," *24/7 Wall Street,* February 27, 2007, www.247wallst.com/2007/02/walmarts_cheap_.html.

26. "Walmart Buys China Grocery Chain," *Wire Services,* October 17, 2006, www.sptimes.com/2006/10/17/Business/Wal_Mart_buys_China_g.shtml.

27. Gogoi, "Walmart's China Card."

28. "Walmart Buys China Grocery Chain."

29. "Walmart Reaches Agreement to Acquire German Hypermarket Chain," *Business Wire,* December 18, 1997, http://www.allbusiness.com/company-activities-management/company-structures-ownership/7024566–1.html.

30. Mark Lander, "Walmart Gives Up Germany—Business—International Herald Tribune," *New York Times,* July 28, 2006, http://www.nytimes.com/2006/07/28/business/worldbusiness/28iht-walmart.2325266.html.

31. Ibid.

32. Ibid.

33. Allan Hall, Tom Bawden, and Sarah Butler, "Walmart Pulls out of Germany at Cost of $1bn," *The Times,* July 29, 2006.

34. Lander, "Walmart Gives Up Germany."

35. Tom Buerkle, "$10 Billion Gamble in U.K. Doubles Its International Business: Walmart Takes Big Leap into Europe," *New York Times,* June 15, 1999, http://www.nytimes.com/1999/06/15/news/15iht-walmart.2.t.html.

36. Ibid.

37. Clark, "Walmart, the U.S. Retailer Taking Over the World by Stealth."

38. Boyle, "Walmart's Painful Lessons."

39. Ibid.

40. Ibid.

41. Mariko Sanchanta, "Wal-Mart Bargain Shops for Japanese Stores to Buy," *The Wall Street Journal,* November 15, 2010, p. B1.

42. "Walmart Announces Central American Investment," September 20, 2005, http://walmartstores.com/pressroom/news/5384.aspx.

43. Gordon Platt, "Walmart Bets Big on Brazil's Market," *Global Finance,* January 1, 2006, http://www.allbusiness.com/public-administration/national-security-international/1138985–1.html.

44. Boyle, "Walmart's Painful Lessons."

45. Ibid.

46. Ibid.

47. Walmart, "Investors: News and Articles," October 22, 2009, http://investors.walmartstores.com/phoenix.zhtml?c=112761&p=irol-newsArticle&ID=1345359&highlight.

48. Ibid.

49. Ibid.

50. Ibid.

51. Ibid.

52. Chuck Bartels. "Wal-Mart has eye on global expansion." MSNBC. June 4, 2010. http://www.msnbc.msn.com/id/37509252/ns/business-us_business/t/wal-mart-has-eye-global-expansion/#.UA9b8bTY-88.

53. Shubh Datta. "Wal-Mart Targets More International Expansion." *Fool.com.* February 9, 2012. http://www.fool.com/investing/general/2012/02/09/wal-mart-targets-more-international-expansion.aspx#.UA9cq7TY-88.

54. Natalie Berg. 2011. "Walmart International Revs Up Growth." Planet Retail. http://www.planetretail.net/Presentations/Walmart-PLMagazine.pdf.

55. "Walmart Sets Up New Subsidiary in China," *ChinaRetailNews.com,* March 24, 2010, http://www.chinaretailnews.com/2010/03/24/3471–Walmart-sets-up-new-subsidiary-in-china/.

56. Ibid.

57. Ladka Bauerova, Chris Burritt, and Joao Oliveira, "The Three-Way Fight for Brazilian Shoppers," *BusinessWeek,* March 25, 2010, http://newsletters.businessweek.com/c.asp?836292&b4a6a1b99cb8d1fb&4.

58. Ibid.

59. Ibid.

60. Ibid.

61. Boyle, "Walmart's Painful Lessons."

62. Ibid.

63. Ibid.

64. Ibid.

65. David Welch, "Wal-Mart Mexico Probe Threatening Global Growth Success: Retail," *BusinessWeek*, April 25, 2012. http://www.businessweek.com/news/2012-04-25/wal-mart-mexico-probe-threatening-global-growth-success-retail#p1

66. Shruti Setia Chhabra, "India Critical for Global Growth: Walmart," *The Times of India,* April 14, 2010, http://timesofindia.indiatimes.com/biz/india-business/India-critical-for-global-growth-Walmart/articleshow/5798939.cms.

67. Boyle, "Walmart's Painful Lessons."

68. "Walmart Actively Seeking Russian Expansion," *Retail.ru,* July 16, 2009, http://en.retail.ru/news/38768/.

69. Ibid.

70. Boyle, "Walmart's Painful Lessons."

71. "Walmart Canada to Open 35 to 40 Supercentres in 2010," *finchannel.com,* February 24, 2010, http://www.finchannel.com/Main_News/Business/59058_Walmart_Canada_to_Open_35_to_40_Supercentres_in_2010/.

72. Ibid.

73. Ibid.

74. Ibid.

75. David Welch, "Wal-Mart Mexico Probe Threatening Global Growth Success: Retail," *BusinessWeek*, April 25, 2012. http://www.businessweek.com/news/2012-04-25/wal-mart-mexico-probe-threatening-global-growth-success-retail#p1.

76. Robb M. Stewart, "Wal-Mart Checks Out a New Continent," *The Wall Street Journal,* October 27, p. B1.

77. Robb M. Stewart, "Wal-Mart Reassesses Massmart Bid," *The Wall Street Journal,* October 29, p. B1.

78. "WalMart Announces Major Reorganization, New Online Initiative," *FoodBiz Daily,* January 29, 2010, http://foodbizdaily.com/articles/96121–walmart-announces-major-reorganization-new-online-initiative.aspx.

79. Ibid.

80. Jonathan Birchall, "Walmart Gears Up for Global Online Push," *Financial Times,* January 29, 2010, http://www.ft.com/cms/s/0/9f944f78–0c67–11df-a941–00144feabdc0.html.

81. Ibid.

82. Mathew Mosk, "Walmart Fires Supplier after Bangladesh Revelation," *ABC News Blotter*, May 15, 2013. http://abcnews.go.com/Blotter/wal-mart-fires-supplier-bangladesh-revelation/story?id=19188673#.Ua3fGEC7Itg.

83. Ulfikar Ali Manik and Jim Yardley, "Another Garment Factory Scare in Bangladesh," *New York Times,* June 14, 2013, p. A11.

84. Steven Greenhouse, "U.S. Retailers Announce Safety Plan," *New York Times,* May 31, 2013, p. B6.

85. Steven Greenhouse, "Obama to Suspend Trade Privileges with Bangladesh," *New York Times,* June 28, 2013, p. B1.

Glossary
术语表

achievement culture A culture in which people are accorded status based on how well they perform their functions.

achievement motivation theory A theory which holds that individuals can have a need to get ahead, to attain success, and to reach objectives.

act of state doctrine A jurisdictional principle of international law which holds that all acts of other governments are considered to be valid by U.S. courts, even if such acts are illegal or inappropriate under U.S. law.

adaptability screening The process of evaluating how well a family is likely to stand up to the stress of overseas life.

administrative coordination Strategic formulation and implementation in which the MNC makes strategic decisions based on the merits of the individual situation rather than using a predetermined economically or politically driven strategy.

alliance Any type of cooperative relationship among different firms.

ascription culture A culture in which status is attributed based on who or what a person is.

assessment center An evaluation tool used to identify individuals with potential to be selected or promoted to higher-level positions.

authoritarian leadership The use of work-centered behavior designed to ensure task accomplishment.

balance-sheet approach An approach to developing an expatriate compensation package that ensures the expat is "made whole" and does not lose money by taking the assignment.

base of the pyramid strategy Strategy targeting low-income customers in developing countries.

bicultural group A group in which two or more members represent each of two distinct cultures, such as four Mexicans and four Chinese who have formed a team to investigate the possibility of investing in a venture.

biotechnology The integration of science and technology to create agricultural or medical products through industrial use and manipulation of living organisms.

born-global firms Firms that engage in significant international activities shortly after being established.

cafeteria approach An approach to developing an expatriate compensation package that entails giving the individual a series of options and letting the person decide how to spend the available funds.

centralization A management system in which important decisions are made at the top.

chaebols Very large, family-held Korean conglomerates that have considerable political and economic power.

charismatic leaders Leaders who inspire and motivate employees through their charismatic traits and abilities.

chromatics The use of color to communicate messages.

chronemics The way in which time is used in a culture.

civil or code law Law that is derived from Roman law and is found in the non-Islamic and nonsocialist countries.

codetermination A legal system that requires workers and their managers to discuss major decisions.

collectivism The political philosophy that views the needs or goals of society as a whole as more important than individual desires (Chapter 2); the tendency of people to belong to groups or collectives and to look after each other in exchange for loyalty (Chapter 4).

common law Law that derives from English law and is the foundation of legislation in the United States, Canada, and England, among other nations.

communication The process of transferring meanings from sender to receiver.

communitarianism Refers to people regarding themselves as part of a group.

conglomerate investment A type of high-risk investment in which goods or services produced are not similar to those produced at home.

content theories of motivation Theories that explain work motivation in terms of what arouses, energizes, or initiates employee behavior.

context Information that surrounds a communication and helps to convey the message.

controlling The process of evaluating results in relation to plans or objectives and deciding what action, if any, to take.

corporate governance The system by which business corporations are directed and controlled.

corporate social responsibility (CSR) The actions of a firm to benefit society beyond the requirements of the law and the direct interests of the firm.

cultural assimilator A programmed learning technique designed to expose members of one culture to some of the basic concepts, attitudes, role perceptions, customs, and values of another culture.

culture Acquired knowledge that people use to interpret experience and generate social behavior. This knowledge forms values, creates attitudes, and influences behavior.

decentralization Pushing decision making down the line and getting the lower-level personnel involved.

decision making The process of choosing a course of action among alternatives.

democracy A political system in which the government is controlled by the citizens either directly or through elections.

diffuse culture A culture in which public space and private space are similar in size and individuals guard their public space carefully, because entry into public space affords entry into private space as well.

direct controls The use of face-to-face or personal meetings for the purpose of monitoring operations.

distributive negotiations Bargaining that occurs when two parties with opposing goals compete over a set value.

doctrine of comity A jurisdictional principle of international law which holds that there must be mutual respect for the laws, institutions, and governments of other countries in the matter of jurisdiction over their own citizens.

downward communication The transmission of information from superior to subordinate.

economic imperative A worldwide strategy based on cost leadership, differentiation, and segmentation.

Eiffel Tower culture A culture that is characterized by strong emphasis on hierarchy and orientation to the task.

emotional culture A culture in which emotions are expressed openly and naturally.

empowerment The process of giving individuals and teams the resources, information, and authority they need to develop ideas and effectively implement them.

environmental scanning The process of providing management with accurate forecasts of trends related to external changes in geographic areas where the firm currently is doing business or is considering setting up operations.

equity theory A process theory that focuses on how motivation is affected by people's perception of how fairly they are being treated.

esteem needs Needs for power and status.

ethics The study of morality and standards of conduct.

ethnocentric MNC An MNC that stresses nationalism and often puts home-office people in charge of key international management positions.

ethnocentric predisposition A nationalistic philosophy of management whereby the values and interests of the parent company guide strategic decisions.

ethnocentrism The belief that one's own way of doing things is superior to that of others.

European Union A political and economic community consisting of 27 member states.

expatriates Managers who live and work outside their home country. They are citizens of the country where the multinational corporation is headquartered.

expectancy theory A process theory that postulates that motivation is influenced by a person's belief that (*a*) effort will lead to performance, (*b*) performance will lead to specific outcomes, and (*c*) the outcomes will be of value to the individual.

expropriation The seizure of businesses by a host country with little, if any, compensation to the owners.

extrinsic A determinant of motivation by which the external environment and result of the activity are of greater importance due to competition and compensation or incentive plans.

fair trade An organized social movement and market-based approach that aims to help producers in developing countries obtain better trading conditions and promote sustainability.

family culture A culture that is characterized by a strong emphasis on hierarchy and orientation to the person.

femininity A cultural characteristic in which the dominant values in society are caring for others and the quality of life.

Foreign Corrupt Practices Act (FCPA) An act that makes it illegal to influence foreign officials through personal payment or political contributions; made into U.S. law in 1977 because of concerns over bribes in the international business arena.

foreign direct investment (FDI) Investment in property, plant, or equipment in another country.

formalization The use of defined structures and systems in decision making, communicating, and controlling.

franchise A business arrangement under which one party (the franchisor) allows another (the franchisee) to operate an enterprise using its trademark, logo, product line, and methods of operation in return for a fee.

geocentric MNC An MNC that seeks to integrate diverse regions of the world through a global approach to decision making.

geocentric predisposition A philosophy of management whereby the company tries to integrate a global systems approach to decision making.

global area division A structure under which global operations are organized on a geographic rather than a product basis.

global functional division A structure that organizes worldwide operations primarily based on function and secondarily on product.

global integration The production and distribution of products and services of a homogeneous type and quality on a worldwide basis.

globalization The process of social, political, economic, cultural, and technological integration among countries around the world.

globalization imperative A belief that one worldwide approach to doing business is the key to both efficiency and effectiveness.

global product division A structural arrangement in which domestic divisions are given worldwide responsibility for product groups.

global strategy Integrated strategy based primarily on price competition.

GLOBE (Global Leadership and Organizational Behavior Effectiveness) A multicountry study and evaluation of cultural attributes and leadership behaviors among more than 17,000 managers from 951 organizations in 62 countries.

goal-setting theory A process theory that focuses on how individuals go about setting goals and responding to them and the overall impact of this process on motivation.

groupthink Social conformity and pressures on individual members of a group to conform and reach consensus.

guanxi In Chinese, it means "good connections."

guided missile culture A culture that is characterized by strong emphasis on equality in the workplace and orientation to the task.

haptics Communicating through the use of bodily contact.

home-country nationals Expatriate managers who are citizens of the country where the multinational corporation is headquartered.

homogeneous group A group in which members have similar backgrounds and generally perceive, interpret, and evaluate events in similar ways.

honne A Japanese term that means "what one really wants to do."

horizontal investment An MNC investment in foreign operations to produce the same goods or services as those produced at home.

horizontal specialization The assignment of jobs so that individuals are given a particular function to perform and tend to stay within the confines of this area.

host-country nationals Local managers who are hired by the MNC.

hygiene factors In the two-factor motivation theory, job-context variables such as salary, interpersonal relations, technical supervision, working conditions, and company policies and administration.

incubator culture A culture that is characterized by strong emphasis on equality and orientation to the person.

indigenization laws Laws that require nationals to hold a majority interest in an operation.

indirect controls The use of reports and other written forms of communication to control operations.

individualism The political philosophy that people should be free to pursue economic and political endeavors without constraint (Chapter 2); the tendency of people to look after themselves and their immediate family only (Chapter 4).

inpatriates Individuals from a host country or third-country nationals who are assigned to work in the home country.

integrative negotiation Bargaining that involves cooperation between two groups to integrate interests, create value, and invest in the agreement.

integrative techniques Techniques that help the overseas operation become a part of the host country's infrastructure.

international division structure A structural arrangement that handles all international operations out of a division created for this purpose.

international entrepreneurship A combination of innovative, proactive, and risk-seeking behavior that crosses national boundaries and is intended to create value for organizations.

international management Process of applying management concepts and techniques in a multinational environment and adapting management practices to different economic, political, and cultural environments.

international selection criteria Factors used to choose personnel for international assignments.

international strategy Mixed strategy combining low demand for integration and responsiveness.

intimate distance Distance between people that is used for very confidential communications.

intrinsic A determinant of motivation by which an individual experiences fulfillment through carrying out an activity and helping others.

Islamic law Law that is derived from interpretation of the Qur'an and the teachings of the Prophet Muhammad and is found in most Islamic countries.

job-content factors In work motivation, those factors internally controlled, such as responsibility, achievement, and the work itself.

job-context factors In work motivation, those factors controlled by the organization, such as conditions, hours, earnings, security, benefits, and promotions.

job design A job's content, the methods that are used on the job, and the way the job relates to other jobs in the organization.

joint venture (JV) An agreement under which two or more partners own or control a business.

kaizen A Japanese term that means "continuous improvement."

karoshi A Japanese term that means "overwork" or "job burnout."

keiretsu In Japan, an organizational arrangement in which a large, often vertically integrated group of companies cooperate and work closely with each other to provide goods and services to end users; members may be bound together by cross-ownership, long-term business dealings, interlocking directorates, and social ties.

key success factor (KSF) A factor necessary for a firm to effectively compete in a market niche.

kinesics The study of communication through body movement and facial expression.

leadership The process of influencing people to direct their efforts toward the achievement of some particular goal or goals.

learning The acquisition of skills, knowledge, and abilities that result in a relatively permanent change in behavior.

license An agreement that allows one party to use an industrial property right in exchange for payment to the other party.

localization An approach to developing an expatriate compensation package that involves paying the expat a salary comparable to that of local nationals.

lump-sum method An approach to developing an expatriate compensation package that involves giving the expat a predetermined amount of money and letting the individual make his or her own decisions regarding how to spend it.

macro political risk analysis Analysis that reviews major political decisions likely to affect all enterprises in the country.

management Process of completing activities efficiently and effectively with and through other people.

maquiladora A factory, the majority of which are located in Mexican border towns, that imports materials and equipment on a duty- and tariff-free basis for assembly or manufacturing and re-export.

masculinity A cultural characteristic in which the dominant values in society are success, money, and things.

merger/acquisition The cross-border purchase or exchange of equity involving two or more companies.

micro political risk analysis Analysis directed toward government policies and actions that influence selected sectors of the economy or specific foreign businesses in the country.

Ministry of International Trade and Industry (MITI) A Japanese government agency that identifies and ranks national commercial pursuits and guides the distribution of national resources to meet these goals.

mixed organization structure A structure that is a combination of a global product, area, or functional arrangement.

MNC A firm having operations in more than one country, international sales, and a nationality mix of managers and owners.

monochronic time schedule A time schedule in which things are done in a linear fashion.

motivation A psychological process through which unsatisfied wants or needs lead to drives that are aimed at goals or incentives.

motivators In the two-factor motivation theory, job-content factors such as achievement, recognition, responsibility, advancement, and the work itself.

multicultural group A group in which there are individuals from three or more different ethnic backgrounds, such as three U.S., three German, three Uruguayan, and three Chinese managers who are looking into mining operations in South Africa.

multi-domestic strategy Differentiated strategy emphasizing local adaptation.

national responsiveness The need to understand the different consumer tastes in segmented regional markets and respond to different national standards and regulations imposed by autonomous governments and agencies.

nationality principle A jurisdictional principle of international law which holds that every country has jurisdiction over its citizens no matter where they are located.

negotiation Bargaining with one or more parties for the purpose of arriving at a solution acceptable to all.

neutral culture A culture in which emotions are held in check.

nongovernmental organizations (NGOs) Private, not-for-profit organizations that seek to serve society's interests by focusing on social, political, and economic issues such as poverty, social justice, education, health, and the environment.

nonverbal communication The transfer of meaning through means such as body language and the use of physical space.

North American Free Trade Agreement (NAFTA) A free-trade agreement between the United States, Canada, and Mexico that has removed most barriers to trade and investment.

oculesics The area of communication that deals with conveying messages through the use of eye contact and gaze.

offshoring The process by which companies undertake some activities at offshore locations instead of in their countries of origin.

operational risks Government policies and procedures that directly constrain management and performance of local operations.

organizational culture Shared values and beliefs that enable members to understand their roles and the norms of the organization.

outsourcing The subcontracting or contracting out of activities to endogenous organizations that had previously been performed by the firm.

ownership-control risks Government policies or actions that inhibit ownership or control of local operations.

parochialism The tendency to view the world through one's own eyes and perspectives.

participative leadership The use of both work- or task-centered and people-centered approaches to leading subordinates.

particularism The belief that circumstances dictate how ideas and practices should be applied and that something cannot be done the same everywhere.

paternalistic leadership The use of work-centered behavior coupled with a protective employee-centered concern.

perception A person's view of reality.

personal distance In communicating, the physical distance used for talking with family and close friends.

physiological needs Basic physical needs for water, food, clothing, and shelter.

political imperative Strategic formulation and implementation utilizing strategies that are country-responsive and designed to protect local market niches.

political risk The unanticipated likelihood that a business's foreign investment will be constrained by a host government's policy.

polycentric MNC An MNC that places local nationals in key positions and allows these managers to appoint and develop their own people.

polycentric predisposition A philosophy of management whereby strategic decisions are tailored to suit the cultures of the countries where the MNC operates.

polychronic time schedule A time schedule in which people tend to do several things at the same time and place higher value on personal involvement than on getting things done on time.

positive organizational behavior (POB) The study and application of positively oriented human resource strengths and psychological capacities that can be measured, developed, and effectively managed for performance improvement in today's workplace.

positive organizational scholarship (POS) A method that focuses on positive outcomes, processes, and attributes of organizations and their members.

power distance The extent to which less powerful members of institutions and organizations accept that power is distributed unequally.

principle of sovereignty An international principle of law which holds that governments have the right to rule themselves as they see fit.

proactive political strategies Lobbying, campaign financing, advocacy, and other political interventions designed to shape and influence the political decisions prior to their impact on the firm.

process theories of motivation Theories that explain work motivation by how employee behavior is initiated, redirected, and halted.

profit The amount remaining after all expenses are deducted from total revenues.

protective and defensive techniques Techniques that discourage the host government from interfering in operations.

protective principle A jurisdictional principle of international law which holds that every country has jurisdiction over behavior that adversely affects its national security, even if the conduct occurred outside that country.

proxemics The study of the way people use physical space to convey messages.

public distance In communicating, the distance used when calling across the room or giving a talk to a group.

quality control circle (QCC) A group of workers who meet on a regular basis to discuss ways of improving the quality of work.

quality imperative Strategic formulation and implementation utilizing strategies of total quality management to meet or exceed customers' expectations and continuously improve products or services.

regiocentric MNC An MNC that relies on local managers from a particular geographic region to handle operations in and around that area.

regiocentric predisposition A philosophy of management whereby the firm tries to blend its own interests with those of its subsidiaries on a regional basis.

regional system An approach to developing an expatriate compensation package that involves setting a compensation system for all expats who are assigned to a particular region and paying everyone in accord with that system.

repatriation The return to one's home country from an overseas management assignment.

repatriation agreements Agreements whereby the firm tells an individual how long she or he will be posted overseas and promises to give the individual, on return, a job that is mutually acceptable.

return on investment (ROI) Return measured by dividing profit by assets.

ringisei A Japanese term that means "decision making by consensus."

safety needs Desires for security, stability, and the absence of pain.

self-actualization needs Desires to reach one's full potential, to become everything one is capable of becoming as a human being.

simplification The process of exhibiting the same orientation toward different cultural groups.

social distance In communicating, the distance used to handle most business transactions.

socialism A moderate form of collectivism in which there is government ownership of institutions, and profit is not the ultimate goal.

socialist law Law that comes from the Marxist socialist system and continues to influence regulations in countries formerly associated with the Soviet Union as well as China.

social needs Desires to interact and affiliate with others and to feel wanted by others.

sociotechnical designs Job designs that blend personnel and technology.

specialization An organizational characteristic that assigns individuals to specific, well-defined tasks.

specific culture A culture in which individuals have a large public space they readily share with others and a small private space they guard closely and share with only close friends and associates.

strategic management The process of determining an organization's basic mission and long-term objectives, then implementing a plan of action for attaining these goals.

strategy implementation The process of providing goods and services in accord with a plan of action.

sustainability Development that meets humanity's needs without harming future generations.

tatemae A Japanese term that means "doing the right thing" according to the norm.

territoriality principle A jurisdictional principle of international law which holds that every nation has the right of jurisdiction within its legal territory.

terrorism The use of force or violence against others to promote political or social views.

Theory X manager A manager who believes that people are basically lazy and that coercion and threats of punishment often are necessary to get them to work.

Theory Y manager A manager who believes that under the right conditions people not only will work hard but will seek increased responsibility and challenge.

Theory Z manager A manager who believes that workers seek opportunities to participate in management and are motivated by teamwork and responsibility sharing.

third-country nationals (TCNs) Managers who are citizens of countries other than the country in which the MNC is headquartered or the one in which the managers are assigned to work by the MNC.

token group A group in which all members but one have the same background, such as a group of Japanese retailers and a British attorney.

total quality management (TQM) An organizational strategy and the accompanying techniques that result in the delivery of high-quality products or services to customers.

training The process of altering employee behavior and attitudes in a way that increases the probability of goal attainment.

transactional leaders Individuals who exchange rewards for effort and performance and work on a "something for something" basis.

transfer risks Government policies that limit the transfer of capital, payments, production, people, and technology in and out of the country.

transformational leaders Leaders who are visionary agents with a sense of mission and who are capable of motivating their followers to accept new goals and new ways of doing things.

transition strategies Strategies used to help smooth the adjustment from an overseas to a stateside assignment.

transnational network structure A multinational structural arrangement that combines elements of function, product, and geographic designs, while relying on a network arrangement to link worldwide subsidiaries.

transnational strategy Integrated strategy emphasizing both global integration and local responsiveness.

two-factor theory of motivation A theory that identifies two sets of factors that influence job satisfaction: hygiene factors and motivators.

uncertainty avoidance The extent to which people feel threatened by ambiguous situations and have created beliefs and institutions that try to avoid these.

universalism The belief that ideas and practices can be applied everywhere in the world without modification.

upward communication The transfer of meaning from subordinate to superior.

validity The quality of being effective, of producing the desired results. A valid test or selection technique measures what it is intended to measure.

values Basic convictions that people have regarding what is right and wrong, good and bad, important and unimportant.

variety amplification The creation of uncertainty and the analysis of many alternatives regarding future action.

variety reduction The limiting of uncertainty and the focusing of action on a limited number of alternatives.

vertical investment The production of raw materials or intermediate goods that are to be processed into final products.

vertical specialization The assignment of work to groups or departments where individuals are collectively responsible for performance.

wholly owned subsidiary An overseas operation that is totally owned and controlled by an MNC.

work centrality The importance of work in an individual's life relative to other areas of interest.

World Trade Organization (WTO) The global organization of countries that oversees rules and regulations for international trade and investment.